THE INTERNATIONAL ENCYCLOPEDIA OF MARKETING

F... ...llege

...ec... - Sou...

WITHDRAWN

THE INTERNATIONAL ENCYCLOPEDIA OF MARKETING

European Marketing Confederation

The original NIMA Marketing Lexicon was realized under the responsibility of the following editorial board:

Doctor Eric Waarts
Doctor John Koster
Doctor Nico Lamperjee
Doctor Ed Peelen

The English translation has been edited by:

Professor Michael Thomas
Professor Stan Paliwoda

Butterworth-Heinemann
Linacre House, Jordan Hill, Oxford OX2 8DP
A division of Reed Educational and Professional Publishing Ltd

ℛ A member of the Reed Elsevier plc group

OXFORD   BOSTON   JOHANNESBURG
MELBOURNE   NEW DELHI   SINGAPORE

First published by Wolters–Noordhoff BV, Groningen, The Netherlands 1993
Second edition 1995
First published in Great Britain 1997

© NIMA, Amsterdam 1993, 1995
© Reed Educational and Professional Publishing Ltd 1997

British Library Cataloguing in Publication Data
A catalogue record for this book is available from the British Library

ISBN 0 7506 3501 0

Printed and bound in Great Britain by Hartnolls Ltd, Bodmin, Cornwall

CONTENTS

FOREWORD

EMC, The European Marketing Confederation, welcomes the opportunity of contributing to the publication of The *International Encyclopedia of Marketing* initiated by the Netherlands Institute of Marketing (NIMA), Founder Member of EMC. The English edition has been heavily supported by The Chartered Institute of Marketing of Great Britain and especially by the contribution of its former National Chairman Professor Michael Thomas. For us, the European Marketing Confederation, such a joint action between CIM, NIMA and EMC is a milestone on the road towards fruitful and efficient cooperation between all the National Associations in Europe.

This encyclopedia is also an important step to serve a good marketing education cause in Europe and provide a reference book for all those professionally involved in the field of marketing. In a profession like ours which is highly diversified and has a major role to play in the European economy, such an initiative can only be fully supported.

EMC's intention is to enhance its role so that the Confederation becomes the main umbrella organization for all marketers, aiming at the improvement of professionalism in our field, as well as the acceptance, within the European Union and Central and Eastern European Countries, of the importance of marketing in the development of Europe.

Dinos Lambrinopoulos
President
European Marketing Confederation

FOREWORD

When we researched our new marketing syllabus with industry and commerce three years ago the first thing business wanted young people joining the discipline to have was an appreciation of the jargon and terminology used in marketing, even before they acquired a knowledge and understanding of the basic principles. If you can't speak the language you cannot even begin to become a practitioner they argued.

I am not suggesting that young marketers should sit down and read this encyclopedia from cover to cover! But the book is an important reference work for English-speaking marketers in understanding the terminology, tools and techniques used in marketing.

No doubt North American and other English-speaking readers will inform the publishers of any of the terms and definitions contained in this book which fail to translate into local usage in their specific areas of the world, thereby helping to expand the material for a new edition in due course!

Professor Michael Thomas of Strathclyde University and a former Chairman of the CIM, who kindly adapted the literal translation from the Dutch, has told me that he had great difficulty with some of the terms, where clearly Dutch usage differed in some respects from the English. But an understanding of diversity and regional differences is crucial to success in international marketing. Thinking global while thinking and acting local is an easy concept, but difficult to implement in practice.

As a relatively modern business discipline, like any other emerging profession, marketing is going through the lengthy evolution of defining its terminology. Indeed, as mass customization and electronic marketing alter the nature of marketing in quick succession the terminology is expanding rapidly. This encyclopedia is an important contribution in codifying this process.

It results from remarkable cooperation between the Netherlands Institute of Marketing (NIMA), the European Marketing Confederation, the two publishers, Wolters-Noordhoff of The Netherlands and Butterworth-Heinemann in the UK, and ourselves. Credit is due to all involved in this collaborative venture.

Plans are being made to translate the material into Spanish as well as possibly Italian, Czech and Hungarian. Commonality of terms but diversity of practice throughout the marketing world is an exciting challenge and opportunity for marketers everywhere.

Steve Cuthbert
Director General
The Chartered Institute of Marketing

1 ESSENTIAL CONCEPTS

Concept overview

brand
business marketing

communication
communication instrument
communication mix
communication policy
competition
competitive advantage
competitor
competitor profile
concentrated marketing
consumer
consumer behaviour
consumer marketing
corporate objectives
customer
customer behaviour

demand
demarketing
differentiated marketing
direct marketing
distribution
distribution mix
distribution policy

end consumer
exchange
exchange objects
exchange subjects
exchange transaction
external environment

final demand

global marketing

industrial sector
industry sector
internal environment
internal marketing
international marketing

management
market
market management philosophies
market orientation
market parties
market research
market segment
market structure

marketing
marketing concept
marketing department
marketing environment
marketing function
marketing instrument
marketing management
marketing manager
marketing mix
marketing objectives
marketing plan
marketing science
marketing scope
marketing strategy
marketing tactics

need
not-for-profit marketing

objective
objectives, hierarchy of
operational marketing management
organization

positioning
price
price instruments
price mix
price policy
product
product concept
product instrument
product/market combination
product/market/technology combination
product mix
product policy
production concept

retail marketing

segmentation
selling concept
services marketing
social marketing concept
strategic marketing management
supplier marketing

target group
target group selection
trade marketing

undifferentiated marketing

Concept descriptions

brand
Branded product which on the basis of bundling of benefits and its extrinsic and/or intrinsic characteristics distinguishes itself from competing articles. These distinctive characteristics offer a certain brand-added value for a relatively large group of consumers.

business marketing (business-to-business marketing, industrial marketing, organization marketing, organizational buying behaviour)
Marketing activities of an organization directed at other organizations. So, these marketing activities are not directed at private persons.

communication
Transferring information. A process in which information is exchanged between people and organizations. During this process a transmitter transfers information (a message) either directly or through a medium, to a receiver. The communication process is completed as soon as the receiver has processed the information. In the course of the communication process, 'noise' may develop which can alter partially or totally the message transferred. In communication, all senses play a part.

communication instrument
A means to transfer information between suppliers, buyers and marketing publics. Communication instruments include the following: advertising, sales force promotions, trade promotions, consumer promotions, sponsorship, direct mail, personal selling, trade fairs and exhibitions.

communication mix
Application, combination and fine-tuning of the communication instruments selected for a specific target group by a particular organization.

communication policy
Analysis, planning, execution and evaluation of activities with regard to communication.

competition
Process occurring between various parties in which each party attempts to achieve its objective and therefore has to compete with other parties. For example, between suppliers offering similar products, each trying to obtain the largest possible share of the market. The competitive process generally has a positive influence on the performance and development of competing parties; however, it may also have a negative influence on the (long-term) profitability of the average competitor.

competitive advantage
Particular advantage of an organization which is relevant for the performance of that organization, and which is processed by competitors to a lesser degree. Such advantages may comprise, among others, technological skills, cost control and service aspects. If the skill is relevant in the long run and cannot be imitated by other organizations, then there is a sustainable competitive advantage. To identify the competitive advantages of an organization one analysis which may be used is the value chain analysis.

competitor
Supplier of a product filling the same or a similar need of a particular group of consumers.

competitor profile
Description of competing parties compared to one's own organization in terms of, amongst others, present activities, objectives, strategies, strengths to capitalize on market opportunities and weaknesses.

concentrated marketing (single segment strategy)
Segmentation strategy where an organization focuses on one or few segments using one particular marketing programme.

consumer
The ultimate user of a product, or service.

consumer behaviour
All activities of customers directly related to acquiring, using and discarding goods, including information processing and decision processes preceding and following these activities. This behaviour can be broken down into four aspects: (1) communication behaviour, (2) purchasing behaviour, (3) consumption behaviour, and (4) dismissive behaviour.

consumer marketing
Marketing activities of organizations aimed at private persons (consumers).

corporate objectives (organizational objectives)
Objectives with respect to the entire company. These company objectives may be either of a quantitative nature (profit, market share, efficiency and/or flexibility) or of a qualitative nature (long run consumer and public welfare, continuity, resistance).

customer
Person or organization who buys, leases or rents goods and services.

customer behaviour
All activities of customers directly related to acquiring, using and discarding goods, including information processing and decision processes preceding and following these activities. This behaviour can be broken down into four aspects: (1) communication behaviour, (2) purchasing behaviour, (3) consumption behaviour, and (4) dismissive behaviour.

demand
Total quantity of products sought in a particular market at a particular moment or over a particular period. Also: need and desire of a group of consumers for particular products or brands, expressed in the desire and the willingness to buy that product or brand.

demarketing
Marketing effort aimed at decreasing the demand by particular groups of consumers for the product so as to ensure quality, brand reliability and buyer loyalty.

differentiated marketing
Segmentation strategy where an organization focuses on one or more segments using focused marketing programmes.

direct marketing
Aimed at establishing a specific transaction and/or obtaining and maintaining a direct relationship between a supplier and consumer typically involving direct communication and direct delivery.

distribution
Bridging differences in place, time, quantity and quality for a specific product between various market parties. In the distribution process several different distribution functions are executed by channel members. The distribution decisions within marketing especially address the question as to who will fulfil which functions (choice of channel), how intensively the product has to be distributed (intensity of the distribution) and which individual distributors will be selected together with the way in which distributors are to be dealt with (push or pull strategy, account management).

distribution mix
Usage, combination and fine-tuning of the distribution channels selected for a specific target group by a specific organization.

distribution policy
Analysis, planning, execution and evaluation of activities relating to distribution channels.

end consumer (final customer)
End or final user of a specific product. Usually this term is used to denote the consumer.

exchange
Free exchange of objects between at least two parties.

exchange objects
That which is exchanged: goods, services, money, information, status, affection.

exchange subjects
The parties participating in an exchange: supplier and consumer.

exchange transaction
Agreement resulting in mutual obligations and rights with respect to the exchange of exchange objects.

external environment
Influences on an organization beyond its control finding their origins outside the organization itself. In this context, a distinction is made between influences from the macro environment and influences from the meso environment. In Anglo-Saxon literature the only distinction made is between macro and micro environment (marketing system). The micro environment (key marketing system) in general comprises both influences from the external meso environment and from the internal environment.

final demand
Demand for goods by final users or end consumers. In most cases this term denotes the demand for goods by consumers.

global marketing
Marketing activities by organizations, aimed at target groups scattered across a large number of countries, endeavouring to accomplish the largest possible uniformity in marketing activities.

industrial sector
Horizontal section in the industry sector. This section refers to organizations fulfilling the same or a similar function in the production process of different varieties of a particular product.

industry sector
All successive participants and their relative position in the manufacturing process of a particular product, belonging to a particular industry sector from original equipment manufacturer (o.e.m.) to end consumer.

internal environment
The internal influences which, in principle, can be controlled by the organization. These influences relate to the organization itself and its various functions, such as organization structure and culture, staff policy, the financial policy, marketing policy, production policy, logistic policy, purchasing policy, research and development policy and the strategic planning process. Generally, in Anglo-Saxon literature the micro environment also comprises the influences which in the Dutch classification are considered to be meso environment factors.

internal marketing
Type of marketing where exchange transactions take place within the organization itself, i.e. marketing activities by sections of an organization directed at other sections of the same organization.

international marketing
Marketing activities (of organizations) aimed at target groups across several markets.

management
Analysis, planning, execution and evaluation of an organization's activities.

market

1 In economics, the market is considered to be the collective demand for and supply of a particular product or particular goods and the total quantities demanded, supplied, respectively, of that product over a certain period in a specific area. The combined action of forces of market parties determines the price of the product in the market.

2 In marketing literature, the market is generally described from the viewpoint of the supplier. Then, the market is the collection of parties demanding a particular product or products ('markets are people').

market management philosophies

Philosophy of an organization as to the way in which the market should be approached. The following concepts are to be distinguished: production concept, product concept, sales concept, marketing concept and social marketing concept.

market orientation

Degree to which an organization takes into account different market parties such as consumers, intermediaries and competitors when deciding on, and executing policies (at all organizational levels).

market parties

All suppliers, buyers, consumers, intermediaries and influencers in a specific market.

market research

Systematically and objectively gathering and analysing data which is essential to determine and resolve marketing problems. Market research forms the link between the consumer, industrial buyer and the general public on the one hand, and the marketeer on the other hand. Information is used to trace and define marketing opportunities and threats; generating, fine tuning and evaluating marketing decisions and activities; monitoring over time the results that have been achieved by marketing; and increasing the understanding of marketing as a process. In market research, the information needs are specified to enable proper analysis; the method of data collection, and the execution of field work are specified. The data is then analysed, and the results, conclusions and implications are communicated.

market segment

Part of a market, i.e. a group of consumers with common properties, for which it may be desirable to apply a specific marketing strategy or marketing mix.

market structure

Typification of a market on the basis of the number of suppliers, consumers and the homogeneity or heterogeneity of the goods traded in. The following market forms may be distinguished: monopoly, monopsony, homogeneous and heterogeneous oligopoly, oligopsony, monopolistic competition (heterogeneous polypoly), complete (free) competition (homogeneous polypoly), and polyopsony.

marketing

All activities carried out by exchange subjects aimed at anticipating, promoting, facilitating, and expediting exchange transactions.

marketing concept

Way in which the market approach can be materialized. This concept assumes that exchange transactions are best achieved by taking the needs of the consumers as a starting point for the activities of the organization.

marketing department

Unit in an organization responsible for implementing the marketing function.

marketing environment

Group of factors affecting the policy of each organization. A major part of these factors lies beyond the control of each distinctive organization, other factors can be affected, and a limited number can be controlled. The marketing environment may be organized in various ways, including the external and internal environment.

marketing function
Organizational function embracing all the various tasks relating to marketing.

marketing instrument
Means used to anticipate, promote, facilitate and expedite exchange transactions. This relates to product, price, communications, distribution and personnel. Traditionally this is the four or five Ps, namely: product, price, promotion (communication), place (distribution) and/or personnel.

marketing management
Analysis, planning, execution and evaluation of the marketing activities of an organization. Marketing management may be of strategic or operational nature.

marketing manager
Person responsible for and in charge of (parts of) an organization's marketing management.

marketing mix
Combination and fine-tuning of the marketing instruments used by an organization, aimed at one or more target groups within a specific product/market/(technology) combination.

marketing objectives
Specific objectives within the framework of the objectives of a company relating to marketing policy. Marketing objectives include: realizing a certain sale, turnover, competitive position or a certain market share.

marketing plan
Plan in which the internal and external environment of a product class, a product group or a brand are analysed, resulting in a SWOT-analysis. Subsequently, one or more objectives are included in the plan, alternative solutions to the problem can be presented and evaluated, and a choice is made from the options outlined, and finally the plan is elaborated and made operational, containing the use of marketing instruments, budgets and action plans. Marketing plans may differ from each other to the extent where they are aimed at strategic or operational issues.

marketing science
Scientific study of those activities aimed at anticipating, promoting, facilitating and expediting exchange transactions.

marketing scope
Marketing activities for certain exchange objects and/or specific exchange subjects or for the use of particular marketing instruments. The scope of marketing includes: business marketing, consumer marketing, services marketing, direct marketing, retail trade marketing, international marketing and not-for-profit marketing.

marketing strategy
The way in which an organization tries to accomplish its long-term marketing objectives. This identifies the direction into which marketing activities are to be developed in order to realize these objectives. It has to do with the product/market combination or target group to be chosen, positioning and is a signpost for the marketing mix.

marketing tactics
Short term, adaptive action (with respect to a certain event) aimed at accomplishing short term objectives (for an instrument or function).

need
Product or service which is necessary for a person's welfare. May be latent (when the person is unaware) or perceived.

not-for-profit marketing (non-profit marketing)
Marketing activities carried out by organizations for educational or charitable purposes without a profit motive.

objective

Result aimed for by an organization in a qualitative and quantitative sense. A distinction can be made between targets at an organizational or business unit level, marketing objectives and marketing instrument objectives. *See also:* objectives, hierarchy of.

objectives, hierarchy of

Objectives may relate to various levels within the organization. With regard to level, usually a distinction is made in objectives for an organization, division and strategic business unit. Objectives for an organization are usually further translated into functional and instrument objectives.

operational marketing management

Analysis, planning, implementation and evaluation of the use of specific marketing instruments designed for a specific target group.

organization (business economy)

All the people, means and activities aimed at achieving certain objectives. Thus an organization distinguishes itself from private persons. For example, manufacturers, retailers and institutions.

positioning

The assigned position of an organization, an SBU, a brand or a product in the perception of consumers in relation to comparable competitors.

price

The exchange value of an article or a service (product) expressed in a unit of account (mostly money). The price may be considered to be the proceeds carrier and an element in the marketing mix.

price instruments

Means which can be used to affect the price/value ratio of exchange objects for consumers, as part of the marketing policy. Price instruments themselves include the following part-instruments: the ex-works price, the contribution margin, wholesaler and retailer margins, trade discounts, the consumer price, consumer discounts, list prices, offer prices, rebates, bonuses, credit mark ups and cash discounts, and the tender price.

price mix

Combination and fine-tuning of the pricing instruments for a specific target group by a particular organization.

price policy

Analysis, planning, implementation and evaluation of activities with regard to the price instruments as part of a marketing policy.

product

The conglomerate of material and immaterial properties of a product or service. This relates to anything that may be offered on a market, for consumption, use, usage or attention, which can fill a specific need. With regard to the constituent parts of the product, Leeflang distinguishes between the physical, extended and total product and Kotler distinguishes between the core benefit offered by this product, the tangible product and the augmented product.

product concept

Way in which the market approach may be materialized. This concept assumes that exchange transactions are best accomplished by paying much attention to quality improvements of the product. The concept is characterized by a large degree of internal orientation. The idea is that a good product sells itself. *See also:* market management philosophies.

product instrument

Means which can be used to have the attributes of the exchange object match the means of the consumers as part of the marketing policy. Product instruments include the following part-instruments: design, style, modelling, brand, packaging and the technical specification of the product, quality, nature and type and the number of products to be manufactured or traded in, expressed in the width, depth, length and height of the range.

product/market combination
Selection of exchange objects and exchange subjects on the basis of a strategic choice of consumer needs that an organization wants to fill, and of consumer (groups) it wants to aim at.

product/market/technology combination
Selection of exchange objects, exchange subjects and technologies on the basis of a strategic choice of consumer needs that an organization wants to fill, of consumer (groups) it wants to aim at, and the way in which (using which technology) it plans to do so.

product mix
Virtual implementation, combination and fine-tuning of the product instruments for a specific target group by a particular organization.

product policy
Analysis, planning, implementation and evaluation of activities with respect to the product instrument as part of a marketing policy.

production concept
Way in which the market approach may be materialized. This concept assumes that exchange transactions are best accomplished by enhancing the efficiency and the capacity of production and distribution. The concept is characterized by a large degree of internal orientation. When the product is cheap and available, it will sell. *See also:* market management philosophies.

retail marketing
Marketing activities carried out by retail businesses.

segmentation
Dividing a market in various (homogeneous) groups of consumers to be distinguished, for which it may be desirable to apply a specific marketing strategy or marketing mix. As a basis for segmentation, four groups of market segmentation criteria may be distinguished: geographical, demographical, psycho-graphical, and behaviouristic segmentation criteria.

selling concept
Way in which the product sales can be accomplished. This concept assumes that exchange transactions can be best materialized by emphasizing communication and distribution efforts. *See also:* market management philosophies.

services marketing
Marketing activities of an organization where the exchange objects to be traded in are services.

social marketing concept
Way in which a marketing approach can be materialized with emphasis on social gain. This concept is supplementary to the marketing concept where social effects of long-term exchange processes are also taken into account. *See also:* market management philosophies.

strategic marketing management
Analysis, planning, implementation and evaluation of marketing activities, with respect to the choice of the product/market/technology combinations, the target groups and the positionings required.

supplier marketing (purchasing marketing, reverse marketing)
Marketing activities by organizations directed at suppliers.

target group (marketing target group)
Group of (potential) consumers which the organization aims at and for which it carries out specific marketing activities.

target group selection (targeting)
Determining the group of existing and potential consumers at which an organization (section) wants to aim and for which it wants to carry out specific marketing activities.

trade marketing
Marketing activities of a producer or distributor aimed at (potential) retailers of his goods.

undifferentiated marketing
A segmentation strategy where the organization, usually for reasons of efficiency, chooses to approach the total market using one marketing programme, irrespective of the differences between consumer (groups).

References and further reading

Assael, H., *Marketing: principles and strategy*, The Dryden Press, Chicago, 1990.

Dibb, S., L. Simkin, W.M. Pride and O.C. Ferrell, *Marketing: concepts and strategies*, European edition, Houghton Mifflin, Boston, 1991.

Heuvel, T. van den, J.H.C. Post and A.L.M. Verbeek, *Basisboek Marketing*, Wolters-Noordhoff, Groningen, 2nd edition, 1991.

Koster, J.M.D., *Grondslagen van de marketingwetenschap*, Stenfert Kroese, Leiden, 1991.

Kotler, Ph., *Marketing Management: Analysis, Planning, Implementation and Control*, Prentice-Hall, Englewood Cliffs, New Jersey, 7th edition, 1991.

Kotler, Ph. and G. Armstrong, *Principles of Marketing*, Prentice-Hall, Englewood Cliffs, New Jersey, 1989.

Kuhlmeijer, H.J. and B.A. Bakker, *Commerciële beleidsvorming*, Stenfert Kroese, Leiden/Antwerpen, 3rd edition, 1990.

Leeflang, P.S.H. and P.A. Beukenkamp, *Probleemgebied Marketing: een management benadering*, Stenfert Kroese, Leiden/Antwerpen, 1987.

Leeflang, P.S.H. and P.A. Beukenkamp, *Probleemvelden in Marketing*, Stenfert Kroese, Leiden/Antwerpen, 1988.

Lilien, G.L., Ph. Kotler and K.S. Moorthy, *Marketing Models*, Prentice-Hall, Englewood Cliffs, New Jersey, 1992.

Verdoorn, P.J., *Het commercieel beleid bij verkoop en inkoop*, Stenfert Kroese, Leiden, 2nd edition, 1971.

Verhage, B.J. and W.H. Cunningham, *Grondslagen van de Marketing*, Stenfert Kroese, Leiden/Antwerpen, 2nd edition, 1989.

Wijnia, S. and J.C.A.M. Wagenmakers, *Commerciële Bedrijfseconomie*, Wolters-Noordhoff, Groningen, 2nd edition, 1993.

2 EXTERNAL ENVIRONMENT

Concept overview

backward integration
boom
branch
brand competition
buyer
buyers' market

captive market
cartel
Chamber of Commerce and Industry
classic distribution channel
company
competition
competitive forces
competitor
competitor profile
concentration curve
concentration process
consumer organization
consumerism
cost structure of the industry
cultural factors
cumulative penetration ratio
cumulative possession ratio
current demand

demand
demand concentration
demand curve
demand equation
demand structure
demanded quantity
demographic factors
depression
deregulation
derived demand
differentiation
direct distribution
distribution channel
distribution link
distribution structure
distributor

economic climate
economic factors
economies of scale
economies of scope
end user
entry barrier
environmental factors
exit barrier
external environment

final demand
forward integration
futures market

generic competition
geographic factors

heterogeneous oligopoly
homogeneous oligopoly
horizontal competition

increased demand
indirect distribution
industrial demand
industry
industry column
initial demand
initial purchase
installed base
institutional factors
integration
interaction
interface
internal environment

joint venture

latent demand
lobby
long distribution channel

macro environmental factors
market
market concentration
market concentration, degree of
market concentration ratio
market form
market fragmentation
market parties
market penetration
market saturation
market segment
market share
market size
marketing environment
micro-environmental matters
middleman
monopolistic competition
monopoly
monopsony

need competition
network
networking

oligopsony
original equipment manufacturer (OEM)

parallelism
Parfitt–Collins test analysis
penetration ratio of non-durables
physical factors

political-legal factors
polyopsony
possession ratio
potential competition
potential demand
potential market
primary demand
product class
product form competition
product group
production coherence
production factors and means
professional organizations
purchase factor market
purchasing frequency
purchasing power
pure competition

recession
relative market share
repeat purchase
replacement demand
replacement purchase

sales market
satisfaction, degree of
secondary demand
selective demand
sellers' market

serviced market
short distribution channel
social class
social status
social-cultural factors
social-economic factors
specialization
spot market
stakeholders
standard of living
strategic alliance
structural overcapacity
subcontracting
substitution
supplied quantity
supply
supply curve
supply function
supply structure
supply surplus

technical factors
total demand
trade organization

usage intensity index
usage intensity rate
user

vertical competition

Concept descriptions

backward integration
The process in which an organization is going to carry out activities in one of more preceding sections of the industry sector.

boom
Stage in the general economic situation characterized by a strong and long-term upsurge of economic activities.

branch (line of business)
Group of organizations in a certain branch of industry showing a large amount of similarity with regard to both production techniques and products supply. For example, the food industry in the retail trade industry or the book industry in the printing trade.

brand competition
Competition between different brands of a particular product which are each other's substitute. *See also:* need competition, generic competition, and product form competition.

buyer
Private person or organization buying, leasing or renting products.

buyers' market
Market situation where the buyers have a stronger position than the suppliers, because the quantity offered exceeds the quantity asked for. *See also:* sellers' market.

captive market (proprietary market)
Market situation where, due to contracts, patterns, or on the basis of loyalty, groups of buyers or, for example, distributors are bound to a specific supplier.

cartel
An agreement between organizations which usually produce similar goods and/or services, making arrangements in order to reinforce their joint position. As a rule cartels include:
– condition cartel: arranging conditions of payment and delivery;
– quota cartel: arranging manufactured quantities;
– area cartel: arranging the division of outlets;
– price cartel: agreeing on minimum prices;
– calculation cartel: where a specific calculation scheme is operated by the partners.

Chamber of Commerce and Industry
Statutory organization aimed at promoting the economic interests of trade and industry, providing information, and keeping an eye on the orderly course of economic affairs and implementing different Acts.

classic distribution channel (conventional channel, traditional channel)
Indirect, long distribution form, where at least two distributors (importer and/or wholesale or retail trade) are involved in the distribution of a particular product.

company (enterprise)
Legally and economically independent organization in which one or more business units are being developed, with the objective of making profit. Enterprises can be distinguished on the basis of legal structure, for example, one-man businesses, private limited companies, co-operative societies and state enterprises; and on the basis of the degree of interweaving, for example, conglomerate or group, parent company and subsidiary company.

competition
Process occurring between various parties in which each party attempts to achieve its own goal and therefore competes with other parties. Competition occurs in many fields. For example, in marketing this process can occur between suppliers offering similar products while each tries to obtain the largest possible share of the market. The competition

process generally has a positive influence on the performance and development of competing parties; however, it can also have a negative influence on the (long-term) profitability of the average competitor.

competitive forces
Forces affecting the nature and the extent of competition in a specific branch of industry. Porter distinguishes five competitive forces, namely: the extent of competition between existing co-suppliers, the negotiation power of the suppliers, the negotiation power of the buyers, the threat of substitutes and the potential entry of new competitors.

competitor
Supplier of a product fulfilling an identical or similar need of a specific group of buyers.

competitor profile
Description of competing parties compared to one's own organization in terms of, amongst others, present activities, objectives, strategies, strengths and weaknesses.

concentration curve
Curve showing the link between the percentage of organizations within a branch of industry on the one hand, and the percentage of the total volume of this industry realized by these organizations on the other.

concentration process
Market process where the number of independent suppliers, buyers or intermediaries decreases, for example, as a result of co-operation, mergers, and acquisitions, or where the largest suppliers take up an ever increasing market share.

consumer organization
Organization of individual consumers. The consumer organization aims at improving the position of consumers in general and its members in particular, and at defending their interests. Ways to accomplish this include providing information to consumers and publishing comparative tests in the monthly consumers' guide and supplying personal advice and legal assistance for members. In addition, the consumer organization endeavours to promote legislation and regulations ensuring consumer rights, for example, with regard to labelling, advertising, warranties and product liability.

consumerism
Political movement among consumers aiming mainly at ensuring and improving consumer rights and reinforcing their position as a market party.

cost structure of the industry
A typical ratio for a specific branch of industry between:
- constant and variable costs;
- costs of capital, labour, raw materials and energy;
- direct and indirect costs;
- cost advantages resulting from economies of scale and series size;
- functional costs, including costs of design, transport, production, marketing, sales, service, research and innovation, human resources, infrastructure.

cultural factors
Macro environmental factors affecting the policy of organizations in a particular field, relating to characteristics of society and social relationships, such as the common values and standards, convictions, needs and desires, the presence of different cultures, subcultures and cultural movements.

cumulative penetration ratio
Ratio indicating the number of buyers in relation to the market potential who have, at least once, bought a non-durable product or brand from the moment of introduction. *See also:* cumulative possession ratio.

cumulative possession ratio (ownership)
Ratio indicating the real number of buyers in relation to the potential number of buyers having bought a particular durable article or brand right from the moment of introduction, at least once. In the Netherlands, for example, the cumulative degree of possession for bicycles is nearly 100 per cent. The actual degree of possession is considerably lower, for example, because elderly people will stop using their bicycles and discard their bicycles at some point of time. *See also:* cumulative penetration ratio.

current demand (market demand)
The customers for a specific product or brand virtually taking part in the exchange process, and particularly the quantities asked by them or the financial value involved.

demand
Total amount of products that is demanded on a specific market at a specific moment or during a specific period.

demand concentration
Process under influence of which an ever increasing part of the total demand originates from an ever decreasing number of consumers.

demand curve
Diagram showing the different quantities of a specific product or specific product group (which will be) demanded at various prices at a particular moment or during a particular period on a particular market (by a particular group of potential buyers). Generally, demand is represented by a descending curve. At higher prices, demand is less than at lower prices.

demand equation
Algebraic equation showing the relationship between the scope of the demand and the variables considered to affect it. A very general demand function is the one in which the quantity of a product asked for is considered to be dependent on the price of that product, given the price of all other products and in otherwise unchanged circumstances.

demand structure
The demand structure of a market is related to the number of consumers, the demand concentration, the demand segments and the market definition. *See also:* supply structure.

demanded quantity
The total quantity of a specific product demanded at a specific moment or during a specific period in a specific market.

demographic factors
Macro environmental factors which (may) affect the policies of all organizations in a particular country for a particular area with respect to the characteristics of its population as a whole, such as: sex, age, race, religion, marital state, demographic pressure, distribution of the population, labour participation, education level, development of the population, and the relative decrease of the number of users in the population. The Office of Population Census Statistics (OPCS) supplies demographic index figures on an annual basis.

depression
Stage in the general economic climate characterized by a long-term and greatly reduced economic activity. *See also*: recession.

deregulation
Process reducing government control over economic activity.

derived demand
Demand for products by organizations resulting in the consequent demand by consumers (final customers) for a specific product.

differentiation
Process in which organizations which originally performed functions in different successive sections of the industry sector pass on one or more of these functions to independently working organizations.

direct distribution (direct channel)
Form of distribution in which the manufacturer supplies direct, without using distributors, to the end consumers. Both the retail trade and the wholesale trade are eliminated in that case. *See also:* indirect distribution.

distribution channel
Successive distributors involved in the distribution of a particular product. A distinction is made between direct and indirect distribution. Direct distribution means that the manufacturer or importer himself delivers products to the end consumer, without using distributors. In the case of indirect distribution one (short channel) or more other distributors supplying each other (long channel) are involved.

distribution link
One or more distributors fulfilling the same trade function within the distribution channel. Thus, the joint exporters form one link. This also applies for the joint importers, the joint agents, the joint commission agents, the joint brokers, the joint wholesale companies and the joint retail businesses, respectively.

distribution structure (distribution pattern)
Nature, number, scope and distribution of the various distributors in a specific area with regard to all goods of a specific product.

distributor (dealer)
Organization fulfilling a trade function in the distribution channel between manufacturer and end user. This may be an exporter, an importer, an agent, a broker, a commission agent, a wholesale trade, a retail trade or a comparable organization.

economic climate
Successive movement in the economic activities which cannot be derived from natural or seasonal factors. *See also:* depression, boom, recession.

economic factors
Macro environmental factors affecting the (economic) operation of all organizations in a specific area, with regard to conditions such as: state of the general economic climate (depression, boom), level of savings and investments, Gross National Income or Gross National Product, inflation, rates of exchange and fluctuations, interest rates and balance of payment.

economies of scale
Cost advantages resulting from the size of the organization and/or the production machinery. The larger the organization, or the scope of production, the lower the constant cost per product unit.

economies of scope
Relative advantages for an organization as a result of the specialization in specific activities, reflected in lower costs per product unit.

end user
The end user or final consumer of a specific product. In most cases this identifies the consumer.

entry barrier
Barrier to the entry of new suppliers in a specific market. Such a barrier is mostly caused by a combination of economic and strategic factors. Think of such factors as scope of investments, effects of scale, technology, etc.

environmental factors (environmental influences)

Influences from the macro, meso and micro environment on an organization which may be essential for the functioning of this organization in its markets and the (strategic) marketing policy. In the analysis stage of the marketing planning process extensive attention is given to the environmental factors relevant for the organization in question.

exit barrier

Barrier for existing suppliers to wind up activities in a certain market. Usually such a threshold is caused by a combination of economic, strategic and also emotional factors.

external environment

For an organization, usually influences beyond their control, arising outside their own organization, for example, competition, technology, availability of raw materials and labour, climate, legislation.

final demand

Demand for products by end users or final consumers. In most cases this denotes the demand for products by consumers.

forward integration

The process in which an organization is going to develop activities in one or more subsequent sections of the industry sector.

futures market

Market in which contracts are traded with regard to goods or currency which will be delivered at a later date. This is distinguished from spot markets, in which goods or currency are traded for immediate delivery.

generic competition

Competition between (suppliers of) different kinds of products which may satisfy an identical need of a certain consumer. This consumer can also fulfil a certain need in a wide variety of ways. Thus, somebody who has decided to go on holiday may have to choose between a camping holiday or holiday in hotels. *See also:* need competition, product form competition and brand competition.

geographic factors

Macro environmental factors affecting the policy of organizations in a specific area, with regard to geographical location, natural conditions, climate, infrastructure (roads, waterways, railroads, airlinks) and the telecommunication infrastructure (means of communication such as telephone, telefax, radio and television).

heterogeneous oligopoly

Market form where a limited number of competing suppliers offer a variant of a specific product within a specific product category.

homogeneous oligopoly

Market form where a relatively limited number of competing suppliers offer markedly similar products (homogeneous).

horizontal competition

Competition between (different) parts of organizations in the same industry sector, or in the same branch of industry or line of business. For example, competition between two manufacturers of bicycles. *See also:* brand competition.

increased demand

Sum of the initial demand and additional demand for a specific durable product or brand in the course of time or in a specific period.

indirect distribution

Distribution form where a manufacturer uses one or more distributors to distribute his products. In indirect distribution, a distinction is made between the short channel and the long channel. *See also:* classic distribution channel.

industrial demand
Demand by organizations for products from other organizations.

industry
Horizontal section in the industrial column. This section relates to organizations fulfilling an identical or similar function in the manufacturing process of various varieties of a specific product. The Central Statistical Office operates a standard classification for branches of industry, including accompanying codes.

industry column
The joint successive participants and their location in the manufacturing process of a specific product from o.e.m. (Original Equipment Manufacturer) to end consumer.

initial demand
Demand for a particular product by non-users or non-owners of that product, proceeding to buy that product for the first time. *See also:* increased demand.

initial purchase
The first time a consumer purchases a specific product brand or new product variant.

installed base
All the items of a specific durable consumption or production article present at a specific moment or in a specific period with all consumers.

institutional factors
Macro environmental factors influencing the policy of organizations in an area with regard to the presence and the importance of various types of institutions, including financial institutions (banks, insurance companies, pension funds, stock exchanges, lending institutions) government and public business organizations (PBOs, such as industrial board, product board) employers and workers organizations, branch and professional organizations, business and industrial services.

integration
Process where organizations are going to develop activities in one or more preceding (backward integration) or successive (forward integration) sections of the industry sector.

interaction (process)
Social process in which two or more people exchange information or interact.

interface
Common grounds between market parties and organizations in the external environment or between departments within an organization.

internal environment
For an individual organization, internal influences which are, in principle controllable. These influences relate to the organization itself and the different departments, including the organization structure and culture, staff policy, financial policy, marketing policy, production policy and logistical policy, purchasing policy, research and development policy and the strategic planning process.

joint venture
Form of co-operation between organizations where these organizations separate part of their company assets which are then joined into a new organization developing an activity or a market for joint account and risk. *See also*: strategic alliance.

latent demand
Non-manifest demand for a particular product in a particular group of potential buyers. Though they may have a need for the product, this need is not yet expressed, because the demanding party does not have sufficient means at his disposal, or because (the demanding party thinks) there is no (such) product (yet) which can fill this need.

lobby

Organized effort of a group of interested parties trying to promote their interests with the government or legislative or regulatory body, usually in an informal way. For example, the cigarette industry and its lobby against a ban on tobacco advertising.

long distribution channel

Indirect, long distribution form where a producer mobilizes at least two distributors for the distribution of his products to the end consumer. *See also:* distribution channel.

macro environmental factors

For an individual organization external influences beyond its control consisting of such factors as geographic, demographic, socio-economic, socio-cultural, economic, technical-technological, political-legal, physical-environmental and constitutional factors.

market

1 In an economic sense. The market consists of all those demanding and supplying a particular product or particular products, and the total amounts of that product demanded, or supplied by them, respectively, during a specific period in a specific area. The combination of forces of market parties also determine the price for the product on the market eventually.

2 In marketing literature the market is generally described from the viewpoint of the customer. Then, the market is the collection of demanding parties for a particular product or particular products ('markets are people').

3 Physical market when suppliers and buyers (intermediaries, if any) assemble to trade, whether or not physically present, products. For example, a weekly market or the stock exchange.

market concentration

Market focus causing the number of independent suppliers or intermediaries to decrease.

market concentration, degree of

Extent to which the number of independent suppliers, buyers or intermediaries is limited in the market for a particular product, or the extent to which the market shares have been divided between the various co-suppliers or buyers. With a larger extent of concentration the influence of an individual supplier or buyer in the market will be greater. Frequently used indicators for the degree of concentration are the C4-index (the sum of the market shares of the four largest suppliers) and the Herfindahl-index (the sum of the square of the market shares of each supplier).

market concentration ratio

Extent to which the number of independent suppliers or intermediaries in the market for a specific product is limited, or the extent to which the market shares have been divided between the various co-suppliers. In a situation where there is a greater extent of concentration of supply, the influence of each supplier in the market will increase. *See also:* market concentration, degree of.

market form (structure)

Characterization of a market on the basis of the number of suppliers, consumers and the homogeneity or heterogeneity of the products traded. The following market forms are distinguished: monopoly, monopsony, homogeneous and heterogeneous, oligopoly, oligopsony, monopolistic competition (heterogeneous polypoly), complete (free) competition (homogeneous polypoly) and polyopsony.

market fragmentation

Phenomenon of markets and market segments disintegrating into progressively smaller segments.

market parties

All suppliers, demanders, intermediaries and influencers in a particular market.

market penetration (purchase penetration, ownership penetration, penetration)
Number of owners or users of a particular product as part of the total number of owners or users in the available market. A distinction is made between durable products where it is about owners, and non-durable products, where it is about users. *See also:* possession ratio, penetration ratio of non-durables.

market saturation
Situation where virtually all potential buyers of a specific product have in effect become consumers and where it is not, or scarcely possible to increase the total amount of products to be sold by stimulating the demand. The total sale of a certain product on that market stagnates or decreases even. For each supplier it, therefore, applies that he can only increase his sale in the market at the expense of the sale of competitors in that market. *See also:* satisfaction, degree of.

market segment
A group of buyers with common properties, for whom it may be desirable to apply a specific marketing strategy or marketing mix.

market share
Relation between the sales or turnover of a specific product brand of a specific supplier in comparison with the total sales or turnover of all suppliers of the product in question in a particular market during a particular period. The market share in units (also called volume market share) relates to the share of the total quantity sold; the market share in turnover concerns the share in revenue.

market size
Size of the current or potential demand in terms of volume or money.

marketing environment
Group of factors affecting the policy of an individual organization. The major part of these factors cannot be controlled by an individual organization, other factors can be influenced, and a limited number is controllable. The marketing environment can be classified in various ways, including the external and internal environment.

micro-environmental matters (factors) (internal environmental factors)
For an individual organization, the internal and in principle controllable influences. These factors have to do with the organization itself and its different functions, including organization structure and culture, staff policy, financial policy, marketing policy, production policy and logistic policy, purchasing policy, research and development policy and the strategic planning process.

middleman (intermediary)
Person or organization who in some way or another acts as an intermediary and renders services in the exchange transactions between suppliers and consumers.

monopolistic competition (heterogeneous polypoly)
Market form where a large number of suppliers each market a differentiated product but with similar function.

monopoly
Market form where only one supplier of a specific product is present in the market.

monopsony
Market form where there is only one buyer for a particular product in the market.

need competition
Competition between different needs of a particular buyer. At a particular moment a buyer cannot spend time on, or place means at the disposal of all needs simultaneously. Thus, at a given moment, someone may have to choose between going on holiday or refurbishing his home. *See also:* generic competition, brand competition, product form competition.

network

Formal or informal complex of relations between various persons and/or organizations who have a common characteristic or interest, or who work together.

networking

The conscious and systematic construction and maintenance of a group of persons and/or organizations.

oligopsony

Market form where there is only a limited number of buyers for a specific product in the market.

original equipment manufacturer (OEM)

Manufacturer who produces/assembles (capital) goods, for which he will use other suppliers, brand products as components. When marketing his own product the manufacturer can then use the suppliers' brand as an (additional) selling argument. An example of this is the slogan 'Intel inside' for computers which have Intel chips/processors built in during assembly.

parallelism (parallelization)

Process where organizations are carrying out activities which so far had not been carried out within the same branch of industry. For example, in the retail trade, nut shops which are going to sell special cheeses as well.

Parfitt–Collins test analysis

Analysis method allowing an estimate to be made of the eventual market share to be obtained in an early stage after the introduction of a non-durable article. In this case three indicators are relevant:

· the cumulative degree of penetration;
· the percentage of recurrent purchases;
· the consumption intensity index.

By multiplying these three indicators with each other an estimate is produced of the eventual market share. For example, with a 40% cumulative degree of penetration, 60% recurrent purchases, and 1.25% consumption intensity index, on the basis of this analysis, an eventual market share of 30% ($0.40 \times 0.60 \times 0.25$) is expected for the new brand.

penetration ratio of non-durables

Ratio indicating the number of consumers in relation to the market potential who have at least once bought a specific non-durable product or brand in a specific period.

physical factors (environmental factors)

Macro environmental factors affecting the policy of organizations in a particular area with regard to scarcity of raw materials, harvest fluctuations, air, water and soil pollution and noise pollution.

political-legal factors

Macro environmental factors influencing the policy of organizations in a specific area with regard to the (political) form of government (democracy, dictatorship), the political stability and integrity, the political constitution of the government, the government policy and associated legal and regulative system.

polyopsony

Market form with many consumers of a specific product in the market.

possession ratio (ownership)

Ratio identifying the real number of buyers in relation to the potential number of buyers, possessing or using at least one article of a particular durable product or brand at a particular moment or in a particular period. *See also:* penetration ratio of non-durables.

potential competition
Suppliers, not yet present in a particular market segment, forming a potential threat for the current suppliers as a result of low entry thresholds in the market in question, the development of attractive substitutes and attractive profit prospects.

potential demand
The not yet manifest demand of consumers interested in a specific product.

potential market (market potential)
That part of all consumers (the total population, all organizations) being interested in a specific product, and which is likely to buy this product in the future, for example, at lower prices for that product or due to an increase in their budgets, or when the familiarity or availability increases or when potential buyers are more and more convinced of the 'benefits' of the product in question.

primary demand
The total demand for a product class in a specific period and in a specific area. For example, the (annual) demand for bicycles or soft drinks in the Netherlands. *See also:* secondary demand.

product class (product category)
A group of products belonging to a specific product class which are closely related to each other with regard to fulfilling the same or a comparable need. A product group consists of various products and product variants. For example, the soft drink product group featuring cola or fruit juice products. Product variants within the fruit juice product group are, for example, apple juice and orange juice.

product form competition (product type competition)
Competition between different technical appearances of one and the same product. For example, competition between instant coffee and filter coffee. *See also:* need competition, generic competition and brand competition.

product group
A group of products belonging to a specific product class which are closely related to each other with regard to fulfilling the same or a comparable need. A product group consists of various products and product variants. For example, the soft drink product group featuring cola or fruit juice products. Within the fruit juice product group there are several product variants (apple juice, orange juice).

production coherence
Phenomenon where two or more products are produced on the basis of the same production process. For example, in an oil refinery various fuels, lubricants, and semi-manufactures for the petro-chemical industry are produced simultaneously.

production factors and means (factors and means of production)
Labour, capital, land, natural resources, management or information.

professional organizations
Association of professionals usually aimed at promoting the interests of its members, and increasing the status of the profession as well as the development of the profession.

purchase factor market
The joint suppliers being potential suppliers for a particular organization.

purchasing frequency (buying frequency, demand frequency)
The number of times that a specific buyer purchases a specific product or brand in a specific period.

purchasing power
Amount of money which consumer(s) can spend on the purchase of products. The purchasing power depends on income, savings, credit and the fixed charges of the consumer, and the extent of inflation.

pure competition (homogeneous polypoly)
Market form (theoretical) in which a relatively large number of suppliers offers a completely identical product in the market.

recession
Decline in economic activity after a period of growth. Recessions affect the purchasing power of consumers and also lead to company closures, higher unemployment, etc. *See also:* depression.

relative market share
The ratio between the market share of an organization and its biggest competitor in the market concern. When the market share of the company is for example, 30 per cent and the market share of its biggest competitor is 20 per cent, then the relative market share is 1.5.

repeat purchase
Second or successive purchase of an article or brand by a customer. *See also:* initial purchase.

replacement demand
The demand of current users of a certain specific durable product for a replacement item because the former item is not used any more or will be discarded. *See also:* initial demand.

replacement purchase
Second or subsequent purchase of a specific durable product or brand to replace a former item which has been discarded. *See also:* initial purchase.

sales market (market, outlet output market)
The joint consumers who are both buyers and potential buyers for a particular organization.

satisfaction, degree of (saturation ratio)
Relationship between the total number of products sold on a specific market since the introduction, and the total number of potential products to be bought, including any additional purchases. *See also:* market saturation, penetration ratio of non-durables.

secondary demand
Demand in units for a specific brand at a specific moment or in a specific period. For example, the amount for Coca-Cola. *See also:* primary demand.

selective demand (specific demand)
Relative demand for a specific brand within a specific product class at a specific moment or in a specific period (market share).

sellers' market
Market situation in which the suppliers have a stronger position than the buyers, because demand exceeds supply. *See also:* buyers' market.

serviced market (served market)
That part of the total market for a product or a service (in terms of buyer groups) on which (part of) an organization focuses.

short distribution channel
Indirect, short distribution form where the producer utilizes only one distributor (retail trade) for the distribution of his products to final consumers.

social class (prosperity class)
Classification of individuals within a social system in a hierarchy of distinctive status classes. This is done in such a way that the individuals within a certain class have more or less the same status, but as compared with the individuals of another class they have a different higher or lower status.

(1) class A: the well-to-do (managers of large companies, high ranking officials, the upper layer of professionals, etc.);
(2) class B1:   the upper layer of the middle group (including managers of middle sized companies, sub-top officials, etc.);
(3) class B2:   the lower layer of the middle group (including managers of small businesses, middle management and officials, etc.);
(4) class C: the less well-to-do (owners of small businesses, low level public servants and office staff, skilled labourers);
(5) class D: the least well-to-do (unskilled labourers, people out of work, etc.);
(6) class E: subsistence level (pensioners, widows, casual workers).

social status

Relative position or a rank within a group assigned to someone on the grounds of role, experience, age, skills or knowledge.

social-cultural factors

Macro environmental factors influencing organizations in a specific area, relating to the nature and number of social classes (usually on the basis of differences in income) and social status, work ethics, work participation, degree of mobility, and number and diversity of the media.

social-economic factors

Macro environmental factors influencing organizations in a specific area on the grounds of a combination of social and economic factors such as division of incomes over the various social classes and income groups, social benefits and the social security system.

specialization

Process in which organizations eliminate activities within the same section of the industry sector (branch of industry or line of business), which up to that moment had been carried out by those organizations. For example, delicatessen shops selling both nuts and cheese, specializing in selling cheese only.

spot market

Market in which goods or currency are traded for immediate delivery. This is distinguished from the term markets, in which contracts are traded with regard to goods or currency which will be delivered at a later date. Prices in spot markets are known as 'spot prices'.

stakeholders (interest groups)

All parties and persons in some way or another interested in an organization, including government, consumers, trade, suppliers, staff and financiers.

standard of living

The level of prosperity of an economic unit (person, household, country), usually reflected in the total number of products (such as food, clothing, furniture, transport and medical facilities) which are consumed by this economic unit.

strategic alliance

Co-operation between two or more organizations. While retaining their independence and identity, they co-operate in a common area of vital importance for the continuity of the separate organizations. Strategic alliances can occur between competitors (horizontal), with suppliers (up-stream), consumers (down-stream) and organizations outside their own market(s) (diversified). The co-operation can be formalized in the shape of, amongst others, joint ventures and consortiums. *See also:* network.

structural overcapacity

Market situation in which the total production capacity of the joint suppliers over a long period exceeds the current demand in that market to a large extent.

subcontracting
The acceptance and execution of (shared) activities by a supplier which were originally accepted for execution by another supplier.

substitution
Process in which a certain object (product brand or market party) on the basis of a change in preference can be replaced with another object comparable in other respects.

supplied quantity
The total quantity of a specific product, offered in a specific market at a specific moment or during a specific period.

supply
The total quantity of goods offered in a specific geographical area at a specific moment or over a specific period.

supply curve
Diagram showing the quantities of a specific product which (could be) supplied by the joint suppliers at different prices at a certain moment or during a certain period, and in otherwise unchanged circumstances.

supply function
Algebraic chart showing the relationship between the quantity offered and the variables considered to affect it. A very general supply function is the one in which the quantity of a product supplied is considered to be dependent on the price of that product, given the price of all other products and in otherwise unchanged circumstances.

supply structure
The supply structure of the market is related to the number of suppliers, the concentration of the supply, the access and exit thresholds of a market and the cost structure of the suppliers. *See also:* demand structure.

supply surplus
Market situation where the total supply structurally exceeds the total demand in a specific market.

technical factors (technological factors)
A group of macro environmental factors influencing organizations in a specific area, with regard to the degree of mechanization and automation of production processes, the development of product technology and the presence of the required (telecommunication) infrastructure and the availability of skilled staff in this respect.

total demand (total sale)
Sum of the increase in demand and the replacement demand for a specific product or brand in the course of time or a specific period.

trade organization
Public corporate body with respect to a horizontal section in an industry sector, namely organizations having an identical or similar function in a specific production process (for example, the Agricultural Board, the Catering Organization). Trade organizations have been given the legal authority to issue regulations and to impose levies on all organizations in that branch of industry. Trade organizations advise the government, provide information for organizations in that branch of industry and may also be charged with the implementation and execution of regulations.

usage intensity index (consumption intensity index)
Index to determine the relative consumption intensity. This figure is determined by the relation between the average consumption of the consumers of a specific brand and the average consumption of all consumers of the product type concerned.

usage intensity rate (consumption intensity)

A consumer's average consumption of a specific non-durable product as compared with the average consumption of all consumers of that product within a specific period.

user

Person using or consuming a product, or organization processing or using a product in the manufacturing process.

vertical competition

Competition between organizations in different sections of the industry sector. For example, competition between bicycle shops and a bicycle importer who, besides supplying bicycle shops, also supplies to end consumers.

References and further reading

CBS, *Statistisch Jaarboek 1992*, CBS-publicaties, 's-Gravenhage, 1992.

Daems, H. and S. Douma, *Concurrentiestrategie en concernstrategie*, Kluwer, Deventer, 1989.

Dibb, S., L. Simkin, W.M. Pride and O.C. Ferrell, *Marketing: concepts and strategies*, European edition, Houghton Mifflin, Boston, 1991.

Heuvel, T. van den, J.H.C. Post and A.L.M. Verbeek, *Basisboek Marketing*, Wolters-Noordhoff, Groningen, 2nd edition, 1991.

Kotler, Ph., *Marketing Management: Analysis, Planning, Implementation and Control*. Prentice-Hall, Englewood Cliffs, New Jersey, 7th edition, 1991.

Kuhlmeijer, H.J. and B.A. Bakker, *Commerciële beleidsvorming*, Stenfert Kroese, Leiden/Antwerpen, 3rd edition, 1990.

Leeflang, P.S.H. and P.A. Beukenkamp, *Probleemgebied Marketing: een management benadering*, Stenfert Kroese, Leiden/Antwerpen, 1987.

Lilien, G.L., Ph. Kotler and K.S. Moorthy, *Marketing Models*, Prentice-Hall, Englewood Cliffs, New Jersey, 1992.

Porter, M.E., *Competitive Strategy: Techniques for Analyzing Industries and Competitors*, The Free Press, New York, 1980.

Porter, M.E., *The Competitive Advantage of Nations*, MacMillan Press, London, 1990.

Scherer, F.M. and D. Ross, *Industrial Market Structure and Economic Performance*, Houghton Mifflin, Boston, 1990.

Verdoorn, P.J., *Het commercieel beleid bij verkoop en inkoop*, Stenfert Kroese, Leiden, 2nd edition, 1971.

Wijnia, S. and J.C.A.M. Wagenmakers, *Commerciële Bedrijfseconomie*, Wolters-Noordhoff, Groningen, 2nd edition, 1993.

3 BUYER BEHAVIOUR

Concept overview

acculturation
active summary
actual self
adaptation
adaptation level
additional demand
additional purchase
adopters
adoption
adoption category
adoption curve
adoption process
adoption, speed of
affect referral
affective component of attitude
affective response
affiliation, the need for
AIDA model
aided awareness
AIO
anticipating socialization
aspiration group
aspiration level
Assael's purchasing behaviour model
assimilation contrast theory
associative memory network
associative value
attention
attitude
attitude change
attitude formation
attitude object
attitude research
attraction effect
attribute
attributed role
attribution theory
autonomous decision
average possession
awareness
awareness analysis
awareness set

baby-boomer
backward conditioning
balance theory
bandwagon effect
basic need
behaviour
behaviour, consistency of
behaviour, determinants of
behaviouristic approach
belief
black box

brand
brand awareness
brand image
brand loyalty
brand personality
brand preference
brand recognition
business buyer
buyer
buyer behaviour
buyer's credit
buying behaviour model
buying motive
buying power
buying process
buying role

cancellation rate
categorization
central cues
central route
central values
characteristics approach
choice criteria
choice set
classic conditioning
classification dominance
coding
cognition
cognitive approach
cognitive capacity
cognitive component of attitude
cognitive consistency theories
cognitive dissonance
cognitive map
cognitive responses
communication
communication behaviour
compatibility
compensatory decision rule
completely planned purchase
complexity
comprehension
conative component of attitude
concept attainment
concept formation
conditioned response
conditioned stimulus
confirmation
conformity
conjunctive decision rule
consideration set
consistency
consistency theory

constructive decision rule
consumer
consumer behaviour
consumer franchise
consumer goods
consumer psychology
consumers' frustration
consumption ideology
consumption package
consumption pattern
consumption quota
consumption time
continuous innovation
convenience goods
cost-consciousness
credence claims
credit
cross-cultural consumer analysis
cues
culture
custom
customer satisfaction monitoring
    programme
cut-off
cyclical behaviour

decay theory
decision-making process
declaratory knowledge
decoding
demand
demonstrative consumption
desire
differential threshold
diffusion process
discontinuous innovation
discretionary income
disjunctive decision rule
dismissive behaviour
disposable income
dissolution
dissonance-reducing behaviour
dogmatism
drive
durable consumer goods
dyadic relationship
dynamic continuous innovation

early adopters
early majority
echoistic observation
ego-defensive function of attitude
elaboration
elaboration likelihood
Elaboration Likelihood Model of
    Persuasion (ELM)
elimination-by-aspects decision rule

emergency goods
emotional motive
empty nester
enculturation
end consumer
end values
Engel, Blackwell and Miniard model
Engel's Law
epidemiological model
episodical knowledge
ergonomics
ethnic patterns
evaluation
evaluation criteria
evaluation of alternatives
evoked set
experience claims
explicit consumer behaviour model
exposure
expressive qualities
extended family
extensive problem-solving purchasing
    behaviour
external search
extinction
extrinsic cues

Family life cycle
final demand
forward conditioning
free disposable income
frequently bought consumer goods
fun shopping
functional approach

generic need satisfaction
Gestalt
Gestalt psychology
Gestalt theory
group
group norm

halo effect
heavy users
hedonist benefits
hedonistic theories
hierarchy of needs
high commitment
high-benefit users
household
Howard & Sheth model

iconic perception
ideal self
identification
image
imagery
imitation effect

implicit consumer behaviour model
impulse goods
impulse purchase
incentive
incidental learning
indifference curve
individualizing
industrial buying process
industrial products
informal group
information environment
information overload
information processing
information, collection of
informational influence
informational motivation
initial purchase
inner-directed consumers
innovation
innovators
installed base
instrumental conditioning
instrumental role
instrumental value
intentional learning
interaction process
interest
interference
interference theory
internal search
intrinsic cues
involvement

knowledge
knowledge function of attitude

labelling
laddering
laggards
late majority
latent demand
Law of closeness
Law of equality
Law of mutual destiny
Law of nearness
lead users
learning
lexicographic decision rule
lifestyle
light users
limited problem-solving purchasing
  behaviour
look and listen, practice of
low commitment
low-balling

market fragmentation
market saturation
massification theory
me-too product
media consumption
medium users
memory
modelling
models of consumer behaviour
monodic approach
monomorphic social influence
motivation
Motivation Research
motivation type
multi-attribute attitude models
multi-stage interaction

need
need for cognition
need, recognition of
need-driven consumers
negative confirmation
Nicosia model
non-adopter
non-compensatory decision rule
non-durable consumption goods
norm
normative influence

on-going search
one-stop shopping
operand conditioning
opinion
opinion leader
optimal stimulating level
optimizing decision rule
outcomes
outer-directed consumers
overt behaviour
owners

partial confirmation
passive rejection
perceived quality
perceived risk
perceived value
perception
perceptual blockage
perceptual organization
peripheral cues
peripheral route
personal factors
personality
personality characteristic
phased decision strategy
polymorphic social influence

polymorphism
positive confirmation
post-consumptives
pre-consumptives
preference
price index number of family
 consumption
price shopping
primacy effect
primary group
proactive inhibition
problem solving
problem solving unit
procedural know-how
processing by attribute
processing by brand
product hierarchy
product-specific need satisfaction
projection
prompting
prospect
psychoanalytic theory
psychography
psycholinguistics
psychological characteristics
psychological surplus value
psychophysiological research
psychophysiology
public opinion
purchase
purchase frequency
purchase, intention to
purchaser
purchasing behaviour
purchasing motivation

rational decision-making
rational motive
rationalization
recency effect
recognition
reference group
reference person
reflex
rehearsal
relational approach
reminder
repeat purchase
replacement demand
replacement purchase
response
retention
retrieval
retrieval set
retroactive inhibition

retrospective questioning technique
risk perception
risk preparedness acceptence
role
role conflict
routing
routinized response behaviour

satisficing behaviour
saturation
schema
schemata
script
search claims
secondary group
secondary needs
selective attention
selective distortion
selective exposure
selective perception
selective recognition of need
selective retention
self-actualization
self-concept
self-designation method
self-monitoring
self-perception theory
self-referencing
self-serving bias
semiotic analysis
semiotics
sensation
sensation seeker
shopping behaviour
shopping goods
short list
significance structure
simple additive decision rule
simplifying decision rule
simultaneous conditioning
situational influence
social class
social facilitation
social inhibition
social status
socialization
speciality goods
stage of life
standard of living
standardized language
status
stimulus
stimulus categorization
stimulus determinants of attention
stimulus discrimination

stimulus generalization
stimulus response model
sub-culture
subjective knowledge
subjective norm
sublimation
subliminal perception
supplier loyalty
supply theories in consumer
  behaviour
support argument
symbolic group
system buying

teleshopping
terminal threshold
time goods
time saving goods
time using goods
transformational motivation
trial
trickle-down theory

two-level choice
type of decision

unaided awareness
unconditioned response
unconditioned stimulus
unsought goods
usage, knowledge of
use/usage behaviour
utilitarian benefits
utility
utility function of attitude
utility maximization

VALS typology
value
value congruency theory
value-expressive function of the attitude
variety seeking behaviour

wants
Weber–Fechner Law
Webster and Wind model
weighted additive decision rule

Concept descriptions

acculturation
Learning a new or 'foreign' culture and adapting to it. *See also:* enculturation.

active summary (synthesis)
Situation in which the consumer makes a link between two important beliefs and evaluation criteria, and uses it to be able to make a choice.

actual self
The image a person has of himself in relation to what he/she really is. This as opposed to how someone would like to be: the ideal self. *See also:* self-concept.

adaptation
Phenomenon whereby the consumers' perception of products/brands changes under the influence of positive expectations created by communication expressions.

adaptation level
The degree of habituation of individuals to certain stimuli (for instance an advertisement for a product). Below a specific level of habituation, these stimuli receive hardly any attention any more. However, if these stimuli are not present, then this is noticed.

additional demand
Demand for a certain durable product or brand by those who already own that product or brand, where an extra item is bought without putting out of use the item already owned, for example, purchasing a second TV set.

additional purchase
Purchase of a certain durable product or brand by someone who already owns that product or brand, when the additional item is bought, without discarding or putting out of use the item already owned.

adopters
Buyers/consumers who try a product (which is new for them) and who decide to buy it and to continue using it.

adoption
Decision by customers to try a product which is new (for them) and who after trial continue to use it.

adoption category
Rogers has distinguished five different adoption categories showing similarities as far as their adoption speed of an innovation is concerned: innovators, early adopters, early majority, late majority and laggards.

adoption curve
Diagram showing the percentage of newly added buyers (adopters) of a product, represented in time. On the basis of the differences in adoption speed, Rogers has distinguished five different adoption categories.

adoption process
Process taking place at the level of the individual consumer passing through various mental and behaviour stages, in trying out (or not) and continuing to use (or not) a product which is new. Traditionally, five stages are distinguished: awareness, interest, evaluation, trial and adoption.

adoption, speed of
Speed at which an individual consumer passes through the (entire) adoption process.

affect referral

Simple decision rule where consumers make a product choice on the basis of overall, general, sentimental judgements with regard to the brands taken into consideration, as opposed to accurately weighing the pros and cons of different brands at an attribute level.

affective component of attitude (sentimental aspect)

That part in the three-component model of attitudes relating to the emotions and feelings (positive or negative) an individual has built up with regard to a specific object. *See also:* cognitive component of attitude, conative component of attitude.

affective response

The feelings, emotions and/or moods evoked in an individual perceiving a stimulus (for example, a commercial or a product).

affiliation, the need for

The desire for affiliation with, friendship with, and acceptance by the members of the social group to which a person belongs (or wishes to belong).

AIDA model

Communication model assuming that individuals pass through four successive stages when processing information and making decisions, namely attention, interest, desire (to own the product/brand) and action (leading to the actual purchasing action).

aided awareness

Extent to which a group of buyers proves to be familiar with the product or brand when the product (or the brand name) in question is shown or mentioned. *See also:* unaided awareness.

AIO

Abbreviation for activities, interests and opinions. Psychographic variables essential in consumer research (into lifestyle and consumption behaviour), focusing on activities, interest and opinions of consumers. *See also:* lifestyle.

anticipating socialization

An individual's adopting standards, values and (purchasing) behaviour of a social group the individual would like to belong to.

aspiration group

Reference group an individual would like to be a member of. This desire is often reflected in the form of anticipated socialization.

aspiration level

What an individual would like to accomplish now or in the future (in terms of performance, property and possibilities).

Assael's purchasing behaviour model

In this model four types of purchasing behaviour are distinguished on the basis of customers' involvement and the differences between the products or brands: (1) complex purchasing behaviour (see also extended problem solving purchasing behaviour), (2) purchasing behaviour aimed at a dissonance reduction, (3) routine purchasing behaviour, and (4) alternating purchasing behaviour which occurs in the case where differences between the alternatives are rather big, but where customers' involvement is small.

assimilation contrast theory

Theory with regard to attitude change, assuming that individuals can only be subject to small changes in their attitudes (assimilation). If the attempt to change the attitude produces too large a contrast between the existing attitude and a presented attitude, then, in accordance with this theory, it can be predicted that the individual will resist the intended change in attitude (for example, presented in a certain advertisement).

associative memory network
A reflection of the idea that knowledge structures of individuals are stored in long-term memory as a group of nodes (the concepts) which may be interconnected in the form of 'memory links' (associations between these concepts).

associative value
Value attributed to an object by an individual on the basis of associations between different objects and the object attributes.

attention
Stage in the information processing procedure in which a certain amount of cognitive capacity is released for and attributed to incoming stimuli (for example, an advertisement). The amount of capacity released depends on these stimuli (intensity, effect of surprise, colour, and so on), on person-specific factors (including interest, need, adaptation level) and on situational environment factors. *See also:* selective attention.

attitude
Acquired, relatively long-term stance taken by someone with regard to persons, activities, products or organizations (= attitude objects). Generally it is assumed that the attitude model consists of three components. A distinction is made between: the cognitive component (the knowledge aspect), the affection component (the sentimental aspect) and the conative component (the behaviour aspect). *See also:* functional approach.

attitude change
Change occurring in (one or more components of) an existing attitude in an individual with regard to certain persons, activities, products or organizations.

attitude formation
Formation and development of a relatively long-term stance/attitude of a certain individual with regard to certain persons, activities, products or organizations.

attitude object
(person, activity, project, organization) with regard to which an individual adopts a certain attitude.

attitude research
Research with regard to the formation of attitudes, extent of durability of these attitudes and/or the way and the conditions in which attitudes may change.

attraction effect
Phenomenon that the attraction of a specific alternative is reinforced if a worse alternative is added to the set of alternatives, or the 'next best' alternative is removed from it.

attribute
Characteristic or property of a product. This term is often used to denote product characteristics that (may) serve as evaluation criteria in the decision-making process of buyers.

attributed role
What is expected of an individual with regard to his behaviour. These expectations are derived from personality characteristics which are supposed to be accompanied by a particular role behaviour, such as age, sex, race, and religion (for example, feminine behaviour, adult behaviour).

attribution theory
Theory assuming that individuals in most cases tend to put down an occurrence or event to a particular cause. Often, an event is put down to an internal or external cause. For example, if a product does not come up to expectations, this can be put down to a fault in the product itself (external attribution) or product misuse (internal attribution).

autonomous decision
Situation in the decision-making process within a consumption household where one of the partners independently makes the eventual choice.

average possession (ownership)

Total number of items of a certain durable product owned or used by buyers divided by the total number of buyers.

awareness (familiarity, realization)

First stage in the decision-making process of buyers with regard to the adoption of a new product. In this stage the consumer becomes aware of the existence of the product.

awareness analysis (familiarity analysis, brand awareness test)

Technique aimed at determining the brand awareness by asking consumers to recollect brand names (unaided awareness) or to recognize brand names (aided awareness).

awareness set

Group of brands (in a product class) known by the consumer.

baby-boomer

Somebody belonging to the relatively large group of consumers born during the baby-boom in the years after the Second World War (1945–1961).

backward conditioning

Form of classical conditioning in which a natural, neutral stimulus (= unconditioned stimulus) is followed by a neutral stimulus which is supposed to evoke a response to be conditioned (= conditioned stimulus). For example, on seeing food (neutral, natural stimulus) a bell starts ringing (conditioned stimulus).

balance theory

Theory with regard to attitude changes in which it is assumed that individuals try to avoid inconsistencies between different (components of) attitudes, and therefore try to reach a balance and consistency in (components of) their attitudes. According to this theory, an individual experiences his environment in the shape of triangular relationships in which persons, ideas and objects function as angular points.

bandwagon effect

Phenomenon where buyers who do not yet have a clear-cut preference for a specific brand, but who do have to make a choice, buy that brand which they think/know to be the most popular brand with other buyers.

basic need

A state of felt deprivation of some basic satisfaction, with regard to vital necessities such as staying alive, food, housing, safety and security. *See also:* need, wants.

behaviour

Key concept in psychology relating to all activities in human organism which can be observed and recorded. In consumer literature behaviour includes: purchasing behaviour, finding information (reading periodicals etc., listening to sales talks or information from friends/acquaintances), saving behaviour, spending behaviour, the way in which products are dealt with, discarding products and lodging complaints. *See also:* consumer behaviour.

behaviour, consistency of

Phenomenon where behaviour of individuals (for example, in supermarkets) remains relatively consistent over a period of time.

behaviour, determinants of

All factors that (may) affect an individual's behaviour, such as culture, age and situation.

behaviouristic approach

Idea that mental processes of individuals cannot be perceived, and therefore are not fit to be studied. In this approach the object of research lies with the relations that can be laid between (perceivable) stimuli and (overt) behaviour responses. *See also:* black box, implicit consumer behaviour model.

belief

Conviction held by an individual being a reflection of the knowledge and perception which that individual has with regard to a specific object. Beliefs are developed on the basis of associations (connections between two nodes in the associative memory network, for example, 'Volvo' and 'safe car', being expressed in: 'Volvo is a safe car'). Such convictions may be based on a personal experience with a product or marketing-communication-manifestations of the supplier, or communication with/of others (independent media, social contacts). Beliefs may be both positive and negative, and may be (partially) correct or (partially) incorrect. *See also:* cognition.

black box

Construction in implicit consumer behaviour models representing non-perceivable mental processes in the decision-making process. The mental processes in the decision-making process such as information processing (for example, in advertising) are non-perceivable and therefore hardly fit to be studied. On the basis of this construction it is assumed that these processes take place in a 'black box'. The only variables in these models are the perceivable stimuli and the (overt) behaviouristic response of the consumers. *See also:* behaviouristic approach, stimulus response model.

brand

A name, term, sign, symbol, mark, lettering or design (or any combination thereof) intended to differentiate a product from its competitors.

brand awareness

Degree (as expressed in a percentage) to which the target group can recognize the brand and/or the properties of that brand within a product class. With regard to the brand name the following classification is made: unfamiliar with; aided familiarity, or recognition of the brand names presented; unaided familiarity, when an individual will reproduce the name of the brand spontaneously, and 'top of the mind awareness', where a consumer mentions particular brands spontaneously in the first place.

brand image

All the images consumers have with regard to a brand, which can influence the behaviour of these consumers towards this specific brand. Part of the brand image is all the characteristics attributed to the brand (see: brand personality), but also characteristics that are associated with the product, and thus 'reflect' on the product (such as: country of origin, the social and environmental responsibility of the manufacturer, the reputation of the proprietor).

brand loyalty

The degree of consumer loyalty to a particular brand, i.e. the intention with which or the extent to which a consumer will buy or will continue to buy the brand in question, irrespective of possible changes taking place with the brand in question and (amendments in) competing products/brands. The consumer may display mostly non-indiscriminate purchasing behaviour, whereby over an ever longer period the same brand article is still bought. Indicators for the degree of brand loyalty include: (1) the number of times a consumer, consecutively, buys the brand in question; (2) the chance that a consumer will buy the brand in question again after a change in price or product.

brand personality

All the attributes of a specific brand in the way they are perceived by the buyers.

brand preference

Priority which a brand takes up in the awareness set of the consumer.

brand recognition

Mental image that a consumer forms in his mind, and on the basis of which a brand is recognized at the moment the consumer encounters it. This image may be composed of sensory patterns (colour, taste, packing), but it chiefly consists of the opinions on the performances of the product.

business buyer (industrial/organizational buyer)
Organization which buys products from other organizations because these products are directly or indirectly necessary for their own production process.

buyer
(1) Person, in the purchasing process, who is responsible for the purchase of products for himself, his household or organization. (2) Person or organization who buys or rents goods.

buyer behaviour
All activities of consumers directly related to acquiring, using and discarding goods, including information processing and decision processes preceding and following these activities. In this behaviour four aspects can be distinguished: (1) communication behaviour, (2) purchasing behaviour, (3) consumption behaviour, (4) dismissive behaviour.

buyer's credit
Situation in which a buyer effects a (partial) pre-payment, before the product is delivered.

buying behaviour model
Model developed to describe, explain, and/or predict purchasing behaviour. *See also:* consumer behaviour, Howard & Sheth model, Assael's purchasing behaviour model.

buying motive
Motive for the buyer to really buy something. The motive may be of a rational or an emotional nature; various buyers may purchase the same product for different reasons (for example, 'replacing the old product', 'because of the low price', 'because of the good quality', 'because of status').

buying power
Amount of money which (a group of) consumer(s) can spend to buy products. Purchasing power is dependent on the consumer's income, savings, credit, standing charges, and the height of inflation.

buying process
The procedural actions playing a role when a product is bought, including the choice of the place where the purchase is effected, signing a purchase agreement, payment, etc.

buying role
In some cases, more than one person is involved in the purchase of products (for example, with organizational purchasing behaviour, and with family purchasing decisions). The people involved may play different roles in the purchasing process, namely: initiator, influencer, gate-keeper, decision-maker, consultant, buyer and user.

cancellation rate
Ratio between the number of initial buyers who do not proceed to a recurrent purchase of a specific product/brand, and the total number of initial buyers.

categorization
Classification of a brand in a person's memory in such a way that the brand is easily recognized and can be evaluated.

central cues
Elements with respect to the content of an (advertising) message serving as a starting point for an individual in the formation and change of a reasoned attitude. *See also:* central route.

central route (central path)
Process in the framework of attitude change where the individual is induced to think about arguments with respect to content. The content of the (advertising) message and the use of relevant arguments play a major role in the formation of a well-reasoned opinion. *See also:* central cues, Elaboration Likelihood Model of Persuasion (ELM), peripheral route.

central values
Essential values in life being of the utmost importance for an individual. These values are essential for the interpretation of human behaviour. *See also:* value.

characteristics approach
Economic analysis of the choice behaviour of buyers, assuming that each product is a bundle/combination of characteristics. Preferences of consumers for each of the alternatives can be estimated by determining the utilitarian functions of each of the characteristics. *See also:* multi-attribute attitude models.

choice criteria (purchasing criteria)
Emotional and/or rational standards used by an individual to make choices.

choice set
Very limited (usually two or three) number of alternatives within the consideration set from which a consumer makes his final purchase choice.

classic conditioning
Kind of learning in which a conditioned stimulus (supposed to evoke a particular response which is conditioned) is linked to an existing natural, unconditioned stimulus (for example, seeing food), until the condition stimulus (for example, the ringing of a bell) in itself is sufficient to evoke the natural, unconditioned response (for example, producing saliva when food is seen).

classification dominance
Impression which a particular supplier manages to realize with a buyer that this supplier's range contains virtually every product which this buyer desires.

coding
Stage in the communication process where words, images, smells, sounds are being selected and used to denote, identify an object (for example, a brand, a message). *See also:* decoding.

cognition
Individual knowledge elements about an object (person, product, organization) in the shape of perceiving, knowing, understanding, being familiar with, remembering, reflected in that individual's beliefs and perceptions regarding the object.

cognitive approach (cognitive learning)
Idea about learning processes of individuals where learning is made operational as a change of knowledge components. In this approach the emphasis lies on understanding mental processes that take place during information processing. This is in contrast with the ideas in the behaviouristic approach (black box). *See also:* explicit consumer behaviour model.

cognitive capacity
Capacity (size and quality) for cognition which an individual has at his disposal at a certain moment in order to be able to process information.

cognitive component of attitude (knowledge aspect)
Part in the three-component model of attitudes that relates to knowledge, perception and beliefs built up by an individual with regard to a specific attitude object. *See also:* affective component of attitude, conative component of attitude.

cognitive consistency theories
Group of theories (including the balance theory, cognitive dissonance theory, consistency theory and value congruence theory) in which it is assumed that people pursue a set of attitudes and in particular knowledge components (knowledge, perception, beliefs), and behaviour which do not mutually conflict. *See also:* cognitive dissonance, consistency.

cognitive dissonance
Condition in which an individual is when he/she has a set of attitudes, and in particular knowledge components and behaviour which are manifestly in conflict with each other. For example, this condition may arise when the individual obtains new information on an object which conflicts with his/her original perceptions and beliefs about that object. *See also:* consistency theory.

cognitive map
1 With regard to brands: Way in which various brands within a product category are stored in the consumer's memory, and the positions these brands take here with respect to each other.
2 With regard to shops: The 'map' buyers have in their minds of places where shops or shopping centres can be found. This is essential when buyers make estimates about the distance they have to cover and the time they have to travel when they want to do their shopping.
3 With regard to the layout of shops: How, in the minds of buyers, a specific shop has been laid out, and in which way the articles are grouped.

cognitive responses
Thoughts (knowledge components, perceptions and beliefs) that spring to mind with an individual in the stage of understanding when information is being processed.

communication
Transferring information. A process in which information is exchanged between people, organizations and equipment. During this process a transmitter transfers information (a message) either directly or through a medium, to a receiver. The communication process is completed as soon as the receiver has processed the information in some way or other. In the course of the communication process, 'noise' may occur due to various causes at different stages. In communication, all senses may play a part.

communication behaviour
Part of buyer and consumer behaviour that relates to the way in which individuals take up, process and possibly pass on information to others.

compatibility
1 Extent to which a product matches the values and experiences of a (potential) adopter.
2 Extent to which a new product matches or can be used in combination with other products already owned/already present.

compensatory decision rule
Method to evaluate alternatives used by buyers in which negatively appreciated attributes of a product can be compensated by other, positively appreciated, attributes of the same product. Examples of compensatory decision rules are: the simple additive decision rule and the weighted additive decision rule. *See also:* non-compensatory decision rule.

completely planned purchase
Purchasing situation in which a buyer does not only buy the product, but also the specific brand he had in mind.

complexity
Extent to which buyers regard an innovation (or a new product) as complex, with regard to its operation or use.

comprehension
Stage in the information processing in which the organization of perceptions and the interpretation of stimuli takes place.

conative component of attitude (behaviouristic aspect)
Part in the three-component model of attitudes with regard to the behaviour aspects (positive or negative) built up by an individual in relation to a specific attitude object,

for example, purchasing intention, or actual purchase. *See also:* affective component of attitude, cognitive component of attitude.

concept attainment
The mental process that takes place when a consumer envisages a brand.

concept formation
The mental process that takes place when a consumer envisages a product category.

conditioned response
Acquired reaction of an organism/human being after confrontation with a specific stimulus. For example, if seeing food (natural, neutral stimulus) is always accompanied by the ringing of a bell (conditioned stimulus) after some time saliva will be produced in the mouth when a bell is rung (conditioned response). *See also:* classic conditioning.

conditioned stimulus
Specific stimulus which (usually in combination with a stimulus which naturally evokes specific behaviour: a natural, neutral stimulus) is used to teach an organism/human being a specific response. *See also:* classic conditioning.

confirmation
Process in which individuals look for support (from their environment: other buyers; or from information: advertising) for the decision they have made with regard to the purchase of a particular (new) product.

conformity
The (degree of) adaptation of an individual to the standards, values, laws, rules and agreements prevalent in a specific social group.

conjunctive decision rule
Non-compensatory strategy in the evaluation of alternatives where cut-off boundaries are established for a limited number of essential product attributes. The alternatives are each assessed in terms of these cut-offs. Alternatives that are unable to accomplish the cut-off criterion of one or more of the attributes are left out of consideration for further evaluation. A high score for one or more of the product attributes is not compensated by a low score (or too low a score) on other attributes. Each of the major attributes must come up to the minimum requirements (cut-off). The conjunctive decision rule is an example of processing by brand.

consideration set
Products or brands that are considered acceptable as alternatives by a consumer and which he/she takes into consideration when satisfying a specific need. *See also:* choice set, evoked set.

consistency
Coherence, similarity, comparability and balance of components of the attitudes of individuals, such as cognitions, feelings and behaviour.

consistency theory
Theory in which it is assumed that components of attitude, such as cognitions, feelings and (purchase/information) behaviour of individuals may not conflict with each other, but must show a mutually consistent coherence. If this should not be the case, cognitive dissonance may result. One of the founders of this theory is Festinger. *See also:* cognitive consistency theories.

constructive decision rule
Method in the evaluation of alternatives in which the buyer joins parts of decision rules stored in his memory to form one new rule on the basis of which a specific choice problem can be solved. Constructed decision rules particularly occur in situations where the consumer cannot fall back on experience (for example, when new or unfamiliar products are involved).

consumer
Private (potential) buyer (natural person) who buys and/or uses products to fill his needs. *See also:* end consumer.

consumer behaviour
All activities of consumers that are directly related to obtaining, using or discarding products, including information processing and decision-making processes that precede and follow these activities. This behaviour can be broken down into four aspects: (1) communication behaviour, (2) purchase/shopping behaviour, (3) consumption behaviour, and (4) dismissive behaviour.

consumer franchise
Advantage that an organization has if it succeeds in binding a (large) group of consumers because these consumers have a strong preference for products or brands of this organization. *See also:* supplier loyalty, brand loyalty.

consumer goods
All goods that are consumed or used by final (end) consumers.

consumer psychology
Part of economic psychology in which attention is paid to consumer behaviour, and in particular the decision-making part in it.

consumers' frustration
Negative tensions that may arise in a consumer as a result of the impossibility to (always) be able to fill all needs that are felt at a certain moment (for example, due to lack of means or because a product is unavailable). In line with the psycho-analytical theory, the consumer may relieve such tensions by way of rationalization, projection, identification, sublimation, or denying that such tensions are present.

consumption ideology
Social meaning attributed to specific products or brands and which are being communicated about.

consumption package (consumption range)
Combination of products considered to be essential by an individual or private household in order to obtain and/or keep a certain standard of living.

consumption pattern
Way in which consumers obtain, use, consume and discard or dismiss products and the habits they have developed doing so (expressed as average, statistic quantities).

consumption quota
Ratio indicating the part of someone's personal income which is used for consumption, related to the total income.

consumption time
Period within which a product is used or consumed.

continuous innovation
A product (in an existing product category), new for consumers, whose market introduction results in the consumers hardly having to change their attitudes and behaviours. For example, the introduction of metal cassettes after the chromium cassettes.

convenience goods
Products for which the consumer, in view of the comprehensive experience he has in buying/using that product, wishes to make relatively little purchase effort. A distinction is made between: (1) fast moving consumer goods (FMCG), (2) impulse goods, and (3) emergency goods.

cost-consciousness
Extent to which a particular buyer thinks he/she is knowledgeable about prevailing (market) prices of a certain product within a certain product category, and in particular, pays attention to and compares prices when purchasing.

credence claims
Claims made by suppliers which cannot be verified or checked by buyers. Acceptance by buyers of these claims is based on belief and trust. *See also:* search claims.

credit
1 Amount of money placed at the disposal of a person or organization by a third party (e.g. a financial institution) in order to broaden spending possibilities. The original amount is to be returned, usually including interest, to the money lender.
2 Situation in which individuals experience such a high degree of satisfaction with a certain object (person, product or organization) that the object in question has a reasonable margin before the individuals' faith is affected.

cross-cultural consumer analysis
Research aimed at investigating the similarities or differences between consumer behaviour in two or more different cultures (countries).

cues
Stimuli offering starting points for consumers in establishing the extent to which a certain product can fill certain needs. *See also:* extrinsic cues, intrinsic cues.

culture
Classical definition: complex entity of knowledge, convictions, arts, laws, standards and values, and other behaviour, skills and habits which is characteristic for the members of a specific society. There are three characteristics: culture (1) is acquired and transferred from generation to generation; (2) knows a strong interwoven link between parts of that culture and (3) is shared by members of the society in question, and is different from other societies.

custom
Fixed, acquired sequence of stimulus and response.

customer satisfaction monitoring programme
Activities of an organization directed at enlarging customers' satisfaction on the basis of regular polls. To this end, it is regularly checked how consumers judge the products and/or accompanying services of the organization. Using these findings, improvements are carried out.

cut-off
Restriction or condition a consumer lays down to product attributes in terms of minimum requirements which the relevant attributes of the alternative product have to come up to. *See also:* conjunctive decision rule, disjunctive decision rule, elimination by-aspects, non-compensatory decision rule.

cyclical behaviour
Phenomenon that a consumer buys a certain product during a specific period, but, after some time, checks what alternatives there are in the market and then (often) switches to another brand.

decay theory
Memory theory assuming that the strength of memory traces declines in the course of time or even disappears completely.

decision-making process (buyer's decision process)
All steps taken by an individual from the moment that a need manifests itself through to the thoughts and feelings which (may) manifest themselves after purchasing a product/or

when using a product. The stages in a (comprehensive) decision-making process are: recognition of need, collection of data, evaluation of alternatives, purchase or non-purchase and after-purchase process.

declaratory knowledge
Subjective information on characteristics of a product stored in an individual's memory. This information does not necessarily have to match objective reality.

decoding
Stage in the communication process where individuals (receivers) select, convert, and use sensorily perceived stimuli (in the shape of images, words, sounds, smells) to identify and denote a specific object (for example, a message, a brand). *See also:* coding.

demand
In marketing: a group of buyers' need and desire for specific products or brands, expressed in the wish and the possibility to buy that product or brand.

demonstrative consumption (conspicuous purchasing behaviour)
Purchasing and using consumer products in order to make an impression on one's environment, or to communicate something about the user's prosperity.

desire
Express wish for a specific object (product/brand) to satisfy a need.

differential threshold
Minimum difference between two stimuli which are just about perceivable by an individual. *See also:* Weber–Fechner Law.

diffusion process
Distribution and acceptance of a new product within a target group. The basis of the diffusion process is formed by the adoption process of individual consumers.

discontinuous innovation
A completely new product for consumers (a new product category) the market introduction of which will result in buyers having to change their attitudes and behaviour patterns considerably. For example, the introduction of the contraceptive pill.

discretionary income
That part of personal income remaining after deduction of the amount which a consumer deems necessary in order to maintain an acceptable standard of living. Usually, this income component is used for savings, or for luxury purchases. *See also:* free disposable income.

disjunctive decision rule
Non-compensatory strategy in the evaluation of alternatives, where cut-off boundaries are established for one or some essential product attributes. The alternatives are each considered in terms of these cut-offs. Alternatives satisfying the cut-off criterion on one or more of the attributes, are taken into further consideration. Each alternative satisfying one of the cut-off criteria is seen as an acceptable alternative. The disjunctive decision rule is an example of processing by brand.

dismissive behaviour
Part of buyer and consumer behaviour in which the buyer stops using the durable product bought and used previously. This relates to the moment and the way in which the buyer puts an end to using the product.

disposable income
Part of the personal income that can actually be spent by the consumer. This is the personal income minus taxes and rates. *See also:* discretionary income, free disposable income.

dissolution
Final stage in the family life cycle in which only one of the partners/spouses has survived.

dissonance-reducing behaviour
Behaviour which is directed at decreasing or eliminating (cognitive) dissonance.

dogmatism
Personality characteristic expressing an individual's rigidity with regard to unfamiliar ideas or products, and/or with regard to information that clashes with attitudes and/or beliefs this individual has.

drive
Internal force arising in an individual as a result of a (sufficiently large) discrepancy between the actual situation and a necessary or desirable situation. This force motivates consumers to come into action after they have become aware of the discrepancy. *See also:* need.

durable consumer goods (commodities, consumer durables)
Consumer goods intended for durable consumption. This usually concerns products at a relatively high price with a high degree of consumer involvement and which are subject to an extensive decision process (such as cars, furniture and washing machines). The usual criterion is that a product will last for at least three years.

dyadic relationship
All the interactions between two parties, for example, buyer and seller.

dynamic continuous innovation
Introduction of a new product or adaptation of an existing product not resulting in consumers having to adapt to a completely different purchasing or consumption pattern (for example, the introduction of the electric toothbrush). *See also:* continuous innovation, discontinuous innovation.

early adopters (early buyers)
Adoption category immediately following the innovators and whose adoption speed is therefore high, but not the highest. On the basis of a normally divided adoption curve, this group, after the first 2.5 per cent of the innovators, constitutes the 13.5 per cent of consumers with the next highest adoption speed. This group is sensitive to trends, actively follows new market developments and tends to follow innovators quickly. The early adopters, however, do not take the initiative in the acceptance and implementation of a certain idea or product. (Rogers 1983)

early majority
Adoption category immediately following the innovators and the early adopters, whose adoption speed is still relatively high. On the basis of a normally divided adoption curve, this group, after the innovators (2.5 per cent), and the early adopters (13.5 per cent), constitutes the next 34 per cent of the consumer population. Although these consumers are sensitive to certain new developments, they do not lead the way in their acceptance and implementation. (Rogers 1983)

echoistic observation
Auditive processing (pattern recognition) of information in sensory memory (short-term memory), where the aspects of a perceived sound are retained on the basis of the physical characteristics (stimuli), such as pitch and volume. It takes a few seconds to forget these aspects. *See also:* iconic perception, memory.

ego-defensive function of attitude
Concept with regard to attitude change assuming that individuals are motivated to protect their self-image from internal feelings of doubt, and therefore avoid some forms of information constituting a threat to this self-image.

elaboration (cognitive processing)

1 Extent of integration between new information and existing knowledge in memory.

2 Number of nodes and links in an associative memory network. *See also:* belief.

elaboration likelihood

Likelihood of cognitive processing of information offered (a particular advertising message).

Elaboration Likelihood Model of Persuasion (ELM)

Model of Petty and Cacioppo describing the processing of persuasive communication: the extent to which an individual processes persuasive communication depends on the individual's motivation and capacity to process the message. If the message is processed on the basis of content and arguments, the central route is followed. Then, the individual is motivated and capable of processing the message. If the individual's motivation and/or capacities are limited, the peripheral route is followed, where the individual goes by the form aspects of the message in particular. *See also:* central route.

elimination-by-aspects decision rule

Non-compensatory decision rule in the evaluation of alternatives, where cut-offs are set for each major product attribute. Then, alternatives are compared with each other on the most important attribute; if different alternatives obtain an assessment above the cut-off level, these are compared with each other on the next important attribute, to a point where only one alternative remains. The elimination by aspects decision rule is an example of processing by attribute.

emergency goods

Consumer products which are purchased if they are urgently required.

emotional motive

Motive on the basis of feelings (such as fear, love, guilt and status) which can control consumer behaviour. *See also:* rational motive.

empty nester

Older adult person whose children do not attend day-time education any more and have already left home.

enculturation

Acquiring, and familiarizing, with a society's culture which a person is part of by birth. *See also:* acculturation.

end consumer

End consumer or end user of a product. In most cases this term is used to denote the consumer.

end values

Values in life that are an individual's most essential values, and that form the origin of his behaviour, for example, safety, love, recognition and security. *See also:* laddering, value.

Engel, Blackwell and Miniard model

Stating that all behaviour of consumers is the result of internal and external variables. The external variables are the environmental stimuli (advertising, information from other people), social influence (culture, reference groups and family), and situational influences (specific situation in which the consumer finds himself); the internal variables are the individual characteristics (motives, values, life style and personality). These external and internal variables jointly influence both the information processing and the decision-making process the consumer goes through.

Engel's Law

'Law' from perceptional theory stating that as an individual's income rises, the percentage of that income spent on food decreases.

epidemiological model
Predictive model with regard to diffusion assuming that diffusion is a process of social interaction where the different successive adoption categories 'contaminate' or 'infect' each other.

episodical knowledge
Information stored in long-term memory placing experiences of consumers in time's perspective. For example, being able to recall the last time one bought shoes.

ergonomics
The (interdisciplinary) science concerned with the physical and environmental factors for product design and layout of the work environment.

ethnic patterns
Standards, values and behaviour of specific ethnic groups within a larger society.

evaluation
Overall assessment of a particular object or a particular activity (for example, an organization, a product bought) on the basis of certain criteria.

evaluation criteria
Standards and specifications on the basis of which individuals assess various alternatives (product/brands) and compare these with each other.

evaluation of alternatives
Stage in the decision-making process in which each of the alternatives is assessed on its specific capability to fill a consumer's specific need(s).

evoked set
Concept introduced by Howard and Sheth, originally meant to indicate the group of products thought acceptable by a consumer for his next purchase. The concept has been further developed and made operational. Nowadays it is more common to use the terms consideration set and choice set.

experience claims
Claims made by a supplier which a buyer can only verify or check by trying out the product.

explicit consumer behaviour model
Consumer behaviour model in which it is stated that individuals' mental processes are capable of being studied, although these take place outside the perception atmosphere. These models describe, explain and/or predict consumer behaviour on the basis of a (limited) number of behavioural variables. With the aid of explicit models attempts are made to gain an insight into the decision-making process of consumers and the factors that influence decision-making. *See also:* behaviouristic approach.

exposure
Part of the information processing with regard to the time that an individual is (sensorily) faced/confronted with stimuli aimed at him through a specific medium in the form of a message (for example, advertising).

expressive qualities
Qualities and characteristics linked with a product or brand expressing a value (for example, status, exclusivity) cherished by the buyer. A product or a brand owes its expressive qualities mainly to marketing communication.

extended family
Core family (private household), complemented with other family members such as grandparents, uncles, aunts, nephews and nieces.

extensive problem-solving purchasing behaviour (EPSP behaviour, extensive problem solving)
Type of purchasing behaviour in which the buyer passes through all stages of the decision-making process in a detailed and accurate fashion. This behaviour concerns, in particular, speciality goods, with the purchase of which the buyer has no or very little experience, whilst the involvement is relatively high.

external search
Way to collect data where the individual obtains information from external sources, such as newspapers, periodicals, advertising, information from friends, acquaintances and sales-people. *See also:* internal search.

extinction
Term from classical conditioning theory indicating that the condition stimulus does not result in a conditioned response any more. This occurs after the condition stimulus has remained unrewarded a couple of times. The individual has been cured of the response association, as it were.

extrinsic cues
Characteristics of a product which, when adapted or changed, do not affect the physical product as such (for example, brand name, price, communication, and image). *See also:* intrinsic cues.

Family life cycle
Development stages a family goes through during its existence. The following stages can be distinguished: (1) young, alone, living outside the parental home; (2) just married/living together, no children; (3) married/living together, with small children, the youngest child younger than six; (4) married/living together, children older than six; (5) married/living together, with children just about to become independent; (6) empty-nest type 1: children have left home, but the bread-winner is still working; (7) empty-nest type 2: children have left home, and the bread-winner is retired; (8) only surviving partner is the bread-winner; (9) only surviving partner is retired.

final demand
Demand for products by end consumers or end users.

forward conditioning
Form of classic conditioning in which the stimulus which is supposed to cause a specific conditioning response (the conditioned stimulus) precedes a neutral, natural stimulus (the unconditioned stimulus). For example, prior to seeing food (neutral, natural stimulus) a bell rings (conditioned stimulus).

free disposable income
Part of an individual's income which remains for consumptive spending after fixed charges such as taxes and rates, and fixed necessary charges (rent, energy, insurances, and so on) have been deducted from the income. *See also:* disposable income, discretionary income.

frequently bought consumer goods (fast moving consumer goods, FMCGs)
Consumer products which are bought frequently and which are used almost every day. The purchase of such goods generally takes a relatively short, if any, decision time. These products have a high turnover and consumption rate (such as foodstuffs, toothpaste and detergents) and have substitutability. *See also:* convenience goods.

fun shopping (recreational shopping)
Situation in which a consumer considers shopping a way of pastime (or recreation). Often, this involves products for which the consumer needs some decision time, and products that do not belong to the basic needs (for example, food).

functional approach
Concept with regard to attitude change assuming that attitudes can be classified on the basis of four functions the attitudes (may) fill for the individual: a utility function, an ego-defensive function, a value expressive function and a knowledge function.

generic need satisfaction (generic demand)
Individuals' pursuit of satisfaction of a very common need. If, for example, someone is thirsty, he can find something to drink in order to quench his thirst. *See also:* product-specific need satisfaction.

Gestalt
Term derived from Gestalt psychology indicating that the whole (the structure perceived) is more than the sum of the separate components (making up the whole). Literally the term Gestalt means: form, shape, configuration. *See also:* Gestalt theory.

Gestalt psychology
German-American school in psychology mainly engaged in experimental research with regard to perception, from the Gestalt concept.

Gestalt theory
Set of generic laws of perception on the basis of which it becomes clear in what way people organize, process and combine to a meaningful whole, on the basis of the raw signals entering through the senses. The four major laws are: (1) the law of equality, (2) the law of proximity, (3) the law of closeness, and (4) the law of common fate.

group
In the restricted sense: two (or more) people with a certain amount of interdependency (the behaviour of one affects the behaviour of the other) and/or ideology. In a wider sense: a collection of individuals having similar characteristics, and/or a common interest, ideal, or ideology, and/or pursuing a common objective.

group norm
Relatively stable expectation with regard to one (or more) behaviour rule(s) for the individual members of a specific group. For this norm some kind of consensus is required.

halo effect
Tendency to judge an object (product, organization, or person) on the basis of only one (conspicuous) characteristic. This judgement is, as it were, transferred to other characteristics of the objects.

heavy users
Users of a specific product or brand consuming considerably larger quantities of it than the average consumption of all users of that product (as measured in a specific period).

hedonist benefits
Value of a consumption object in terms of emotions, sensory stimuli, or aesthetic considerations.

hedonistic theories
Group of theories stating that the major objective people strive for is experiencing pleasant stimuli or avoiding unpleasant experiences.

hierarchy of needs (Maslow's pyramid of needs)
Maslow's motivation theory assumes that individuals try to satisfy their needs according to a set, hierarchic pattern. Individuals cannot experience and satisfy higher needs, until, to a large extent, lower needs are satisfied. The five hierarchic levels in Maslow's pyramid of needs are: (1) physiological needs, (2) need for safety and security, (3) social needs (affiliation), (4) need for recognition and respect, and (5) need for self-development (self-actualization).

high commitment (high involvement)

Strong degree in which an individual considers a specific object (for example, a particular product/brand) relevant for himself. Decision-making under high involvement (for example, with products with a relatively high risk such as cars and stereo equipment) implies extensive problem solving purchasing behaviour.

high-benefit users

Users of a product experiencing a strong, unfilled need, or subjecting a specific product (attribute) to higher demands than on an average is done by buyers.

household

Community of persons, with or without family-ties, usually living in one dwelling unit (under one roof).

Howard & Sheth model

Consumer behaviour model in which endogenous variables are broken down into perception determinants, and choice and learning determinants. The Howard & Sheth model breaks down purchasing behaviour into extensive problem solving purchasing behaviour, restrictive problem solving purchasing behaviour and routine purchasing behaviour. The differences between these types of purchasing behaviour can be reduced to the amount of knowledge and experience the consumer has with (the purchase of) a product, and the effort the consumer is prepared (or has to) make. *See also:* explicit consumer behaviour model.

iconic perception

Visual processing (pattern recognition) of information in sensoric memory on the basis of physical properties of stimuli such as colour, brightness and shape. *See also:* echoistic observation, memory.

ideal self

All characteristics an individual would like to have, i.e. how a person would like to be. *See also:* actual self, self-concept.

identification

Following the examples of individuals who have a similar pattern of needs.

image

The joint, whether or not imagined, subjective representations, ideas, feelings and experiences by a person or a group of persons with respect to a certain object (product, person or organization).

imagery

Process in which sensory information and experiences are represented in working memory.

imitation effect

Phenomenon that individuals allow themselves to be influenced by the (purchasing) behaviour of other individuals. In consequence the speed of the adoption process increases as the number of adopters increases.

implicit consumer behaviour model

Consumer behaviour model in which it is assumed that mental processes of individuals take place outside the perception atmosphere, and are therefore not fit to be studied. Thus, the behaviour is not explained, but only described or predicted. Such a model does not include (or it includes only few) behaviour variables/behaviour details to describe/predict behaviour. Implicit models give no insight into the decision-making process as such. These models make links between perceivable stimuli and overt behaviour expressions (responses) only. *See also:* behaviouristic approach, stimulus response model.

impulse goods

Consumption goods that were bought spontaneously (without being planned), often after the consumer encountered these products (shelf, display). *See also:* convenience goods.

impulse purchase
Purchase of a product by a consumer who has not gone through a well-considered decision-making process; impulse purchases are often made when consumers see a product on the shelf in the shop or encounter it during a sales promotion.

incentive
Reward (in the shape of a price discount, present, trip, or the like) a buyer receives as an extra stimulus to show the (purchasing) behaviour desired.

incidental learning
Learning which takes place by accident, without the subject intending to learn something during information processing. Often, what individuals learn from advertising messages results from incidental learning. *See also:* intentional learning.

indifference curve
Curve on which each point represents a combination of different quantities of 'two' different products or product attributes having the same use for a certain individual.

individualizing
Term indicating the trend that individuals are less and less bothered by standards, values, and traditions prevailing in the society or culture they are part of. Due to this trend, it is becoming more and more difficult to predict consumer behaviour and/or to divide markets into (sufficiently large) homogeneous market segments. *See also:* market fragmentation.

industrial buying process
Stages an organization goes through when purchasing raw materials, (capital) goods and/or services for its own operations. The following stages can be distinguished: (1) determining the necessity to buy; (2) determining the offer selection criteria and peripheral conditions; (3) making enquiries asking for offers; (4) assessing offers; (5) negotiating with suppliers; (6) the purchasing decision and (7) delivery, installation, implementation and evaluation. In addition, it is customary to distinguish the following purchasing situations: new task, modified rebuy, and straight rebuy.

industrial products
Goods or services bought by organizations to be used in the production of a semi-manufactured article or a manufactured article, or in the delivery of a service.

informal group
Relatively unstructured reference group consisting of acquaintances, friends and/or colleagues.

information environment
Joint data which is at the disposal of an individual in a specific situation and under particular circumstances.

information overload
Situation which arises when the quantity of (obtained/collected) data for a particular process of choice is too large for the individual's cognitive capacity.

information processing
A process in which a stimulus is perceived, interpreted and stored in memory, in order to be able to use the information (possibly at a later stage) as an aid for a decision to be taken. McGuire distinguishes five stages in information processing: exposure, attention, understanding, acceptance and retention.

information, collection of
Stage in the decision-making process of individuals in which they are motivated to activate knowledge which is stored in memory (internal search) or try to absorb information from the environment (external search).

informational influence

Influence from others (friends, acquaintances, experts) on an individual's attitudes and behaviour. These other persons are considered valuable sources of information by the individuals.

informational motivation (negative motivation)

Negative motive to buy a product. This motive can find its origin in experiencing problems, such as a headache, wanting to smoke and taking up less tar/nicotine, wanting to drink without getting too much alcohol in the blood. The motivation to buy products is to solve or to avoid these problems, or to take away dissatisfaction. *See also:* motivation type.

initial purchase

The first time a buyer buys a specific product, brand or new product variant.

inner-directed consumers

Group of consumers classified on the basis of the VALS-typology, who tend to have their (purchasing) behaviour controlled by personal standards and values rather than by the environment standard. *See also:* outer-directed consumers, VALS typology.

innovation

Idea or product which is considered new by potential adopters.

innovators

Adoption category with the highest adoption speed. On the basis of a normally divided adoption curve, this concerns the first 2.5 per cent of consumers who adopt a certain innovation. Since the innovators are the first to purchase a new product, they often cause a trend. (Rogers 1983)

installed base

The joint quantity of items of a particular durable consumption or production good which, in a specific period, is present with or used by all buyers. *See also:* owners, average possession.

instrumental conditioning

Type of learning by way of trial and error. Thus habits are formed under the influence of the positive and negative effects which a specific type of behaviour has.

instrumental role

Role behaviour in decision-making and purchasing processes based on knowledge about functional attributes, such as financial aspects, performance characteristics and conditions of purchase.

instrumental value

The value an individual attaches to a particular object on the basis of physical properties, and the ensuing consequences. For example, a Volvo has sturdy bumpers, and a car with sturdy bumpers is less vulnerable to damage. *See also:* laddering, utilitarian benefits, value.

intentional learning

Conscious and motivated learning process aimed at a specific object. *See also:* incidental learning.

interaction process

Social interaction in face-to-face contacts between two or more individuals, for example, between a salesperson and the buyer, or between buyers themselves.

interest

Stage in the adoption process with regard to the acceptance of a new product, in which the consumer actively tries to find information about the product.

interference

Searching and activating information from long-term memory is made more difficult due to information which was received recently, or due to older information which was stored earlier.

interference theory

Memory theory assuming that forgetting information is due to acquiring and processing new information.

internal search

Type of data collecting in which the individual uses knowledge which is stored in memory.

intrinsic cues

Characteristics of the physical product on the basis of which an individual assesses a product. In this case, a distinction can be made between functional cues (related to the advantages expected by the consumer, such as taste, fragrance, energy consumption), structural cues (related to the way in which functional cues are realized, such as size and shape) and aesthetic cues (which help creating an attractive and distinctive brand, such as design and use of colour). If intrinsic cues are adapted or changed, a change is materialized in the physical product as such. *See also:* extrinsic cues.

involvement

The extent to which a potential (potential buyer) expects the choice and purchase of a product or brand to have major consequences and risks for him. In particular, involvement affects the purchase efforts a consumer wants to make. The involvement of the buyer can be influenced by the type of product, the person and the situation.

knowledge

Information stored in a certain individual's memory which can be retrieved.

knowledge function of attitude

Concept with regard to attitude changes in which it is assumed that individuals feel a need to get to know and understand the people and objects they encounter. Attitude categories include this knowledge and this understanding, so that attitudes also serve as a 'memory stepping-stone'.

labelling

Technique for behaviour modification in which a person is assigned a label (for example: 'You are someone who likes quality'), hoping that the person will show the (purchasing) behaviour corresponding with this label.

laddering (analysis of the structure of meaning)

Technique aimed at obtaining insight in the (hierarchic) meaning structure of an object in the consumer's memory. This structure of meaning consists of the perceived product qualities ('A Volvo has sturdy bumpers'), this results in ('A car with sturdy bumpers is less vulnerable), and the eventual values of life ('safety') (pursued by the consumer). *See also:* end values, instrumental value.

laggards

Adoption category with the lowest adoption speed. On the basis of a normally divided adoption curve, this group constitutes the last 16 per cent of the consumer population. Consequently, this group is very reserved with regard to accepting and implementing certain new ideas or products (Rogers 1983).

late majority

Adoption category consisting of the group of consumers having the lowest adoption speed, except for the laggards. On the basis of a normally divided adoption curve, this group constitutes 34 per cent of the consumer population. This group is relatively insensitive to certain new ideas and products, and is slow in their acceptance and implementation. (Rogers 1983).

latent demand

Unexpressed demand for a particular product by a particular group of non-buyers. They may have a need for the product, but this need is not yet manifested in a real demand, because the demander does not yet possess sufficient means, or because (the demander thinks that) there is no (such) product (yet) that can fill this need.

Law of closeness

Law of observation resulting from the empirical fact that people show a tendency to form a complete image of an object ('to finish' the image), even when the perceptual field lacks elements. *See also:* Gestalt theory.

Law of equality

Law of observation resulting from the empirical fact that people show a tendency to interpret (two or more) identical stimuli as belonging together (even if they do not have any interrelationship). *See also:* Gestalt theory.

Law of mutual destiny (Law of common destiny)

Law of perception resulting from the empirical fact that people show a tendency to interpret two (or more) stimuli making the same movement or moving in the same direction as belonging together. *See also:* Gestalt theory.

Law of nearness (Law of proximity)

Law of observation resulting from the empirical fact that people show a tendency to see (two or more) stimuli that are closely together (in space or in time) as one entity. *See also:* Gestalt theory.

lead users

Type of consumers having (latent) needs which, at this moment, do not (yet) play a major role, but may do so in the future.

learning

Gathering information and transforming this information into knowledge; the process in which experience leads to changes in attitudes, in particular knowledge and/or behaviour.

lexicographic decision rule

Non-compensatory decision rule in the evaluation of alternatives in which the different alternatives are compared with each other on the most important attributes. If more alternatives receive the highest appreciation, they will be compared with each other on the one but most important attribute, until only one alternative remains. The lexicographic decision rule is an example of processing by attribute.

lifestyle

During a specific timespan, a reasonably consistent and characteristic way of life of a certain (group of) individual(s), on the basis of core values, standards and behaviour. Different lifestyles can be characterized on the basis of such differences or similarities between (groups of) consumers as having money or spare time; in activities, interests and opinions (AIOs) or on the basis of behaviour, activities, interests and opinions (central values) of individuals in VALS-typifications.

light users

Users of a particular product or brand consuming considerably smaller quantities of that product or brand than the average consumption of all consumers of a product (as measured in a particular period).

limited problem-solving purchasing behaviour (limited problem solving)

Form of purchasing behaviour in which the buyer does not fully or extensively pass through the stages in the decision-making process. This behaviour occurs when products are bought which the buyer has already had some experience with. For the purchase of those products only a limited number of information sources are consulted, a limited number of alternative considered and/or a limited number of evaluation criteria are used.

look and listen, practice of (viewing and listening habits)
Pattern of viewing and listening behaviour concerning the specific programmes individuals watch on television and/or listen to on the radio, including the moments and/or the way in which they watch these media, listen to these media, respectively.

low commitment (low involvement)
The extent to which an individual considers a specific object (for example, a particular product/brand) relevant for him/her self. Decision-making under low involvement (for example, with products whose alternatives hardly differ from each other (such as is the case in most fast-moving consumer goods) implies limited problem solving purchasing behaviour, or routine purchasing behaviour.

low-balling
Technique for behaviour modification in which a low price is announced for a product/brand, and subsequently the price is raised after the consumer has become interested in the product.

market fragmentation
Situation in which, due to the large degree of individualization, it is difficult to discern economically viable large and relatively homogeneous market segments.

market saturation
Situation in which almost all potential consumers of a specific product/brand have effectively become buyers, and in which it is not or hardly possible to increase the total turnover of the product/brand by stimulating the consumption intensity and/or additional demand.

massification theory
Idea that the distinction between blue collar workers (social class A) and middle class white collar workers (social class B2) is gradually disappearing. *See also:* social class.

me-too product
Products which may be new for a particular company, but which is only a new brand or a new variant of an existing product for the consumers, and whose entire proposition is an emulation of a very successful competing brand.

media consumption
Number of media (radio, television, newspapers and periodicals) that an individual uses, and the time and attention spent on each of these media.

medium users
Users of a particular product or brand, whose consumption level lies between that of light users and heavy users.

memory
Part of the cognitive system in which information is processed and knowledge is temporarily or permanently stored. Usually the operation of memory is explained on the basis of a so-called multi-storage model. In this model a distinction is made between:
1 sensory memory, where 'raw' stimuli enter through the senses and are processed within seconds to interpretable patterns and which are remembered exactly;
2 short-term memory (working memory), where entering information is combined and compared with knowledge already stored in long-term memory; this working memory, within which 'thinking processes' take place, has a very limited information processing capacity and
3 long-term memory, where knowledge material can be stored for a longer period.

modelling (vicarious learning)
Way of learning, in which an individual observes other people's behaviour and consequences, and familiarizes him/her self with it.

models of consumer behaviour

A group of models used to try to describe, explain and/or predict consumer behaviour prior to, during or after purchasing a product. Well-known models include the Nicosia model, the Howard & Sheth model, and the Engel, Blackwell & Miniard model.

monodic approach

Term used in innovation diffusion research to denote that personal and social characteristics of individual consumers are focused on.

monomorphic social influence

Normative and/or informational influence from individuals in the environment relating only to a specific product.

motivation

The driving forces in an individual, underlying the actions aimed at the filling of needs. *See also:* purchasing motivation.

Motivation Research

Research (often associated with Ernest Dichter) from 1940–1960 (mainly in the US) in which the studies of consumer behaviour focused primarily on the sentiments and the subconsciousness of the individual. This approach finds its origin in psychoanalytic motivation and personality theories.

motivation type

Classification by Rossiter and Percy in informational and transformational motivation, which, in combination with a low or high involvement, leads to a classification of products by motivation type and decision type.

multi-attribute attitude models

Models in which it is assumed that the final attitude of an individual with respect to a particular object is a function of the beliefs about the attitudes of this attitude object, and the relative interest that the individual attaches to each of these attributes. *See also:* weighted additive decision rule.

multi-stage interaction

Situation in the communication process in which the message of a certain supplier is initially aimed at influential persons or organizations in the environment (opinion leaders). Subsequently, these opinion leaders will influence potential buyers. In that case it is assumed that both the individual looking for information and the influential persons from his/her environment are influenced by (the same) media.

need

A state of felt deprivation of some basic satisfaction. If the individual is aware of this deprivation, there is a manifest need; if the individual is not (yet) aware of the situation, there is a latent need. In many cases, products may fill needs felt. *See also:* basic need, wants.

need for cognition

Personality characteristic which is the cause of the need an individual has to acquire, process, and evaluate information, and the pleasure derived from it (inclination to think).

need, recognition of

Stage in the decision-making process in which individuals realize that there is a discrepancy between the actual situation and a necessary or desirable situation; if the perceived discrepancy is large enough, the drive will be evoked to trigger off a decision-making process.

need-driven consumers

Group of consumers classified on the basis of the VALS-typology showing a (purchasing) behaviour which is more characterized by filling (basic) needs than by specific preferences for products or brands.

negative confirmation
Term used with operand conditioning to denote that the chance for repetition of behaviour decreases considerably if such behaviour has negative consequences. *See also:* operand conditioning.

Nicosia model
Explicit consumer behaviour model in which information processing and purchasing processes are represented in the shape of a flow chart.

non-adopter
Buyer who has decided not to buy a specific new product/brand.

non-compensatory decision rule
Decision rule in the evaluation of alternatives by buyers in which the negative assessment of the specific product attribute cannot be compensated by a positive assessment of another attribute of the same product. Non-compensatory decision rules include: the lexicographic, the conjunctive, the disjunctive and the elimination-by-aspects decision rules. *See also:* compensatory decision rule.

non-durable consumption goods (non-durables)
Consumer products with a relatively short lifespan, such as clothing and shoes. The usual criterion is that the product does not last longer than about three years. *See also:* frequently bought consumer goods.

norm
Written (explicit) or unwritten (implicit) rule of behaviour.

normative influence
Pressure exerted by a reference group or person on an individual to adapt to the group norm.

on-going search
Type of external search in which information acquisition takes place on a regular basis, independent of incidental needs of the consumer.

one-stop shopping
Specific purchasing behaviour of consumers who prefer to do much shopping (in particular convenience and shopping goods) in one location. The retail trade can meet this need by settling in shopping centres or shopping malls, by erecting larger (self-service) department stores, hypermarkets, or by engaging in co-operative organizations.

operand conditioning (instrumental learning process)
Type of learning by means of trial and error in which habits are formed in reaction to the positive or negative consequences of behaviour. The nature and intensity of these consequences affect the frequency or the chance of a specific type of behaviour occurring in the future, in a direct way.

opinion
Subjective judgement of an individual, whether or not based on objective knowledge components.

opinion leader
Individual who, in one or more fields, informally has a strong influence on attitudes, and in particular on other individuals' behaviour.

optimal stimulating level
Level of surprise, newness and complexity which individuals strive for in their personal experiences with other people and products. Individuals who are characterized by a high level of stimulation are more open for new products, and will be prepared to take risks at an earlier stage than individuals with a low stimulating level.

optimizing decision rule
Decision rule in which a buyer evaluates each alternative product or brand on the basis of all major product attributes, and chooses the product or brand with the highest (weighted) score on the sum of the attributes. *See also:* simplifying decision rule.

outcomes (after purchase experiences)
Result of the decision-making process in which the buyer checks whether or not the chosen and bought alternative (sufficiently) fills the needs and comes up to the expectations that were present prior to the purchase.

outer-directed consumers
Group of consumers classified on the basis of the VALS-typology who allow their (purchasing) behaviour to be influenced strongly by the standards and values of the people in their environment. *See also:* inner-directed consumers, VALS typology.

overt behaviour
Behaviour which can be observed without the aid of recording machinery or instruments.

owners
All buyers using, or having at home, at least one item of a specific durable consumption or production article.

partial confirmation
Diagram of positive confirmations of a particular kind of behaviour, in which specifically desired response sometimes is, but at other times is not awarded.

passive rejection
Situation in which an individual decides not to use a particular new product/brand (innovation), without having tried or used that product.

perceived quality
Quality attributed to a product or brand by the buyer on the basis of different intrinsic or/and extrinsic cues belonging to that product.

perceived risk
Individual assessment of the (financial, functional, physical, social and psychological) consequences of someone's own behaviour, for example, as a result of purchasing a certain product or brand. *See also:* risk perception.

perceived value
Subjective appreciation of a product by an individual. A condition to proceed to buying a specific product is that the subjective appreciation (as expressed in financial terms) of a certain individual for that product is, at least, equal to, or higher than the price to be paid.

perception
Mental activity in which an individual selects, processes and integrates sensory stimuli into an experience or a meaningful and coherent image of a particular object or an action. Perception comprises the information processing stages of exposure, attention and understanding.

perceptual blockage
Process in which, subconsciously, particular stimuli are filtered or completely excluded from perception because these stimuli present threatening information or are inconsistent with someone's needs, values, beliefs or attitudes.

perceptual organization
Subconsciously arranging stimuli in groups or configurations according to the Gestalt principles of observation. *See also:* Gestalt theory.

peripheral cues
Form aspects of a (advertising) message offering starting points for an individual to form/ change an attitude. *See also:* central route, Elaboration Likelihood Model of Persuasion, peripheral route.

peripheral route
Process within the framework of attitude change in which an individual is not induced to start thinking about arguments of content, but in which form aspects in the communication are more important than the content (an attractive source, the number of arguments instead of the content of the arguments, atmospheric image). *See also:* central route, Elaboration Likelihood Model of Persuasion, peripheral cues.

personal factors
Number of descriptive (demographic) and psychological (personality) characteristics of persons which are supposed to have an influence on consumer behaviour.

personality
The total number of psychological and behaviouristic characteristics which make an individual unique and distinct from the individuals.

personality characteristic
An individual's inclination to react to stimuli from the environment in a consistent and specific way. Examples are: indolence, frugality, (social) fear, need for recognition.

phased decision strategy
Process in which initially a certain decision rule is used to reduce the number of alternatives in the choice set to a conveniently arranged amount, and then applies (a) different (combination of) decision rule(s) to make the definitive choice.

polymorphic social influence
Normative and/or informational influence with regard to different products/product categories, and which is caused by individuals in the environment.

polymorphism
Phenomenon that an individual is an innovator with respect to different products/product categories.

positive confirmation
Term used in operand conditioning, indicating that if a person's special type of behaviour has positive consequences, the chance of repetition of this behaviour increases substantially.

post-consumptives
Group of individuals with a strongly developed socially and environmentally oriented consciousness rejecting consumption society and being in favour of small-scale and environmentally friendly production.

pre-consumptives
Group of individuals spending relatively little money on consumption of goods or services, because they do not have enough money at their disposal, or because they live frugally.

preference
Situation in which a particular object (person, organization, product, brand) is considered better or more attractive by a particular individual than any comparable alternatives.

price index number of family consumption
Index, prepared by the central statistical bureau, representing the changes in the cost of living. The index is based on the prices of several products essential for subsistence, such as housing, food, clothing, shoes, personal care, and transport.

price shopping
Purchasing behaviour in which price motives form a major factor in purchasing decisions and choice of shops.

primacy effect
The information obtained first, or the information presented at the beginning of a (advertising) message has more effect (more weight) in the interpretation than information which is presented at a later stage. *See also:* recency effect.

primary group
Group consisting of people from the immediate environment of an individual exerting the most and direct influence on that individual's behaviour. Often, this refers to family members and (good) friends. *See also:* secondary group.

proactive inhibition
Form of interference in which learning or remembering new information is made more difficult due to knowledge already present in memory. *See also:* retroactive inhibition.

problem solving
The thinking process and the well-reasoned actions aimed at filling needs.

problem solving unit
Group of specialists in an organization formed to sell a product to another organization. The problem solving unit (PSU) is the counterpart of the DMU, and may consist of incumbents of different levels and coming from various disciplines in order to understand the specific desires of the purchasing organization.

procedural know-how
Way in which information, stored in an individual's memory, can be used in the decision-making process.

processing by attribute
Collecting and processing information on products or brands on the basis of (relevant) product attributes. The alternatives are compared with each other by comparing each of the relevant attributes.

processing by brand
Collecting and processing information on products or brands by checking which attributes each product or brand has. The starting point is to envisage each alternative in terms of the most essential attributes.

product hierarchy
Memory structure of the buyer in which different brands in a product category are arranged on the basis of preferences or the brands.

product-specific need satisfaction
An individual's pursuit to satisfy a highly specific need with a particular product or brand. Rather than having something to drink and quench his thirst (non-specific need), someone might fancy a beer, or a Heineken (a very specific need). *See also:* generic need satisfaction.

projection
Blaming one's own faults on others or on products or organizations that allegedly do not function properly. *See also:* consumers' frustration.

prompting
Technique to modify behaviour in which a buyer is induced to consider buying a product by calling attention to a product's existence (for example: 'We have a wonderful tie to match', when the buyer has just bought a suit).

prospect
Potential buyer; person or organization with whom mutual communication exists, but who has not yet decided to buy.

psychoanalytic theory
Motivation and personality theory stating that motivation and personality of individuals is formed by the interplay of the 'id' (subconscious: the source of psychic energy in which maximum pleasurable sensations are pursued), the 'ego' (part of the personality in which rational considerations take place on the basis of the principle of reality), and the 'super ego' (the voice of the conscious, reminding the individual of rules of decency and morale). This theory was founded by Freud; applications of this theory in consumer behaviour can be found in the Motivation Research Tradition.

psychography
Research into the psychological characteristics of groups of individuals which (may) influence the decision-making process, or purchasing behaviour.

psycholinguistics
Study of psychological factors playing a role in observing, processing, and interpreting language.

psychological characteristics
The joint personality characteristics in terms of standards and values, needs, attitudes, beliefs, preferences, interests, habits which distinguish a person (or a group) from other persons (or groups); together with the behaviour characteristics the psychological characteristics make up an individual's personality.

psychological surplus value (added value/overvalue)
Difference in an individual's appreciation of a particular product with specific intrinsic cues and the same product without these intrinsic cues.

psychophysiological research
Research aimed at physiological behaviour responses associated with mapping (intra) psychological processes (information processing or decision processes). Examples of techniques used in such research include: ECG (Electro Cardiogram: recording of the heartbeat), EEG (Electro Encephalogram: recording of the electric activity of the brain), GSR (Galvanic Skin Response: recording of the conductivity and/or resistance of the skin), and pupillometry (recording of the reactions of the eye pupil.

psychophysiology (psychophysics)
Interdisciplinary field of research in which notions from psychology and physics are combined in order to be able to study and make links between the objective input of stimuli and the subjective reactions on it.

public opinion
All the individual ideas on a subject that are in the centre of public interest, aggregated on a population (for example, the opinions of the Dutch population on the environmental impact of using cars).

purchase
Stage in the buyer's decision-making process in which he/she acquires the product desired by means of an action (usually after having made a choice from several alternatives).

purchase frequency
The number of times a particular consumer buys a particular product or brand during a particular period.

purchase, intention to
Customers' degree of willingness and inclination to buy a specific product in a specific period.

purchaser
Staff member in an organization who is in charge of the purchase of products. As a rule the purchaser is part of the DMU.

purchasing behaviour (buying behaviour/buyer behaviour)
Part of buyers' or consumers' behaviour relating to the factual purchase of products and the location where and the frequency at which the products are bought. The purchasing behaviour is dependent on such elements as the types and kinds of product bought, the consumer's motivation and involvement when buying a certain product, and the experiences the buyer has using and buying that specific product. *See also:* limited problemsolving purchasing behaviour, extensive problem-solving purchasing behaviour.

purchasing motivation
The driving force(s) present in any individual behind his actions aimed at satisfying needs, in this case the motive for the actual purchase. This motive may find its origin in a negative motivation (solving problems, avoiding problems and eliminating dissatisfaction), a neutral motivation (continuing satisfaction), or positive motivation (sensorial satisfaction, or intellectual stimulus). *See also:* motivation type.

rational decision-making
Problem solving based on carefully weighing and evaluating (functional) attributes.

rational motive
Motivation for behaviour exclusively based on well considered, consistent and logical formation of a judgement. In consumer behaviour, such a formation of judgements hardly occurs. *See also:* emotional motive.

rationalization
The reasoning away of needs not to be filled and/or replacing these by needs which can be filled. Very often, this causes a distortion of perception and/or opinion. *See also:* consumers' frustration.

recency effect
The most recent information, or the information presented at the end of a message, has more effect (more weight) in the interpretation than information presented earlier. *See also:* primacy effect.

recognition
Retrieving information stored in memory, for example, as a result of a learning process. A method to search the content of memory for the result of the learning process is to determine what the individual can remember (recollection) and what has been forgotten. In this method the individual is given a group of names, words and/or symbols, and he is asked to indicate which of these names, words or symbols he recalls.

reference group
Group of people having a substantial influence on the attitudes, and in particular the (purchasing) behaviour of a specific individual, because this individual associates himself or compares himself with that group.

reference person
Person having a substantial influence on the attitudes, and in particular (purchasing) behaviour, of a specific individual, because this individual associates himself or compares himself with that person.

reflex
Autonomous, uncontrollable, natural reaction (response) of an organism/individual on a stimulus. For example, withdrawing a hand as soon as it touches a hot object.

rehearsal
Mental activity in which information is rehearsed in short-term memory to allow the information to take root in long-term memory.

relational approach
Strong attention for communication networks with innovation-diffusion research, influence of socio-structure variables on the diffusion process in a social system.

reminder (recall)
Becoming aware of information stored in long-term memory.

repeat purchase
Second or consecutive purchase of a product, or brand by a consumer.

replacement demand
The demand of current users of a specific durable product for a similar replacement item, because the old item is not used any more or will be discarded.

replacement purchase
Second or subsequent purchase of a particular durable product or brand to replace a previous item after it has been discarded.

response
An individual's reaction to a specific stimulus or cue.

retention
Stage in information processing in which information is transferred from short-term memory to long-term memory, and is stored there for a longer period.

retrieval
Process in which information stored in long-term memory is retrieved and activated.

retrieval set
Group of alternatives (products, brands, suppliers) being available, after information has been retrieved and activated from long-term memory.

retroactive inhibition
Form of interference in which retrieving and using information from long-term memory is made more difficult due to new knowledge which has just been stored in memory. *See also:* proactive inhibition.

retrospective questioning technique
Technique to map search processes of individuals by asking them to report on activities which have taken place during the decision-making process.

risk perception
All the risks that an individual expects to run as a consequence of particular actions, for example, purchasing a particular product or brand. Usually, individuals are aware that they cannot oversee all the consequences of their actions. With regard to buying products, the following risks may be distinguished: (1) social risk: the environment may react negatively on the purchase; (2) physical risk: the product may damage health; (3) psychological risk: to what extent does the product correspond with the user's self-image or personality; (4) functional risk: to what extent does the product offer what was promised (in advertising, or by the seller and other informants); (5) financial risk: the product may be too expensive in relation to what it offers, and (6) time risk: the chance that time is spent on the purchase of a product which eventually does not come up to the expectations. *See also:* perceived risk.

risk preparedness acceptence
Risks which individuals are prepared (or are able to) to take in their dealings, for example, when trying a new product or brand. To a greater or lesser extent, individuals may be prepared to take risks.

role

All the standards, expectations and behaviour associated with occupying a functional position within a specific group. In the context of a specific social situation, a person may have different roles which can each be relevant.

role conflict

Situation in which the expectation of the environment conflicts with an individual's idea of a role, or if there are conflicting behaviour and expectation patterns as a result of occupying different roles at the same time.

routing

Sequence of (shelf) presentation of the range of articles in a particular shop or with different shops, or the walking route followed in a particular shop or to different shops.

routinized response behaviour

Kind of (recurrent) purchasing behaviour in which the buyer does not entirely, or to a very limited extent, pass through the stages in the decision-making process. In that case, the purchasing decision is based on habits the buyer has developed in his experiences with the product or brand. These habits signify the decision-making process. In particular in routine purchasing behaviour, one (or more) stages in the decision-making process might be skipped altogether. Routine purchasing behaviour has to do with convenience goods, in particular where there is a low involvement.

satisficing behaviour

In practice, it is impossible to be able to take into consideration all appropriate alternatives in a decision-making process. On the basis of this assumption, it is supposed that individuals do not strive for the best, maximum realistic solution, but for an acceptable solution for their problems, reflected in their purchasing behaviour.

saturation

In marketing: complete satisfaction of buyers' needs in a market.
In perception theory: intensity of a colour.
In psychology: phenomenon in which an individual cannot absorb more information (for example, as a result of information overload).

schema (scheme, plan)

Knowledge structure of a higher order in an individual's memory composed of networks of associations around an object, person, idea, organization, product, brand or situation. *See also:* schemata.

schemata

Components which the associative memory network is composed of.

script

Specific scheme of the standard sequence in which sequential types of behaviour should take place. For example: tasting wine in a ritual fashion.

search claims

Claims made by a supplier with regard to a particular product or brand which can be fully verified and checked by an individual using external information collection. *See also:* credence claims.

secondary group

Group consisting of people exerting a less direct influence on the attitude and the behaviour of a certain individual, than people from the primary group. Often these are people with whom the individual maintains a less frequent, or less intensive contact. *See also:* primary group.

secondary needs (psychogenic needs)

Needs finding their origin in functioning within a particular culture, or membership of a particular group, such as the need for respect, prestige, affection and power.

selective attention
Phenomenon that an individual does not pay attention to all stimuli (for example, the subjects presented by the media), or does not pay attention to them to the same extent. The selection of stimuli (subjects) is based on interests or specific needs.

selective distortion
Selective perception and explanation of facts, messages or characteristics by an individual. This perception and explanation differ per individual under influence of opinions adopted earlier, and set attitudes. *See also:* rationalization.

selective exposure
Individual selection of stimuli (messages and media) which a person wishes to be exposed to. Individuals do not expose themselves to all stimuli (for example, media): they select those stimuli that match their interest, and from which they think they can obtain information relevant for them.

selective perception
Collective indicating that people cannot or do not wish to process all information from their environment, and therefore do not expose themselves to all stimuli and/or pay only limited attention to them. *See also:* selective attention, selective exposure.

selective recognition of need
Activating a specific need by linking it to a specific product/brand within a specific product category.

selective retention
Phenomenon that not all information perceived by an individual and stored in memory is available for processing at a later stage. Obviously, that which an individual can or wishes to remember is either consciously or unconsciously filtered.

self-actualization
The pursuit to build up, understand and maintain a personal system of values within which there is scope for optimum self-development. *See also:* hierarchy of needs.

self-concept (self-image)
The joint impressions, knowledge and expectations somebody has about himself with regard to personality, social environment in which he is and the relationships he has. Usually, in this case, a distinction is made between the actual self and the ideal self.

self-designation method
Research method in which people are asked to indicate to what extent they act as a reference person for others.

self-monitoring
Personality quality on the basis of which a person follows his own behaviour (critically) and assesses it.

self-perception theory
Theory in which it is assumed that in some situations people learn what attitudes and emotions they (apparently) have by observing their own behaviour ('I have bought this product, so, obviously, I think it is a good product').

self-referencing
Personality quality on the basis of which an individual feels a strong inclination to relate information to himself and to interpret it using his own experiences.

self-serving bias (defensive attribution)
Phenomenon that individuals attribute causes to events, and in such a way that their own person(ality) undergoes a positive stimulus from it. For example: if a product does not come up to their expectations, then the supplier or the manufacturer is to blame, if the product performs better than expected, this is due to their smart choice. *See also:* attribution theory.

semiotic analysis

Qualitative research technique studying the symbolic meanings of objects (products and communication/messages) in their usage.

semiotics

(Symbolic) value and meaning of objects (products and communication/messages) for individuals.

sensation (perception)

The immediate and direct activation of receptors in the senses (ears, eyes, nose, mouth, skin) as a reaction to simple stimuli (for example, an advertisement, packaging, colour, design, brand name), and transferring these sensory data through the nervous system to the brain. The ability to perceive stimuli varies with the quality of the senses and with the number and the intensity of the stimuli encountered.

sensation seeker

Individual with a strong need for constant stimulation, which is expressed in his behaviour.

shopping behaviour

Part of consumer behaviour relating to purchasing behaviour of consumers, such as visiting frequency, expenditure in a particular shop and/or shopping centre; this also includes the route which buyers follow in the shop and/or between the shops. *See also:* routing.

shopping goods

Product for which a buyer is prepared to make a certain purchasing effort by comparing the price and/or quality attributes of the goods on offer.

short list

Number of possible suppliers who, after a general initial evaluation round, are preferred by a buying organization.

significance structure (means–end structure)

Systematic representation of the way in which a buyer experiences a product. Three to six levels of significance are distinguished. These vary from product attributes via consequences to instrumental values and end-values. Consequences represent the functional and emotional advantages of a product for the individual, the values relate to what is pursued or considered valuable in life. *See also:* laddering.

simple additive decision rule

Compensatory decision rule used by consumers when evaluating alternatives in which the consumer counts the number of times the alternative scores favourably on one of the major choice criteria. The alternative scoring the largest number of points is most likely to be bought.

simplifying decision rule

Decision rule in which a buyer evaluates the alternatives on the basis of only one essential product attribute. *See also:* optimizing decision rule.

simultaneous conditioning

Type of classic conditioning in which influencing of behaviour is created by offering the conditioned stimulus and the unconditioned stimulus at the same time. For example: when watching food (neutral, natural stimulus) a bell is ringing (conditioned stimulus).

situational influence

Influence of the circumstances in the environment in which the decision-making processes and purchasing behaviour of consumers takes place. The origin of these influences is restricted in time and place and is independent of the buyer and the product characteristics.

social class (prosperity class)
Classification of individuals within a social system in a hierarchy of distinctive status classes. This is effected in such a way that the individuals within a specific class have more or less the same status, but as compared with the individuals of another class, have a higher or lower status. Most Dutch marketing research agencies operate five classes, namely:
(1) class A: the well-to-do (managers of large companies, high ranking officials, the upper layer of professionals, etc.);
(2) class B1: the upper layer of the middle group (including managers of middle sized companies, sub-top officials, etc.);
(3) class B2: the lower layer from the middle group (including managers of small businesses, middle management and officials, etc.);
(4) class C: the less well-to-do (owners of small businesses, low level public servants and office staff, skilled labourers);
(5) class D: the least well-to-do (unskilled labourers, people out of work, etc.);
(6) class E: subsistence level (pensioners, widows, casual workers).

social facilitation
Situation in which an individual's behaviour is stimulated by the presence of other people. For example: watching other people enjoying a good meal results in the viewer developing an appetite.

social inhibition
Situation in which an individual's behaviour is inhibited by the presence of other people. For example, having a meal at home is accompanied by other behaviour than having a meal in a restaurant together with other people.

social status
Relative position of a rank within a group assigned to someone on the grounds of role, experience, age, skills or knowledge.

socialization
Absorbing a culture including all standards, values and symbols belonging to it.

speciality goods
Products for which a buyer is willing to make a high purchasing effort because no or only few purchasing experiences either have been gained with them yet, or because these products are special and/or available from only one or a few shops.

stage of life
Stage in an individual's life from infant, toddler, pre-schooler, schoolchild, adolescent/teenager, pre-adult, adult, senior, elderly to the very old person.

standard of living
The level of prosperity of an economic unit (person, household, country), usually reflected in the product inventory (such as food, clothing, furniture, transport, and medical facilities) bought by this economic unit.

standardized language
Technical language often used by the members of a buying centre in a company.

status
The relative prestige that is attributed to an individual as a member of a specific group or a social system.

stimulus (sensory input)
Any kind and quality of input/stimuli for one of the senses. Examples of stimuli for buyers are: products, packagings, brand names and advertising messages.

stimulus categorization
Classifying a stimulus on the basis of concepts which have been stored in memory during the understanding stage of information processing.

stimulus determinants of attention
Characteristics of a stimulus (for example, an advertising message) that influences attention, such as colour, size and location of the advertising message.

stimulus discrimination
In the classic conditioning theory, the situation in which an individual learns how to distinguish a particular stimulus from other stimuli and how to react to the stimulus in question with a specific response. *See also:* stimulus generalization.

stimulus generalization
In classic conditioning, the situation in which a new stimulus, which strongly resembles the existing (un)conditioned stimulus, evokes the same response with an organism. *See also:* stimulus discrimination.

stimulus response model
Model enabling the description and prediction of the behaviour of organisms/people. In such a model links are made between perceivable stimuli and overt reactions (responses).

sub-culture
Part of a culture within which members' own standards and values prevail which are usually not valid for the culture as a whole.

subjective knowledge
An individual's assessment with regard to his own expertise in specific fields. For example, how knowledgeable does he think he himself is with regard to purchasing (specific) products.

subjective norm
Component from Fishbein's reasoned behaviour theory indicating what convictions an individual has on the behaviour expected from him, and the extent to which he is prepared to conform to this normative pressure.

sublimation
Conversion and manifestation of a suppressed need into a socially accepted form of behaviour. *See also:* consumers' frustration.

subliminal perception (sub-threshold perception, subception)
Sensory recording of stimuli by an individual, the intensity of which is so weak, that this recording does not penetrate the receiver's consciousness.

supplier loyalty
Motivated, hard to change habit in preference for a specific supplier of products. In practice, this means that a consumer is inclined to go on buying from the same supplier(s).

supply theories in consumer behaviour
Notion that the purchasing behaviour of consumers should not only be studied as a function of perceptions of products at the moment (just) before the purchase, or as a function of the spending opportunities, but that also the consumer's past should be analysed in terms of stock on hand and stock policy. In this respect a distinction can be made between (1) the stock of psychological preferences and habits developed and (2) the stock of physical goods available.

support argument
Cognitive response of a buyer in the form of an approving reaction to the claims that are made, for example, in (an advertising) message.

symbolic group
Reference group a particular individual identifies himself with by adopting the attitudes, standards, values and (purchasing) behaviour, despite the improbability that this individual will ever become a member of this group. *See also:* aspiration group.

system buying
Buying an overall solution (turn-key solution) consisting of joint components.

teleshopping
Preparing and executing the purchasing decision at home, such as placing the order and taking receipt of the order using catalogues, telephone, videotex, audiotex, order forms, and other response facilities.

terminal threshold
The point at which an increase in intensity of a stimulus does not affect someone's sensual perceptions any more.

time goods
Products which can be classified on the basis of the consequences they have for the way in which the consumer spends his time. *See also:* time saving goods, time using goods.

time saving goods
Products which, when used, produce time savings for the consumer (time-extensive), such as electric lawn mowers, TV-dinners, dishwashing machines. *See also:* time goods, time using goods.

time using goods
Products that require the consumer to invest time (time-intensive), such as travelling, watching TV, practising sports and recreation. *See also:* time goods, time saving goods.

transformational motivation (positive motivation)
Positive motivation to buy a product. These motivations may find their origin in the pursuit of a more pleasant life, such as fine food, drinking, looking beautiful and attractive, or going on holiday. The motivation to buy products is to fulfil this desire, for example, by taking salt, drinking fashionable beverages, buying beautiful clothes, using make-up. *See also:* motivation type.

trial
Stage in the adoption process with regard to the acceptance of a new product, in which the consumer tries the product out (on a limited scale).

trickle-down theory
Theory of social influencing, in which it is assumed that lower social classes pursue behaviour which is common to higher social classes.

two-level choice
Concept assuming that a buyer often has to make a double choice: firstly on the level of the product class (which product), and secondly on the product level (which brand).

type of decision
Classification of purchase decisions (Rossiter & Percy) on the basis of low or high involvement which, combined with a negative or positive purchasing motivation, leads to a classification of products. *See also:* motivation type.

unaided awareness (active awareness, spontaneous awareness)
Extent to which a buyer is familiar with a product or brand without the product (or brand name) being shown/mentioned. This active buyer awareness of a product or brand is determined on the basis of such questions as: 'Which products or brands do you know in the product category . . . ?' *See also:* aided awareness.

unconditioned response
Natural reaction of organisms/humans on a specific natural stimulus (for example, getting saliva in the mouth (response) on seeing food (stimulus). *See also:* classic conditioning, reflex.

unconditioned stimulus
Natural stimulus evoking a specific natural reaction (response) with an organism/human being. For example, withdrawing the hand (response) from excessive heat (stimulus). *See also:* classic conditioning, reflex.

unsought goods
Type of goods which the consumer may or may not know, but for which he usually has no intrinsic motivation to buy (for example, funeral insurance policies).

usage, knowledge of
Information stored in memory on how a product may be used, and what is needed (in other products) to be able to use the product.

use/usage behaviour (consumption behaviour)
Part of buyer and consumer behaviour relating to all the actions of a buyer linked to consuming and/or using a product. *See also:* consumer behaviour.

utilitarian benefits
Advantages having to do with objective, functional product characteristics which a buyer obtains when he buys a product. *See also:* instrumental value.

utility
Extent to which a specific product can fill a specific (human) need.

utility function of attitude
Concept in consumer behaviour with regard to attitude change stating that individuals develop attitudes with regard to products or brands, because these attitudes can be practicable (useful) with choice processes in the future.

utility maximization
Principle assuming that choice processes of individuals can be reduced to their pursuit of such a distribution of their budget between the purchase of different (quantities of) products, that the total utility which is derived from the different (quantities of) products is as high as possible.

VALS typology
Value and lifestyle typology, consumer typology on the basis of behaviour, activities, interests, and opinions. Using 36 criteria, various groups of consumers may be distinguished in this way, on the basis of lifestyle. The most important of these are the inner-directed, the outer-directed and the need-driven consumers.

value
In economics: the meaning of goods and services for prosperity purposes. A distinction is made between the practical value, the value an object has because it satisfies a need when used and the exchange value or market value, the value an owner may receive from someone else by parting with the object.
In psychology: the relative permanent judgement (the subjective appreciation) of a (group of) people on what is important in life to pursue (end values) or on what behaviour is most appropriate to accomplish the end values (instrumental values). *See also:* end values.

value congruency theory
Theory assuming that there should be a consistent ratio between the values an individual deems important and the values (expressive, instrumental) he derives from particular objects (for example, products, brands).

value-expressive function of the attitude

Concept with regard to attitude change in which it is assumed that in attitudes not only a number of general ideas with regard to standards and values is expressed, but also the lifestyle of an individual.

variety seeking behaviour

Purchasing behaviour characterized by regularly changing brands, because the individual needs variety.

wants

Desire for specific satisfiers of needs. *See also:* basic need, need.

Weber–Fechner Law

'Law' in perceptional theory stating that the number of stimulus changes which is necessary to exceed the differential threshold is dependent on the intensity of the stimulus which is perceived first: as the intensity of the initial stimulus is greater, a bigger amount of change is necessary before a difference is perceived.

Webster and Wind model

Model in which organizational/industrial purchasing behaviour is described and in which four factors are distinguished that affect the purchasing decision behaviour. These are: the environment, the organization, the inter-personal and the personal determinants.

weighted additive decision rule

Compensatory decision rule in the evaluation of alternatives in which the subjective assessment of performances of a product on the choice criteria can be weighted on the basis of the relative consequence (for the buyer) of each of these criteria. *See also:* multi-attribute attitude models.

References and further reading

Assael, H., *Consumer Behavior & Marketing Action*, PWS-Kent, Boston, 1992.

Boom, E.J. and A.A. Weber, *Consumentengedrag*, Wolters-Noordhoff, Groningen, 1993.

Engel, J.F., R.D. Blackwell and P.W. Miniard, *Consumer behavior*, The Dryden Press, New York, 1990.

Festinger, L., *The theory of cognitive dissonance*, Stanford University Press, 1957.

Howard, J.A., *Consumer Behavior in Marketing Strategy*, Prentice-Hall, Englewood Cliffs, New Jersey, 1989.

Howard, J.A. and J.N. Sheth, *The Theory of Buyer Behavior*, Wiley, New York, 1969.

Koutsoyiannis, A., *Modern Microeconomics*, MacMillan Press, London, 2nd edition, 1983.

Loudon, D.L. and A.J. Della Bitta, *Consumer Behavior: Concepts and Applications*, McGraw-Hill, New York, 1988.

Mowen, J.C., *Consumer Behavior*, MacMillan, New York, 1987.

Petty, R.E. and J.T. Cacioppo, *Communication and Persuasion: Central and Peripheral Routes to Attitude Change*, Springer Verlag, New York, 1986.

Rogers, E.M., *Diffusion of innovations*, The Free Press, New York, 1983.

Rossiter, J.R. and L. Percy, *Advertising and Promotion Management*, McGraw-Hill, New York, 1987.

Schiffman, L.G. and L.L. Kanuk, *Consumer Behavior*, Prentice-Hall, Englewood Cliffs, New Jersey, 3rd edition, 1987.

Solomon, M.R., *Consumer behavior*, Allyn and Bacon, Boston, 1992.

Wierenga, B. and W.F. van Raaij, *Consumentengedrag*, Stenfert Kroese, Leiden, 1987.

4 MARKETING RESEARCH

Concept overview

absolute frequency
accuracy
action research
ad hoc hypothesis
ad hoc research
AGB/Attwood panel
AID
alternative hypothesis
ambiguous question
analysis of variance
analysis phase
angulometer
area sample
association test
ASSPAT method

back data
barometer research
Bayes' theorem
Bayesian decision analysis
bias
bimodal distribution
binomial distribution
bipolar scale
bivariate distribution
bivariate regression analysis
blind product test
Bogardus scale
branded test
budget research

cagi
canonical correlation coefficient
capi
categorical system
cati
causal chronological model
causal connection
causal research
census
central tendency criterion
central-limit theorem
chi-square test
class
classical probability
classifying
cluster analysis
cluster sample
co-variance
cohort
cohort analysis
communication method of data collection
confidence interval
constant sum scale

construct
construct validity
consumer panel
content-validity
continuous research
continuous variable
control group
convenience sample
convergent validity
corporate marketing research
correlation
correlation coefficient
correspondence analysis
coverage errors
criterion validity
critical area
critical value
Cronbach alpha
cross tabulation
cross-modality comparison
cross-sectional research
cumulative distribution function
cumulative frequency distribution
cumulative frequency polygon
curtosis
customer satisfaction survey
cyclical fluctuations

databank
decile
decision tree
Delphi method
demographic characteristics
dependent samples
dependent variable
descriptive research
descriptive statistics
desk research
deviation margin
dichotomous scale
discrete variable
discriminant analysis
disproportional stratified sample
disproportionate sample
distribution panel
dummy variable
duplicate sample
dustbin research

eccentricity
electro-dermagraphy
empirical research
encoding
ESOMAR

estimate
expected value
experiment(al) research
experimental condition
experimental group
experimental variable
expert research
exploratory research
exponential smoothing
external data
external source
extrapolation
eye camera

face-to-face interview
factor
factor analysis
factor loading
factor score
field experiment
fieldwork
fieldwork agency
fieldwork checking
fieldwork fraud
filter question
first-order interaction
focus group discussion
fractile
frequency density
frequency distribution
frequency polygon
funnel approach
fusion technique

galvanometer
generalization
generalizing survey results
geographic characteristics
geometric mean
graph
graphic scale

histogram
Homals
household panel
hypothesis

in-depth interview
in-home-use-test
in-store-test
incentive
independent samples
independent variable
index number
inductive statistics
initial measurement
internal data

internal source
international market research
interval level
interview
interviewer bias
intrapolation

job classification

Kolmogorov–Smirnov test
Kruskal–Wallis test

laboratory experiment
left skewed
Likert scale
Likert scale item
Lisrel
logit analysis
loglinear analysis
longitudinal research

magnitude estimation
mall intercept
manipulation check
Mann–Whitney test
market research plan
market research process
Marketing Decision Support System
    (MDSS)
Marketing Information System (MIS)
marketing research
matching
mean
mean absolute deviation
measurement level
measures of variability
median
median test
metric measurement level
modal class
mode
monadic research
moving average
multi-client research
multi-dimensional scaling
multiple correlation coefficient
multiple determination coefficient
multiple-item scale
multivariate analysis of variance

n
Natural grouping
Nielsen Store Audit
no-bias
nominal measurement level
nomogram
non-coverage error
non-metric measurement level

non-parametric test
non-random sample
non-response
non-sampling error
non-verbal response
normal distribution
null hypothesis

observation errors
observation method of data collecting
octile
omnibus research
one-dimensional scale analysis
one-tailed probability
one-tailed test
open-ended question
opinion research
oral interview
ordinal measurement level
outlier
overcoverage error
overrun probability

paired comparison
panel
pantry check
parametric test
partial correlation coefficient
passer-by research
pay-off table
Pearson correlation coefficient
percentile
physical characteristics
picture graphic
pie chart
pilot survey
pooling
population
population research
postal research
postcode segmentation
prediction validity
primary data
Princals
principal component analysis
probability
probability distribution
projective technique
proportionate stratified sample
protocol
psychophysiology
pupillometer
purposive sample

qualitative research
quantitative research
quartile

quartile distance
quasi experiment
questionnaire routing
quota sample

random number
random sample
randomization
range
rank correlation coefficient
ratio measurement level
regression analysis
relative frequency
reliability
reminder
reply scale
reply tendency
representative
research briefing
research design
research fatigue
research goal
right of inspection
right skewed
round-robin product test

sample allocation
sample distribution
sample frame
sample frame errors
sample research
sample size
sampling distribution
sampling error
SAS (Statistical Analysis System)
scale
scaling technique
scanning
scattergram
seasonal fluctuation
secondary data
self-completion
semantic differential
semi-structured interview
sentence completion
sequence effect
sequential sample
sign test for paired samples
significance level
significant result
simple random sample
skewed distribution
skewness measure
snowball sample
socially desirable response
socio-economic characteristics
split-half reliability coefficient

SPSS (Statistical Package for the Social Sciences)
spurious correlation
standard deviation
standard error
standard normal distribution
standardization
Stapel scale
start-address method
statistic analysis module
statistical testing
stochastic variable
story telling
stratification
stratified cluster survey
stratified sample
structured interview
structured question
structured questionnaire survey
subjective probability
symmetric distribution
systematic sample

t-test for one sample
t-test for paired samples
t-test for two samples
tachistoscope
telephone survey
telescope effect
test design
test market
test measure
test/retest reliability
thematic apperception test (TAT-test)
third-person technique

time sequence analysis
time series
time series analysis
total error
trend
true experiment
two-tailed probability
two-tailed test
type I error
type II error

UAC-code
undertaking discernment
uniform distribution
unimodal distribution
unipolar scale
unstructured interview
urbanization, degree of

validity
variability
variance
variation coefficient
verbal scale
verification question

weighted mean
weighted sample
weighting
Wilcoxon test for paired samples
word association

yes-bias

z score
z-test for one sample
z-test for proportions

Concept descriptions

absolute frequency
The number of times a particular value (or class) occurs. *See also:* frequency distribution.

accuracy
The degree of confidence interval; the term indicates the size of the margin in which the real value of the parameter (for example, the average turnover) in the population is likely to lie.

action research
Type of research, particularly developed in sociology, with the objective of implementing results of the research, if possible, already when the research is being carried out, after which these changes are also subjected to the current research process.

ad hoc hypothesis
Hypothesis not prepared prior to a research, but in the course of the research or during the interpretation of the results.

ad hoc research
Collecting and processing data occasionally, in order to solve a specific, one-off problem. *See also:* continuous research.

AGB/Attwood panel
Consumers panel set up and managed by the AGB-Attwood marketing research agency. The most important AGB/Attwood panel consists of a representative sample of approximately 5,000 households. For a large number of consumption goods the respondents have to keep a diary to record the number of purchases. Apart from the product, also the brand, quantity purchased, packing size, price paid, place of purchase and day of purchase need to be recorded. At present, panel members, when recording their purchases at home, can use a reading pen which can read the UAC-codes of the articles.

AID
AID (*a*utomatic *i*nteraction *d*etection), statistical technique with which by means of analysis of variance a gradual search is made for variables which can give an optimum explanation of the variance in the dependent variable. The end result is a tree structure of variables. Through the AID technique, interactions between variables can be detected. For stable results, the technique can only be applied on large samples (1,000 or more).

alternative hypothesis (research hypothesis)
The hypothesis (indicated by H_a or H_1) which is accepted when the null hypothesis must be rejected. The alternative hypothesis contains the assumption on the value of a variable or the correlation between the variables. Usually the following wording is applied: 'there is a difference between . . . and . . .' or 'there is a positive correlation between . . . and . . .'.

ambiguous question
Question which the interviewee can interpret in different ways. *See also:* bias.

analysis of variance
Statistical technique used to test if two or more means are equal to each other. The technique is applied on data with an interval or ratio measurement level. Example: is the average amount spent monthly on recreation equal for secondary modern, comprehensive school and grammar school pupils? Analysis of variance is often abbreviated to ANOVA (*a*nalysis *o*f *va*riance).

analysis phase
The stage in the research process in which the collected data are linked up and interpreted. In the case of quantitative data, statistical techniques are used to analyse the data.

angulometer
Apparatus used to measure at what angle recognition of an object is easiest.

area sample

Special type of cluster sample in which the area sample is formed by a map or plan of an area, and in which the clusters consist of blocks on the map, for example, city districts, provinces, regions.

association test

A projection technique in which the respondent is asked for his associations with a verbal stimulus (a word, a sentence).

ASSPAT method

Abbreviation for *ass*ociation *pat*tern method. In this method the respondent is presented with a pattern of boxes in which columns are formed by, for example, brands, and rows by statements. A sample statement is: 'cheap'. The interviewee is supposed to place a cross at the statements he thinks appropriate for the brands. The outcome is a pattern in which crosses indicate which brands are associated with which statements. In the analysis of these data such methods as correspondence analysis may be applied.

back data

Old data offered for sale by market research agencies (at a low price) after having obtained permission for sale from the client.

barometer research

Continuous research with the objective to accurately monitor changes in the market. For example: the corporate image barometer measuring changes in companies' images in time.

Bayes' theorem

Rule developed by Thomas Bayes to change the (objective or subjective) probability of the occurrence of an event in the light of new information. The Bayes' theorem can be used in market research to assess the question as to whether or not it makes sense to gather additional market data, given the cost of collecting that data and the risk reduction of the decision to be expected.

Bayesian decision analysis

Way of structuring and solving decisions under risk by means of a pay-off table or decision tree.

bias

Systematic (non-incidental) distortion in the answers of interviewees as a result of the interviewer's influence, the wording of the question, the situation in which the person is interviewed, and so on. Examples of bias: yes-bias, no-bias, giving socially desirable answers. *See also:* reply tendency.

bimodal distribution

Frequency distribution with two peaks. *See also:* unimodal distribution.

binomial distribution (Bernoulli distribution)

A binomial divided variable is the number of times of 'success' in independent repetitions of the process, in which each repetition results in either of the two possible outcomes: 'success' or 'no success'. Example: the number of times 'three' comes on top when throwing an untampered dice twenty times is a binomial divided variable.

bipolar scale

Response scale in which the two extreme values of the scale are identified by opposite word pairs. An example of a scale of five: very positive 1 2 3 4 5 very negative.

bivariate distribution

The frequency distribution or probability distribution formed by the combination of two variables. Example: the bivariate frequency distribution of age and income produces, for each combination of age and income, the number of persons meeting this combination.

bivariate regression analysis

Regression analysis with only one independent variable.

blind product test

Type of market research into the preference of consumers for one or more products with regard to physical characteristics such as taste, smell and quality. During this test the products have been stripped of all non-physical characteristics such as brand name, packing and price. *See also:* branded test.

Bogardus scale

A scale developed by Bogardus used to measure attitudes in respect of persons of a different race, a different religion, a different nationality, and so on. The Bogardus scale is an example of the Guttman scale. The subsequent items decrease as far as the respondent's privacy is concerned. Example: What would you think of a Japanese person as: son in law (very good . . . very bad); as a neighbour; as chairman of the judo club; as an inhabitant of your city?

branded test

Type of market research into the preference of consumers for one or more product alternatives/different brands, in which all characteristics of these brands can be observed by the consumers and the brand is revealed (as opposed to a blind test, in which the product alternatives are stripped of all non-physical characteristics). *See also:* blind product test.

budget research

Research into the income and expenditure of households and persons. Budget research is carried out by such agencies as the Central Statistical Office (UK).

cagi (computer assisted graphical interviewing)

Type of computer guided questioning in which (high quality) graphic stimuli or answer modalities are used on the computer screen. Especially suitable for communication research.

canonical correlation coefficient

The Pearson correlation coefficient between two sets of variables. Each set is characterized by a linear combination of a number of variables. The canonical correlation coefficient is used in discriminant analysis and canonical correlation analysis.

capi (computer assisted personal interviewing)

Face-to-face research with the help of (portable) computers. The advantages of computer guided questioning such as routing, consistency checks, customizing of question wordings and so forth, applied to the face-to-face situation.

categorical system

Classification of a group of elements on the basis of such a system of characteristics of the elements that each element can be classified unambiguously. Categorical systems can be used, for example, to form strata and clusters.

cati

*C*omputer *a*ssisted *t*elephone *i*nterviewing.

causal chronological model

Kind of chronological analysis in which fluctuations in time of the dependent variable are explained by fluctuations in time of independent variables. Example: A model in which the changes in the weekly turnover of beer are explained by the weather changes (temperature, hours of sunshine) and the advertising expenditure for beer.

causal connection

Cause–result relationship between two or more variables. In order to admit that there is a causal connection between variables, there should be:
1 a relation between the variables,
2 a chronological order between cause and result, and
3 no other possible causal factor.

causal research (testing research)
Research in which it is assumed that the relevant variables are known, and in which also the correlation between variables is clearly specified. The aim of causal research is to test (to reject, or to confirm) the supposed relations and to measure the strength of the relation or the size of the effect. *See also:* descriptive research, exploratory research.

census
Collecting data on all inhabitants in a particular area.

central tendency criterion (centre measure, location criterion)
Such a criterion indicates around which number the observations are grouped. Frequently used criteria for central tendency are: the mean, the median and the mode. To be distinguished from dispersion measurements such as variation width and standard deviation.

central-limit theorem
If random samples of size n are drawn from a population distribution with a mean μ, and standard deviation σ, when n is big, the distribution of the sample mean will roughly show a normal distribution with expected value π and standard deviation $\sigma/\sqrt{n}$ (the standard error). The approximation of the normal distribution will improve as n increases.

chi-square test
The chi-square test is a non-parametric test which can be applied in two situations, namely (1) in a cross table and (2) in a sample.
ad 1. Application with the objective to check whether a significant correlation exists between rows and columns in a cross table. Conditions for applicability
  · two or more independent samples;
  · data on a nominal measurement level or higher;
  · up to 20 per cent of the cells in the cross table with a theoretical frequency less than 5, and not a single cell with a theoretical frequency less than 1. Categories may be joined in order to meet this condition.
Example: the relation between the 'prosperity' variable and the 'EC-nationality' variable can be tested using a chi-square test.
ad 2. Application with the objective to check whether there is a significant difference between a given theoretical frequency distribution and an observed distribution. In this context the term adaptation test or also goodness-of-fit test is used. Conditions for applicability
  · one sample;
  · data on a nominal measurement level or higher;
  · a theoretical (= expected) frequency in each category of no less than five.
Example: the frequency distribution of prosperity in the sample is compared with the frequency distribution of prosperity in the population, as reflected in the prosperity data in the 'Marktanalytisch Vademecum'. In this way the representativeness of the sample for the prosperity variable can be examined.

class
Collection of identical or more or less equal measurement values. The distance between the bottom limit (= lowest observation within the class) and the top limit is called class interval. Then, a class limit is the value between the two subsequent classes.

classical probability
The relative frequency, i.e. the probability that a specific event will take place. To be distinguished from subjective probability.

classifying
Arranging objects in clear-cut and mutually exclusive categories. *See also:* categorical system.

cluster analysis
Statistical technique meant to arrange a large number of objects (such as consumers, companies, countries) into a limited number of clusters (groups), in such a way that

objects within a cluster resemble each other more than object outside that cluster. For example, the technique can be applied in market segmentation in which clustering could be applied by age, interests, hobbies, viewing and reading habits, etc.

cluster sample

Sample in which the sample frame is split into groups (so called clusters) after which a random sample is drawn from the clusters. Subsequently, each element from each cluster drawn is interviewed (one-stage cluster sample). After drawing a number of clusters, it is also possible to draw a random sample of elements from each cluster drawn (two-stage cluster sample). Example: in order to produce a sample of students at polytechnics from the sample frame of polytechnical schools (one school is one cluster) a sample of schools is drawn. Subsequently, each student of a polytechnic drawn is interviewed (one-stage sample), or, within a school, a sample of students from the school in question is drawn (two-stage sample).

co-variance

Statistical criterion indicating to what degree two variables vary correspondingly (co-vary). When the co-variance is calculated for standardized variables, the Pearson correlation coefficient is generated.

cohort

A collection of persons who experienced the same event in the same time interval. Examples: birth cohort 1970–1980 (all persons born in the period 1970–1980), the flower-power cohort (seized by the flower-power movement during adolescence).

cohort analysis

Statistical methods to separate the effects of period (year), age and cohort. Suppose that elderly people drink less coke than youngsters. A question to be asked could be, is this an age effect (as a person grows older he is less fond of coke), or is it a cohort effect (elderly people were not exposed to coke in the sensitive period of their lives in which preferences for beverages are developed).

communication method of data collection

Collecting data by asking people questions. Examples of this are questionnaire, group discussion, open interview. *See also:* observation method of data collecting.

confidence interval

In a random sample this indicates the degree of probability that the actual value of the parameter in the population (for example, the average of the coefficient) will lie within the boundaries of the interval. 95 per cent or 99 per cent confidence intervals are frequently used.

constant sum scale

Scaling technique in which a respondent is supposed to distribute a fixed number of points between a number of products or brands, for example, by preference or taste, in such a way that a larger number of points stands for a higher preference, or better taste, respectively.

construct

Theoretical idea or concept which is not immediately observable, such as attitude versus environment, involvement, intelligence. Measurements are often carried out by means of a multiple-item scale.

construct validity

The degree to which measuring a construct in a set of mutually theoretical relationships correlates, as expected, with other constructs. Construct validity, therefore, can only be determined in an empirical cycle.

consumer panel
Fixed group of households or consumers in which data is collected continuously (for example, daily, weekly, monthly) on purchasing habits and behaviour patterns. *See also:* distribution panel, panel.

content-validity (face-validity)
The degree to which the items in a multiple-item scale together cover all aspects of the construct to be measured. A test to measure teacher training college students' arithmetic skills which does not contain fractions, for example, is not content valid. Content validity is sometimes called face validity, because it is judged subjectively (at sight) if the content of an item is compatible with a construct.

continuous research
Research which is repeated at regular intervals in the same form, with the aim to record changes in time. *See also:* ad hoc research.

continuous variable
Variable in which the readings form a continuum: for each two random readings a third reading can be found which lies between the first and the second. *See also:* discrete variable.

control group
In an experiment, sample group which is not exposed to the experimental condition of the experimental variable (though having the relevant characteristics of the experimental group).

convenience sample
Non-random sample in which convenience plays a major part when selecting the elements in the sample.

convergent validity
Degree to which measuring a construct correlates with an external criterion which is measured simultaneously. It is a form of criterion validity. An example is a pregnancy test: it does not predict if someone will become pregnant, only if someone is pregnant at the moment when the test is performed.

corporate marketing research
Marketing research on behalf of an organization as a whole. Not for a specific part of the company or for a specific product.

correlation
Relationship between two or more variables.

correlation coefficient
Statistical criterion for the strength of the relationship between variables. Well-known coefficients are: the Pearson correlation coefficient and the Spearman-rank-correlation coefficient.

correspondence analysis
Exploratory statistical technique to detect relationships in large cross tabulations, and to represent these relationships in a two-dimensional picture.

coverage errors
Errors generated when the sample frame does not correspond with the population. To be distinguished are overcoverage and undercoverage.

criterion validity (pragmatic validity)
The extent to which the measurement of a construct is correlated with an external criterion (for example, a characteristic or specific behaviour). In this case, the external criterion can be measured at the same moment as the construct (concurrent validity) or it can be measured in the future (predictive validity).

critical area
The collection of data of the test quantity in which the null hypothesis (H_0) is rejected. Thus, the critical area contains the values of the test quantity which are not in the confidence interval.

critical value
Value which bounds the critical area.

Cronbach alpha
Coefficient developed by Cronbach indicating a measurement's reliability by means of a multiple-item scale. The size of Cronbach alpha is determined by the average correlation between the items (as the items in the scale show a stronger positive correlation, Cronbach alpha increases) and the number of items (more items lead to a larger alpha). The alpha lies between 0 (totally unreliable) and 1 (fully reliable).

cross tabulation
A table in which at least two variables are crossed. The rows of the table are formed by values (or classes) of the one variable, whereas the columns represent the values (or classes) of another variable. At the intersection of rows and columns the absolute and/ or relative frequencies of each combination of the values (or classes) are shown.

cross-modality comparison
Procedure applied in magnitude scaling in which the respondent judges the same stimulus on two response scales (two modalities). The aim is to check to what degree the respondent succeeds in estimating ratios between stimuli. *See also:* magnitude estimation.

cross-sectional research
Sample research in which the observations relate to one period. Unlike panel research and chronological analysis.

cumulative distribution function (cumulative frequency distribution)
Represents the relationship between a specific value of a variable and the percentage (the relative frequency) of the observations below that specific value.

cumulative frequency distribution
Represents the relationship between the upper boundary of a class and the total number of observations below that specific boundary. The cumulative frequency of a class boundary is calculated by adding the frequencies below the class boundaries.

cumulative frequency polygon (ogive)
Frequency polygon in which the cumulative frequency distribution is represented graphically. Here, however, the dots which are connected by means of the lines are located over the class boundaries and not over the class midmarks, as in a non-cumulative frequency polygon.

curtosis (curvature)
Measurement indicating how peaked a distribution is by comparing it with the form of the normal distribution with the same standard deviation. The curtosis is 0 when the distribution corresponds with the normal distribution. The curtosis is positive (> 0) when the distribution is higher in the middle than the normal distribution, and the curtosis is negative (< 0) when the distribution is flatter in the middle than the normal distribution.

customer satisfaction survey
Research in which the satisfaction with the products supplied takes a central place. Factual experiences, concrete reactions and contact evaluations are more important than attitudes, image and other, more general characteristics.

cyclical fluctuations
Movements around the trend in a chronological sequence caused by long-term influences (for example, ten-year cyclical fluctuations).

databank
Component of a *Marketing Decision Support System* (MDDS) enabling data to be stored in a computer in a systematic, conveniently accessible way, and to retrieve these data selectively.

decile
A cumulative frequency distribution can be broken down into fractiles. A breakdown into ten equal parts is called a breakdown in deciles (the first decile through to the tenth decile). The first decile of a cumulative frequency distribution is the value below which 10 per cent of the observations lie, the second decile indicates the limit below which 20 per cent of the observations lie, and so on. Usually, the fifth decile is called the median.

decision tree
Way to structure a decision problem under uncertainty by showing, from the left to the right, a chronological sequence of decisions and probabilities. In the tree structure which is formed in this way, usually decisions are indicated by boxes and probabilities by circles.

Delphi method
Method of data collection named after the Greek town of Delphi, where priests predicted the future. In this method, in a number of rounds, experts' opinions are collected. The experts give their independent opinions. At the end of each round the experts are confronted with the opinions of others, primarily in order to acquire a higher degree of consensus. The method can be used, for example, to gain an insight in highly uncertain market developments.

demographic characteristics
Basic characteristics connected to a person or a household. Examples of demographic characteristics are: age, sex, marital status, religion, size of family, and duration of marriage.

dependent samples
Samples are called dependent when on the basis of the value of observation X a statement can be made on the value of observation Y. A frequently occurring situation of dependent samples is one in which the same person is repeatedly subjected to measurements, for example, in a panel (repeatedly measuring purchasing behaviour with the same respondents) or when a respondent judges a beer of brand A first, followed by a beer of brand B. The distinction between dependent and independent samples is essential for the choice of the statistical test.

dependent variable (criterion, effect, variable to be explained)
Identification of a variable the values of which (variance) are supposed to be dependent on the values (variance) of the independent variable(s).

descriptive research (explanatory research)
Research in which it is assumed that the relevant variables are well-known, but in which the hypotheses are worded in a general way. Often, results of descriptive research have to do with: measurements of relative frequencies, measurements of the degree of correlation between variables and comparisons between groups (for example, the comparison 'buyers' versus 'non-buyers' on a large number of variables). Descriptive research is an intermediate form between exploratory research and causal research, and therefore features characteristics of both kinds of research.

descriptive statistics
That part of statistics which is concerned with processing and representing facts in such a way that the data is neatly arranged. The description of the data takes place by means of statistical ratios (such as mean, median, standard deviation), by means of figures (such as frequency polygon, histogram) or by means of tables (frequency table, cross table). *See also:* inductive statistics.

desk research

Collecting and processing existing data (secondary data). The data may originate from both internal and external sources.

deviation margin

Deviation between the actual situation and the research outcome as a result of accidental sample deviations. The expected maximum size of the deviation margin depends on the desired reliability of the statement, the sample size and the research outcome itself.

dichotomous scale

A scale type including only two scale values. Examples: sex, yes/no, buyer/non-buyer. In statistical procedures the dichotomous scale may be seen as an interval-scaled variable.

discrete variable

Variable in which only specific values are possible. Examples: sex (man, woman), number of children (0, 1, 2, . . .). The opposite of continuous variable.

discriminant analysis

Statistical technique in which, as in regression analysis, the variance of one dependent variable is explained by the variance in one or more independent variables. Discriminant analysis distinguishes itself from regression analysis in that the dependent variable is scaled dichotomously or nominally, whereas with regression analysis the dependent variable is interval-scaled or ratio-scaled. The object of the analysis is a classification of objects (or individuals) in mutually excluding classes on the basis of a collection of 'discriminating' variables. The interesting question in this case is, which variables are most important, i.e. discriminating, and in which class will an object fall, given an interplay of characteristics.

disproportional stratified sample

A stratified sample in which the ratios of the strata in the sample are unequal to the ratios of the strata in a population (the sample frame). Example: if in the sample frame 15 per cent of the students attend higher vocational education, this group may be overrepresented in the sample by drawing for example, 35 per cent higher vocational education students, or it may be underrepresented by drawing, for example, 10 per cent higher vocational education students.

disproportionate sample

Sample in which the distribution of one or more characteristics does not correspond with the distribution of those characteristics in the population.

distribution panel

Fixed group of retail organizations in which, permanently, (weekly, bi-monthly, and so on) a number of data is collected. Data collected include turnover figures and prices of products and brands, and the number and type of displays in the shops. *See also:* Nielsen Store Audit.

dummy variable

Discrete variable which can take only one of two values, usually 0 and 1. Used to enable dichotomously, nominally or ordinally scaled variables to be taken as independent variables in regression or discriminant analysis.

duplicate sample

Together with the first sample, a second sample is drawn simultaneously in comparable circumstances.

dustbin research

Researching the contents of dustbins in order to gain an insight into consumption behaviour of households. A cleaner type of dustbin research is acquired by asking household members to put the packings of particular products in separate rubbish bags or bins, so that their use can be measured.

eccentricity
The relative location of a unit (for example, a person or a data-point) in the joint unit. In descriptive statistics eccentricity of observations is indicated by the Z-value, which indicates the distance from the unit to the mean, measured in standard deviations. A heavily eccentric data-point is called an outlier.

electro-dermagraphy (galvanic skin response)
Measuring skin resistance. The instrument used to measure skin resistance is called a galvanometer.

empirical research
Research aimed at confirming or rejecting hypotheses or theories by testing them in a controllable and repeatable way against perceivable facts.

encoding
Conversion of answers to non pre-coded or partly pre-coded questions to solid numerically manageable codes. This generally labour-intensive process takes place using a code book.

ESOMAR
European Society for Opinion and Marketing Research, aiming to promote the development of marketing and marketing research.

estimate
Statistical quantity used in sample research to estimate the unknown value of a parameter in the population. The average length of the persons in a random sample with size n is an estimate of the average length in the population.

expected value
Value resulting when in a probability distribution each outcome is multiplied by the chance of that probability, and after that the multiplication products are added up. As used in the analysis of decision trees and Bayesian decision analysis.

experiment(al) research
Form of causal research in which the impact of the manipulation of the dependent variable(s) is measured by manipulating the experimental variable(s). At the same time attempts are made to control the impact of interfering variables as much as possible. The degree of control in an experiment can differ (see true experiment and quasi experiment). Further, experiments can be differentiated in laboratory experiments and field experiments.

experimental condition
The level of the experimental variable. For example: in case of an experimental variable 'pressure of time' three conditions could be distinguished: 'no pressure of time', 'high pressure of time', and 'very high pressure of time'.

experimental group
Sample group in an experiment exposed to the experimental condition of the experimental variable of which the effect is to be measured. To be distinguished from control group.

experimental variable
The variable of which a causal effect on the dependent variable is measured in an experiment. The experimental variable has a number of experimental conditions, i.e.: levels. To distinguish them from environment variables; this relates to all variables which may interfere with the relation between the experimental variable and the variable to be explained.

expert research
Collecting information on a specific subject by means of interviewing experts in that field. *See also:* Delphi method.

exploratory research
Research aimed at acquiring insight into the issue of the subject to be researched. The essence of the, initially, often wide and vague problem is thus more clearly outlined.

So, more accurate issues and hypotheses can be worded. Exploratory research is also a form of pre-research following descriptive and test studies. Often, in exploratory research qualitative methods such as in-depth interviews and group discussions are used. *See also:* causal research, descriptive research.

exponential smoothing
Chronological analysis in which recent observations count heavier to predict future values. The degree to which recent observations count more than earlier observations is determined by the smoothing constant.

external data
Data originating from an external source.

external source
Source of secondary data outside the organization for which the survey is carried out. Examples: Nielsen, Attwood, scientific periodicals. *See also:* internal source.

extrapolation
Determining values of a variable outside the observation field on the basis of data inside the observation area.

eye camera
Camera used to follow a person's eye movements, for example, when watching an advertisement or commercial, in order to find out what the person watches, when and for how long.

face-to-face interview
Structured or unstructured oral interview in which the interviewer is physically present with the respondent.

factor
In the factor analysis context: a linear combination of variables.

factor analysis
Statistical technique to represent the information in a large number of variables as correctly as possible, on the basis of the correlations between variables, by means of a (small) number of new variables. These new variables are called factors. If it appears that with relatively little loss of information the number of original variables can be strongly reduced to a smaller number of factors, then this enables a better arranged presentation of the data. Factor analysis uses variables measured on interval or ratio-scaled variables.

factor loading
In the factor analysis context: the correlation between the variable and the factor.

factor score
In the factor analysis context: a respondent's score on a factor; this is a combination of original scores on the variables.

field experiment
Form of causal research in which the influence of the experimental variable(s) on the dependent variable(s) is determined. Unlike the laboratory experiment, a field experiment is carried out in a realistic situation. In order to enable the best possible determination of the experimental variable, any interfering variables are controlled as much as possible (by matching or randomization). The degree of control of these interfering variables is usually smaller than in a laboratory experiment, in consequence of which the internal validity of a field experiment can be a problem. Due to the realistic situation in which the experiment takes place the external validity of a field experiment will usually be larger than in a laboratory experiment. Example: measuring the effect of shelf height on choice behaviour by applying variation in the shelf height in an existing supermarket.

fieldwork
The way in which primary data is collected in an interview or in a field experiment (approaching respondents, interviewing, sending letters of gratitude, etc.).

fieldwork agency
Agency specializing in the execution of face-to-face fieldwork.

fieldwork checking
Measures executed to check whether fieldwork is carried out in accordance with the instructions and codes provided. According to the VMO guidelines 15 per cent of fieldwork should be checked.

fieldwork fraud
Filling in answers when the intended respondent has in fact not at all or only partly been questioned for the questionnaire.

filter question
Question used to select the desirable group of respondents for (part of) the interview. For example: in a CD purchasing behaviour survey, the filter question is posed if the respondent owns a CD-player or not. Subsequently, only owners of CD-players are subjected to (the rest of) the interview.

first-order interaction
Interaction between variables in which the effect of a variable A on variable B depends on the values of variable C.

focus group discussion
Qualitative research into the form of an open-ended discussion of eight to twelve persons with a panel chairperson. The interaction between the persons in the discussion is important. The chairperson stimulates this discussion without influencing its content.

fractile (quantile)
A fractile is a breakdown of a cumulative frequency distribution in such a way that each part contains an equal percentage of the observations. If the frequency distribution is broken down into four equal parts, these are called quartiles; when broken down in eight parts, they are called octiles, and when broken down in ten parts, they are called deciles. With a breakdown in 100 equal parts, the parts are called percentiles. In that case the fifth percentile is the value of the variable covering the first 5 per cent of the observations arranged by size.

frequency density
The frequency density of a class is the absolute frequency of the class divided by the class range. The frequency density is used in unequal class ranges. *See also:* histogram.

frequency distribution
A frequency distribution of a variable indicates how often each variable (or class) of the variable occurs. On the basis of the frequency distribution the mean, median, standard deviation, skewness and so on of the distribution is calculated. The representation of a frequency distribution in table form is called frequency table.

frequency polygon
Chart of a frequency distribution in which the frequencies are indicated by means of dots. Subsequently, the dots are linked by means of straight lines. The dots are located over the class midmarks. The frequency polygon is alternative for the histogram. *See also:* cumulative frequency polygon.

funnel approach
Method to determine the order of questions in a questionnaire in which the initial questions are general questions, after which gradually more and more specific questions on the subject are posed.

fusion technique
Method of relating characteristics, although measured during different research involving different interviewees, to each other. The most comparable interviewees/units are put on a par with regard to characteristics which were included in both sets of research. The quality of the fusion is, amongst others, dependent on the strength of the relation between the characteristics to be related and the common characteristics used for the fusion.

galvanometer
Instrument that measures the electrical resistance of the skin. *See also:* electro-dermagraphy.

generalization
Declaring the results of a sample survey valid for the population. *See also:* generalizing survey results.

generalizing survey results
Projecting assessments from a sample survey on the level of the population. For example: when in a research into the attitude regarding public transport tickets for students it appears that 30 per cent (± 4 per cent) of the students take a positive stance with regard to the public transport ticket, this means that of a 600,000 student population there are 200,000 (± 24,000) students with a positive attitude in respect of the ticket. *See also:* generalization.

geographic characteristics
Geographic characteristics such as degree of urbanization, province and climate, which, for example, can be used as a segmentation variable.

geometric mean
The geometric mean (GM) of n observations $x_1, x_2, \ldots x_n$ is: $GM = \sqrt[n]{X_1 \times X_2 \times X_3 \times \ldots X_n}$.

graph
Graphic representation of the relation between two variables in the shape of a continuous line. Often used to reflect the developments of a certain variable over time.

graphic scale
Unipolar or bipolar response scale in which the respondent is asked to place a cross or other symbol on a line.

histogram (bar chart)
Graphic representation of the frequency distribution of a continuous variable. In a histogram a number of columns are drawn which are contiguous. Classes are represented on the x-axis and the frequencies of equal class intervals on the y-axis. With unequal class intervals, frequency densities are to be put on the y-axis. In a histogram the frequencies are proportional to the surfaces of the columns. With equal class intervals this means that the frequency is proportional to the height of the column. With unequal class intervals, this means that the frequency density is equal to the height of the column. *See also:* frequency polygon.

Homals
*Hom*ogeneity analysis by means of *a*lternating *l*east *s*quares. Computer program to execute correspondence analysis.

household panel
Consumer panel in which the household as a whole is the unit of analysis, rather than the individual members of the household.

hypothesis
Statement on the value of a variable or on the relation between two or more variables. A hypothesis can be tested for tenability by means of research. *See also:* alternative hypothesis, null hypothesis.

in-depth interview
An unstructured personal interview in which the interviewer tries to have the interviewee talk freely about a particular subject. The object is to get to know basic motives and opinions in this way.

in-home-use-test
Survey in which the respondent can try a product in his/her own surroundings, after which judgement takes place. The product can be tested without brand or specific packing (blind product test), or with brand and/or packing (as marketed product test, branded product test).

in-store-test
Field experiment taking place in a shop or store.

incentive
Reward offered to an interviewee to compensate for the time and effort put into the research. Very common in qualitative research. Less common in quantitative research. One of the risks considered is the possibility that a selective response is created by an existing (or not) interest for the incentive given.

independent samples
Samples are called independent when on the basis of the value of observation i (for example, respondent i) nothing can be said about the value of observation j (for example, respondent j). Suppose that one sample of size n is drawn, and subsequently the observations from that sample are arranged by sex. In that case there are two independent samples, a sample of men (with size n_1) and a sample of women (with size n_2), and $n = n_1 + n_2$. In a sample arranged by education with the classes 'high', 'middle', 'low', three independent samples will result. The research into independent and dependent samples is important in the choice of the statistical test.

independent variable (exogenous variable)
Identification of a variable, the variance of which is considered a constant, which needs no further explanation in the specific research. Independent variables are used to explain the variance in the dependent variable.

index number (ratio)
The relationship between two numbers, expressed as a percentage. It is a measurement for the size of the change of a variable, for example, the change in time. When the basic value of the index is set at 100, the values exceeding 100 indicate a rise, whereas the values below 100 indicate a fall of the variable.

inductive statistics
That part of statistics which is concerned with the question to what extent a result which is found in a sample can be generalized with regard to (is also valid for) the population from which the sample was drawn. Some characteristic concepts are: null hypothesis and alternative hypothesis, testing, test measure, sample distribution. *See also:* descriptive statistics.

initial measurement
The measurement of the dependent variable(s) in an experiment before the experiment variable(s) has (have) been influenced. An experimental set-up in which this takes place is called a 'before-after' set-up. An experimental set-up in which no initial measurement takes place is called an 'after-only' set-up.

internal data
Data originating from an internal source.

internal source
A source of secondary data within the organization for the benefit of which the research is carried out, such as: market research already present, representatives' reports, production and stock figures. *See also:* external source.

international market research
Market research with the objective to collect data in various countries for the support of international marketing decisions.

interval level (interval scale)
Type of scale in which there is not only an arrangement between the scale values, like for instance with the ordinary scale, but in which also the distances between the subsequent scale values are equal. However, there is no fixed zero point yet, like with the ratio scale. Example: temperature in degrees Celsius, in which the difference between 0 and 20 degrees is twice the size as the difference between 20 and 30 degrees. However, 20 degrees is not twice as hot as 10 degrees Celsius. The term interval level is more correct than the term interval scale. *See also:* ratio measurement level.

interview
Conversation between an interviewer and a respondent. Interviews can be distinguished by their degree of structure (unstructured, semi-structured and structured) and by the way they are carried out (personal, written, by telephone, taped or untaped).

interviewer bias
Systematic error in an interview caused by the fact that the respondent is influenced by the characteristics or behaviour of the interviewer. Thus, the sex, age, race or frequent frowns on the interviewer's face during an interview may systematically affect the respondent's answer.

intrapolation
Determining values of a variable within the observation area.

job classification
Classification of jobs in several mutually excluding classes, with the aim to categorize a multitude of jobs in a convenient arrangement.

Kolmogorov–Smirnov test
Non-parametric test which can be applied in two situations, namely (1) with one sample, and (2) with two independent samples.
ad 1. The objective is to check whether there is a significant difference between a theoretical and an observed frequency distribution. Applicable when there is:
· one sample
· data on at least an ordinal measurement level.
Example: the frequency distribution of the education distinguished in the classes 'low', 'intermediate' and 'high' in the sample is compared with the frequency distribution of education in the population, as represented in statistical data. In this way, the representativity of the sample for the education variable can be researched. Also it can be tested, for example, if an observed distribution can be seen as a normal distribution (test on normality).
ad 2. The objective is to check whether the frequency distribution of one sample differs significantly from the frequency distribution of another sample. Applicable if there is/are:
· two independent samples,
· data on at least an ordinal measurement level.
Example: the frequency distribution of the education of men, distinguished in the classes 'low', 'intermediate' and 'high' is compared with that of women in order to check if there is a difference in education level between men and women.

Kruskal–Wallis test
Non-parametric test directed at checking if the medians of k-independent samples differ significantly from each other. Applicable if there are/is:
· three or more independent samples
· an independent variable on at least an ordinal measurement level
· a nominally independent variable.

laboratory experiment

Controlled experimental research in which the effect of the experimental variable (n) on the dependent variable(s) is determined. In order to be able to conclude that the experimental variable is the only variable which causes the effect, any influence from other variables is eliminated as much as possible by carrying out the experiment in a stringently controlled situation. Owing to this approach, the laboratory experiment usually has a higher internal validity. However, due to the artificiality and unnaturalness of the experimental situation the external validity may be a problem. *See also:* quasi experiment, field experiment.

left skewed (negative skewed)

Skewed distribution in which the arithmetic mean is smaller than the median. With a one peak distribution the peak is situated right of the centre and the distribution has a long end to the left. In this case, the skewness is negative (< 0) and it will be more negative as the peak of the distribution is situated more to the right.

Likert scale

A multiple-item scaling technique, designed by Likert, in which, for example, a respondent's attitude is measured by calculating the sum score for each respondent on a number of Likert scale items. These scale items are to be considered relevant for the construct to be measured.

Likert scale item

Rather extremely positively or negatively worded statement (called item) of which a respondent is to indicate on a scale of five to what extent he or she agrees with the statement. Example: our company produces in a very environmentally friendly way. Do you: (1) totally disagree; (2) disagree; (3) neither agree nor disagree; (4) agree; (5) totally agree?

Lisrel

General model of structural comparisons developed by Jöriskog and Sörbom with which complex patterns of causal relationships between variables can be analysed. Lisrel stands for *li*near *s*tructural *rel*ations.

logit analysis

Statistical technique, comparable with regression analysis, in which the dependent variable, however, is a dichotomous scale.

loglinear analysis

Statistical technique to analyse the correlations between two or more variables of a nominal measurement level.

longitudinal research

Research into the values of variables as they occur during a particular period of time. Often panels and subsequent independent samples are used.

magnitude estimation

Scaling technique from psycho-physics in which a respondent has to indicate for a particular characteristic (for example, taste) what the ratio is of stimulus B, as compared with a particular reference stimulus A. Subsequently, stimuli C, D, E etc. have to be compared with A. The mutual ratio can be expressed in a figure, the length of a line, squeezing a handheld dynamometer, and so on. For example, when tasting beer: 'If you reward Heineken's crispiness with 100 points, how many points would you give to Buckler? And, in comparison with Heineken, how many points would you give to Bavaria Malt?'

mall intercept

Method of collecting data in which interviewers ask passers-by in a shopping centre to co-operate in a research. A proper application of this method is a quota sample.

manipulation check

A measurement in an experiment in which it is checked whether the difference created by the researcher in the experimental conditions is also experienced as such by the sample. In other words: has the researcher manipulated the experimental variable correctly?

Mann–Whitney test

Non-parametric test intended to determine if two populations from which the samples were taken have the same form (in particular with regard to the central tendency). Applicable if there is/are:

· two independent samples
· data on an ordinal measurement level

Example: a product is assessed by a 'heavy user' sample and a 'light user' sample of the product. Each respondent judges the product on a scale of five. By means of the Mann–Whitney test it can be determined if the judgement of the 'heavy users' differs significantly from the judgement of the 'light users'.

The Mann–Whitney test can be seen as a good, non-parametric alternative for the t-test for the difference between two means. The Mann–Whitney test is similar to the Wilcoxon test for two independent samples.

market research plan

Plan of a market research project that, apart from a description of the intended research process, contains a specification of time planning, required budget and executors.

market research process

Subsequent stages in setting up and executing a market research exercise. Often, the following stages are distinguished:

· formulating the research target, issues and research questions;
· determining the information required and sources of information;
· collecting data;
· analysing and interpreting data
· communication of findings, conclusions and recommendations.

Marketing Decision Support System (MDSS)

Interactive computer system which helps marketing decision-makers to use data and models in order to solve poorly structured problems. By means of a MDSS a decision-maker can retrieve and analyse data from a databank or Marketing Information System (MIS) and compile new information fairly easily. When analysing the data, the decision-maker chooses from a number of models stored in the model bank of the MDSS. The models can be calculated with the aid of techniques from the statistical method bank. The major goal of an MDSS is to accomplish an improvement of the marketing decisions (enhancement of effectivity).

Marketing Information System (MIS)

System, often with the use of a computer, enabling both internal and external data, primary and secondary information to be stored and retrieved (databank). The objective of an MIS is to collect, process and store data and information. This is done in such a way, that only relevant information is available for the user in a neatly arranged and practicable form (for example, standard reports) and at the right moment. The advantage of applying an MIS lies in higher efficiency of the administration and in faster communications. *See also:* Marketing Decision Support System.

marketing research

Systematically and objectively looking for and analysing data which are essential for determining and solving marketing problems. Marketing research forms a link between the consumer, the industrial buyer and the general public on the one hand, and the marketeer on the other hand. Information is used to detect and define marketing opportunities and marketing threats; generating, fine-tuning, and evaluating marketing decisions and marketing activities, chronological follow-up of the results accomplished by marketing; and extending the understanding of marketing as a process. In marketing research information necessary to be able to analyse the above mentioned subjects is specified; the method of data collection is specified; the execution of field work is taken care of; the data is analysed, and the results, conclusions and implications are communicated.

matching
A method used in experimental research which ensures that the experimental group and a control group match each other on particular variables. Ideally one might want to use identical twins which are allocated randomly to either group. Example: suppose we wanted to match by the variable 'use' with the classes: 'heavy users' and 'light users'. We would then take two persons of the same class (for example, two 'heavy users'), of which one is randomly allocated to the experimental group and the other to the control group and so on. In this way 'heavy users' and 'light users' are distributed proportionally between the two groups, so that the 'use' variable will not influence the outcome of the experiment. *See also:* randomization.

mean (arithmetic mean)
The arithmetic mean of a set of numbers is the sum of all the numbers in this set divided by the total number of elements.

mean absolute deviation
The mean of the absolute deviations of the different observations in respect of the measure for the central tendency. Measures for central tendency are: mean, median or mode. Usually, the mean will be chosen as a measure of central tendency in calculations of the mean absolute deviation. In that case, the formula reads:

$$MAD = \frac{\sum_{i=1}^{n} |x_i - \bar{x}|}{n}$$

measurement level
Variables can be measured on a dichotomous, nominal, ordinal, interval and ratio measurement level. A variable's measurement level determines the type of calculation and the type of statistical techniques that can be applied to the data. Thus, for example, there is no point in calculating a mean of sex (a variable on a nominal measurement level).

measures of variability
Statistical ratios that characterize the variability of the observations. Major measures of variability are: variation width, quartile interval, standard deviation and variance.

median
The middle observation (the middle number) when all observations have been arranged by size. Therefore, at least 50 per cent of the observations is less than or equal to the median and at least 50 per cent is greater than the median. With an even number of observations, the median is the average of the middle two observations. The calculation of the median requires data on, at least, an an ordinal measurement level. *See also:* central tendency criterion, quartile, fractile.

median test
A non-parametric test, intended to check if the median of one sample is significantly different from the median of the other sample. Applicable when there is/are:
· two independent samples
· data on at least an ordinal measurement level.

metric measurement level
Concerns variables measured on an interval or ratio scale.

modal class
The class having the highest frequency density. With equal class intervals, it is the class which occurs most frequently.

mode

The value of a variable occurring most frequently; the most probable value of a probability distribution. In frequency distributions, the mode is the middle of the modal class. *See also:* mean, median.

monadic research

Method of data collection in which only one stimulus at a time is judged by a respondent. *See also:* paired comparison.

moving average

The arithmetic mean of the last N-values in which the last N-values move one period again and again. Example: the average turnover during the weeks 1–13; 2–14; 3–15, etc.

multi-client research (syndicated research)

Research with various clients, concerning a common problem, for example, a branch problem. The clients will receive the complete report for inspection.

multi-dimensional scaling

Collection of techniques intended to place objects (products, brands) and/or subjects (consumers) in a multi-dimensional space. In this way positioning of objects in combination with preferences (ideal points) of subjects can be understood.

multiple correlation coefficient

Measurement in a multiple regression analysis, represented as R, for the size of the linear correlation between the dependent variable on the one hand, and the joint independent variables on the other hand. *See also:* multiple determination coefficient.

multiple determination coefficient

Measurement in a multiple regression analysis, being the square of the multiple correlation coefficient, represented as R^2, which indicates the percentage of explained variance of the dependent variable in a multiple regression analysis.

multiple-item scale

Measuring a construct by submitting a number of questions or statements (items) to a respondent and subsequently calculating the sum score on the items for each respondent. Common when a person's attitude in respect of a product or brand is measured and in measuring personality characteristics.

multivariate analysis of variance

Analysis of variance with more than one dependent variable. Abbreviated to MANOVA (*m*ultiple *an*alysis *o*f *va*riance).

n

'n' indicates the sample size which means that the result reported is based on a limited number of interviewees. An unusual n is n = 1, which indicates that an announcement is made which is not based on a representative research, but on an opinion, a preconception of the 'researcher'.

Natural Grouping

Technique in which, by means of gradual, binary splitting up, a group of stimuli – for example, brands – is described. On the basis of the resulting breakdown distances between the stimuli are calculated and represented graphically in more dimensions, with the aid of correspondence analysis.

Nielsen Store Audit

Research using store panels executed by A. C. Nielsen (a global research agency). The research takes place with representative samples of shops from various lines of business: food store (Food index), chemists (Drug index), tobacconists (Tobacco index), off-licence shops (Liquor index) and DIYs (do-it-yourself shops). For each article the stock on hand and purchases are recorded on a bi-monthly basis. Nielsen's customers receive a survey (total, by district, by shop type) of the consumer turnover (number and price), the stocks, and the distribution spread.

no-bias

Reply tendency in which the respondent, after having given 'no' as an answer to a number of questions, is inclined to answer 'no' to each following question, irrespective of the content of that question. The same effect can be seen when the respondent 'agrees' with statements he is supposed to give his opinion about, on a response scale running from 'totally disagree' to 'agree'. *See also:* yes-bias.

nominal measurement level (nominal scale)

Type of scale in which there is no arrangement between the scale values. The only goal of the scale is to distinguish the scale values. For example: city, type of company (industrial, service, agriculture), car makes (Audi, Peugeot, Ford). The term nominal scale is less correct than nominal measurement level.

nomogram

Graphic display showing the accuracy at different reliabilities and different sample sizes. Due to use of computers enabling convenient, exact calculations, nomograms are not much used any more.

non-coverage error

Coverage error which results if the sample frame does not contain all the elements of the population.

non-metric measurement level

This concerns variables measured on a nominal or ordinal scale.

non-parametric test

A statistical test is called non-parametric if it does not require much of the form of the distribution of the variable(s) in the population. Non-parametric tests are suitable for data on a nominal or an ordinal measurement level. They can also be applied on data of an interval or ratio measurement level when the distribution of the variable(s) does not meet the demands of a parametrical test. Well known non-parametric tests are: sign test, median test, chi-square test, Kolmogorov–Smirnov test, Mann–Whitney test, Wilcoxon test and Kruskal–Wallis test.

non-random sample (targeted sample)

Sample in which the components of the population have not been chosen randomly, but in a different way.

non-response

The percentage of elements of the sample of which no or incomplete information has been obtained. Results from: refusal to co-operate in the research, being unable to co-operate (ill, and so on), being unavailable or being unwilling or not in a position to answer specific questions in the questionnaire. Non-response is a non-observation error.

non-sampling error

Inaccuracy in the results which is not due to the random composition of the sample (the sampling error), but to observation errors and non-observation errors.

non-verbal response

Non-verbal means of reaction. One can think of facial expressions, posture, eye movements, changes in skin resistance and so forth. Non-verbal reactions are often unconscious and are recorded in market research (especially qualitative research), as these reactions do not show a bias (see: socially desirable response). Another application concerns target groups who possess verbal skills to only a slight degree or not at all, such as children.

normal distribution (Gauss-distribution)

A normal distribution is a distribution of a continuous chance variable. The non-distribution is graphically displayed by a smooth, symmetric curve having a centre peak. The distribution has the familiar bell shape. A major characteristic of the normal distribution is that mean, median and mode coincide. The normal distribution is fully determined with two parameters, mean (expected value) μ, and standard deviation σ; this is symbolically indicated by N (μ, σ). *See also:* standard normal distribution.

null hypothesis

The null hypothesis (identified by H_0) is the hypothesis to be tested which after testing is, or is not, rejected in favour of the alternative hypothesis. Usually the wording of the null hypothesis reads 'there is no relationship between . . . and . . .'; and the alternative hypothesis reads 'there is a relationship between . . . and . . .'.

observation errors

The joint errors in a research due to wrongly interpreted questions, inappropriately worded questions, processing errors (coding errors and so on), interviewer's biases, and so on. To be distinguished from non-observation errors.

observation method of data collecting

Systematic recording of observations with persons or of material matters (such as turnover figures and prices). Observation can be done by persons or by means of machines (such as video, scanning cash register, galvanometer). *See also:* communication method of data collection.

octile

A cumulative frequency distribution which can be broken down into fractiles. A breakdown in eight equal parts is called a breakdown in octiles (the first octile through to the eighth). The first octile is the value below which 12.5 per cent of the observations lie. The second octile indicates the limit below which 25 per cent of the observations lie, etc. The second octile can also be called quartile and the fourth octile is the median.

omnibus research

Sample research carried out by a research agency in which different clients can ask their own questions in one joint questionnaire. A respondent who is interviewed in an omnibus research may, therefore, be asked questions on a wide range of subjects, for example, on using his car, on smoking and on baby shampoo. The costs of an omnibus research is divided proportionally between the clients, and each client will only have access to the outcomes of his own questions. To be distinguished from multi-client research.

one-dimensional scale analysis

Group of techniques meant to distinguish objects (such as products and brands) and/or subjects (consumers) by one dimension only.

one-tailed probability

The probability in a one-tailed test. The one-tailed probability is half of the two-tailed probability. This means that if the p-value (one-tailed) is printed in a computer output, the number in question must be multiplied by two if a two-tailed test is carried out.

one-tailed test

A test of the null hypothesis (H_0) in which the alternative hypothesis (H_a) contains a 'greater than' or 'less than' sign. Therefore, in the H_a direction is given to the difference or the correlation. If H_a contains a 'greater than' sign, a test is called 'right-sided'; if it contains a 'less than' sign a test is called 'left-sided'.

Example H_0: 'there is no difference between men and women in the average attitude with respect to the XYZ company': ($H_0{:}\mu_m = \mu_v$). Example H_a: 'men adopt a more positive stance with respect to the XYZ company than women' ($H_a{:}\mu_m > \mu_v$). *See also:* two-tailed test.

open-ended question
Question in which the interviewee does not have to choose between a number of pre-set answers, but may word the answer completely freely in his own words. *See also:* structured question.

opinion research
Research aimed at obtaining information with regard to opinions on various matters among the (general) public.

oral interview
Interview carried out orally, either by telephone (ear-to-ear) or in direct personal contact (face-to-face). To be distinguished from a written questionnaire interview.

ordinal measurement level (ordinal scale, order scale)
Scale type in which there is an order of rank between the scale values, but in which no equal distance between the subsequent scale values is assumed. The figures allocated to the scale values are only numbers of rank. They do not imply to indicate that the difference between scale values 2 and 3 is equal to the difference between scale values 4 and 5. Examples: response scales (never, seldom, often, always), education (secondary, modern, comprehension school, higher vocational education, university), size of company (less than 10 employees, 11–200 employees, more than 200 employees). The term ordinal scale is less appropriate than the term ordinal measurement level.

outlier
Observation the size of which is so different from the other observations that a researcher can decide that this observation is to be considered a special case, for example, by removing it from the analysis or by giving it extra weight. *See also:* eccentricity.

overcoverage error
Coverage error which arises when the sample frame contains elements that do not belong to the population. Example: a list of intermediate vocational schools contains also a number of higher vocational or comprehensive schools.

overrun probability
The smallest value of the significance level which a decision-maker can choose for which the sample results lead to rejection of the null hypothesis. The null hypothesis is rejected if the overrun probability is smaller than the significance level chosen by the decision-maker. *See also:* one-tailed probability, two-tailed probability.

paired comparison
Method of data collection in which respondents are asked to make a choice from two stimuli, again and again, on the basis of one characteristic. *See also:* monadic research, round robin product test.

panel
Fixed group of units (persons, households, shops, businesses, and so on) in which, permanently or very frequently, research takes place with regard to the same variables. In this way changes in time can be detected. *See also:* consumer panel, distribution panel.

pantry check
Observation at home with the consumer in which ownership of a specific product or brand is recorded by the interviewer. In the case of consumption goods, also stock on hand and packaging sizes may be recorded.

parametric test
Test requiring the distribution of the variable in the population to comply with specific characteristics, for example, that this variable is to be normally divided. A parametric test requires data on at least an interval measurement level. Well-known parametric tests are the F-test, the t-test and the z-test. *See also:* non-parametric test.

partial correlation coefficient

The correlation coefficient between two variables after corrections have been carried out for the impact of one or more variables.

passer-by research

Type of observation in which in a specific location, for example, the entrance of the shopping centre or a car-park, the number of persons per time unit is counted and if necessary arranged on relevant characteristics for the survey, such as sex, hair length, type and make of means transport.

pay-off table

Table used in the Bayesian decision analysis containing three elements. A number of alternatives from which a choice is to be made, the condition of the environment (called statement of nature) and the outcome (consequences) of each alternative with each environment condition. Also used in game theory in which the possible strategies of the adversaries are considered to be the environment conditions.

Pearson correlation coefficient

Statistical measurement between -1 and $+1$ developed by Pearson indicating the direction ($+$ or $-$) and the strength of the linear correlation between two variables. The variables must be interval-scaled and ratio-scaled. Also called: product moment correlation coefficient.

percentile

A cumulative frequency distribution can be broken down into fractiles. A breakdown in 100 equal parts is called a breakdown in percentiles (the first percentile through to the 100th percentile). The first percentile is the value below which 1 per cent of the observations lie, the 17th percentile indicates the limit below which 17 per cent of the observations lie, and so on. The 50th percentile is usually called the median.

physical characteristics

In market research, physical characteristics, for example age and sex, which are often used for background data. *See also:* demographic characteristics, geographic characteristics, socio-economic characteristics.

picture graphic

Graphic representation of a frequency distribution in which the absolute frequency is represented by means of an appealing image.

pie chart

Graphic representation of a relative frequency distribution in which the percentage of a class is proportional to the size of the corresponding segment of the pie.

pilot survey

Small-scale research in which any problems in the execution of a survey can be pinpointed. In a pilot survey the questionnaire is also tested. A pilot survey serves to detect errors and omissions in the survey design or the questionnaire.

pooling (notary public statistics)

Kind of research in which the participants (the pool) send their data to a fixed point where this data is collected and processed to a full-size survey. Because of the confidentiality of the individual participants' data and the purity of the procedure a notary public may be asked to act as supervisor. Pooling may provide an understanding of, for instance, the size of the market. Often applied to the industrial market.

population (universe)

The collection of elements about which statements are to be made within the framework of a sample survey. Example: car owners, households with at least one child under five, Italian restaurants. *See also:* sample frame.

population research
Full scale screening of parts of the population in which no sample is drawn, but in which all elements from the relevant part of the population are meant to be interviewed.

postal research
Written research in which the questionnaire is sent by post to respondents and in which the completed questionnaire is also returned by post.

postcode segmentation
System in which personal and household data is linked to the postcode, so that the postcode may be of assistance when segmentation is required. Applied to such things as Geo-Market profile.

prediction validity
The extent to which the measurement of the construct correlates with an external criterion in the future; how well the measurement predicts what it is supposed to predict. Prediction validity is a kind of criterion validity. Example: to what extent does an average final examination mark in grammar school correlate with a successful university student career? If there is a strong correlation, then the final examination mark is a valid measurement for 'university potential'.

primary data
Data collected for a specific research goal, either by the organization itself, or by third parties by order of the organization. To be distinguished from secondary data.

Princals
A method and a computer program with which *principal* component analysis can be executed on variables measured on a nominal, ordinal or interval scale. Princals is an abbreviation of *Principal c*omponent analysis by *al*ternating *l*east *s*quares.

principal component analysis
Variant of factor analysis.

probability
The relative frequency of incidence of a particular event, in the long run in an identical and independently repetitive process. 'The chance of getting a six when throwing a pure dice is 1/6' means that in the long run, (after very many throws) the relative frequency with which a 6 is thrown equals 1/6. *See also:* subjective probability.

probability distribution (probability density)
Distribution in which an accompanying chance is attributed to each possible outcome of a stochastic variable. The sum of the chances equals 1. There are discrete (for example, the binomial) and continuous (for example, the normal) probability distributions. *See also:* cumulative frequency distribution, stochastic variable.

projective technique (indirect questioning technique)
Group of techniques used in motivation research in which a respondent is faced with an ambiguous stimulus (a word, a picture, a part of a sentence), and which the respondent may react to freely. The assumption is that in the reaction to, the structuring of, and giving meaning to the contents of the ambiguous stimulus, the respondent reveals something of his values, motives, needs, or personality. Projective techniques include: third person technique, word association test, sentence completion, story telling, thematic apperception test.

proportionate stratified sample (proportionate allocation)
A stratified sample in which the ratios of the strata in the sample equal the ratio of the strata in the sample frame. Example: if in the sample frame 15 per cent of the students attend higher vocational education, then it is made sure that the sample also contains 15 per cent higher vocational education students.

protocol

Documents, usually during qualitative research, in which the answers of the respondents are literally recorded. The protocol can be used with the research report. In a quantitative research the answers to open questions can be recorded in a protocol.

psychophysiology

Science which is concerned with the research into the relationship between an objective physical stimulus (for example, the sugar content of Coca-Cola) and the subjective sensation of the stimulus (the perceived sweetness of Coca-Cola). Major researchers in this field were L. Fechner and S.S. Stevens. *See also:* magnitude estimation.

pupillometer

Apparatus measuring the changes in the size of the pupil (pupil dilatation) of the eyes. It is assumed that the size of the pupil increases as a person's interest in an object increases.

purposive sample (judgement sample)

Non-random sample in which the elements are selected which are considered 'typical of the population'. Examples: choosing a specific city for a test market, interviewing a number of experts on a specific subject.

qualitative research

In market research an often small-scale research in which the observations usually are not expressed in figures. Qualitative research can be applied as preliminary research in order to structure the problem for quantitative research. In addition, qualitative research can be applied to understand and explain the results which have been found in quantitative research. Thus, qualitative and quantitative research are complementary forms of research.

quantitative research

Research in which the information is expressed in figures enabling statistical analysis. *See also:* qualitative research.

quartile

A cumulative frequency distribution can be broken down into fractiles. A breakdown into four equal parts is called a breakdown into quartiles (the first, the second, third and fourth quartile). The first quartile is the value below which 25 per cent of the observations lie. The second quartile is the value below which 50 per cent of the observations lie. The second quartile is usually called the median.

quartile distance

The length of the interval within which the middle 50 per cent of the observations lie. The quartile distance can be determined by taking the difference between the third and the first quartile.

quasi experiment (pre-experiment)

Experiment characterized by the fact that only the result of a specific event will be measured. The events themselves will not be interfered with. A major characteristic of a quasi experiment is that it is not possible to randomly allocate groups to an experimental condition (very often a control group is lacking, or has not been composed randomly).

questionnaire routing

The order in which respondents go through the questions on a questionnaire. This can vary strongly due to the use of filter questions (see filter question). For example: Respondents who possess brand A (filter question: do you use brand A?) will get questions on this brand, others won't.

quota sample

Non-random sample in which the population is divided into a number of strata on the basis of variables which are considered important, after which from each stratum a specific and specified quota of elements can be selected. The interviewer is told how many persons he is to interview in a particular stratum, so the number of men and the number of women, the number having a high income, etc. The interviewers are free to choose who they are going to interview, as long as the quota requirements are met. Often, the sample should preferably have the same proportions of elements as the population. Example: an interviewer is told to interview a quota of 50 men between 25 and 40, bearded, and 100 men between 25 and 40, without beard.

random number
A number generated without any pattern or plan. *See also:* random sample.

random sample
Sample in which the elements of the sample frame are drawn randomly and in which each element has a predefined chance of ending up in the sample.

randomization
Randomly allocating samples (and conditions) to the experimental and the control group, so, each person has the same chance of ending up in the experimental group.

range (dispersion range)
The difference between the largest and the smallest observation.

rank correlation coefficient
Statistical measurement between −1 and +1 developed by Spearman indicating the direction (+ or −) and the extent of correlation between two variables. The variables should be measured on, at least, an ordinal level. Also called Spearman rank correlation coefficient.

ratio measurement level (ratio scale)
Scale type with a fixed initial point and equal distances between the subsequent scale values. Examples: temperature in degrees Kelvin, age, income, travelling distance in km, turnover, market share. The term ratio scale is less correct than the term ratio measurement level.

regression analysis
Statistical technique in which a variance of one dependent variable (measured on an interval or a ratio scale) is explained by the variance in one independent variable (simple regression) or more variables (multiple regression). Regression analysis supplies information on the impact of the separate explanatory variables on the dependent variable, together with the extent to which the variance of the dependent variable is explained. In market research regression analysis is frequently applied. In this way a market share can be explained from pricing and advertising share. *See also:* discriminant analysis.

relative frequency
The frequency of a value (or class) of a variable as expressed in a percentage of the total.

reliability
The extent to which repeated measurements will produce the same outcomes. The repeated measurement is to be carried out in comparable circumstances. Example: to what extent does the attitude score differ if the same person is re-interviewed two weeks after the first measurement. Major methods to determine the reliability of a measurement are the test-retest reliability, Crombach-alpha, and the split-half reliability coefficient.

reminder
Repeated request to complete and return a questionnaire.

reply scale (response scale)
The categories in which the respondent is supposed to give his answer to a statement or a claim. Sometimes all categories are named, and sometimes unipolar or bipolar response scales are made in which categories are indicated with boxes, with figures, or with a line.

reply tendency
Deviation in a person's reply to a specific question arising from the fact that a series of questions is answered. Reply tendencies may be yes-bias and no-bias. *See also:* bias.

representative
Term used for samples to indicate that the sample is a proper reflection of the population on a number of characteristics.

research briefing
The information and peripheral conditions which a research agency receives from a client for the set-up of a research plan. Information is given on, for example, the product, the market, the marketing problem, the target, the target group and the research budget.

research design
Part of the market research process in which the method, the means and the procedure to obtain the necessary primary data is specified.

research fatigue
Phenomenon occurring among people who have often been approached as part of market research. Research fatigue can express itself in non-response and/or deviant reply patterns. With the latter one can think of partial non-response (don't know, won't say), but also of reply patterns influenced by learning experience (people avoid answers which they suspect will lead to further questions). Research fatigue especially occurs among research intensive segments, for example, among doctors.

research goal
The wording of the goal or goals that are to be accomplished with the aid of research.

right of inspection
Interviewees right to inspect the data collected on them, as well as the right to demand that these are in whole or in part deleted from the file.

right skewed (positively skewed)
Skewed distribution in which the arithmetic mean is greater than the median. In a one-peak distribution the peak lies left of the midmark and the distribution has a long end to the right. The skewness, in this case, is positive (> 0) and will be more positive as the peak of the distribution is situated further to the right.

round-robin product test
Comparison of all possible pairs of stimuli from a set of stimuli. Suppose, in a survey with five products, product A is compared and judged against products B, C, D and E. Subsequently product B is compared with C, D and E, followed by a comparison of C with D and E. So in the case of five products, ten paired comparisons are made.

sample allocation
Determining the number of elements drawn from each sub-group (stratum or cluster) of the population. This may be a proportional or a disproportional allocation. *See also:* disproportional stratified sample.

sample distribution
The frequency distribution of the variable in the sample. The sample distribution should not be confused with sampling distribution.

sample frame
The concrete list of elements (persons, household, companies, etc) from which a sample is drawn. A telephone directory, a list of companies addresses, a list of intermediate vocational schools may form the basis of the sampling frame.

sample frame errors
Errors originating when elements of the population have been included incorrectly in the sample frame. Examples: an address occurring twice, a wrong telephone number, a person living alone instead of living together with someone else.

sample research
Acquiring information on the entire population by means of researching part of that population (the sample). The objective is to generalize the findings for the entire population.

sample size
The number of elements in the sample. The sample size depends on such things as the variation of the characteristic in the population to be researched, the desirable accuracy and the desirable reliability of the outcome.

sampling distribution
The frequency distribution of a statistical quantity (such as mean, proportion, median) arising when all possible random samples of size n are drawn from a population. It is the probability distribution of the test quantity. The sampling distribution is essential in each statistical test procedure. To be distinguished from sample distribution.

sampling error
Inaccuracy in the result of a sample research resulting from the fact that only one sample is made and not the entire population is researched. This error is due to a random composition of the sample. In random samples the size of this error can be calculated, in non-random samples this is not possible. *See also:* non-sampling error.

SAS (Statistical Analysis System)
Widely used software package to run statistical analyses. Available as a main frame version and as a pc-version.

scale
Carefully composed collection of statements meant to measure a specific construct. Is also used to indicate response scales and for the measurement level of a variable. *See also:* multiple-item scale.

scaling technique
Method to build up a scale. That scale can then be used to measure (scale) subjects and/ or objects. There are one-dimensional and multi-dimensional scaling techniques.

scanning
Recording the turnover by means of scanning and reading of the UAC-code at the cash register. Scanning provides an insight into the turnover, the stock, the moment of purchase, the chosen till, etc. *See also:* distribution panel.

scattergram
Cloud of dots which is formed by plotting the observations of the one variable on the X-axis against the observations of the other variable on the Y-axis. The data requires at least an interval measurement level.

seasonal fluctuation
Chronological movement caused by seasonal influences.

secondary data
Existing data which have not been collected for the research goal in question. Secondary data may be both internal and external data. Examples: representatives' reports (internal source of secondary data), data from the central statistical bureau or from a consumer panel (external sources of secondary data). *See also:* primary data.

self-completion
Research method in which the answers are recorded by the interviewees themselves without interference from the interviewer. Self-completion mostly occurs in written research. The method is particularly suitable for researches asking for sensitive information.

semantic differential (Osgood-scale, semantic contrast pairs)
Scaling technique designed by Osgood in order to measure a person's opinion on an object (product, brand, company, person) using a number of word pairs such as good, bad; cheap, expensive. Usually a response scale of seven is used. By means of the semantic differential a profile of the object can be obtained.

semi-structured interview
Interview with a questionnaire which is partly structured and partly unstructured. *See also:* interview.

sentence completion
Projective technique in which a respondent is asked to complete an incomplete sentence with the first words that come to his mind. Example: people who spend their holiday in Greece are . . .

sequence effect
A type of bias whereby the order in which the questions are asked influences the response. For example: a question on the judgement of product X can be influenced when a previous question already gave the respondent information on this product. Sequence effects can also occur when the questionnaire is very long. When answering more questions, the respondent will develop a routine which can lead to reply tendencies. In the latter example the effect can be limited by varying the order in which the questions are asked (split-run). *See also:* reply tendency.

sequential sample
Sample procedure that starts off with a relatively small sample. When the outcome is sufficiently clear, the research is stopped. If not, an additional sample is drawn to complement the first sample, etc.

sign test for paired samples (paired sign test)
Asymmetric test aimed at finding out if there is a significant difference between the first and the second measurement. The null hypothesis assumes no difference between the measurements. Applicable in the case of:
· two dependent samples
· data at least on an ordinal measurement level, so that it can be indicated for each pair which observation is the largest.
For example: each person in the sample compares the taste of brand A with the taste of brand B and indicates which of the two they like best. By means of the sign test it can be determined if brand A is found to be significantly better or worse than brand B. *See also:* t-test for paired samples, Wilcoxon-test for paired samples.

significance level (unreliability threshold)
The probability that the null hypothesis (H_0) is appropriately rejected; in other words: rejecting H_0, whereas H_0 is true (a so-called type I error with probability α). Frequently used significance levels are: $\alpha = 0.10$, $\alpha = 0.05$, $\alpha = 0.25$ and $\alpha = 0.01$.

significant result
Test result in which it is decided to reject the null hypothesis. The decision to reject the null hypothesis (H_0) depends on the choice of the significance level α. Frequently tests are carried out at a significance level of 5 per cent.

simple random sample
Random sample in which each element from the sample frame has an equal *and calculated* chance to be drawn.

skewed distribution (asymmetric distribution)
Frequency distribution which is not symmetric with regard to the arithmetic mean. A major characteristic of a skewed distribution is that mean and median do not converge. In a symmetric distribution, the mean is equal to the median. A skewed distribution may be left skewed and right skewed. The degree of skewness is measured by means of the skewness ratio. An example of a skewed distribution is the distribution of income: there are relatively many people with low incomes in relation to the number of persons with high incomes.

skewness measure
Ratio for the degree of asymmetry of a frequency distribution. If skewness is 0, then distribution is symmetric.
See also: skewed distribution, left skewed, right skewed.

snowball sample
Non-random sample starting off with a small group of respondents in which each respondent mentions one or more elements (possible other respondents) meeting a specific criterion. Subsequently the new elements mentioned are included in the sample. They too are asked to mention new elements, etc. This procedure may be used for hard to trace respondents, as would be the case for a sample of cocaine users.

socially desirable response
A bias in the reply to a question, in which the respondent either consciously or subconsciously does not give his real opinion, because of perceived social pressure. It is also possible that the respondent will give a more extreme reply rather than a moderate reply, because he expects to obtain additional social approval with it. The social pressure in this case consists of the interviewer, reference groups, the general public opinion, etc. Some examples of subjects that may easily lead to socially desirable reply include questions on discrimination and prejudices, prohibited behaviour such as theft and tax evasion, alcohol and drugs consumption, environmentally friendly behaviour and money spent on charity.

socio-economic characteristics
Characteristics of a person or a household, such as income, job, education, and social class. On the basis of socio-economic characteristic a division can be made by prosperity (also called the *social economic status* (SES)

split-half reliability coefficient
Method to measure the reliability of a multiple-item scale. The number of items is randomly divided in two parts, so that two scales result. Of the two parts the sum score for each respondent on the items is calculated. In this way two measurements of the construct are obtained. The correlation coefficient between sum scores is called the split-half reliability coefficient; it is an indication of the reliability of the measurement.

SPSS (Statistical Package for the Social Sciences)
Frequently used software package to run statistical analyses. Available both as a mainframe version and a pc-version.

spurious correlation
Correlation between two variables without any causal connection. The statistically found spurious correlation disappears or strongly decreases if it is controlled on the effect of a third variable.

standard deviation
A degree of variability which indicates the extent of dispersion around the arithmetic mean. The standard deviation is the root from the variant. The standard deviation can be calculated for variables at interval or ratio measurement level. A distinction is to be made between the standard deviation in the population (σ) and the standard deviation of the sample(s) for these quantities. The formulas for these quantities (with continuous variables) read:

$$\sigma = \sqrt{\frac{\sum_{i=1}^{N}(x_i - \mu)^2}{N}}$$

$$\hat{\sigma} = s = \sqrt{\frac{\sum_{i=1}^{n}(x_i - \bar{x})^2}{n-1}} \cdot \sqrt{\frac{N-n}{N-1}}$$

where:

σ, s = the standard deviation in the population, in the sample, respectively

x_1 = observation i

$\mu, \bar{x}$ = population, sample mean, respectively

N, n = population, sample size, respectively

$\dfrac{N-n}{N-1}$ = finiteness correction

If the population standard deviation is unknown, it can be estimated by s where $\hat{\sigma} = s$ ($\hat{\sigma}$ = the estimated population standard deviation). The finiteness correction is equalled to 1 if the sample size n is less than 5% of the population size $N(n < 0{,}05N$; applies for proportions too).

The formulas for the population standard deviation (σ_p), sample deviation (s_p) of a proportion, respectively, read:

$$\sigma_p = \sqrt{\pi(1-\pi)}$$

$$\hat{\sigma}_p = s_p = \sqrt{p(1-p)} \cdot \sqrt{\frac{N-n}{N-1}}$$

where:

σ_p, s_p = the standard deviation of the proportion p in the population, in the sample, respectively

π, p = proportion in the population, in the sample, respectively

If the population standard deviation is unknown, it can be estimated from a sample, by s_p, where $\hat{\sigma}_p = s_p$ ($\hat{\sigma}_p$ = the estimated population standard deviation)

standard error

The standard error is the standard deviation of the sample distribution. Frequently used is the sample distribution of the mean. The formula of the standard deviation of the sample mean (identified by $\sigma_{\bar{x}}$) is:

$$\sigma_{\bar{x}} = \frac{\sigma}{\sqrt{n}}$$

where:

σ = population standard deviation

n = sample size

The standard error of the sample mean is estimated in the sample using the formula:

$$\hat{\sigma}_{\bar{x}} = S_{\bar{x}} = \frac{s}{\sqrt{n}} \cdot \sqrt{\frac{N-n}{N-1}}$$

where:

$\hat{\sigma}_{\bar{x}}$ = estimated standard deviation of the sample mean

$S_{\bar{x}}$ = standard error of the sample mean from a sample

s = sample standard deviation

n, N = sample, population size, respectively

$\dfrac{N-n}{N-1}$ = finiteness correction (see note under standard deviation)

The standard error of a *proportion* (indicated by $\sigma_{\bar{p}}$) is:

$$\sigma_{\bar{p}} = \sqrt{\frac{\pi(1-\pi)}{n}}$$

The standard error of a *proportion* is estimated in a sample using the formula:

$$\hat{\sigma}_{\bar{p}} = S_{\bar{p}} = \sqrt{\frac{p(1-p)}{n}} \cdot \sqrt{\frac{N-n}{N-1}}$$

where:
$\hat{\sigma}_{\bar{p}}$ = estimated standard error of a proportion
$S_{\bar{p}}$ = calculated standard error

standard normal distribution (z-distribution)
Basic distribution of the normal distribution. The distribution has a mean (expected value) of 0 and a standard deviation of 1. The distribution is symbolized by N(0,1). Through standardization, each normal distribution can be converted to a standard normal distribution. *See also:* z-score, normal distribution.

standardization
A variable can be standardized by deducting the mean from each observation and dividing it by the standard deviation. This results in z-scores. Due to standardization, variables measured on different units can be compared more easily. Also, this allows for outliers to be detected.

Stapel scale (scalometer)
Variant on the semantic differential, developed by Stapel, in which instead of bipolar, unipolar response scales are used with an even number of reply categories (often ten).

start-address method (random-walk method)
Method of selecting respondents for a sample. According to chance a street with a home number is pulled as a start address. Thereupon the pollster will select addresses on the basis of specific instructions, for example, the first house number plus 15, turning right at the first side road, upon refusal the next house number is taken, etc. This procedure can be regarded as a cluster sample taking.

statistic analysis module
Component of a *M*arketing *D*ecision *S*upport *S*ystem (MDSS) containing a great variety of statistical methods and techniques which can be used to perform (complex) analyses of the data in the system's databank.

statistical testing
Using a statistical test to determine whether a test quantity/measure (correlation, a difference found between means, the regression coefficient, and so on) found in an empirical research is statistically significant. *See also:* inductive statistics.

stochastic variable (probability variable)
A variable is called stochastic if it can assume several different values, each with a specific probability. An example of a discrete stochastic variable is the number of cars that a dealer sells on a monthly basis. An example of a continuous stochastic variable is the weight, in grammes, of a detergent packet at the time of packing. The joint values of a stochastic variable together with the accompanying probabilities is called a probability distribution.

story telling
Projective technique in which a respondent is asked to tell or write a story on the basis of a drawing, cartoon, or picture.

stratification
Splitting up a sample frame on the basis of one or more characteristics, in such a way that each element belongs to one stratum only. Attempts are made to stratify in such a way that the strata are as homogeneous as possible.

stratified cluster survey
Combination of a stratified sample and a cluster survey. A sample frame of clusters is divided in strata and then a random sample of clusters is drawn from each stratum. Subsequently all the elements of a cluster are interviewed (one-stage cluster survey) or a random sample of elements is drawn from each cluster (two-stage cluster survey). Example: for an investigation into shoplifting by secondary school pupils, the list of

secondary schools is first divided in three strata: protestant, catholic, and public secondary schools. Subsequently a sample of schools is drawn from each stratum, after which the pupils of a school drawn are interviewed.

stratified sample (articulated sample)
A sample in which the sample frame is split into groups (called strata) after which a random sample is drawn from each group. Example: students are stratified by type of education in three strata: intermediate vocational education, higher vocational education and university students, after which a random sample is drawn from these three strata.

structured interview (formal interview)
Interview with a questionnaire in which the questions, reply options and the order of the questions are fully fixed. In principle, each respondent is interviewed in the same way. *See also:* structured questionnaire survey, interview.

structured question
A question in which a respondent is presented with a number of options which he must choose from. *See also:* open-ended question.

structured questionnaire survey
Sample survey in which people are interviewed in a standardized way with a structured or semi-structured questionnaire. The main objective of such surveys is to obtain quantitative data.

subjective probability (Bayesian probability)
The extent to which a person believes a particular event will happen, reflected in a probability. The subjective probability indicates how likely a person considers a specific event.

symmetric distribution
Distribution having the same shape on both sides of the median. An example of the symmetric distribution is a normal distribution. *See also:* skewed distribution.

systematic sample (survey)
Random sample in which each kth element is drawn from the sample frame. It is assumed that there is no arrangement relevant for the research of the elements in the sample frame. For example: Drawing each tenth or each hundredth address from the telephone directory.

t-test for one sample
Parametric test aimed at checking if the mean for one sample differs significantly from the supposed mean. Applicable when
 · the data is measured on at least interval level;
 · the population standard deviation is unknown;
 · the distribution of the variable in the population is either normal or symmetrical, or the distribution of the variable in the population is asymmetric but so great that the central limit theorem applies.
Example: checking if the average age in the sample corresponds with the CBS data on the average age in the population (in which the standard deviation in the population is estimated with the sample). *See also:* chi-square test, Kolmogorov–Smirnov-test, z-test for one sample.

t-test for paired samples (paired t-test)
Parametric test aimed at testing if there is a significant difference between the first and the second measurement. The null hypothesis assumes no difference between the measurements. Applicable when:
 · the data is measured on at least an interval level;
 · there are two dependent samples;
 · the population standard deviations σ_1 and σ_2 are unknown;
 · the distribution of the differences between the scores is normally or symmetrically distributed, or the distribution of the variables in the population is asymmetric, but n is so great that the central limit theorem (n > 30) applies.

Example: in a sample each respondent's attitude with regard to product XYZ is measured before and after exposure to a tv-commercial featuring the product. With the aid of the paired t-test it is checked if the attitude in respect of the product has significantly changed under the influence of the tv-commercial. *See also:* sign test for paired samples, Wilcoxon-test for paired samples.

t-test for two samples
Parametric test aimed at checking if two means differ significantly. In the null hypothesis it is assumed that the mean in one sample equals the mean in another sample. Applicable when
- the data is measured on at least interval level;
- the samples are independent;
- the population standard deviations are unknown;
- the variables in the population are normally or symmetrically distributed, or the distribution of the variables in the population is asymmetric but so great that the central limit theorem applies.

Example: checking whether the average consumption of beer (in litres/month) differs between men and women. *See also:* Mann–Whitney test, Kolmogorov–Smirnov test.

tachistoscope
Apparatus which shows images, packings, and so on during a very short period, where the duration of the exposure may be varied. After the exposure the respondent is asked to indicate what he has seen and how he interprets this. The tachistoscope can be used for such matters as packaging research or advertising research.

telephone survey
Interview of respondents over the telephone. *See also:* cati.

telescope effect
A bias when answering questions, in which the respondent (mostly unconsciously) provides wrong information if asked when an event occurred. There are two forms: backward telescoping in which the respondent remembers the event happening not as long ago as was actually the case, and forward telescoping in which the event is placed in history longer ago.

test design
The procedure and implementation for collecting data in experimental research.

test market
Field experiment in a small part of the entire market, meant to test out the marketing mix chosen, for example, when a new product is launched. Attempts are made to have the test market be as representative as possible for the market as a whole.

test measure
A variable of probability the value of which is determined from the sample. Using the value of the test measure it is checked whether the null hypothesis is to be confirmed or rejected. A test measure frequently used is the sample mean. *See also:* standard error.

test/retest reliability (stability)
Method to determine the reliability of a measurement by repeating this measurement after a while (for example, two weeks) with the same persons and correlating the scores. The mean of a frequency distribution with classes is calculated by:

$$\bar{x} = \frac{\sum_{i=1}^{k} f_i x_i}{n}$$

where:

f_i = number of observations in class i
x_i = midmark of class i
k = number of classes
n = total number of observations

The calculation of the mean requires data to be at least at interval level. *See also:* weighted mean, geometric mean.

thematic apperception test (TAT-test)

Projective technique in which a respondent is asked to tell or to write down a story on the basis of a series of pictures submitted to him.

third-person technique

A projection technique used for sensitive subjects in which the question is worded in the third person ('they', 'he', or 'she', or passive voice). Meant to have the respondent give his own opinion, like: 'What do your co-workers in this company think of the manager?' rather than: 'What do you think of the manager?'

time sequence analysis

Time series analysis in which attempts are made to explain the value of a variable (only) from observations of the same variables in other periods. Example: attempts are made to predict the demand for a product in the coming months on the basis of the demand in previous periods.

time series

Series of measurements of the same variable recorded at different moments. Sometimes the values observed belong to time intervals (a week, a month) and not to moments. Example: a monthly turnover of a specific brand from 1980 through to 1990.

time series analysis

Analysis aimed at explaining the development of a variable in time. In this context a distinction is made in time sequence analysis and causal time series models.

total error

The sum of the sampling error and all non-sampling errors in a sample research.

trend

The general tendency of a time series in the course of time. To be distinguished from cyclical, seasonal and accidental fluctuations.

true experiment

Experimental set-up in which the researcher controls who is exposed when to which experimental condition and when, and with whom the effects are measured. An essential characteristic of a true experiment is having an experimental group and a control group being composed on the basis of matching or randomization. The influence of any interfering variables is kept under control as much as possible in a true experiment by means of randomization. A true experiment may concern both a laboratory and a field experiment.

two-tailed probability

The probability with a two-tailed test. The two-tailed probability is twice as large as the one-tailed probability. This means that if the p-value (two-tailed) is printed in a computer output, the figure in question is to be divided by two when a one-tailed test is carried out.

two-tailed test

Testing the null hypothesis (H_0) in which the alternative hypothesis (H_a) contains the 'not equal to' sign. In H_a no direction is given to the difference or the correlation. Example: H_0: 'there is no difference between men and women in the average attitude with respect to the XYZ company': ($H_o:\mu_m = \mu_v$), with as H_a: 'there is a difference between men and women in the average attitude with respect to the XYZ-company' ($H_a:\mu_m \# \mu_v$). *See also:* one-tailed test.

type I error
Rejection of the null hypothesis, although the null hypothesis is in fact correct. The probability of a type I error is indicated by α. *See also:* significance level.

type II error
Acceptance of the null hypothesis, although the null hypothesis is in fact correct. The probability of a type II error is indicated by β.

UAC-code
*U*niform *A*rticle *C*oding: bar coding on the packing of article in order to facilitate scanning.

undertaking discernment (power of distinction)
The probability that the null hypothesis is appropriately rejected. The power of distinction equals (1–ß), where ß indicates the probability of a type II error.

uniform distribution
Probability distribution in which each possible outcome may occur with equal frequency. Example: probability distribution of roulette.

unimodal distribution (one-peak distribution)
Frequency distribution with one peak. *See also:* bimodal distribution.

unipolar scale
Response scale in which only one of the extremes of the scale has been named.

unstructured interview (informal interview)
Interview in which only one checklist with subjects to be discussed or open-ended questions is used. In principle all the questions of the checklist will be dealt with in the course of the interview, but the extent to which and the order may differ between respondents. The object is to create a conversation between interviewer and interviewee in which the latter vents his opinion on the subject in his own words. Due to the lack of structure of the interview, the interviews may show a marked difference for each respondent. *See also:* in-depth interview, projective technique.

urbanization, degree of
Arrangement of municipalities on the basis of urbanization:
- · Agglomerate: Amsterdam, Rotterdam, The Hague and peripheral municipalities.
- · other large and intermediate sized cities: the core city counts more than 50,000 inhabitants and the commuter municipalities.
- · small cities: urbanized countryside with 5,000 to 50,000 inhabitants, the cities have less than 20 per cent of agricultural population.
- · country side: towns with more than 20 per cent agricultural professional population or the municipalities with less than 5,000 inhabitants.

validity
The degree to which that what is measured corresponds with that which is meant to be measured. Examples: Is somebody's socio-economic status validly measured by determining his income and his profession? How valid is it to measure brand preference on the basis of the quantity sold of the various brands if during the research some brands were regularly sold out? Methods to gain an insight in validity are: content validity, predictive validity, and construct validity.

variability (spread, dispersion)
The degree to which the individual observations differ from the central tendency. Variability identifies the degree of variation within a distribution. Two ranges of figures may have the same mean, but a different variability. Criteria for variability are: variety width, quartile interval, standard deviation and variance.

variance
Squared standard deviation. Just as the standard deviation there is a population variance and a sample variance. *See also:* standard deviation.

variation coefficient
The standard deviation divided by the arithmetic mean times 100. In this way the variation is expressed in a variable in a percentage of the mean. The variation coefficient requires data on a ratio measurement level.

verbal scale
Response scale consisting of words from which the respondent is to make a choice. Example: fully agree, agree, disagree, fully disagree.

verification question
Question in a survey meant to check the consistency of an answer to a previous question which is equal or very similar to this question. *See also:* manipulation check.

weighted mean
In the arithmetic mean each observation has the same weight when the mean is calculated. In a weighted mean the observations differ as far as the weight is concerned which is attributed to the observations.

weighted sample
If the composition of the sample does not correspond with the composition of the population as far as certain variables are concerned, the sample may be brought into line with the real composition of the population by weighting.

weighting
When processing a research, the deviation of the sample with regard to the population can be corrected by means of weighting. This concerns corrections of response differences between groups (differential non-response). Weighting means that a weight is allocated to respondents (and their answers). Respondents belonging to underrepresented groups are allocated weights of more than 1, respondents belonging to overrepresented groups are allocated weights of less than 1. The weighting is reported in the justification for the research, in which in particular the size of the weights is indicated. *See also:* weighted sample.

Wilcoxon test for paired samples
A non-parametric test aimed at checking if there is a significant difference between the first and the second measurement. The null hypothesis assumes no difference between the measurements. Applicable when there are/is:
- two dependent samples
- data on at least an ordinal measurement level, so that for each pair it can be indicated which observation is the largest and
- the possibility to arrange the difference between the paired samples (ordered metric).

The Wilcoxon test has more power of distinction than the sign test as the magnitude of the differences between the pairs is included in the calculation, whereas the sign test only considers the sign of the difference. The Wilcoxon test can be seen as a good non-parametric alternative for the t-test for paired samples. Example: each person in a sample compares the taste of brand A with the taste of brand B, and assigns a score for each of these brands on a scale of five. Using the Wilcoxon test, it can be checked if brand A is found to be significantly better or worse than brand B. *See also:* t-test for one sample, t-test for paired samples.

word association
Projective technique in which a respondent listens to a series of words and then has to mention the first word that comes to mind.

yes-bias
Reply tendency in which the respondent, after having given 'yes' as an answer to a number of questions, is inclined to answer 'yes' to each following question, irrespective of the content of that question. The same effect can be seen when the respondent 'agrees' with statements he is supposed to give his opinion about on a response scale running from 'totally disagree' to 'agree'.

z score (standard score)

Difference between a specific value x_1 and the arithmetic mean of the distribution, expressed in units of the standard deviation. The formulas read:

(population)

(sample)

distribution of the z-score has an average of 0 and a standard deviation of 1 (but is not necessarily normally distributed). *See also:* eccentricity, standardization.

z-test for one sample

Parametric test with one sample, with the objective to test whether the mean in the sample differs significantly from a supposed mean. Applicable when
- the data is measured on at least interval level;
- the population standard deviation is known;
- the variable in the population is normally or symmetrically distributed, or the distribution of the variable in the population is asymmetric but so great that the central limit theorem applies.

Example: checking if the average age in the sample corresponds with the OPCS data (in the UK) on the average age in the population.

z-test for proportions

The z-test for proportions is a parametric test with the objective to check whether
1. with one sample, the sample proportion differs significantly from the assumed population proportion;
2. with two independent samples, if the two proportions differ significantly from each other.

ad 1. Z-test for one sample. Applicable when
- the data is measured on a dichotomous level;
- the population standard deviation is known;
- np or $n(p-1)$ is greater than 10 (n = sample size, p = sample proportion)

Example: checking if the percentage of car owners in the sample corresponds with the OPCS data on car ownership in the population.

ad 2. With two independent samples. Null hypothesis: $p_1 = p_2$. Applicable when
- the data is measured on a dichotomous level;
- the population standard deviations are known;
- np_1 and np_2 are greater than 10 (n = sample size, p = sample proportion).

Example: checking if the percentage of beer-drinking women differs from the percentage of beer-drinking men.

References and further reading

Aaker, D.A. and G.S. Day, *Marketing Research*, Wiley, New York, 1980.

Churchill, G.A., *Marketing Research*, The Dryden Press, Chicago, 1991.

Green, P.E., D.S. Tull and G. Albaum, *Research for marketing decisions*, Prentice-Hall, Englewood Cliffs, New Jersey, 1988.

Huizingh, E., *Inleiding SPSS/PC + 4.0 en Data Entry*, Addison-Wesley Publishing Co., Amsterdam, 1991.

Kooiker, R., *Marktonderzoek*, Wolters-Noordhoff, Groningen, 5th edition, 1997.

Lehman, D.R., *Market Research and Analysis*, Irwin, Homewood, Boston, 1989.

Moors, J.J.A. and J. Muilwijk, *Steekproeven, een inleiding tot de praktijk*, Agon Elsevier, Amsterdam, 1975.

Schreuder, F., *Handboek gegevensanalyse met SPSS/PC+*, Academic Service, Schoonhoven, 1991.

Siegel, S., *Nonparametric Statistics*, McGraw-Hill, London, 1956.

Swanborn, P.G., *Schaaltechnieken*, Boom, Meppel, 1982.

Tull, D.S. and D.I. Hawkins, *Marketing Research: measurement and method*, Macmillan Publishing Company, New York, 1990.

Zwan, A. van der and J. Verhulp, *Grondslagen en techniek van de marktanalyse*, Stenfert Kroese, Leiden, 1980.

Zwart, P.S., *Methoden van Marktonderzoek*. Stenfert Kroese, Leiden, 1993.

5 MARKETING PLANNING AND STRATEGY

Concept overview

acquisition
anticipating change

BCG portfolio analysis
behaviour segmentation
benchmarking
benefit segmentation
best practice
build strategy
business definition
business process re-engineering
business unit strategy
bypass attack strategy

capability
cash cow
co-operation strategy
competitive advantage
competitor profile
concentrated marketing
confrontation matrix
consortium
contingency plan
contraction defence strategy
core competence
corporate objectives
corporate strategy
cost leadership
cost leadership strategy
counter segmentation
counter-offensive strategy
cycle management

demarketing
demographic market segmentation
differentiated marketing
differentiation strategy
disinvestment strategy
distinctive competence
diversification strategy
dual planning

effectiveness
efficiency
encircling strategy
entry barrier
exit barrier
experience curve

first entrant advantage
five-forces model
flanking attack strategy
focus strategy
frontal attack strategy
functional objective
functional strategy

game theory
gap analysis
General Electric portfolio analysis
generic competitive strategy
geographic segmentation
growth strategy
growth-gain matrix
growth-share matrix
guerilla-attack strategy

harvest strategy
hold strategy

instrument objective
integration strategy
investment strategy

joint venture

key success factor

learning curve
learning organization
life-style segmentation

macro segmentation
management
market arena
Market Attractiveness Business
    Assessment analysis (MABA analysis)
market challenger
market challenger strategy
market development strategy
market follower
market follower strategy
market leader
market leader strategy
market niche
market orientation
market segment
market segmentation
marketing audit
marketing implementation
marketing management
marketing mix
marketing myopia
marketing objectives
marketing performance
marketing plan
marketing planning
marketing programme
marketing strategy
merger
micro segmentation
mission
mobile defence strategy
mobility barrier

Nash equilibrium
network
networking
niche strategy

objective
objectives, hierarchy of
operational management
operational marketing management
organizational culture
overall cost leadership

parallelism strategy
penetration strategy
planning hierarchy
portfolio analysis
position defence strategy
positioning
pre-emptive defence strategy
prisoner's dilemma
product/market combination
product/market/technology combination
  (PMT-combination)
Profit Impact on Market Strategy
  (PIMS)
psychographic market segmentation

re-active change
relative market share
revolutionary change

SBU (strategic business unit)
scale effects

scenario
scenario planning
scope
segmentation strategy
served market
seven S's model
space matrix
specialization strategy
strategic alliance
strategic flexibility
strategic group
strategic issue
strategic market management
strategic market plan
strategic market planning
strategic marketing management
strategic options
strategy
SWOT analysis

tactics
target group
targeting
Total Quality Management

undifferentiated marketing strategy

value activities
value chain
value system
value-based planning

zero-sum games

Concept descriptions

acquisition
The term acquisition is used when orders are obtained (order, client acquisition) and when another organization is acquired (takeover).

anticipating change (pro-active change)
Strategic change anticipating future changes in the organization's environment. *See also:* re-active change.

BCG portfolio analysis
Boston Consulting Group portfolio analysis. One of the well-known portfolio analysis techniques. Basically the SBUs (or products) are evaluated in terms of only two criteria: market growth and relative market share. On the basis of the analysis, investment strategies for the SBUs or products (build, hold, harvest, divest) are derived. *See also:* General Electric portfolio analysis.

behaviour segmentation
Market segmentation in which the market is divided into consumer groups on the basis of their consumption or response with regard to a specific product offer, and for whom it may be desirable to apply a separate market approach. Behaviour segmentation criteria may include: consumption situations (for example, coffee for breakfast, in the afternoon, after dinner or to mark special occasions), and consumption status (buyers, ex-buyers, potential buyers).

benchmarking
Comparing the performances and work methods of one's own organization on a regular basis with those of leading competitors and/or prominent organizations in other branches of industry.

benefit segmentation
Market segmentation in which consumer groups are distinguished on the basis of what they look for as an advantage or essential function when buying a product. The market for toothpaste can, for example, be segmented into consumer groups who are particularly interested in 'clean teeth', or 'fresh breath', or 'no tartar'.

best practice
An excellent execution of a business function by an organization against which another organization in the same market or another market wants to compare itself so as to learn from it.

build strategy
Investment strategy for an SBU (or product) aimed at enlarging relative market share. *See also:* investment strategy.

business definition
Definition of the scope of an organization (or sub-division) on the basis of four dimensions, namely: consumer functions (what advantage is offered to the consumer), consumer groups, technology (in which way is the consumer function realized) and the level in the industry sector where the organization (unit) operates.

business process re-engineering
The adaptation of business processes to create an optimum. By structuring the business processes around the consumers, activities which initially would have been distributed by the organization, are now often concentrated in one person or department. In order to realize this, a drastic adaptation of the information structure and flows is also necessary. Business re-engineering is aimed at achieving, amongst other things, larger efficiencies and short reaction times.

business unit strategy
Strategy by which an organization sub-division (SBU) aims to compete in a particular market.

bypass attack strategy
Strategic term derived from military science in which the attacking side attacks the adversary indirectly by settling in one or more areas in the enemy's neighbourhood. In marketing this concept means a competitor-oriented strategy in which an organization attacks a competitor by taking the same product to a geographically nearby market, or to take a different product to the same geographical market, or offers a new technology with the same functionality on the same market. The aim of this strategy is to divert consumers from the organization attacked, and to move the marketing battle to the adversary's battlefield.

capability
The ability of an organization to make use of its specific means and skills. *See also:* core competence, distinctive competence.

cash cow
SBU (or product) with a high relative market share greater than 1 in a market with a low growth level.

co-operation strategy
Strategy which is all about the co-operation between someone's own organization (unit) and other organizations. Examples are joint ventures, strategic alliances, mergers and take-overs.

competitive advantage (differential advantage)
Specific skill of an organization which is relevant for that organization's performances and which is owned to a lesser degree by competitors. This includes technological expertise, cost control or aspects of service. If the skill is relevant for a longer period and cannot be emulated by other organizations, then this is called a sustainable competitive advantage. To identify the competitive advantages of an organization such methods as value chain analysis can be used.

competitor profile
Description of competing organizations compared to one's own organization in terms of, amongst other things, present activities, objectives, strategies, and strengths and weaknesses.

concentrated marketing
Segmentation strategy in which an organization aims at one or very few segments using one specific marketing programme.

confrontation matrix
Confrontation of internal strengths and weaknesses with external opportunities and threats of an organization (unit). This will expose 'likely strengths' and 'risky weaknesses'.

consortium
Formal temporary co-operation between two or more organizations in which more than adequate means are brought in to realize collective objectives. A consortium is not a separate entity, but consists of the contribution by the parties concerned. An example is the consortium of the channel tunnel project in which amongst others, banks and construction companies were involved.

contingency plan
Plan indicating what must be done in case of possible contingencies ('what/if'), for example, serious market disturbances.

contraction defence strategy

Strategic term from military science in which the side attacked withdraws to a smaller area which can be defended better. In marketing this term means a competitor-oriented strategy in which an organization sheds activities and concentrates on a number of key (core) activities as a result of which it will be easier for the organization to defend itself against attacks by competitors.

core competence

The specific knowledge and skills, the technical and management systems, and the standards and values which are fundamentally characteristic to an organization. It is the collective learning process of the organization which can result in a competitive advantage. *See also:* capability, distinctive competence.

corporate objectives

Objectives embracing the entire company. These corporate objectives may be either of a quantitative (profit, market share, efficiency and/or flexibility objectives), or of a qualitative nature (long-run consumer and public welfare, continuity, resistance).

corporate strategy

Strategy concerning the entire company. Attention is paid to the mission with the central question which role the organization will and can play in which market, taking into account its stakeholders, its core competencies and the choice as to how this mission can be realized.

cost leadership

Situation in which an organization realizes structural overall cost advantages as compared with competing suppliers.

cost leadership strategy (cost focus strategy)

Generic competition strategy aimed at obtaining and maintaining overall structural cost advantages compared with competing suppliers. *See also:* focus strategy, differentiation strategy.

counter segmentation

Approach in which a company consciously joins two or more segments in their marketing approach resulting in a broader segment base and enabling it to use the marketing instruments in a more efficient way.

counter-offensive strategy

Strategic term from military science in which the side attacked defends itself by opening a counter attack. In marketing, this term means a competitor-oriented strategy in which the organization attacked opens the counter attack, for example, by implementing a price reduction, by stepping up promotional activities, by introducing a new 'fighting brand', etc.

cycle management

Type of management in which much attention is given to reducing operational and development cycles as part of a time-based competition strategy.

demarketing

Marketing efforts by one or more suppliers aimed at reducing the total demand, or the demand from specific consumer groups for their product so as to maintain quality of the brand and technical support.

demographic market segmentation

Market segmentation in which the market is divided into demographically defined consumer groups for which it may be desirable to apply a separate market approach. Demographic criteria include: age, segments, size of household, family cycle, income, job, education, religion, race, and nationality.

differentiated marketing

Segment strategy in which an organization aims at various segments using different customized marketing programmes.

differentiation strategy

1. One of the three generic competition strategies distinguished by Porter. The strategy is aimed at offering goods or service packages which are considered unique in the entire industry. The uniqueness may, for example, be the technological capability of an organization (Motorola in the communications industry). 2. Strategy in which activities of an organization within a section of the industry sector are cast off. This strategy is the opposite of an integration strategy.

disinvestment strategy

Investment strategy for an SBU directed at eliminating the SBU or products from that SBU.

distinctive competence

The unique combination of knowledge and skills, technical and management systems, and standards and values which, with regard to competitors, can lead to competitive advantage. *See also:* capability, core competence

diversification strategy

Strategy (Ansoff) aimed at growth in which new products are offered to new consumers. Within the diversification strategy the following distinction is made: concentric diversification, horizontal diversification and conglomerate diversification. In the first case synergy in the technological and commercial area is pursued in the search for new buyers and products. In horizontal diversification synergy is present on either of the two aspects. The latter lacks any relationship with the old activities.

dual planning

Type of strategic planning in which short-term and long-term plans are developed and executed in a parallel manner. A dual plan consists of specific action plans aimed at using short-term possibilities, and strategic initiatives aimed at the longer term, such as organizational changes, strategy development and the development of competencies.

effectiveness

The extent to which objectives are realized.

efficiency

The relationship between the means applied and the results accomplished.

encircling strategy

Strategic term from military science in which the attacking side encircles the adversary completely and thus forces him to deploy his defence on all fronts. In marketing the term means a competitor-oriented strategy in which an organization attacks a competitor on many fronts simultaneously. For example, in all geographical markets with a range of products which is at least equally large, at the same or lower prices and with at least comparable distribution and promotional activities.

entry barrier

Barrier making it difficult for an organization to penetrate a line of business, such factors as size of investments, scale effects, required technology and production skills.

exit barrier

Barriers preventing existing suppliers from leaving a particular market. Such barriers are usually caused by a combination of economic, strategic emotional and contractual factors.

experience curve

A curve indicating the relationship between the experience gathered in manufacturing products (cumulative production), and the accompanying cost price per product unit. The curve is descending; the cost of production, labour, marketing, R&D, purchase and so on decline as a result of an increase in experience. *See also:* learning curve.

first entrant advantage
Strategy aimed at being the first (pioneer) to enter the market to realize competitive advantage.

five-forces model
Model developed by Porter in which structural profitability is explained by the degree and nature of the competition with regard to a sector of industry. This competition is determined by five affecting competitive forces:
1 the degree of internal competition
2 the power of suppliers
3 the power of consumers
4 the threat of potential entering parties
5 the threat from possible substitutes.

flanking attack strategy
Strategic term from military science in which the attacking side attacks the adversary on one or more weakly defended areas. Within marketing this term means a competitor-oriented strategy in which an organization attacks a competitor in a small area, exactly on the spot where the competitor is weak and its own organization can operate strongly. For example, by attacking in a specific area where the competitor scores relatively poorly.

focus strategy
One of the three generic competition strategies distinguished by Porter. The strategy is aimed at offering the product supply to only a small part of the market, for example, a market segment. Cost focus strategy and differentiation focus strategy are distinguished. *See also:* differentiation strategy, cost leadership strategy

frontal attack strategy
Strategic term from military science in which the attacking side attacks the adversary in the area where he is strongest. In marketing the terms means a competitor-oriented strategy in which the attacking organization attacks a competitor on its core activities.

functional objective
Objective to be realized by a functional unit in an organization.

functional strategy
Strategy for a functional unit in an organization, such as marketing, R&D, production, purchasing, and logistics.

game theory
Theory on the way in which organizations or individuals behave in competitive situations. These situations occur when parties ('players') have opposite interests, and, at the same time, are interdependent. The interdependency arises when the consequences of an action by one of the parties are dependent on the actions of the other parties. The basis for the game theory was made by Von Neumann and Morgenstern (1944).

gap analysis
Analysis of the discrepancy between the (turnover) objectives of the organization (unit) and the results expected with the policy unchanged. In the analysis the total discrepancy is examined more thoroughly and differentiated by component parts.

General Electric portfolio analysis
One of the well-known product portfolio analysis techniques. SBUs (or products) are to be evaluated in terms of several criteria which are related to market attractivity and the organization's market position (business position). On the basis of the analysis, investment strategies for SBUs or products (build, hold, harvest, divest) are derived. *See also:* BCG portfolio analysis, Market Attractiveness Business Assessment analysis.

generic competitive strategy

General strategy with regard to the way in which an organization, or divisions within that organization, wish to distinguish themselves, in principle, from the competitors. Porter (1980) distinguished three generic competitive strategies which might lead to success: (1) overall cost leadership, (2) differentiation and (3) focus. The generic competitive strategy chosen will be the starting point for such things as marketing strategies and product strategies.

geographic segmentation

Market segmentation in which the market is divided into geographically defined consumer groups for whom it may be desirable to apply a separate market approach. Geographical criteria may include: countries, regions, cities, suburbs, and so on.

growth strategy

Investment strategy aimed at increasing the turnover and/or sales and/or market share. Several growth strategies are distinguished. Ansoff, for example, identifies the following: penetration, diversification, market development and product development strategies.

growth-gain matrix

A less known portfolio analysis technique of the Boston Consulting Group. In a matrix (containing four cells) the market growth of an SBU (product) is established against the growth of the production capacity (or turnover growth) and it is determined to what degree the organization division can keep pace with the market growth, or can keep running ahead of it, or runs up arrears. In the matrix a diagonal line runs from bottom left to top right. Business units (products) which are positioned below this diagonal line improve their market position and vice versa, business units above the diagonal line lose their market position. *See also:* BCG portfolio analysis.

growth-share matrix

One of the well-known Boston Consulting Group portfolio analysis techniques. *See also:* BCG portfolio analysis.

guerilla-attack strategy

Strategic term from military science in which the attacking side carries out multiple surprise attacks on the adversary in different very small areas and if necessary withdraws after the attack. The – often small – attacking side concentrates the attack time and again completely on such a small area that the adversary cannot sufficiently defend himself. It withdraws before the adversary can relocate his defence, and carries out another surprise attack on the adversary in a different small area. In marketing the term means a competitor-oriented strategy in which the organization carries out a large number of subsequent small attacks on different activities or niches of the competitor, in order to confuse him, if necessary demoralize him, and thus conquer a permanent spot in the market.

harvest strategy

Investment strategy for an SBU in which the investments are withdrawn and no further support is offered, the intention being simply milk the profits and run down this product line totally. Objective of this strategy is generating cash flows. A reduction of the relative market share is accepted if this has a positive effect on short term cash flows or profits. *See also:* investment strategy.

hold strategy

Investment strategy for an SBU in which investments have such a level that the relative market share is maintained. *See also:* investment strategy.

instrument objective

Specific objective within the framework of marketing objectives concerning a separate marketing instrument. Instrument objectives include: product objectives, price target objectives, communications objectives and distribution objectives. *See also:* objectives, hierarchy of.

integration strategy
Strategy in which an organization (unit) joins its activities with the activities of organizations below, above, or next to it in the industry sector. In case an upward or downward extension takes place, it is called vertical integration (forward or backward), otherwise it is called horizontal integration. This is the opposite of differentiation strategy.

investment strategy
'Strategy' (objective would be a better term) is worded in terms of the (relative) market share to be pursued. On an SBU level the investment strategy is usually derived from a portfolio analysis. Generally, four investment strategies are distinguished: build strategy, divest strategy, harvest strategy, and hold strategy.

joint venture
Form of co-operation between organizations in which part of each company's capital is brought together in a new organization which develops an activity or market for joint account and risk.

key success factor (critical success factor)
Skill or means which may be of critical importance to enable successful operation in a market.

learning curve
Relationship (displayed graphically) of the between the accumulated production and labour cost per product unit. When product experience increases, labour cost per product unit may fall. *See also:* experience curve.

learning organization
An organization aimed at creating, obtaining and distributing information and which will adapt its behaviour to new knowledge and insights. Generative learning is characteristic to the learning organization, in other words, the organization discovers and adapts through action. This is to be distinguished from so-called adaptive learning, whereby behaviour is adapted on the basis of examples and consequently the mirror function plays an important role.

life-style segmentation
Market segmentation on the basis of the characteristic life-style, spending time and money, of groups of consumers. For example, a cigarette manufacturer may break down the market into life-style segments representing 'adventurers', 'high societies', and 'trendy people'. *See also:* psychographic market segmentation.

macro segmentation
Form of market segmentation in business marketing, in which, as a first step in the segmentation procedure, the total market is divided into consumer groups having common characteristics not directly linked to the purchasing behaviour of organizations, such as size, line of business, SIC-code, and location. In the next stage each of the macro segments may be divided further into subsegments. *See also:* micro segmentation.

management
Analysis, planning, implementation and evaluation of activities. *See also:* strategic marketing management, operational management.

market arena
Indicates the field in which the organization competes with other organizations. The playing field can be defined in different ways with the help of, amongst others, the product/market/technology combination.

Market Attractiveness Business Assessment-analysis (MABA analysis)
One of the portfolio analysis techniques. During the MABA analysis SBUs (products) are judged in terms of market attractiveness and strengths of the organization unit. The market attractiveness is generally determined by the market size, growth, competition,

consumers satisfaction, price level in the market, profitability of the suppliers in the market, government interference, the sensitivity of the financial results to economic trends, capital intensity, the novelty of the technology and the possibilities to protect these. The 'business strengths' are related to the size, growth and market share of the SBU (the product), the loyalty of the consumer, the sales margins, the distribution, the technological skills, patents, marketing, flexibility and organizational skills. *See also:* BCG portfolio analysis, General Electric portfolio analysis.

market challenger
The organization (unit) which as far as market share is concerned is usually second or third in the market and which wants to improve its position by attacking the market leader and/or other suppliers in the market. *See also:* market challenger strategy.

market challenger strategy
Strategy for organizations which as far as market share is concerned are usually the second or third and who want the improve their position by attacking the market leader and/or other suppliers in the market.

market development strategy
Ansoff strategy aimed at growth and in which the same products are sold to new consumer groups (markets).

market follower
The organization (unit) which is not a market leader and which wants to improve its market position (market share) without competing directly with the market leader.

market follower strategy
Strategy for non-market leaders aimed at improving their own market position (market share) without competing directly with the market leader. In general, market followers will have to keep their costs down and their quality and service up; they will have to enter new markets quickly.

market leader
The organization (unit) in the market which usually has the largest market share or the one usually preceding others to pass on price changes or product innovations. Usually has the highest degree of market penetration and the highest promotional expenditures.

market leader strategy
Strategy for market leaders aimed at maintaining the dominant position in the market by enlarging the primary demand or by defending or enlarging market share.

market niche
The organization (unit) aiming at one specific segment in the market and answering consumer requirements within these segments very precisely.

market orientation
Degree to which an organization takes into account the different market parties and interest groups such as suppliers, consumers, intermediaries, competitors, share holders and key figures in the social surroundings when deciding on and executing its policy (on all organizational levels).

market segment (segment)
Part of a market, i.e., a group of consumers with common properties, for whom it may be desirable to apply a specific marketing strategy for a marketing mix.

market segmentation (segmentation)
Breaking down of a market into different (homogeneous) groups of consumers to be distinguished, for which it may be desirable to apply a specific marketing strategy or marketing mix. As a basis for segmentation four groups of market segmentation criteria might be distinguished: the geographic, the demographic, the psychographic and the behaviouristic segmentation criteria.

marketing audit

A comprehensive, systematic, preferably independent, and periodically recurrent thorough investigation and evaluation of the marketing function and activities of an organization (division). *See also:* marketing performance.

marketing implementation

The execution of marketing programmes in accordance with fixed time schemes, budgets, task divisions and accountabilities of different encumbrance.

marketing management (commercial policy, commercial policy making)

Analysis, planning, execution and evaluation of an organization's marketing activities. Marketing management may either be of a strategic or an operational nature.

marketing mix

Combination and fine-tuning of the marketing instruments used by an organization which are aimed at one or more target groups within a specific product/market (technology) combination.

marketing myopia

Myopia = near-sightedness. Statement by Levitt indicating organizations which are blinded by the excellence of (their) own product(s). In consequence they do not give enough attention to the market and to consumer requirements in particular.

marketing objectives

Specific objective within the framework of company objectives concerning marketing policy. Marketing objectives are, for example, materializing a specific turnover, sale, competitive position or specific market share.

marketing performance

The quality of the marketing efforts. A distinction is to be made in the effectiveness (accomplishing objectives) and efficiency (the relationship between results and means applied) of the performance. When determining marketing performance, the environment may also be taken into account: to what extent did it have a positive or negative impact on the results attained. *See also:* marketing audit.

marketing plan

Plan (policy statement) in which the internal and external environment of a product class, a product group or a brand are analysed, resulting in a SWOT-analysis and usually a definition of a problem. Subsequently one or more objectives are added to the plan, alternative solutions to the problem may be presented and evaluated and a choice may be made from the options. These may eventually be included in an operational plan containing the application of marketing instruments, budgets, and action schemes. Marketing plans may mutually differ to the extent in which they are directed at either strategic or operational problems. *See also:* SWOT analysis.

marketing planning

Management activity aimed at analysing and diagnosing the present and future internal and external environment, preparing a SWOT-analysis, a marketing problem definition, one or more objectives, alternative solutions, their evaluation and choosing the most appropriate solution. The option chosen is prepared and included in an operational plan containing the application of marketing instruments, budgets, and action schemes. *See also:* marketing plan.

marketing programme

Preparing the marketing strategy and producing concrete action plans with a limited duration.

marketing strategy

The way in which an organization tries to accomplish its long-term objectives. The strategy indicates into how marketing activities are to be developed in order to realize these objectives. Refers to the product/market/technology combination of the target group, the positioning to be chosen, and management of the marketing mix.

merger
Formal joining together of two or more organizations into one new entity.

micro segmentation
Form of market segmentation in business marketing in which market segments are further broken down into subsegments based on similarities in purchasing behaviour of the organizations, the size of the decision making unit, the degree of purchasing complexity. *See also:* macro segmentation.

mission
The role and the ambition of the organization in the operational area it has defined (see: business definition). The mission usually reflects the organization's philosophy and culture, also, attention is often paid to the quality of the competitors. 'What is our business and what should it be?' 'Being number 1 in the market!' The mission statement is a formal description of the mission of the organization. This includes the market in which the organization wishes to compete, the strategic ambitions of the organization and the philosophical way in which the organization wants to realize these ambitions.

mobile defence strategy
Strategic term from military science in which the side attacked defends itself by going on to move and occupy new areas so that the attacking party does not get enough opportunity to execute the attack in a co-ordinated manner. In marketing the term means a competitor-oriented strategy in which the defending organization keeps on entering new markets or launching new products, and thus making it more difficult to be attacked in a co-ordinated way.

mobility barrier
Factors making it difficult for an organization to change its strategic position, which means to move from one strategic group to another, due to such factors as effects of scale, required technology and production skills.

Nash equilibrium
Central concept from game theory. Specific combination of the strategic choices of each of the players in which none of them is inclined to unilaterally change his/her strategy.

network
Formal or informal complex of relations between various people and/or organizations who have a common characteristic or interest, or work together.

networking
The conscious and systematic construction and maintenance of a network of people and/or organizations.

niche strategy (market niche strategy)
Strategy of an organization (unit) aimed at one specific segment in the market and which very carefully anticipates the desires of the consumers within this segment.

objective
Goal pursued by an organization in a qualitative or quantitative sense. A distinction can be made between objectives at organizational or business unit level, marketing objectives and marketing instrument objectives. *See also:* objectives, hierarchy of.

objectives, hierarchy of
Objectives may relate to different levels within the organization. As far as the level is concerned, usually a distinction is made between objectives for an organization, a division, and a strategic business unit. Usually, these organization (division) objectives are then translated into functional and instrument objectives.

operational management

Analysis, planning, execution and evaluation of an organization's daily recurrent activities. Generally, the objectives for operational management are derived from the objectives at higher levels in the organization. Usually, operational management relates to logistics, administration and marketing.

operational marketing management

Operational management with regard to the marketing function. *See also:* operational management.

organizational culture

Values, standards, symbols and behaviour shared by participants in an organization, expressed in relationships, communications and styles of management, and so on.

overall cost leadership

One of the three generic competition strategies distinguished by Porter. The strategy is aimed at acquiring a permanent and substantial head start in cost in respect of the competing organizations in the entire line of business. Organizations will try as much as possible to avail themselves of scale efficiency, strict cost control, etc. The lower cost is often reflected in lower market prices than those of competitors.

parallelism strategy

Strategy in which an organization (unit) adds activities from other industry sectors to its business, but at the same level of the industry sector. For example: a foodstuff retailer adds personal care articles to his range. *See also:* specialization strategy.

penetration strategy

Investment strategy (Ansoff) which is pursued to accomplish a higher turnover/higher market share in markets in which the organization is already operational, using the current products.

planning hierarchy

Coherent system of organization plans. For example, Year One of the plan for the organization is constructed on the basis of a long-term plan. Subsequently, the yearly plan can be further specified in a marketing plan. The marketing plan is then attuned to, or forms the input for functional plans such as purchase plans, stock plans, personnel plans, production plans, and financial plans.

portfolio analysis

Analysis which can be used to define the strategy for an organization with more strategic business units. Characteristic is that the concern strategy arises from the integration of the separate investment strategies of the SBU (or product). In that case attention is paid to the correlation between the strategies of the separate SBUs (or products) and to the investment limitations.

position defence strategy

Strategic term from the military science in which a party defends its field in advance by setting up all kinds of means of defence around its own field, for example, by building ramparts, laying mine fields, and so on. Position defence has a dual goal: (1) to make any attack less attractive to an adversary and (2) to be able to defend itself better in case of an attack. In marketing the term means a competitor-oriented strategy in which an organization tries to screen its market by implementing all types of protective means, such as creating a large consumer loyalty, blocking distribution channels and so on.

positioning

The realized (relative) position of an organization, an SBU, a brand or a product in the perception of consumers, in respect of comparable competitors.

pre-emptive defence strategy
Strategic term from military science in which a side to be attacked starts the attack in the field of the adversary, even before the adversary has been able to start the attack in the field of the defending organization. In marketing this term means a competitor-oriented strategy meant to defend one's own position. This is done by attacking a (potential) competitor even before he/she has started attacking the organization, for example, by introducing products on the competitor's market.

prisoner's dilemma
Group of situations within game theory in which (1) for each player the result of the optimum strategy for himself is higher than the optimum strategy for the collective, and (2) when all players choose the optimum strategy for themselves, they would be worse off than if they had all chosen the optimum strategy for the collective. This situation frequently occurs in marketing practice. Thus, a price discount by only one of the competing suppliers of a product may be favourable for the performance of that organization, however, when all competitors allow the same price discount, the result of the entire line of business may be affected negatively.

product/market combination
Selection of exchange objects and exchange subjects on the basis of a strategic choice of consumer requirements which an organization wants to supply and of consumer (groups) they want to focus on.

product/market/technology combination (PMT-combination)
Selection of exchange objects, exchange subjects and technologies on the basis of a strategic choice of consumer requirements that an organization wants to supply, of consumer (groups) it wants to focus on and in which way (using which technology) it wants to do this.

Profit Impact on Market Strategy (PIMS)
Empirical database containing a large number of variables about various aspects of a large number of business units. The variables relate to such things as product quality, degree of vertical integration, market growth, capital intensity, stage of life cycle in which the line of business is, return on investment, and cash flow. With the aid of the database, analyses can be carried out to find out the effect of strategic variables on, for example, the return on investment or the cash flow.

psychographic market segmentation
Market segmentation in which the market is broken down with the aid of lifestyle characteristics in consumer groups for whom it may be desirable to apply a separate market approach. Psychographic criteria that may be used include: combinations of personality characteristics, life styles, attitudes, and so on.

re-active change
Strategic change as a result of changes in the surroundings which have already occurred. *See also:* anticipating change.

relative market share
One of the variables from the Boston Consulting Group portfolio analysis. The relative market share is the market share of the SBU (product) divided by the market share of the largest competitor of that SBU (product). The relative market share provides an insight into market relations.

revolutionary change
Change accompanied by a redefinition of the work method of the organization, including the degree to which the needs of the consumers are being satisfied, the basis to compete and the accompanying critical success factors. Revolutionary change can be both anticipatory and reactive.

SBU (strategic business unit, strategic company unit)

A more or less autonomous organizational unit which is part of a larger organization. It may concern a product, a product line, or a division. The unit has a separate consumer group and is confronted with specific competitors. The SBU is the smallest unit in an organization and can undertake strategic market planning activities independently. Ideally, an SBU should be able to operate independently of the organization and it should have a manager who is responsible for the strategic market planning and the profit, and who has decision-making authority with regard to the factors influencing the SBU's performance. Despite its independence, the SBU has to serve the objectives of the entire organization.

scale effects (advantage of scale)

Efficiency advantages reflected in a falling unit price which occurs when the operative scale is enlarged. The cost advantages may be found both in the field of production, marketing, R&D, and in other function areas.

scenario

Postulated sequence of any future situation in which an organization may find itself.

scenario planning

Developing one or more scenarios and judging the (corporate) strategy in the various future environment situations that have been outlined in the scenarios.

scope

Range of the corporate activities in terms of dimensions of the business definition, namely: technology, consumer functions, consumer groups, and the level in the industry sector on which the organization (unit) operates.

segmentation strategy

Determining on the basis of a segmentation analysis whether one or more segmentations are to be approached in a concentrated, differentiated or undifferentiated way.

served market

That part of the total market for an item or a service (in terms of consumer groups) on which an organization (division) focuses.

seven S's model

Method (developed by McKinsey) to describe and assess organizations as a whole or in part. The model includes seven variables which can each be used as a management instrument. The seven variables are 'structure' (formal and informal organization structure), 'strategy', 'systems' (internal procedures and regulations), 'staff' (quality of the people), 'style' (the organization and management culture), 'skill' (the organization's strong and weak points), and 'shared values' (culture of the organization and of the participants in the organization).

space matrix (strategic position and action evaluation matrix)

An analysis instrument, developed by Dickel, which, with the help of four factors, can characterize the overall strategic profile of an organization as being aggressive, defensive, conservative or competitive.

specialization strategy

Strategy in which an organization (unit) limits its operational field to specific (part) activities within a specific segment of an industry sector. It is the opposite of a parallelism strategy.

strategic alliance

Co-operation between two or more organizations. While retaining their independence and identity, they co-operate in a common area of vital importance for the continuity of the separate organizations. Strategic alliances can occur between competitors (horizontal), with suppliers (up-stream), consumers (down-stream) and organizations outside their own market(s) (diversified). The co-operation can be formalized in the shape of, amongst others, joint ventures and consortiums. *See also:* network.

strategic flexibility
Ability of an organization to change as a result of alterations in the surroundings in the areas of, among others, core competencies, distinctive competencies, and product/market/technology combinations. Strategic flexibility is connected with the learning ability of individuals within the organization. The organization structure is characterized by, among others, relatively few hierarchic structures, and planning, controlling and checking procedures.

strategic group
Group of organizations within an industry having a similar strategic profile, which means having comparable strategic characteristics such as the generic competitive strategy, the range of articles and the degree of innovation. Generally speaking, competitive forces between the strategic groups are different. For strategic analysis it means that a separate analysis (for example, using the five-forces model) is to be carried out. *See also:* five-forces model.

strategic issue
Development which is very likely to have a substantial influence on the organization's performance.

strategic market management
Analysis, planning, organization, evaluation, and control of activities determining the organization's long-term direction. It concerns the fine-tuning now and in the future between the environment, the stakeholders and the core competences of the organization. In general, the objectives in strategic market management are concerned with the higher levels in the organization. *See also:* objectives, hierarchy of, strategic market planning.

strategic market plan
Document describing the strategic market planning of an organization or a strategic business unit. It may include organization objective(s), the current and future internal and external environment, the portfolio analysis, the investment strategy, the functional strategies, such as marketing strategy and the evaluation of strategic alternatives. *See also:* strategic market planning.

strategic market planning
Management activity aimed at determining the organization objective(s) analysing and diagnosing the current and future internal and external environment, the portfolio analysis, determining the investment strategy, setting up and choosing alternative functional strategies, including the marketing strategy, evaluating separate plans on target congruency, available means and quality, and finally planning the execution, organization and evaluation and control.

strategic marketing management
Analysing, planning, executing and evaluating marketing activities, concerning the choice of the product market technology combinations, the target groups, and the desired positionings.

strategic options
Options from which an organization (unit) can choose within the framework of its strategy definition. In the field of marketing, options are distinguished concerning the dependency in respect of other organizations, the position of the organization in the industry sector or in respect of competitors, investments (investment strategies), or the business definition of the organization.

strategy
The way in which an organization tries to accomplish its long-term objectives taking into account an important development, or changes in the environment. A strategy can find its reflection in a behaviouristic pattern, a (desirable) position, a plan or a perspective. Strategies may be distinguished on different levels: the corporate strategy, the business unit (SBU) strategy, and the functional strategy.

SWOT analysis
Summarizing analysis of the Strengths, Weaknesses, Opportunities and Threats of an organization unit, sometimes geared to a specific brand or product. Can also be used as SWOTI
in which the I stands for Issues. Issues can be located with the help of the competition
matrix.

tactics (marketing tactics)
Short-term, adaptive action (in respect of a particular event in the environment) directed
at accomplishing short-term goals (for instrument or function). *See also:* strategy.

target group
Group of (potential) consumers which the organization focuses on and for which it
engages in specific marketing activities.

targeting (target group determination)
Determining the collection of (potential) consumers which an organization (division)
wants to focus on and for which it wants to engage in specific marketing activities.

Total Quality Management
Analysis, planning, execution and evaluation of activities within the entire organization
(in all units and at all levels) aimed at obtaining the standards of quality and improving
the quality. Often demands adaptation of attitude and behaviour of employees within the
organization.

undifferentiated marketing strategy
Segmentation strategy in which the organization, usually on the basis of efficiency considerations, chooses to approach the total market using one marketing programme, irrespective of the differences between the (groups of) consumers which may occur.

value activities
Activities, distinguished by Porter, within the value chain of an organization. These activities can be divided into primary activities (incoming logistics, production, outgoing logistics,
marketing & sales and service), and supporting activities (infra-structure, human resource
management, R&D and procurement).

value chain
Analysis method developed by Porter meant to identify competitive (dis)advantages of an
organization. Characteristic of the approach is distinguishing the strategically important
areas or functional areas of an organization in which major added values can be realized.
For each division, cost developments and possibilities of differentiation are analysed in
comparison with competing organizations.

value system
A system of linked value chains (see: value chain) of which an organization can be part
(for example, the linking of the value chain of the supplier(s) with the value chain of a
'processing organization', and subsequently with the value chain of a link in the distribution chain.)

value-based planning (strategic value management)
Approach in which maximization of the economic value of an organization (division) is
pursued for shareholders. Various models and concepts have been developed to calculate
the height and composition of the economic value on the basis of discounted cash flows.
On the basis of these calculations, recommendations are prepared on methods to increase
the economic value.

zero-sum games
Specific situation in game theory in which any profit of one player is fully compensated
by losses suffered by the other player(s). In marketing this occurs, among others, in the
battle for market shares. The market share profit made by one of the organizations must
be at the complete expense of the market share of other organizations.

References and further reading

Aaker, D., *Strategic Market Management*, Wiley, New York, 2nd edition, 1988.

Abell, D.F., *Managing with Dual Strategies*, Free Press, New York, 1993.

Abell, D.F. and J.S. Hammond, *Strategic Market Planning*, Prentice-Hall, Englewood Cliffs, New Jersey, 1979.

Ansoff, H.I., *Implanting Strategic Management*, Prentice-Hall, Englewood Cliffs, New Jersey, 1984.

Axelrod, R., *The Evolution of Cooperation*, Basic Books, New York, 1984.

Bonoma, T.V., *The Marketing Edge: making strategies work*, The Free Press, New York, 1985.

Chandler, A.D., *Strategy and Structure*, MIT Press, Cambridge, 1962.

Daems, H. and S. Douma, *Concurrentiestrategie en concernstrategie*, Kluwer, Deventer, 1989.

Day, G.S., *Market-Driven Strategy: Processes for Creating Value*, The Free Press, New York, 1990.

Kotler, Ph., *Marketing Management: analysis, planning, implementation and control*, Prentice-Hall, Englewood Cliffs, New Jersey, 7th edition, 1991.

Krijnen, H.G., *Strategie en Management*, Wolters-Noordhoff, Groningen, 3rd edition, 1992.

Mintzberg, H. and J.B. Quinn, *The Strategy Process, concepts, context, cases*, Prentice-Hall, Englewood Cliffs, New Jersey, 2nd edition, 1991.

Neumann, J. von and O. Morgenstern, *The Theory of Games and Economic Behavior*, Princeton University Press, 1944.

Porter, M.E., *Competitive Strategy: Techniques for Analyzing Industries and Competitors*, The Free Press, New York, 1980.

Porter, M.E., *Competitive Advantage: Creating and Sustaining Superior Performance*, The Free Press, New York, 1985.

Porter, M.E., *The Competitive Advantage of Nations*, MacMillan Press, London, 1990.

Porter, M.E., *Competition in Global Industries*, Harvard Business School Press, Boston, 1990.

6 PRODUCT AND BRANDS POLICY

Concept overview

adopters
adoption
adoption category
adoption curve
adoption process
adoption speed
after sales service
aided brand awareness
alphanumeric brand
as marketed product test
Aspinwall classification
assessor
assortment consistency
assortment depth
assortment height
assortment length
assortment mix
assortment reorganization
assortment width
augmented product

Bass model
bastion brand
battle of the brands
blanket family brand
blanket family brand strategy
blind product test
brand
brand added value
brand article
brand associations
brand awareness
brand damage
brand dilution
brand equity
brand extension
brand extension strategy
brand image
brand line extension
brand loyalty
brand name
brand name spectrum
brand parity
brand preference
brand strategy
brand stretching
brand switching
brand switching matrix
brand switching probability
brand umbrella
brand valuation
branded product
branded test
by-product

cannibalization
CE marking
certification
collective brand
comparative product test
complementary goods
concept development stage
concept testing
conjoint analysis
consumer goods
convenience goods
Copeland classification
core assortment
core product
corporate endorsement
counterfeiting
credence product attributes

decline stage
Delphi research method
diffusion process
discount brand
discount manufacturer owned brand
distinctive product advantage
distributor owned brand
down-grading
dualistic brand strategy
durable consumer goods

early adopters
early majority
economic life cycle
essential commodities
experience product attributes
expert research
expressive product characteristic
expressive product function
extrinsic product attributes

fad
fashion product
fast moving consumer goods (FMCGs)
form brand

generic brand
go-error
goods
grading
gross weight
growth stage

has-been brand
heterogeneous products
homogeneous products

idea generation stage
image

imitation
imitation coefficient
imitation effect
impulse goods
indifferent goods
individual brand
individual brand strategy
industrial goods
innovation coefficient
innovators
instrumental product feature/characteristic
instrumental product function
integral quality care
intrinsic product attributes
introduction stage
ISO
ISO 9000 certificate
ISO 9000 standard

label
laggards
late majority
leader
licence
life cycle
line filling
line stretching
logo
loss-leader
luxury products

main product
manufacturer owned brand (MOB)
market stretching
Markov model
maturity stage
me-too product
monadic product test
multi-dimensional product space

net weight
NEWS
non-durable consumer goods

objective quality

packaging
packing
paired comparison
patent
perceptual mapping
peripheral assortment
physical product
position, to
positioning
pre-sales service
premium brand
prestige article

private label
product
product benefit
product class
product design
product development process
product differentiation
product elimination
product feature
product form
product group
product information
product innovation
product instrument
product liability
product life cycle (PLC)
product line
product mix
product modification
product policy
product quality
product range
product recall
product specification
product tampering
product tinkering
product type
proposition
prototype

quality management
quality mark

repositioning
Research & Development (R&D)
retailer brand

screening stage
search product attributes
series brand
service
services marketing
shopping goods
speciality goods
standard brand
status product
stop error
sub-brand
subjective quality
substitutes

tangible product
tare
taste test
test market
total product
trade mark
trading down

trading up
transport package
type name

UAC-code
unaided brand (name) awareness
unique selling proposition (USP)

unsought goods
up-grading

venture team

warranty
wholesaler owned brand

Concept descriptions

adopters
Buyers/consumers who have accepted a product (new to them) and have decided to buy and continue to use it.

adoption
Decision by buyers/consumers to accept a new (for them) product, and to go on using it.

adoption category
Five different adoption categories, showing similarities as far as their adoption speed of an innovation is concerned: innovators, early adopters, early majority, late majority and the laggards.

adoption curve
Graphical display of the percentage of newly arrived adopters of a product, represented in time. On the basis of the differences in adoption speed, Rogers has distinguished five different adoption categories.

adoption process (acceptance process)
Process taking place at the level of the individual consumer whereby he/she passes through various mental and behavioural stages when trying out (or not) and continuing to use (or not) a new product. Traditionally, five stages are distinguished: awareness, interest, evaluation, trial and adoption.

adoption speed
Speed at which an individual consumer passes through the (entire) adoption process.

after sales service
Service with regard to a specific product whereby after-care is emphasized. Part of the full product.

aided brand awareness (passive brand awareness)
The percentage of the target group stating that they recognize (know) a specific brand, indicated by the researcher.

alphanumeric brand
Brand or sub-brand represented in a number/figure. For example the brand 4711 (Eau de cologne) or the sub-brands of BMW, the 500 series, or of Levi Strauss the 501, or of Miele the 220i Hoover.

as marketed product test
Kind of market research with potential consumers into their preference for, and acceptation of a new product. The product is tested in the shape in which it could be marketed, in that it is tested 'as a whole'. This means that not only the physical product is researched, but also the associated pricing, packaging, commercial, etc.

Aspinwall classification
Classification of goods by Aspinwall into red, orange, and yellow goods, on the basis of purchasing frequency, gross margin of profit and service needs. Developed for stock control. Is comparable to the Copeland classification in convenience, shopping, and speciality goods, respectively.

assessor
A pre-test market instrument developed by Silk and Urban focusing on the prediction of the (market share) position of a new product in respect of existing choice-alternatives/substitutes. Especially meant for fast moving consumer goods.

assortment consistency
The nature and degree of relationship between the product groups carried in the assortment.

assortment depth
The average number of products and product types within the product groups of an assortment.

assortment height
The unweighted average price level of the products in the assortment.

assortment length
The average stock (at the distribution point) of the products carried in the assortment. Also: the total number of products the assortment is composed of.

assortment mix
The composition of the assortments in terms of product groups, products and product types expressed in a specific assortment width, depth, height, length, and consistency.

assortment reorganization (pruning)
Literally: cleaning up the assortment. Eliminating the product groups, products or product types from the assortment which, from a business economics point of view or in relation to the business concept, are not (or no longer) acceptable to be maintained in the assortment.

assortment width
The number of different product groups within the assortment.

augmented product
The augmented product comprises, in addition to the tangible product, all those properties of a product which are not physically perceivable, including service, guarantee, and image.

Bass model
Mathematical model, developed by Bass, used to describe diffusion processes, and to predict penetration developments of new products. Typical of the model is that both the so-called innovation phenomenon and the so-called imitation phenomenon are used. For example: someone might, spontaneously, decide to buy a DAT recorder (innovation phenomenon), but he or she may also be induced to buy as a result of interaction with others who already own a DAT recorder (imitation phenomenon). *See also:* imitation coefficient, innovation coefficient.

bastion brand
Strongest and often the first brand of an organization and therefore the most profitable in the brands portfolio of a company. Within the brand strategy a bastion brand can be protected against attacks from competitors by cover brands and fighter brands.

battle of the brands
Expression for the battle between manufacturers' brands and wholesalers/distributors' brands.

blanket family brand (umbrella brand)
Brand name an organization uses for different products within specific or varied product groups. For example, in one specific product group, Vauxhall, Ford and Rover for cars, Philips for electrical appliances and Addis for household articles. For products in various product groups: for example, Hoover, Sony, St Michael of Marks & Spencer for both clothes and meat products.

blanket family brand strategy (monolithic brand strategy)
Brand strategy whereby an organization uses one brand name and one visual style for products in different product groups. For example: Philips (light bulbs, televisions, CD players) and Yamaha (motor bikes, pianos).

blind product test
Type of market research into the preference of consumers for one or more products with regard to physical characteristics such as taste, smell and quality. During this test the

products have been stripped of all non-physical characteristics such as brand name, packing and price. *See also:* branded test.

brand
In the legal sense (Benelux Trade Marks Act): 'accepted as brands are: names, drawings, prints, stamps, figures, letters, shapes of goods or packaging, and all other signs serving to distinguish the products (goods and/or services) of a company'. For brand in the marketing sense. *See also:* branded product.

brand added value
The contribution of a brand (name) together with its related (intrinsic and extrinsic) characteristics to the appreciation of the consumers for the product as a whole.

brand article (brand)
Branded article which on the basis of its extrinsic and/or intrinsic characteristics distinguishes itself from competing articles. The objective of these distinctive characteristics is to create a certain brand-added value for a relatively large group of consumers. *See also:* premium brand, distributor owned brand.

brand associations
The associations a brand evokes in a consumer. These associations can be related to physical aspects of the product itself, but they can also be related to more immaterial aspects.

brand awareness
Extent to which the target group is capable of recognizing a product/brand, and/or the features (characteristics) of it within a product class. In this case a distinction is made between unaided brand awareness, and aided brand awareness.

brand damage
Damage to the brand image and therefore the brand-added value of a product, for example, as a result of negative publicity surrounding the brand in question. Brand damage often results in a decrease of the consumer's confidence in a brand, which can lead to a drop in the market share.

brand dilution
Phenomenon in which a brand after a lapse of time evokes ever less clearly defined associations. This term is often used to indicate that a brand does not evoke specific product associations any more. Brand dilution can occur, among others, as a result of carelessly chosen brand expansion or where the brand name is now synonymous with the product class.

brand equity (brand capacity)
The strategic and financial value which a brand may possess for the producer. Although 'brand equity' originally concerns the brand value to the producer, this term is sometimes also (unjustly) used to indicate the brand value to the consumer. *See also:* brand added value.

brand extension (trans-categorial brand extension)
Brand strategy whereby a brand authorized dealer uses the brand name of a specific product in a specific product group also for the brand authorized other product group(s). For example, Bic (originally disposable pens, afterwards also razor blades and lighters). Linera (initially margarine, afterwards also cheese, jam, etc), Porsche (originally cars, now also: lighters, sunglasses).

brand extension strategy (brand stretching strategy)
Brand strategy in which an organization markets and adds to the assortment other products using the name of an already existent and successful brand of that organization. *See also:* line stretching.

brand image

Sum of the impressions consumers have of a brand, which may influence the behaviour of these consumers with regard to the brand in question. Part of the brand image are all the characteristics attributed to the brand (see: brand personality), but also qualities associated with the brand, which therefore 'radiate' on the brand (such as: country of origin, social and environmental responsibility of the manufacturer, the reputation of the organization).

brand line extension

Brand strategy whereby a brand authorized dealer uses a brand name already carried for product variations within the same product group. Distinction can be made between horizontal line extensions (extensions with the same price/value relation as the original brand; for example, different flavours) and vertical line extensions (extensions with a different price/value relation than the original brand; for example, different models of a car brand).

brand loyalty

The degree of consumer loyalty to a particular brand, i.e. the intention with which or the extent to which a consumer will buy or will continue to buy the brand in question, irrespective of possible changes taking place with the brand in question and (amendments in) competing products/brands. The consumer may display mostly non-indiscriminate purchasing behaviour, whereby over an ever longer period the same brand article is still bought. Indicators for the degree of brand loyalty include: (1) the number of times a consumer, consecutively, buys the brand in question; (2) the chance that a consumer will buy the brand in question again after a change in price or product.

brand name

Brand or sub-brand represented in a word or letters (language). For example the brands Levi Strauss, Mars, M&M, BMW.

brand name spectrum

Continuum which brand names can be divided into, varying from descriptive names (such as Vidal Sassoon's Wash & Go), associative/suggestive names (such as Finimal), to fantasy names (such as Kodak).

brand parity

Equality of different brands within a product group perceived by consumers.

brand preference

(Degree of) preference for a specific brand (article) to other brands, i.e. the priority which a brand takes in the awareness set of the consumer.

brand strategy

Strategy executed by a brand authorized dealer (manufacturer or trade) with regard to the type and number of brands or brand names under which the organization wishes to market products. Hereby, the organization tries to distinguish itself from its competitors and commit its consumers by exploiting one (or more) product(s) in a consumer recognizable brand. An organization can exploit one or more brands in one product group or various product groups (whereby the different brand articles correspond to different desires and needs of the consumers). For example: Unilever uses, among others, the brands Blue Band, Becel, Bona, Lätta and Linera in the Dutch low-fat margarine market.

brand stretching

Brand strategy meaning that a brand name already carried, will be used for other products/ product variations. In brand stretching a distinction can be made between (brand) line and brand extensions.

brand switching

The switching of a consumer in two successive purchases from brand A to brand B.

brand switching matrix
Table in which the brand switching probability(ies) between various brands is represented. Is an essential part of, for example, Markov models.

brand switching probability
The probability that the consumer, in two successive purchasing events, switches from brand A to brand B. This probability is applied in such models as the so-called Markov models.

brand umbrella
A group of individual brands under the joint brand name of an organization. For example, Croma, Tipo and Uno with Fiat as an umbrella, or Walkman and Triniton with Sony as an umbrella.

brand valuation
A financial sum expressing the value which a brand represents in the market or within a certain product group. This value is often put on a par with the net cash value of future profits that can be realized with this brand.

branded product (branded article)
Legal/technical term. Product/article which in some way or other distinguishes itself from a brand (name, symbol, sign, colour, design, packaging) of other products/articles.

branded test
Type of market research into the preference of consumers for one or more product alternatives/different brands, in which all characteristics of these brands can be observed by the consumers and the brand is revealed (as opposed to a blind test, in which the product alternatives are stripped of all non-physical characteristics). *See also:* blind product test.

by-product
Term to distinguish principal products in the assortment on the basis of the economic importance of those products for the organization. In the case of a by-product, the difference between returns and costs, in general, is lower than with a main product. A by-product usually results from the production process of a principal product and therefore any price fetched for the by-product will constitute a contribution.

cannibalization
Literally: eating the same species. In marketing jargon this term is used when the sale of a new product takes place at the expense of an already existing and similar product of the same organization. Car manufacturers upgrade on existing model and so owners seeking a replacement often trade down.

CE marking
The CE brand (Conformité Européenne) is a technical hallmark valid in all EU member states, concerning environmental protection, safety, health and other consumer protection. In future the gradual technical harmonization within the EU will replace and surpass the national hallmarks (such as BSI (UK)).

certification
Obtaining an official certificate proving one complies with a certain threshold standard (for example ISO 9000 standard).

collective brand
Brand, owned by the collective brandholder, of which several organizations are allowed to make use so long as a minimum number of quality demands have been met.

comparative product test
Type of market research in which the preference and acceptance of (potential) buyers for a specific product are investigated. The product to be researched is explicitly compared to similar products. *See also:* paired comparison.

complementary goods
Goods which out of necessity are used as complements to each other. On the basis of this characteristic the mutual, cross price elasticity is smaller than zero. Complete complementarity exists, for example, between a left shoe, and a right shoe. A reduced form of complementarity exists between a car and, for example, petrol, LPG or diesel. *See also:* indifferent goods, substitutes.

concept development stage
Stage in the product development process in which a product idea is developed to a summary of the characteristics that could be given to the new product.

concept testing
Research into the feasibility of several product concepts. A technique often applied in this stage is the conjoint analysis. *See also:* concept development stage.

conjoint analysis (trade-off analysis)
Market research technique which can be used in the concept development stage of the product development process. The essence of this technique is to discover the relationship between product characteristics (attribute levels) and consumer preferences. Respondents are asked to indicate an order of preference within a number of product concepts offered each showing a different combination of characteristics.

consumer goods
All goods used or consumed by end-users.

convenience goods
Product sort in the Copeland classification. The consumer is prepared to make only very little purchasing effort for these goods. Usually it concerns fast moving and routinely bought goods (for example, foodstuffs). *See also:* Copeland classification.

Copeland classification
Copeland distinguishes different categories of goods on the basis of the necessity or the willingness of the consumers to make larger or smaller purchasing efforts to buy these goods. He distinguishes: convenience goods (products for which consumers are willing to make only little purchasing effort), shopping goods (for which they are prepared to make some purchasing effort, they do some 'shopping'), and speciality goods (consumers put in great purchasing efforts).

core assortment
That part of the assortment which consists of articles with a relatively high rate of turnover. Usually those products are considered to belong to the core assortment which represent the top 20 per cent of all articles carried, in terms of turnover. *See also:* peripheral assortment.

core product (core need)
Considering the product in terms of functions for the consumer: the product as filler of a specific consumer need. For example: a manufacturer of electric drills supplies as a core product the possibility for the consumers to drill holes in hard material (Levitt). Kotler made a distinction between core benefit (= core product), tangible product, augmented product being the three composite parts of a product.

corporate endorsement
Marketing of a product by an organization using the organization's own name (for example, Philips) or an individual brand name which differs from that of the organization, whereby the organization is clearly stated as the consignor. For example, Perla Coffee from Albert Heijn. When introducing a new brand, an organization may sometimes (temporarily) emphasize the link with the parent company (in order to procure a speedier acceptance of the new brand). For example: Kylian beer and Lingen's Blond beer by Heineken.

counterfeiting
Illegally copying/forging brand products. For example: fake Rolexes and fake Lacoste shirts sold as such or priced as 'lookalikes'.

credence product attributes
Attributes of a product which the consumer also after purchase/consumption cannot judge adequately. When the vast majority of the attributes of a product considered important by the consumer, even after purchase cannot be assessed adequately, it is also referred to as 'credence products' (for example, the services of a surgeon) *See also:* search product attributes, experience product attributes.

decline stage
Last stage of the product life cycle: period prior to its elimination in which its sales decline continously.

Delphi research method
Type of market research often applied in an early stage of the product development process in which in a number of rounds of expert opinions are collected. Initially, the experts give their opinion independently of each other. At the end of each round they are faced with the other experts' opinions. Subsequently they might adjust their own opinion. Questionnaire rounds continue unless some form of consensus is achieved on the issues.

diffusion process
Distribution and acceptance of a new product within a target group. The basis for the diffusion process is formed by the adoption process of individual buyers.

discount brand (C brand)
Brand with a lowly perceived quality level of which price buyers are the main target group.

discount manufacturer owned brand
Branded (manufacturer's) article especially in the range of fast moving consumer goods with a low perceived price and quality level, a low name reputation and a small market share within a certain geographical area. The distribution range of these articles in that area is usually minor. Producers/suppliers of discount brands usually do not exert marketing efforts aimed at the final consumers. The marketing responsibility for the discount brand is usually handed over entirely to the distributors/trade by the supplier.

distinctive product advantage (comparative, competitive product advantage)
Unique quality of a product which competing products do not own, and which, is appreciated by consumers. *See also:* unique selling proposition.

distributor owned brand (dealer brand, own label)
Brand which is owned by a distributors organization (retail trade/wholesale trade) identified by the name this organization has given to this brand, and which (mainly) is sold through the retail or wholesale outlets.

down-grading
Consciously reducing the service and/or quality level of a product, assortment or shop formula (outlet). Often accompanied by a price reduction.

dualistic brand strategy (endorsed brand strategy)
Brand strategy whereby an organization exploits a group of individual brands within a product group, whereby a collective brand name is used alongside the individual brand name. This collective brand name often is the name of the organization. The individual brands can have a different price/value relation (vertical line extensions), for example, Fiat: Uno, Punto, Tipo and Croma of the individual brands can all have approximately the same price/value relation. For example, with General Motors in the USA: the brands Chevrolet, Pontiac, Oldsmobile, Buick and Cadillac. In the latter case the individual brands are often accommodated within more or less independent subsidiary companies.

durable consumer goods (consumer goods, consumer durables)
Goods used by consumers who can use the same article more than once and over a long period of time (for example, cars, refrigerators, washing machines). Usually, the criterion is that the product lasts at least three years.

early adopters (early buyers)
Adoption category immediately following the innovators and whose adoption speed is therefore high, but not the highest. On the basis of a normally divided adoption curve, this group, after the first 2.5 per cent of the innovators, constitutes the 13.5 per cent of consumers with the next highest adoption speed. This group is sensitive to trends, actively follows new market developments and tends to follow innovators quickly. The early adopters, however, do not take the initiative in the acceptance and implementation of a certain idea or product (Rogers 1983).

early majority
Adoption category immediately following the innovators and the early adopters, whose adoption speed is still relatively high. On the basis of a normally divided adoption curve, this group, after the innovators (2.5 per cent), and the early adopters (13.5 per cent), constitutes the next 34 per cent of the consumer population. Although these consumers are sensitive to certain new developments, they do not lead the way in their acceptance and implementation.

economic life cycle
The period in which a durable consumer or production good (from a business economic point of view) can still be used in a cost effective way: at the point where the cost price (per unit) to substitute the item is permanently lower than to continue using the item in question, the economic life cycle of that item has come to an end.

essential commodities
Products on which the relative expenditure increases slower than the income of a consumer rises. The income elasticity of the demand for these products is, therefore, positive, and lies between 0, and 1. *See also:* luxury products.

experience product attributes
Attributes a product has which the consumer can only assess after purchase or usage of the product. When the majority of the attributes considered important by the consumer can only be judged after purchase of the product, then this is also called 'experience products' (for example, wrapped food products). *See also:* search product attributes, credence product attributes.

expert research
Type of market research in which the researcher uses the knowledge, opinions and expectations of persons who are (professionally) very familiar with the field to be researched.

expressive product characteristic (symbolic product characteristic)
Product characteristics may be of an instrumental or an expressive nature. The expressive characteristics of a product include those attributes which a consumer can use to express, amongst other things, his/her personality and/or lifestyle. For example, the design of a tie.

expressive product function (symbolic product function, hedonic product function)
Product functions can be of an instrumental or an expressive nature. In the case of the expressive function it is all about fulfilling the expressive needs of the consumer. This function is fulfilled by one or more expressive product characteristics. Thus, the expressive function of a design of a tie may be to fulfil the wearers need to belong to a specific (aspiration) group.

extrinsic product attributes
(Visible) attributes of a product which can be physical in nature (packaging) or non-physical in nature (price, brand name, etc). *See also:* intrinsic product attributes.

fad
A fashion that is taken up with great enthusiasm, characterized by rapid sales growth and equally rapid decline (e.g. the Rubik Cube).

fashion product
Product with a relatively short product life cycle as a result of the fashion sensitivity of consumers, and the short-lived fashion trends. A fashion product is linked up with a particular movement, way of behaviour, way of clothing, and so forth.

fast moving consumer goods (FMCGs)
Consumer goods characterized by a high consumer purchasing frequency. These are often convenience goods with a high turnover rate and low margins per unit.

form brand
Brand in which the form of a product or the packing (also) has been registered as the brand (for example, the Coca-Cola bottle) to distinguish it from a brand image and a brand name.

generic brand (unbranded article)
Unbranded product, with a nondescript, often virtually unprinted white packing.

go-error
(The cost of) the mistake which is made when the (continued) development of a new product is mistakenly carried on.

goods
Products of which the specific characteristics are substantially of a material (tangible) nature. *See also:* service.

grading
Function of trade in which products are divided into (standard) quality and/or weight categories.

gross weight
Total weight of a product, i.e. including the weight of that product's packaging. *See also:* net weight, tare.

growth stage (expansion stage)
The second stage in the product life cycle: period in which the sale initially grows rapidly (rapid growth stage, expansion stage), and subsequently grows at a slower rate.

has-been brand
Brand that often had a substantially larger market share and a larger name awareness in the past than is the case now. Some 'has-been brands' are taken out of the market after a lapse of time, others have new life breathed into them (so called 'brand revitalization'), for example, Bush (domestic electrical equipment).

heterogeneous products (heterogeneous goods)
Products which are considered to be different by consumers.

homogeneous products (homogeneous goods)
Products which are considered completely identical by consumers.

idea generation stage
Stage in the product development process in which (as many) ideas (as possible) are generated for any new products.

image
The joint imaginative (or not) subjective representations, ideas, feelings, and experiences of a person or a group of persons with regard to a particular object (product, person or organization).

imitation
Is used in such circumstances as the atmosphere of products and diffusion processes. *See also:* imitation coefficient, me-too product.

imitation coefficient
A parameter from, amongst others, the Bass model indicating the extent to which consumers follow each other when buying a specific new product. For example: someone might decide spontaneously to purchase a DAT recorder (the probability of this happening is described by the innovation coefficient), but he may also be induced to purchase as a result of communication with others who already own a DAT recorder (described by the imitation coefficient). *See also:* innovation coefficient.

imitation effect
Phenomenon that individuals allow themselves to be influenced by other individuals' (purchasing) behaviour. As a result the speed of the adoption process increases as the number of adoptions increases.

impulse goods
Goods which, in general, are bought by consumers on the spur of the moment, and often only after having been confronted with them.

indifferent goods (independent goods)
Goods for which the demand for one item is not at all, or hardly (measurably) influenced by, or linked with the demand for another item. As a result the cross price elasticity between these goods is (almost) equal to zero. The demand for shoes, for example, will not at all relate to the demand for spaghetti. *See also:* complementary goods, substitutes.

individual brand
Brand which is used exclusively for one product, such as Unilever's Jif, Omo, Persil and Blue Band.

individual brand strategy (multi-lithic brand strategy, branded brand strategy)
Brand strategy in which an organization launches products which all have their own brand name, onto the market. When the organization carries only one brand, the brand name is then often the same as the name of the organization. Examples of organizations with various individual brands in several product groups are Unilever, and Procter & Gamble.

industrial goods
All the goods used in industrial production to produce final goods.

innovation coefficient
Parameter from, amongst others, the Bass model indicating the extent of the 'spontaneous' adoption of a new product. For example: someone might decide spontaneously to buy a DAT recorder (the probability of this happening is represented by the innovation coefficient), but he may also be induced to buy as a result of the interaction with others who already own a DAT recorder. *See also:* imitation coefficient.

innovators
Adoption category with the highest adoption speed. On the basis of a normally divided adoption curve, this concerns the first 2.5 per cent of consumers who adopt a certain innovation. Since the innovators are the first to purchase a new product, they often cause a trend (Rogers 1983).

instrumental product feature/characteristic (functional product feature/characteristic)
Product features may be either of an instrumental or of an expressive nature. The instrumental features of a product include those attributes with which the consumer can fill a functional, technical need. For example, size and strength of a garden spade.

instrumental product function (functional product function)

Product functions may be either of an instrumental or of an expressive nature. In case of the instrumental function it is all about filling functional, technical consumer needs. This function is filled by one or more instrumental product features. Thus, the instrumental feature of a garden spade is moving soil.

integral quality care

Integrated quality policy, whereby in coherence and a responsible way care is carried for the ISO 9000 standard, labour circumstances and the environment.

intrinsic product attributes

(Invisible) attributes of a product that when changed, change the physical product itself as a result. Intrinsic product attributes are, for example, taste and aroma of food products. *See also:* extrinsic product attributes.

introduction stage

The initial stage in the product life cycle: the period immediately following the introduction of a new product in which the growth in sales is still small and, in general, the profit is negative.

ISO

International Organization for Standardization

ISO 9000 certificate

Proof an organization can obtain if its products, procedures and production processes meet the ISO 9000 standard.

ISO 9000 standard

Quality standard, determined by the ISO with regard to the objective/technical quality of products, procedures and production processes.

label

Part of the packaging (or added to the packaging) of a product, containing printed information in which, amongst others, the product's nature and composition are described.

laggards

Adoption category with the lowest adoption speed. On the basis of a normally divided adoption curve, this group constitutes the last 16 per cent of the consumer population. Consequently, this group is very reserved with regard to accepting and implementing certain new ideas or products (Rogers 1983).

late majority

Adoption category consisting of the group of consumers having the lowest adoption speed, except for the laggards. On the basis of a normally divided adoption curve, this group constitutes 34 per cent of the consumer population. This group is relatively insensitive to certain new ideas and products, and is slow in their acceptance and implementation (Rogers 1983).

leader (traffic builder)

Article within the assortment used especially to attract customers, or to generate traffic.

licence

A permission granted by the licensor (patent keeper) to another company in order to, either for or without payment, manufacture a specific product (patent right) of the licensor and/or sell it within a specific area.

life cycle

Period during which a durable good can perform well. Technical life cycle and economic life cycle can be distinguished. The shorter of the two life cycle concepts, either the technical or the economic life cycle, is considered the factual life cycle.

line filling
Type of assortment extension in which expansion of the product line takes place by adding products or product types within the original product line.

line stretching (product extension strategy)
Type of assortment extension in which expansion of the product line takes place by adding new products or product types within the same product group, but outside the original product line.

logo
A characteristic symbol which can consist of a combination of certain letters, words, images, colours and illustrations, represented as one entity. The aim of the logo is to distinguish a brand from other brands and to act as a sign of recognition for the consumers. In fact, a logo is the design of an image, name, and form block for communicative expressions. Examples: AH, V&D, the LaCoste crocodile, the Apple apple.

loss-leader
Article in the assortment offered at cost price or lower meant to attract customers.

luxury products
Products (goods) on which the (relative) expenditure increases rapidly as the income of the consumers rises. The income elasticity of the demand for these products is, therefore, positive, and greater than 1. *See also:* essential commodities.

main product
Term to distinguish by-products in the assortment on the basis of the economic importance of those products in the organization. In the case of a main product the difference between return and costs, in general, is larger than in the case of a by-product.

manufacturer owned brand (MOB)
Brand identified by the name given to it by the producer/manufacturer, and which he also owns.

market stretching
Strategy extending the maturity stage of the product life cycle by entering new markets or stimulating more frequent or alternative use of the product.

Markov model
Stochastic brand choice model enabling the acquisition of an understanding of the purchasing process of consumers. Essential in this model are the transgression probabilities between brands (i, and j) indicating the probability that a consumer or a group of consumers, in the initial purchase, buys a specific brand (i), and in their subsequent purchase buys a different brand (j).

maturity stage (stabilization stage, saturation stage)
A third stage in a product life cycle. Period in which the growth of product sales declines and sales stabilize.

me-too product
A marketed imitation product without any specific distinctive product advantage following an already existing, usually successful, product of another supplier.

monadic product test
Form of market research in which a (complete) product is tested with the consumer without the consumer being asked to make a comparison with other/comparable products.

multi-dimensional product space
Products may be described by locations in a multi-dimensional space in which the space dimensions are formed by the product attributes relevant to recognize the differences and similarities between the products. The more the products resemble each other, the closer they lie to each other in a multi-dimensional space.

net weight
Weight of the product without the weight of the packing of that product. *See also:* gross weight, tare.

NEWS
Model with which, in an early stage, the turnover to be accomplished, and the associated market share, can be predicted for a new product. In this case the emphasis lies on the influence of advertising on the adoption process. NEWS stands for *n*ew *p*roduct *e*arly *w*arning *s*ystem.

non-durable consumer goods
Consumer goods having a (relatively) short life cycle. The usual criterion is that the product does not last longer than three years.

objective quality (technical quality)
Degree to which a product complies with measurable criteria.

packaging
primary-packaging: the packaging necessary to keep the product together or to ensure the quality.
secondary-packaging: usually meant to offer either extra protection (for example, box for toothpaste tube) and/or to enable communicative elements to be added (such as paper packaging around plastic packing of vacuum packed coffee).
additional packaging: packaging such as the cylinder around a bottle of whisky.

packing
Part of the tangible product. It is the material in which an article is wrapped. A distinction is made between primary packaging, secondary packaging, external packing, packaging for transport, and label.

paired comparison (paired product test)
Comparative product test in which the products to be compared are offered to the respondents in pairs, with the request to show preference for one of both alternatives each time.

patent
A legal concept. On the basis of a patent (legal) protection is obtained from imitation of a technical innovation.

perceptual mapping
Technique in which an attempt is made to represent consumer perceptions with regard to product attributes in a multi-dimensional product space.

peripheral assortment (supplied assortment, fringe assortment)
The part of the assortment consisting of articles with a relatively low turnover speed. Usually, those products are considered to belong to the peripheral assortment, which do *not* belong to the top 20 per cent of the articles carried, in terms of turnover. *See also:* core assortment.

physical product
The joint physical characteristics of the product (such as weight, dimension, taste, smell and speed).

position, to
(An organization's) conscious efforts to realize a particular relative position of the organization, an SBU, a brand or a product in the perception of consumers, in respect of comparable competitors.

positioning
The realized (relative) position of an organization, an SBU, a brand or a product in the perception of consumers, in respect of comparable competitors.

pre-sales service
Service with regard to a particular product whereby care is being emphasized, even before the product is sold or delivered.

premium brand (manufacturer owned premium brand)
(Manufacturer's) brand article especially in the range of fast moving consumer goods with a (constantly) highly perceived price and quality level, an extensive name reputation and a broad advertisement support, and a relatively large market share within a certain geographical area. These brand articles are often distinguished by a large distribution range within that area (according to the Cebuco, between 70 and 80 per cent). *See also:* brand article.

prestige article (prestige product)
1 Article with a strong quality or service image which has been included in the assortment because of the assortment strategy, despite the fact that it does not, or hardly yields any direct profit.
2 Article with a strong quality or service image that provides the buyer/user prestige because of the strong expressive qualities, which is the main reason why it is bought. *See also:* status product.

private label
Products which, from the manufacturer's point of view, are marketed by order of third parties, and, using a different brand name from the personal brands of that manufacturer, are marketed by these third parties using the brand names chosen by themselves. *See also:* distributor owned brand.

product
The joint material and immaterial qualities of an article or service. This concerns everything that can be offered on a market, for consumption, use, attention, in order to be able to fill a specific need. With regard to the composite parts of the product, Leeflang distinguishes between the physical, augmented and total product, and Kotler distinguishes between the core benefit, tangible product, and the augmented product.

product benefit
Product attribute seen by consumers as an essential distinctive characteristic of the product in question.

product class (product group, product category)
A group of product categories from which the consumer may choose to fill a particular or comparable need. Thus, the transport product class (providing the transport need of consumers) includes the product group cars, motor bicycles, mopeds, and bicycles.

product design
Technical and commercial development (design) of a product concept into a physical product.

product development process
The process that takes place (within an organization) with regard to marketing a new product from the development of ideas to the introduction of new product or product types for new or existing markets. Generally, this process distinguishes seven stages, namely: idea generation stage, screening stage, concept development stage, strategy development stage, physical product development stage, test stage, and product introduction stage.

product differentiation
1 With regard to assortment policy: offering different types of a product which may be attractive for different consumer (groups). A distinction is made between horizontal product differentiation (different product types with the same quality) and vertical product differentiation (different product types in a range of quality levels).

2 With regard to positioning: distinguishing the personal product with respect to competing products, and making the consumers aware of the differences between the products in question.

product elimination
Eliminating a product from the market for good.

product feature (product characteristic)
Material or immaterial characteristic of a product.

product form
A specific technical appearance of a group of products within a product class.

product group
A group of products belonging to a specific product class which are closely related to each other with regard to fulfilling the same or a comparable need. A product group consists of various products and product variants. For example, the soft drink product group featuring cola or fruit juice products. Product variants within the fruit juice product group are, for example, apple juice and orange juice.

product information
1 Usually data, specified by law, on qualities, content, composition, and use of a product which are stated on the product, the packaging, the label or on an instruction leaflet. *See also:*
2 Neutral, i.e. non-advertising, information on (technical) characteristics and application possibilities of a (new) product released in, for example, the form of press releases in order to stimulate free publicity.

product innovation
A product which is fundamentally new for both potential consumers and for the organization.

product instrument
Means which can be applied to have the attributes of the exchange object match the needs of the consumers as part of the marketing policy. Product instruments include the following part-instruments: design, development, brand, packaging, and the technical specifications of the product, the quality, nature, type, and number of products to be produced or to be traded, expressed in the breadth, depth, length, and height of the assortment.

product liability
The liability of the supplier (producer or trade) as a result of improper functioning of the product manufactured or delivered by him/her.

product life cycle (PLC)
(The graphical display of) the course of a product's sales over time. These sales can be studied at different (product) levels (product class, product group, product, product type). Generally, four (standard) stages are distinguished within the PLC: introduction stage, growth stage, maturity stage, and end stage. Sometimes the growth stage is also broken down into a 'rapid growth' stage, and a 'declining growth' stage.

product line
The group of products and product types offered by a particular organization.

product mix
Actual application, combination and fine-tuning of the product instruments for a specific target group by a particular organization. Consists of, amongst others, the physical product itself, the packaging, possible brand name and label information. In retail trade marketing the product mix concept is used as a synonym for assortment mix.

product modification
A change in the product mix, i.e. a change in the tangible or non-tangible elements of a product. The result is neither fundamentally new for the market, nor fundamentally new for the organization.

product policy
Analysis, planning, execution, and evaluation of activities regarding the product instruments as part of marketing policy.

product quality
Degree to which a product complies with the demands resulting from use or consumption. *See also:* subjective quality, objective quality.

product range (assortment)
The joint product groups, products, product types, and brands offered by a (production or trade) organization.

product recall
Recalling products to the factory/distributor in connection with failures found.

product specification
Specification by a producer or consumer with regard to mainly the technical and/or functional aspects of a product.

product tampering
The intentional damage of brand products by third parties with the objective to stop consumers from buying the brand product in question. For example: (threatening to) poison food products.

product tinkering
Lowering the quality of the intrinsic characteristics of a brand article by a manufacturer. For example: the use of cheaper materials.

product type
A specific type of supply of a product, within a product or product group, to be distinguished on the basis of specific product features (for example, ground coffee within the coffee product, the hot beverages product group).

proposition
That which a supplier (producer/trade) offers to consumers in the market, including the image which suppliers pursue, consisting of instrumental and expressive product aspects (including brand and brand image), price aspects, distribution aspect, communication aspects and personal aspects.

prototype
First test model of a new product capable of performing all technical functions provided.

quality management
Analysis, planning, execution and evaluation of activities in the entire organization (in all parts and at all levels), aimed at maintaining and improving quality and realizing quality standards. This often demands the adaptation of attitude, knowledge and behaviour of all employees in an organization.

quality mark (collective mark)
Mark serving to ensure one or more common characteristics of products/goods. Such marks emanate from different organizations (for example, quality, technical safety) Examples: British Standards Institute (BSI) Kitemark, Woolmark, Good Housekeeping Seal of Approval.

repositioning
Conscious effort of the supplier to change the positioning of a brand.

Research & Development (R&D)
Functional department or area within an organization in charge of investigating, researching, and, where possible, developing improvements of the technical aspects of the production and product development process.

retailer brand (retailer owned brand)
Distributor brand owned by a retail organization and sold (almost) exclusively through that organization.

screening stage
Stage in the product development process in which the ideas that were developed in the idea generation stage are assessed on their technical and commercial feasibility.

search product attributes
Attributes of a product which the consumer can assess before purchasing the product. When the vast majority of the attributes of a product considered important by the consumer can be assessed before purchase, it is also referred to as 'search products' (for example, furniture). *See also:* experience product attributes, credence product attributes.

series brand
Brand name consisting of a prefix or suffix of the original brand, combined with a new brand or sort name. For example, the series brand names derived from McDonald's such as McFrites, MacBurger, McChicken.

service
Product of which the specific characteristics are essentially of an intangible nature or provision of services with regard to a particular product in which the emphasis lies on care, follow-up, including checking, maintenance, and repair.

services marketing
Marketing activities of an organization in which the exchange objects to be traded are services.

shopping goods
Product type in the Copeland classification. For these goods, the consumer is prepared to go to some length before proceeding to buying the goods. Usually, a limited number of products or brands (for example, clothing), if necessary in different shops, is compared with each other before the actual choice is made. *See also:* Copeland classification.

speciality goods
Product type in the Copeland classification. For these goods, the consumer is prepared to go to great length before proceeding to purchasing them. Often, this has to do with products having a high involvement, and a low initial information level with the consumer (for example, first purchase of motor car, house, or concluding mortgage). *See also:* Copeland classification.

standard brand
(Manufacturer's) brand article especially in the range of fast moving consumer goods with a lower perceived price and quality level than an A brand, a lower name reputation, less advertisement support and a relatively limited market share within a certain geographical area. These brand articles are often distinguished by a lower distribution range within that area (according to the Cebuco < 65 per cent). *See also:* brand article.

status product
Article with a strong radiation effect which, because of the strong expressive function, supplies the user/consumer status, which is the very reason why it is bought. *See also:* prestige article.

stop error
(The cost of) the mistake which is made when it is erroneously decided not to continue the development of a new product.

sub-brand
Addition to a family brand indicating a specific (type/sort) product (variation). A sub-brand can consist of a word (brand) or an alphanumeric brand. For example, the sub-brand Mondeo of Ford, the sub-brands Punto, Tipo of Fiat, Civic, Accord and Prelude

of Honda (word brands), or the sub-brands 501 of BMW, 200D of Mercedes, 501 of Levi Strauss (alphanumeric brands).

subjective quality (perceived quality)
Value judgement on the suitability of the use of a product. Judgement is passed on the basis of various quality indicators and in the context of previous experiences, quality awareness, usage objectives, risk calculations and other personal and situational circumstances.

substitutes
Goods which are interchangeable, and can be used in each other's place. On the basis of this, the mutual, cross price elasticity is greater than 0. When the price of one article declines, the quantity demanded of the other article (of which the price remains the same) will decline. *See also:* complementary goods, indifferent goods.

tangible product
Those components of the product which are physically perceivable (not only the 'physical product' but also the packing, the quality, the styling). *See also:* core product.

tare
Weight of only the packing of a product. *See also:* gross weight, net weight.

taste test
Type of market research in which taste (perception) is researched to see if a product matches the requirements of potential consumers.

test market
A form of (experimental) market research in an advanced stage of the product development process in which the developed product and the associated market activities (or variations of it) are marketed and tested on a limited scale and in a limited area.

total product
The augmented product plus the qualities allocated to and derived from it by the consumer. For the consumer, this includes all instrumental, and expressive features, and all associated elements, such as warranty, packing, advertising, and pricing.

trade mark
A legal term, covering words, symbols or marks that have been legally registered by a company. A brand name or corporate logo must be registered for a company to have the proprietary right to use it.

trading down
Adding to the assortment one or more articles with a relatively lower price and/or quality in relation to the original assortment.

trading up
Adding to the assortment one or more articles with a relatively higher price and/or quality in relation to the original assortment.

transport package
Packing required for storage, identification or transport (for example, additional protection).

type name
Collective name indicating the production area or the production method of a product within a particular product group. The type name often has legal protection. For example, in the case of wine, the name of the area of origin (appellation d'origine) functions as the type name (Bordeaux, Elzas wine etc). Type brands are also found among dairy products.

UAC-code
Electronically readable bar code on the packing, labels, or articles, by which the goods can be identified (the *u*niform *a*rticle *c*oding). The European coding system is identified by EAN, *E*uropean *a*rticle *n*umber.

unaided brand (name) awareness (active brand (name) awareness, spontaneous brand (name) awareness)
The percentage of the target group which (spontaneously) recalls a certain brand after being requested to sum up a lists of brands known within a certain product class or group.

unique selling proposition (USP)
Exclusive sales argument regarding a proposition which the competition is unable or unwilling to use.

unsought goods
Goods which the consumer may know, but which he is not motivated to buy (for example, funeral policies).

up-grading
Consciously raising the service and/or quality level of a product, product assortment or shop formula.

venture team
In the framework of product policy, a project organization form for the product development process in which a team is formed consisting of staff from different departments and/or from different disciplines.

warranty (guarantee)
Part of the augmented product. The supplier offers warranty during a fixed period with regard to failures or defects in (specifically identified parts of) the product offered.

wholesaler owned brand
A specific type of a distributor brand owned by a wholesale organization, and which is (almost) exclusively sold within that organization and/or affiliated organizations.

References and further reading

Aaker, D.A., *Managing Brand Equity*, The Free Press, New York, 1991.

Crawford, C.M., *New Product Management*, Irwin, Homewood, Ill., Inc., 2nd edition, 1987.

Moore, W.L. and E.A. Pessemier, *Product Planning and Management, Designing and Delivering Value*, McGraw-Hill, New York, 1993.

Riezebos, H.J., *Brand-Added Value/Merkmeerwaarde: theorie en empirisch onderzoek naar de waarde van merken voor consumenten*, Dissertatie, Eburon, Delft, 1994.

Rogers, E.M., *Diffusion of innovations*, The Free Press, New York, 1983.

Urban, G.L. and J.R. Hauser, *Design and Marketing of New Products*, Prentice-Hall, Englewood Cliffs, New Jersey, 1993.

Urban, G.L., J.R. Hauser and N. Dholakia, *Essentials of New Product Management*, Prentice-Hall, Englewood Cliffs, New Jersey, 1987.

Wierenga, B. and W.F. van Raaij, *Consumentengedrag*, Stenfert Kroese, Leiden, 1987.

Wind, Y., *Product Policy: concepts, methods and strategy*, Addison-Wesley Publishing Co, Mass., 1980.

Zeithaml, V.A., A. Parasuraman and L.L. Berry, *Delivering Service Quality: balancing customer perceptions and expectations*, The Free Press, London, 1990.

7 PRICE POLICY

Concept overview

absolute price change
absolute price difference
acceptable costs
active price policy
adaptive pricing
advantages of scope
average fixed costs
average gross margin
average gross profit
average return
average variable costs
avoidable costs

bait pricing
barriers to entry
bent sales curve
bonus discount
break-even analysis
break-even point
break-even ratio
break-even sales
break-even turnover

capacity
cash discount
catalogue price
circular reactions
co-operative price setting
commission
competition-oriented pricing
competitive bidding
consolidation strategy
consumer price
consumer surplus
contrary demand curve
contribution accounting
contribution margin
cost centre
cost-benefit analysis
cost-orientated pricing
cost-price
cost-price plus method
cross-price elasticity of the demand
current capacity utilization
customer-oriented pricing

degree of actual capacity utilization
demand curve
differential cost-price
differentiation value
difficult comparison effect
direct costing method
direct costs
direct price change

discontinuous decline in demand
discount
discount-pricing
down-grading
dual pricing
dumping

economic value
economic value analysis
economies of buyer focus
economies of scale
efficiency in transfer pricing
end benefit effect
equilibrium price
Every-Day-Low-Price strategy (EDLP)
expansion price strategy
expected value method
external cost efficiency

fair price
firm bidding
fixed costs
fixed pricing
flexible break-even-analysis
flexible pricing
forward looking costs
full competition
functional discount

going-rate pricing
gross margin
gross profit
growth discount

harvest strategy
heterogeneous oligopoly
homogeneous oligopoly
horizontal price fixing

incremental costs
index of consumer prices
indirect costs
indirect price change
integral selling price
internal cost efficiency
internal transfer prices
introductory price
inventory effect

joint prices

leader
learning advantages
learning curve
loss-leader pricing
low-balling

margin
margin generator
margin stability
marginal analysis
marginal costs
marginal return
mark-up
market follower price policy
market mechanism
market share objective
market share pricing
market zone
maximum capacity utilization
me-too pricing
minimum price
monopolistic competition
monopoly

net profit
net profit margin
neutral price strategy
non-monetary price
non-price competition

odd pricing
offer
oligopoly
one price selling (OPS)
opportunistic price setting
opportunity costs
optimum price
over-capacity
overhead costs
overpricing

panel price research
passive price policy
pay-back-period
penetration price strategy
perceived quality
perceived-value pricing
predatory pricing
premium pricing
prestige buyers
prestige products
prestige zone
price
price acceptance
price action
price as quality indicator
price awareness
price behaviour
price bundling
price buyers
price cartel
price competition

price differentiation
price discrimination
price distance
price elastic demand
price elastic supply
price elasticity coefficient
price elasticity of demand
price elasticity of supply
price inelastic demand
price inelastic supply
price instrument
price knowledge
price leader
price limits
price mechanism
price mix
price objective
price offer
price perception
price policy
price/quality buyers
price/quality effect
price/quality relationship
price regulations
price research
price rigidity
price sensitivity
price setting
price stability
price strategy
price threshold
price/value relationship
price-lining
price-list
price-off
price-trade-off research
product introduction strategy
product line pricing
productivity strategy
profit
profit maker
profit margin
promotion discount
promotion zone
psychological pricing
public tender
put-out pricing

quality buyers
quantity discount

recommended prices
recommended resale price (RRP)
reference price
reference value

refund campaign
relative break-even sales change/or per cent
relative price change/or per cent
relative price difference/or per cent
replacement costs
retail contribution margin
retrenchment strategy
return on investment (ROI)
returns objective
reverse pricing

sales price
sales response
sales response curve
sales response research
sealed bid
seasonal price reduction
sequential penetration strategy
shared cost effect
simulation method
simulation test markets
skimming price strategy
special deal
standard cost price
substitute awareness effect

substitutes
sunk costs
sunk investment effect
sunk investments

tender system
test market method
total constant costs
total costs
total expenditure effect
total returns
total variable costs
trade discounts
turnover bonus
turnover generator

under-capacity
unique value effect
unit or absolute break-even sales change
up-grading

value perception
variable costs
velocity of stock turnover
vertical price fixing
volume zone

wholesale contribution margin

Concept descriptions

absolute price change
Change in prices, expressed in money. *See also:* relative price change/or per cent.

absolute price difference (absolute or unit price distance)
Difference in prices, expressed in money. *See also:* relative price difference/or per cent.

acceptable costs
The actual maximum acceptable cost price which can be calculated if on the basis of inverse pricing backward calculations are made (taking into account a certain marginal profit) from the price of the competition (market price) or a consumer price required or viable in the market.

active price policy
Competition-oriented price policy in which especially price instruments are used as competitive weapons.

adaptive pricing
Competition-oriented method of pricing in which especially smaller companies with a viable marketing position adapt their prices to those of the (larger) competitors, or to the current market prices. They will not trigger off any changes in price themselves. *See also:* market follower price policy.

advantages of scope (economies of scope) (scale)
Using synergy effects, organizations can profit by advantages in the atmosphere of common costs or overhead costs, using a well balanced product portfolio. *See also:* internal cost efficiency.

average fixed costs
The joint fixed costs divided by the size of production, or the constant cost per product unit.

average gross margin
The gross margin (in money or percentages) per product unit. The average gross margin is usually displayed in a percentage of the total return less the direct or variable costs.

average gross profit
The total gross profit divided by the number of products sold, or the gross profit per product unit.

average return
The total return divided by the number of products sold; the return per product unit. If this concerns one product, then the average return equals the price. For different products or assortment the average return is an indicator for the average price level of those products or the assortment.

average variable costs
The joint variable costs divided by the production size or the variable costs per product unit.

avoidable costs
Costs considered relevant in the framework of pricing, because they have not (yet) been made, or can be undone or are still avoidable. For example, the (future) depreciations on a means of production. On the basis of the current market value of the means of production the cost associated with it can be avoided.

bait pricing
Pricing relating to a special offer or loss-leader designed to bring customers into the store. Usually they will be weaned off the 'bait' and sold on a 'switch', another brand of higher value and quality. *See also:* psychological pricing.

barriers to entry
Competition-oriented method of pricing in which the price is (temporarily) set so low that any competitors do not enter the market.

bent sales curve
Specific shape of the sales curve for an individual supplier in a homogeneous oligopoly, as a result of the reactions of competitors. The competitors do follow the price decreases of the supplier, but they do not or only to a limited extent follow the price rises.

bonus discount
Reduction (afterwards) of the selling price by the supplier because the buyer has achieved a particular performance (example: reaching a particular quantity purchased in a specific period).

break-even analysis
Determining the critical size of production and sale at which the total return of the quantity of products (at a specified selling price) is exactly equal to the total cost of production and sale of that quantity (total cost = total return).

break-even point (critical point)
The point (in a chart) at which neither profit nor loss is made. At this point the size of the production and/or the sales are such that the total cost are exactly equal to the total return at a specific price (total return = total cost).

break-even ratio
Ratio with which the required increase or decrease of the production and the turnover after a change in price can be calculated in order to reach a break-even point again.

break-even sales (critical sales)
The critical sales at which for a given selling price the total return is exactly equal to the total cost of production and sales (total cost is total return).

break-even turnover (critical turnover)
The critical turnover at which for a given selling price the total return is exactly equal to the total cost of production and sales (total return = total cost).

capacity (normal utilization of)
The optimum utilization of the production capacity in relation to the cost price of the product. Usually the standard utilization is approximately 80 per cent of the maximum production capacity. *See also:* degree of actual capacity utilization, standard cost price.

cash discount
Discount granted to buyers for cash payment or payment within a specified term.

catalogue price (list price)
Fixed price for a particular product as included in a catalogue or price list.

circular reactions
Reactions from competitors (often to a specific pricing of one of the suppliers) in a heterogeneous oligopolistic market form.

co-operative price setting
Method of competition-oriented pricing in which several large organizations with a relatively large and viable market position together implement price changes (whether or not based on formal agreements). If one organization changes the price (price leader), then the others will follow with a comparable price change (market followers). *See also:* price cartel.

commission
Fixed amount or percentage of the selling price or turnover or profit which the distributor or a reseller receives as a compensation for services rendered.

competition-oriented pricing
Method of pricing whereby the price level of the (major) competitors is taken as a starting point. Examples: discount pricing, dumping, going-rate pricing, market follower pricing, me-too pricing, premium pricing, put-out, and stay-out pricing.

competitive bidding
Modelled on different price levels, submitting an offer price that best suits the company according to its current needs.

consolidation strategy
Alternative (price) strategy in the declining stage of the product life cycle. Using specific investments, the company tries to materialize a stronger position in declining markets, or market segments, by realizing the cost advantage. By means of price competition, weaker competitors are ousted from the market. Due to 'shake-out' in consequence of the retrenchment or harvest strategy of the competitors, the company can realize a larger market share in a restructured market.

consumer price
Price which the consumer is charged (usually including VAT).

consumer surplus
The part of the potential return in a market which a supplier does not receive because there are always consumers who would be prepared to pay a higher price than the actual market price.

contrary demand curve
Special course of the demand curve as a result of the decline in the decrease (increase) of the quantity demanded with a fall (rise) of the prices.

contribution accounting
Method of analysis whereby the profitability of a product is determined on the basis of the direct costing method (see direct costing method).

contribution margin (coverage contribution)
The difference between the selling pricea and the variable costs. The contribution is a (profit) mark up (in money or percentage) on the variable or direct costs, which are supposed to cover the constant or indirect and the profit (usually per product unit). *See also:* gross margin.

cost centre
The article or the service the return from the sale of which is supposed to compensate (partly) the costs made.

cost-benefit analysis
An analysis method in which the costs to be made (of the production or a campaign) are weighted against the returns (to be expected) (from turnover or from that campaign).

cost-orientated pricing
Method of pricing based on the cost-price (integrated approach) or the variable costs (differential approach).

cost-price (average total costs, costs per product unit)
The total or integrated costs (constant costs and variable costs or indirect, and direct costs) divided by the size of production or the cost per product unit.

cost-price plus method (integrated cost calculation, cost-plus pricing)
Cost-oriented method of pricing on the basis of a specific (profit) mark-up on the cost-price (full costing) in percentage terms.

cross-price elasticity of the demand (cross-price elasticity)
The (relative) change in percentage terms of the quantity demanded of a specific product in relation to (= divided by) the (relative) change in price of a competing product in percentage terms. If the cross-price elasticity is greater than 0, then it is concerned with substitutes (the quantity asked for decreases when the price of a competing product declines). If this is less than 0, then it concerns the complementary products (the quantity of a product asked for rises, if the price of the competing product falls). If the cross-price elasticity equals 0 then it concerns indifferent products (do not have anything to do with each other).

current capacity utilization (actual capacity utilization)
The real utilization of the production capacity. *See also:* degree of actual capacity utilization.

customer-oriented pricing (demand-oriented pricing)
Method of pricing based on the prices which the (potential) consumers are prepared to pay for the product, taking into account the psychological aspects of the price. (Examples: bait pricing, inverse pricing, odd end prices, perceived value pricing, price differentiation, price discrimination, psychological pricing.) *See also:* price behaviour, price perception.

degree of actual capacity utilization
Ratio in percentage terms between the actual utilization and the maximum utilization of a production unit (machine or man capacity).

demand curve
Graphical display of different quantities of a specific product or a specific product group which will be demanded at different prices at a specific moment in a specific market (by a specific group of potential buyers). In general, the demand curve shows a declining tendency. At higher prices there is less demand than at lower prices.

differential cost-price
Cost-price which is charged on the basis of the extra costs (of production, and sales) which have to be made to be able to supply the product. *See also:* marginal costs.

differentiation value
In the framework of the economic value analysis, a calculation of the cost advantages, or disadvantages, linked to the purchase, and the use of a different product than has been bought or used so far. Example: purchasing an energy-saving light bulb saves on electricity consumption, but causes costs because other sockets may have to be mounted.

difficult comparison effect
Factor affecting the price sensitivity of the consumers, and which is caused by the difficult comparability of usually technically complex products. As the product specifications become more technical, and more complex, the (not so knowledgeable) consumers will find it more difficult to compare substitutes. Therefore their price sensitivity decreases.

direct costing method (differential approach, variable cost calculation)
Cost calculation in which the variable costs only are differentiated by a cost unit (for example, a product). The constant costs are not allocated to separate cost units, but will jointly be charged to the profit and loss account.

direct costs
Costs which are allocated directly to the production or sale of a specific product. *See also:* variable costs.

direct price change
(Openly or secretly) changing the price or value ratio of a specific product by changing (one of) the price components. For example, (openly) changing the price, but also changing the discounts, margins, and terms of payment. Thus, a producer or a supplier may henceforth allow 1 per cent discount or require cash payment, rather than, for example,

allowing 2 per cent discount for payment within ten days. In such a case there is a disguised (direct) price rise.

discontinuous decline in demand
Irregular decline in the demand curve resulting from price thresholds as a result of which some parts of the demand curve are more price elastic (horizontally), and other parts are more price inelastic (vertically). In the more horizontal parts of the curve, the quantity demanded is influenced more strongly by price changes than in the more vertical parts.

discount (rebate)
Reduction of the normal selling price or list price.

discount-pricing
Method of consumer and competition-oriented pricing in which, for a specific product, a (slightly) lower price is asked than is done by the market leader.

down-grading
Consciously decreasing the service and/or quality level of a product, assortment or shop formula, for example, by lowering the quality of the supply, cutting down on the lay-out, and lowering prices.

dual pricing (staged pricing)
System of pricing in which in addition to a fixed amount (due once or periodically) a contribution per unit or per usage is charged. For example, in addition to the membership fee of the library, a contribution is charged per book borrowed, or in addition to the admission fee to a discotheque an amount per drink.

dumping
Competition or cost-oriented pricing in which a specific supplier markets his products at a price which is substantially lower than the average market price. In some cases even, prices are used which are lower than the cost-price. Sometimes, this is done on competitive grounds, for example, in order to rapidly conquer a specific market share, or on cost grounds, for example, in order to increase the profitability or the cash flow at short notice.

economic value (replacement value)
The actual value of a means of production or stock, calculated on the basis of costs which have to be made to substitute the means of production or stock. This is the economic replacement value.

economic value analysis (replacement value analysis)
Analysis method in which an organization, from the point of view of a buyer, makes a comparison between the economic value of different products for that buyer. In doing so, not only the price differences are paid attention to when the article is bought (reference value), but also the differences in costs or values which the properties of those products mean for that buyer (differentiation value). For example: higher acquisition costs combined with cost advantages as a result of better efficiency or quality, or cost disadvantages, for example, as a result of (higher) switch-over costs.

economies of buyer focus
Marketing strategy whereby an organization focuses on only a small number of consumers (groups) using a limited number of products. Such a strategy saves on the costs of communication/promotion and distribution/sale.

economies of scale (scale advantages)
Cost advantages as a result of the size of the organization and/or the production machinery. The larger the organization, the production size, the lower the constant cost per product unit.

efficiency in transfer pricing
Pricing of (components of) products by the different departments in an organization or by different links in a distribution channel with respect to each other, with which, owing

to the eventual selling price an optimum sale or turnover will be realized for all departments, or organizations in question in that distribution channel.

end benefit effect
Factor influencing the price sensitivity of buyers which is determined by the extent to which a product together with other products materializes a specific desired end result. Consumers are more sensitive to the price of a product as this price constitutes a major part of the total cost to materialize a specific end result. Example: when buying a (relatively expensive) car, the buyers are less price sensitive to the price of additional products or accessories when these are bought simultaneously with the car, than when these were bought separately.

equilibrium price
The price which will arise, or would arise, if after the (free) operation of the market mechanism the size of the supply and the demand with that price are in balance with each other.

Every-Day-Low-Price strategy (EDLP)
Strategy adopted by retailers of offering permanently low prices as a matter of corporate policy.

expansion price strategy
A buyer and competition-oriented pricing when a new product is launched, where for one or more products a price is determined which is relatively so low that it enables the market share to be extended substantially. *See also:* penetration price strategy.

expected value method (expected value method)
Method of pricing in case of tender, taking into account the profit at different possible offer prices, and the estimated probability that at each of these prices the order is landed.

external cost efficiency
Bringing about cost advantages by careful selection and management of – external – relations with customers and suppliers. Examples: economies of scale by logistic integration, efficiency in transfer pricing. *See also:* internal transfer prices.

fair price
Price for a specific product which is experienced as 'fair' by buyers or consumers.

firm bidding
Submitting a (private) tender in which suppliers are not allowed to change their tender at a later stage. *See also:* tender system.

fixed costs (constant cost(s))
Production costs which, at a specific production capacity, do not vary with the size of the production and are independent. Often, these costs were made in the past or are still to be paid, even though the production has been halted (compare indirect costs). At a specific production size, these costs on an average are constant per product unit.

fixed pricing
Method of pricing in which a fixed margin of profits is applied on the cost-price for all products. *See also:* cost-price plus method, flexible pricing.

flexible break-even-analysis
Method whereby the potential result is calculated for a number of different prices. This is done by calculating the potential number of units of a product to be sold (resulting in the total profit), and the total cost accompanying the production size for each price.

flexible pricing
Method of pricing in which different margins of profit are applied on the cost-price for different products. *See also:* cost-price plus method.

forward looking costs
In the framework of pricing relevant costs which (will have to be) are made in the future in order to be able to launch the product, and keep it in the market. *See also:* avoidable costs.

full competition
Market form in which many suppliers offer the same (homogeneous) product. None of the individual suppliers is free to determine his own price. The (market) price is a fact for each individual supplier.

functional discount
Discount or extra margin for the trade or middlemen meant to have them fulfil distribution functions.

going-rate pricing
Method of competition-oriented pricing in which the market price, the average price level for the same or comparable products in the line of business are followed.

gross margin
Difference between the retail price and the variable costs (in the retail trade usually the purchase price) of a product or product group. The gross margin can be expressed in an absolute money sum or a percentage of the retail price. *See also:* contribution margin.

gross profit
Total profits minus purchase and direct production costs.

growth discount (bonus/premiums rebate)
Discount allowed to the industry or trade by a supplier or producer when the sale of a specific product to that company in a particular period has risen substantially. The size of the growth discount, may, for example, be linked up to the percentage by which the sale or turnover has grown.

harvest strategy
Alternative (price) strategy in the decline stage of the product life cycle. The organization withdraws from the market or from the industry, in stages and completely. The aim of this is to be able to use the means which come available for investments in other, more profitable market segments. The fields where the organization will withdraw first are the fields where it occupies a weak position. In this case the organization will operate a pricing of a kind in which the income is maximized. *See also:* retrenchment strategy.

heterogeneous oligopoly
Market form in which a limited number of competing suppliers within a specific product category each offer a type of a specific product. In this market form, each supplier has a limited freedom to determine his own selling price. *See also:* circular reactions, oligopoly.

homogeneous oligopoly
Market form in which a relatively limited number of competing suppliers offer completely identical products (homogeneous). In this market form, none of the individual suppliers is free to determine his own selling price. The market price is a fact for each individual supplier. *See also:* oligopoly.

horizontal price fixing
Agreements between joint suppliers (at industry level) to supply their products at fixed prices.

incremental costs
In a framework of pricing relevant costs which increase as a result of a price change. Usually these are the variable or the direct costs (that vary with the size of the production). Some constant costs, however, can also be incremental, for example, the costs of having a price list or menu card printed when prices change.

index of consumer prices
Measure to indicate the price development in one or more sectors. The prices are expressed in a ratio while a particular period is chosen as a basic period (then the index in the basic period is 100).

indirect costs
Costs which cannot (simply) directly be allocated to the manufacture of a particular product.

indirect price change
Changing (openly or secretly) the price/value ratio for a particular product due to a change of non-price components. For example, supplying (openly) more or less the same product at the same price, but also changing terms of delivery and sale (disguised).

integral selling price
Method to calculate the selling price of a product based on the integral cost using the cost-price plus method.

internal cost efficiency
Realizing (production) cost advantages with respect to the competition as a result of benefits of scale, product-portfolio advantages and/or the occurrence of learning/experience advantages

internal transfer prices
Fixed prices for products for internal delivery between different company divisions or company units.

introductory price
Price which is used when a new or rejuvenated product is launched.

inventory effect
Factor influencing the price sensitivity of the buyers which is determined by the possibility to keep the product in stock. If a stock can be kept of a product, the buyers are very price sensitive in the short run. By 'hoarding', a price rise can be avoided temporarily.

joint prices (price bundling)
Form of pricing in which complementary products (which have to be used together) are priced in relation with each other. For example, the joint pricing for the razor, and the separately available special blades for that razor.

leader (customer draw, bait, traffic builder)
Article in the assortment which is offered to customers, often at a very low price, to generate traffic.

learning advantages (experience advantages)
As more experience is gained in producing a specific product, the production cost per unit of that product will decline. As a result of learning/experience effects, it will be possible to produce quicker, better or cheaper.

learning curve (experience curve)
Graphical display of the decline of the production costs as a result of the occurrence of learning/experience advantages.

loss-leader pricing
Assortment price policy (in particular in retail trade) in which some articles in the assortment are offered at cost-price, or even below, as baits to increase the total turnover.

low-balling
Technique for behaviour modification in which a low price is announced for a product/brand and subsequently the price is raised after the consumer has become interested in the product.

margin
The difference between the costs, and returns in money or percentages (per product unit). The margin is mostly determined in the form of a mark-up in money or percentages (on the cost price, purchase or selling prices). The margin forms the profit of the producer or the intermediate trade. *See also:* gross margin, contribution margin.

margin generator
Article which has a relatively high margin for the producer or the distributor.

margin stability
The producer's or distributor's pursuit to maintain the margin fairly stable in the long run.

marginal analysis
Method of pricing in which, under the condition of profit maximization, that price is chosen for a product at which the marginal return is equal to the marginal cost (MR = MC) at that particular production and turnover size.

marginal costs
The additional costs as a result of extending the production with one (indefinitely small quantity of) extra product.

marginal return (marginal profit)
The extra profit result of the sale of one (indefinitely small quantity of) extra product.

mark-up
In percentage terms, (profit) mark-up on the full cost price of the variable/direct costs, to cover only the (gross) profit or the constant/indirect costs, and the (gross) profit, respectively.

market follower price policy (follow the leader pricing)
Form of competition-oriented pricing (especially in an oligopoly) in which the market leader's price policy is followed. However, this is dangerous as the followers are unaware of the market leader's cost structure.

market mechanism
The impact which price changes have on the size of demand and supply. In general, higher prices lead to more supply and a decline in the quantity asked for, whereas lower prices cause a decrease in supply and an increase in demand. *See also:* equilibrium price.

market share objective
Marketing objective to realize a particular market share or to maintain a particular market share (if necessary at the expense of short-term profit). Sometimes, this objective is also used as a price objective.

market share pricing
Pricing with a particular market share as an objective. *See also:* market share objective, price objective.

market zone
That part of the total market in which buyers have similar specific requirements with respect to the product quality in relation to the price, which affects the quality and intensity of the distribution required. *See also:* prestige zone, promotion zone, volume zone.

maximum capacity utilization
The maximum number of products that can be manufactured using the existing production capacity (capital and labour). The degree of utilization is 100 per cent. On the basis of cost considerations a standard utilization is to be preferred to a maximum utilization.

me-too pricing
Competition-oriented method of pricing in which the same price is asked for a product as the product which is used by the (major) competitor for that product.

minimum price
The lowest consumer price at which the retail trade is allowed to sell a producer's particular branded product. If the retailer offers this branded product below the minimum price he will be debarred from delivery of this product by the supplier. In many cases the minimum price is equal to the purchase price plus value added tax and costs the retailer incurs in the sale of the product.

monopolistic competition
Market form where a large number of suppliers each market a different but similar product. In this market form, each supplier has a limited freedom in determining his own selling price.

monopoly
Market form where only one supplier offers a specific product. In this market form, this supplier has a fairly large freedom in determining his own selling price. This freedom is limited by substitutes, by the threat of entry by other competitors, and by government intervention.

net profit
The total return less the total cost (indirect and direct, constant and variable costs).

net profit margin
net profit expressed as a percentage of the retail price.

neutral price strategy (normal price strategy)
Combined introduction and price strategy in a specific market zone in which the price right from the beginning is set at the eventual level (possibly combined with a short price campaign). Conditions in this case are: the consumers are of an average price sensitivity, there is moderate competition and the relationship between constant and variable costs is more or less equal.

non-monetary price
All sacrifices not to be expressed in money which consumers have to undergo in order to be able to buy the product. Examples are the distance that the consumers have to bridge, the time and effort he has to sacrifice (time threshold), and the fear or uncertainty he has to conquer (psychological barrier).

non-price competition
Form of competition in which the emphasis of marketing policy lies on other elements from the marketing mix than the price. There is a passive price policy.

odd pricing
Prices differing only little from each other, in an absolute sense, but which do differ much in the consumer's experience (subjectively): non-rounded prices like $1.95 or $3.95 create the illusion that they are lower than the rounded amounts of $2 or $4, psychologically it may be important for the buyer to make the purchase.

offer (supply)
The (written) offer of a supplier to supply specific products or services in which the price and other conditions/terms (of sale and delivery) are stated. *See also:* competitive bidding.

oligopoly
Market form in which only major suppliers offer a (homogeneous or heterogeneous) product. Depending on the degree of heterogeneity of the product, each supplier in this market form is more or less free to determine his own selling price. *See also:* heterogeneous oligopoly, homogeneous oligopoly.

one price selling (OPS)
System of price fixing, especially when selling durable consumer goods such as cars, whereby a relatively low retail price is used. This price, or the delivery of all sorts of extra accessories for the same price, is non-negotiable.

opportunistic price setting
Competition-oriented method of pricing in which an organization always lowers its price slightly earlier or increases it slightly later than the price of its (major) competitor. As a matter of fact, this is price competition. In each price change, attempts are made to do the competition out of a small piece of market share.

opportunity costs
The (calculated, theoretical) costs which arise because means of production are used in a specific direction. (Any) added return or profit in the use of these means of production for other goals is therefore not realized. This loss of return or profit can also be regarded as costs.

optimum price
In the framework of the NSS price sensitivity meter, the price for a product which is acceptable for a substantial part of the (potential) buyers. They experience that price for the product as cheap, fair or expensive. The remaining part of the (potential) group of buyers, however, resist this price because the one half of it thinks the product too cheap at this price and the other half thinks the product too expensive.

over-capacity
Too much excess production capacity means that actual production costs are higher in proportion to the percentage of excess unused production facilities.

overhead costs
Costs which cannot be allocated direct to the manufacture of a particular product. Usually it concerns the cost of (higher) management. *See also:* indirect costs.

overpricing (overprice setting)
The retail trade setting a consumer selling price which is higher than is desired by the producer or supplier as a result of the trade's tendency to charge higher margins in the absence of competition.

panel price research
Method of (price) research in which by means of (shop, consumer) panels the real price behaviour or the real sale is determined.

passive price policy (non-price competition)
The emphasis of the marketing policy lies on other elements from the marketing mix than the price. There is non-price competition.

pay-back-period
Period in which the cost of a particular investment (for example, the expenses for the development and introduction of a new product) is recovered by an organization.

penetration price strategy
Combined introduction and price strategy in a specific market in which the price for a product is initially set very low, and is gradually increased in a later stage (whether or not combined with product differentiation). Conditions for such a strategy are: very price sensitive buyers, many (potential) competitors, relatively low variable costs or large contribution margin.

perceived quality
The quality of a product or brand perceived or expected by potential buyers. In this case the price can be used as an indicator for the quality.

perceived-value pricing
Method of consumer-oriented pricing whereby the pricing of a product is based on the subjective appreciation of the (potential) buyers for the product benefits in relation to the price of that product and the price of competitive articles. *See also:* value perception.

predatory pricing
Competition-oriented method of pricing in which the price (whether or not temporarily) is set at such a low level by a particular organization that the competition runs into major trouble, or is ousted completely from the market. *See also:* put-out pricing.

premium pricing
Method of competition-oriented pricing in which a (slightly) higher price is asked for a product than is used by the (major) competitors.

prestige buyers
Buyers who buy expensive, prestige products in order to acquire status. Special attention is paid to the esteem that the product provides the buyer, and to a lesser degree or not at all to the price. *See also:* quality buyers, prestige zone.

prestige products (status products)
Products that are bought or used because they give the user prestige or status.

prestige zone
That part of a total market where the buyers want a prestigious, luxury product which is distributed exclusively or selectively, and is sold at relatively high prices. *See also:* prestige buyers.

price
The exchange value of an article or a service (product) expressed in a monetary price.

price acceptance
Indicates the extent to which buyers experience the prices asked for a product as reasonable. *See also:* price behaviour, price limits, price perception.

price action (discount action)
A temporary, short-lived action in which the supplier (producer or trade) allows a discount on the normal selling price to realize more sales with existing buyers and/or to induce new buyers to buy the product.

price as quality indicator
The price is often considered to be a measure (indicator) of the product's quality. So a high price is associated with a high quality, whereas a low price suggests a low quality.

price awareness (price consciousness)
The extent to which consumers or buyers are aware of the prevailing market prices for a particular product and in particular the degree in which they pay attention to the price when buying articles. *See also:* price behaviour, price perception.

price behaviour
Indicates the real behaviour of the consumers with regard to purchasing of products at specific prices. By means of (panel) research (for example, AGB-Attwood, Nielsen) price behaviour can be researched. *See also:* price perception.

price bundling
A form of consumer-oriented price policy in which the product and a number of separate, optional components of a product (which can also be bought separately) are supplied cheaper together as one (cheaper) package. *See also:* psychological pricing.

price buyers
Buyers who, when buying a product, pay special attention to the price of that product, and to a lesser degree to the (supposed) quality. *See also:* volume zone.

price cartel (price agreement)
Mutual agreements on the price policy by price suppliers in an oligopolistic market form, including agreements on the (height) of the price, method of price calculation, and discounts to be granted.

price competition
Form of marketing policy in which especially the price is used as a competition weapon. In this case there is an active price policy.

price differentiation
Using different prices (based on differences in cost price) for different models/types of a particular product.

price discrimination
Using different prices for the same product (not based on differences in the cost-price) in different markets (buyer groups, geographical places or moments) based on differences in price sensitivity.

price distance
The difference between prices expressed in money or percentages. *See also:* absolute price difference, relative price difference.

price elastic demand
The buyers react strongly to relatively small price changes: in terms of percentage, the quantity demanded changes (relatively) more than the (relative) price change in terms of percentages. The total return (TR) increases in case of a price reduction, and decreases in case of a price rise. The price elasticity of demand is then < -1 (or in an absolute sense: $> |-1|$).

price elastic supply
The suppliers react strongly to relatively small price changes: in percentage terms, the quantity offered changes (relatively) more than the (relative) price change in percentage terms. The price elasticity of supply is then > 1.

price elasticity coefficient
Number indicating the ratio between a relative price change and a relative change in the quantity of product offered or demanded. *See also:* price elasticity of supply, price elasticity of demand.

price elasticity of demand
The (relative) change in the quantity demanded (q_v) of a specific product in percentage terms in relation to (= divided by) the percentual (relative) change in price of that product in percentage terms. The price elasticity of demand, in general, is negative (lower prices lead to a larger quantity demanded, higher prices lead to a smaller quantity demanded).

Formula: $E^p_{q_v} = \dfrac{dq_v/q_v}{dp/p} = \dfrac{dq_v}{dp} \cdot \dfrac{p}{q_v}$

price elasticity of supply
The (relative) change in percentage terms of the quantity offered (q_a) of a specific product in relation to (= divided by) the (relative) change in price for that product in percentage terms. The price elasticity of supply, in general, is positive (lower prices lead to a smaller quantity offered, and higher prices lead to a rise in the quantity offered).

Formula: $E^p_{q_a} = \dfrac{dq_a/q_a}{dp/p} = \dfrac{dq_a}{dp} \cdot \dfrac{p}{q_a}$

price inelastic demand
There are limited reactions of suppliers to relatively large price changes: in terms of percentages the quantity offered changes (relatively) less than the (relative) price change, in terms of percentages. The total return (TR) falls in the case of a price reduction and rises in the case of a price rise. The price elasticity of demand lies between 0 and -1.

price inelastic supply
There are limited reactions of suppliers to relatively large price changes: in terms of percentages the quantity offered changes (relatively) less than the (relative) price change, in terms of percentages. The price inelastic supply lies between 0 and $+1$.

price instrument
Means which can be used to influence the price/value ratio of the exchange object for the consumers, as a component of the marketing policy. Within the price instruments, the following instruments may be distinguished: the ex-works price, contribution margin, retail and wholesale margins, trade discounts, consumer price, consumer discounts, list prices, offer prices, rebates, bonuses, credit allowances and cash discounts, and the tender price.

price knowledge (price familiarity)
The extent to which (potential) buyers (think they) are familiar with the different prices which are used for the brand or product researched, and for the different competing brands or products. *See also:* price behaviour, price perception.

price leader
A supplier in the market who (usually in a oligopoly) has a relatively large influence on the price policy of the remaining suppliers. Often, the price policy of the price leader is followed (at a distance) by the other suppliers. *See also:* competition-oriented pricing, market follower price policy.

price limits
The two extreme prices which are still acceptable for buyers of a product. At higher prices the product is thought too expensive and at lower prices the quality of the product is not trusted any more. *See also:* price acceptance, price as quality indicator.

price mechanism
Phenomenon that higher prices, in general, lead to a decrease in the quantity demanded, and an increase in the quantity supplied, and, vice versa, that lower prices, in general, lead to an increase in the quantity demanded, and a decrease in the quantity supplied. To a larger or lesser extent, the price height, and the price fluctuations determine both the size of the quantity demanded and the size of the quantity supplied. *See also:* market mechanism.

price mix
Factual application, combination, fine tuning of the price instruments for a specific target group by a specific organization.

price objective
Objective for price policy indicating what the organization wants to accomplish with the pricing for different products. In this case a distinction can be made between pure price objectives, such as price perception or price behaviour, and impure price objectives, such as (margin of) profit, return, turnover, market share.

price offer
(Temporarily) offering to buyers a product at a lower price, for example, by marking down articles as follows: 'was $20, now $17.50' or 'get 3, pay 2', or delivering more product, extra service or better terms of sale payment for the same price, for example, 'now 50 grammes extra for the same price' etc.

price perception
The subjective appreciation or experience of the price (height) which comprises such elements as price knowledge, price acceptance, and price sensitivity. Price perception is decisive for price behaviour.

price policy
Analysis, planning, implementation, and evaluation of activities with regard to the price instruments as components of marketing policy.

price/quality buyers
Buyers who, when buying a product, pay special attention to the price in relation to the (supposed) – objective – quality of that product: they want 'value for money'.

price/quality effect
Factor influencing the price sensitivity of the buyers which is determined by the (supposed) relationship between the price for a product and the – objective – quality. As the (supposed) product quality is higher, the buyers tend to become less price sensitive. But also: as the price is higher, a higher – objective – product quality is assumed, and the buyers are less price sensitive.

price/quality relationship (price/performance ratio)
The ratio between the price of a product, and the – objective – product quality.

price regulations
The phenomenon that joint producers, or the trade, voluntarily or due to government regulations, limit the freedom in price policy with regard to the height of the price or other (price) conditions.

price research
Internal and/or external research which an organization carries out itself or has carried out to support the price strategy and the price policy to be executed.

price rigidity
Situation of very stable actual (market) prices, occurring in an oligopoly as a result of circular reactions to be expected from the competitors, and the consequently 'bent' course of the individual sales curve for each supplier in this market.

price sensitivity
Indicates to what extent buyers react to price changes. *See also:* price elastic demand, price behaviour, price perception.

price setting (pricing)
Determining the level of the price, the height of the price, and the additional implementation of the price policy within a price strategy chosen.

price stability
The producer's or supplier's pursuit to maintain a fairly constant price in the long run.

price strategy
The part strategy of the marketing strategy relating to the marketing variable price. Relates to the general price level, the introduction strategy, and either price competition or price stability.

price threshold (threshold price)
Price at which a specific product is in relatively slow demand. At a price immediately below (or above) the price threshold, relatively more is sold. *See also:* odd pricing, psychological pricing.

price/value relationship (ratio)
The relationship between the price of a product and the subjective appreciation of the benefits which this product has for the buyer. *See also:* value perception.

price-lining
Form of product line pricing in which the entire assortment is offered under a limited number of price levels. *See also:* product line pricing.

price-list
List of the prevailing prices for the various products marketed by an organization. *See also:* catalogue price.

price-off (price offer campaign)
Temporary discount allowed by a producer or retailer during a specific promotional campaign in order to stimulate the sale of a product.

price-trade-off research
Method of price research in which the interest of different, separate product qualities and product benefits are tested in relation to different possible prices.

product introduction strategy
The marketing strategy and the (price) strategy connected with it which is used when a (new or renewed) product is launched.

product line pricing (full-line pricing)
Form of product line pricing in which the different parts of the assortment which belong together in some way or other (on the basis of consumption and/or use relationship) are priced in relation with each other. The aim is to accomplish the largest possible sale of, or profit on the entire assortment rather than on separate products in the assortment.

productivity strategy
Method of cost saving in which, with unaltered costs, more is produced.

profit
Increase of the net capital caused by operational activities. In accountancy terms the profit can be calculated from the profit and loss account, as the balance of turnover and costs over a specific period. From the balance sheet the profit can be determined on the basis of the increase in the size of the net worth in a specific period, corrected for other acquisitions or redemptions of capital. In a business economics sense there are several valuation standards to calculate the profit.

profit maker
Article which, due to a relatively large sale, possibly in combination with a relatively high margin, makes a major contribution to the (gross) profit of the (distributive) trade.

profit margin
The gross or net profit per product unit expressed in money or in percentages.

promotion discount
Discount granted to the trade by a supplier or producer. In fact this is not a real discount. It is about partially or entirely contributing to the cost of promotional material of the trade for the product in question.

promotion zone
That part of the market where buyers (price/quality buyers) want a product of an average quality at a reasonable price, whereas this product is selectively and intensively distributed.

psychological pricing
Determining selling prices, taking into account the different psychological aspects of the price. *See also:* odd pricing, price bundling.

public tender (system/open)
Publicly announcing and inviting producers or suppliers to submit their tenders.

put-out pricing
Competition-oriented method of pricing in which the price is (temporarily) set so low that the competition is ousted from the market. This is equivalent to 'dumping' but if the intended effect is to oust a competitor it is predatory pricing.

quality buyers
Consumers who, when buying a product, pay close attention to the (alleged) good quality of it. *See also:* prestige buyers.

quantity discount
Discount granted by the producer or supplier to the industry, or trade, on the basis of order size. The larger the order, the higher the discount.

recommended prices (list prices)
The retail price desired by the producer which the retail trade is recommended to charge.

recommended resale price (RRP)

The price that the producer charges to his buyers for his product but which may be discounted by intermediaries in the distribution channel.

reference price

A perception existing with consumers or buyers about the acceptable price (height) for a specific product with which perceived prices (of competing products) are compared. *See also:* fair price.

reference value

Concept essential in the economic value analysis relating to the buying price of that product which a consumer considers the best conceivable alternative for the product he uses now. The reference value is equal to the buying price of this alternative, possibly corrected for differences in quantity used.

refund campaign

A promotional action or price campaign (usually in combination with a coupon or mailing campaign) in which the end consumer can receive directly from the producer or the wholesaler a price discount or a compensation in money.

relative break-even sales change/or per cent

Calculation method of the required increase or decrease of the manufacture, and sale, in percentages, in order to reach a break-even point again after a price change.

relative price change/or per cent

Change in prices, expressed in percentages. *See also:* absolute price change.

relative price difference/or per cent

Difference in prices, expressed in percentages. *See also:* absolute price difference.

replacement costs

Costs which have to be made to replace means of production or stocks.

retail contribution margin

Compensation (in money or percentages) the retail trade charges on the purchase prices or the selling prices (exclusive of VAT) of a particular product or particular product group.

retrenchment strategy

Alternative (price) strategy in the decline stage of the product life cycle. The organization withdraws entirely or partly from a number of markets or market segments in order to be able to focus on those markets or market segments where the position of the organization is stronger.

return on investment (ROI)

(In terms of percentages,) the ratio between the returns of the net assets or loan capital invested in an organization, and the net assets or loan capital.

returns objective

Organization objective to accomplish a preset return on the (invested, net or loan) capital. Sometimes, this objective is also used as (non-pure) price objective. *See also:* price objective.

reverse pricing (end-price-minus method)

A consumer-oriented method of pricing in which the producer selling price is calculated by backward calculation from the consumer price wanted, the prices charged by the competitors or the price which is viable in the market, taking into account the normal wholesale or retail margins.

sales price (selling price)

The price at which a particular product or a particular service is bought by a producer or the trade.

sales response

The response of consumers to the application of one or more marketing variables, i.e. the price, measured in terms of purchasing intention or factual purchasing behaviour. It is indicated how many consumers (say they will) buy a product at different prices.

sales response curve

Graphical display of the quantities of a specific product which could be sold at different prices by an individual organization to a specific group of consumers (under unchanging conditions). In general, the sales response curve shows a descending tendency when prices are indicated on the vertical axis and quantities are indicated on the horizontal axis. In the case of higher prices the quantity which can be sold will be lower than in the case of lower prices.

sales response research

Method of research in which the reaction of consumers is measured on one or more marketing variables, in this case the price. It is researched how many buyers (will) buy a product, or not, at different prices.

sealed bid (closed offer)

Issuing offers in public tender, which offers are opened, and made public simultaneously.

seasonal price reduction

Discount granted by a supplier or producer to the industry or distributors in order to accomplish a (better) spread of the sale in time of a specific seasonal product.

sequential penetration strategy

Combined introduction-price strategy in a particular market or market zone in which the price for a product is, initially, set low to attract the most price sensitive consumers. Subsequently, in combination with product differentiation (product replacing or assortment stretching) the price is set higher to attract the less sensitive buyers.

shared cost effect

The influence brought about by the fact that a buyer contributes only partially to the price. As the part that the buyer has to pay for a product is smaller in relation to the total price of that product, his price sensitivity will decrease. For example: being less price sensitive if the restaurant bill is paid jointly, or less sensitive to the cost of illnesses which is (completely or partly) paid by an insurance company.

simulation method

Method of market research in which it is tried to simulate the normal, real purchasing situation as closely as possible.

simulation test markets

In different shops (test markets) elements of the marketing mix or combinations of it are tried out (products, prices, packaging, communication).

skimming price strategy

Combined introduction-price strategy in a particular market or market zone in which the price for a product is, initially, set high to attract the least price sensitive consumers. Conditions for such a strategy are: few price-sensitive buyers, little competition in the introduction period, relatively high variable costs (or small contribution margin).

special deal

Discount on the normal selling price granted by a producer or supplier to the trade, which in fact is not a real discount. In particular, it concerns here support in the costs in the shop layout, supplying material for the shelf layout or extra display material.

standard cost price

The cost price at a standard utilization of the production capacity, usually about 80 per cent of the total production capacity.

substitute awareness effect
Factor influencing the price sensitivity of the buyers, and which is determined by the degree in which the buyers are aware of the substitutes offered in the market. As buyers are more aware of, and have more knowledge of (potential) substitutes, their price sensitivity is greater.

substitutes
Products that on the basis of consumption and/or use relationship could be each other's competitors, or identical products of competing suppliers.

sunk costs
In the framework of pricing, costs which are not considered relevant. These costs were made in the past, and in that sense are lost.

sunk investment effect
Influence on the price sensitivity of the consumers of investments made in the past. The bigger the sunk investment, the less price sensitive the consumers are for the current (then relatively low) costs of maintenance or repair.

sunk investments
Investments which were made in the past. For a part these expenses are sunk costs, sometimes another part may (still) be considered avoidable costs.

tender system (competitive bidding)
Method of pricing in which suppliers can submit a tender to supply a specific product to particular specifications. The offer includes the prices and other terms and conditions of the delivery. *See also:* competitive bidding.

test market method
Method of market research applicable for price policy in which by means of total measurement (complete test market), or partial measurement using a random sample (limited test market) the sales possibilities at different prices are researched.

total constant costs (total fixed costs)
All production costs that, at a specific production capacity, do not vary with the size of the production, and so are independent of the actual size of the production. Often, these costs were made in the past or have yet to be paid, even though the production has been halted (compare indirect cost). At a specific production size, on an average these costs are constant per product unit. *See also:* overhead costs.

total costs (full costs, costs)
The joint (production) costs comprising the sum of the joint constant and the joint variable costs, or the joint indirect and direct costs.

total expenditure effect
Factor influencing the price sensitivity of consumers which is determined by the relative (large) size of expenditure for a specific product, both in money as in terms of percentages of the income. The larger the expenditure on a product, the more benefits a consumer may obtain if he can buy this product at a cheaper price from a competing supplier. So the buyer is more price sensitive as the purchase price of a product is higher and this covers a relatively large part of the income (extensive inquiry, familiarizing and comparing).

total returns (turnover)
All returns from the sale of a specific product, or the number of products sold multiplied by the return price.

total variable costs
All production costs which, at a specific production capacity, vary along with the size of the production, and so are dependent on the actual size of it. Often, these costs can be directly allocated to separate products. The variable costs tend to proceed to zero when the production is halted. *See also:* direct costs.

trade discounts
Discounts which are granted to the trade to reward cost savings, stimulus to increase the turnover or the sale, or to give a direction to the sale or to influence the way they fill their functions and their performances (directional discount).

turnover bonus
Discount granted by a supplier or producer to those industrial customers or distributors who realize a particular turnover or sale in a particular period with the product of that supplier or producer. A general rule is that the larger the quantity bought, the higher the bonus received.

turnover generator
Article that generates much return for the distributors owing to its relatively large turnover.

under-capacity
Low capacity of the production machinery. The standard utilization lies substantially lower than the actual degree of utilization. Structurally, the degree of utilization is too high.

unique value effect
Factor influencing the price sensitivity of buyers which is determined by one or more unique qualities of a product which make this product clearly distinct from other products. As the unique value of the product is greater, the price sensitivity of the buyers is less.

unit or absolute break-even sales change
Calculation method of the necessary increase or decrease of the production and turnover in units, in order to return to a break-even point after a change in price.
Formula: Break-even sales change = break-even ratio × original sales.

up-grading
Consciously increasing the service and/or quality level of a product, assortment or shop formula, for example, by increasing the quality of the supply, improving the (shop) layout and increasing the prices.

value perception
The subjective appreciation of the quality (of the different product characteristics, attributes, advantages) by the (potential) buyers of a product in relation to the price. *See also:* perceived quality.

variable costs
The production costs which, at a specific production capacity, vary with the size of the production, and so are dependent on the actual volume of production. Often, these costs can be directly allocated to separate products. The variable costs tend to proceed to zero when the production is halted. *See also:* direct costs.

velocity of stock turnover (circulation rate of stock)
The number of times that the average stock of a company is sold in one particular period, for example, one year.

vertical price fixing
System of price agreements for products in which producers can enforce the retail price to be used by retailers.

volume zone
The major part of the total market, the mass market, where consumers pay special attention to a relatively low price in relation to the perceived product quality, and where there is an intensive distribution.

wholesale contribution margin
Margin (in money or in percentages) which the distributive trade charges on the purchase price or the selling price of a particular product or a particular product group as a compensation for the function they carry out.

References and further reading

Kuhlmeijer, H.J., *Prijsbeleid – Handleiding voor Studie en Praktijk*, Kluwer Bedrijfswetenschappen, Deventer, 1989.

Livesey, F., *Pricing*, Macmillan, London/Basingstoke, 1976.

Monroe, K.B., *Pricing: making profitable decisions*, McGraw-Hill, series in Marketing, Oxford, 1979.

Nagle, T.T., *The Strategy & Tactics of Pricing*, a Guide to Profitable Decision-making, Prentice-Hall, Englewood Cliffs, New Jersey, 1987.

Rogers, L., *Pricing for Profits*, Basil Blackwell, Oxford England/Cambridge USA, 1990.

Simon, H., *Price Management*, Elsevier Science Publishers/North Holland, Amsterdam, 1989.

8 DISTRIBUTION POLICY

Concept overview

ABC method
account management
account manager
administered marketing channel system
agent
Aspinwall classification
assortment
assortment building function
assortment consistency
assortment depth
assortment height
assortment length
assortment width
auction
availability
average turnover share

backward integration
breaking bulk
broker
buying share

cabotage
captive distribution
cash and carry wholesaler
category management
channel captain
channel competition
channel conflict
collection trade
consignment
contractual market channel system
contribution margin
conventional marketing channel
Copeland classification
copy
copy briefing
copy platform
customer service

dealer
dealer development
dealer support
differentiation
direct distribution
direct-product-profitability (DPP)
direct-product-profitability method
distribution
distribution analysis
distribution centre
distribution channel
distribution channel decision
distribution diagram

distribution functions
distribution instrument
distribution intensity
distribution management
distribution mix
distribution outlet
distribution policy
distribution position
distribution strategy
distribution structure
distributive trade
distributor
distributors-portfolio-analysis (DPA)
double target group approach
drop shipper
dual channel strategy

economic order frequency
economic order quantity
EDI (Electronic Data Interchange)
end user
European Article Numbering (EAN)
exclusive distribution

FIFO (first-in-first-out)
forward integration
franchising
full function or service wholesaler

grading

handling costs
horizontal cartel
horizontal marketing system

in-store communication
in-store promotions
incentive
indirect distribution
indirect long channel
indirect short channel
institutional approach
integrated marketing system
integration
intensive distribution
inter-channel competition
inter-channel conflict
intra-channel competition
intra-channel conflict
inventory function
inventory system
inventory turnover

jobber
just in time (JIT)

LIFO (last-in-first-out)
limited distribution
logistics
logistics management

mail order company
mail order sale
market coverage
market reach
market share
materials handling
materials management
merchandise display
merchandiser
merchandising
middleman
missionary salesman
multi-brand dealer
multi-channel distribution

normal inventory level

order acquisition
order keeping
order picking
order picking method
order processing
order size
order taking

parallel-import
Pareto rule
performance bonus
physical distribution
physical distribution management
point of purchase (POP)/point of sale
    (POS)
POP activities
POP display
prestige good
price distribution
public warehousing
pull strategy
purchase co-operation
purchase organization
push strategy

quantity discount
rebate system
reciprocity
reliability of delivery
retail
retail audit
retail marketing
route plan
route planning

safety stock
sales outlet
sales share
selection indicator
selective distribution
service distribution
service level
service merchandiser
service merchandising
single brand dealer
single channel strategy
sorting-out
speculative trade
storage method

trade margin
trade marketing
trading down
trading up
transhipment
transport system
turnover bonus
turnover share

Uniform Product Coding (UPC)

van seller
vertical cartel
vertical differentiation
vertical marketing system
vertical price fixing

warehouse
warehouse system
wholesale marketing
wholesale organization
wholesaler owned brand

Concept descriptions

ABC method
Article classification method in which products types or product goods in the assortment are subdivided into fast moving articles (A-articles), articles for which there is an average demand (B-articles), and articles that are in slow demand.

account management
Specific marketing approach by a producer or supplier directed at the (major) distributors (accounts) of his products. Due to increasing concentration, especially in the retail trade, the distributors' power and expertise, as well as professionalism have grown. As a consequence they know their own needs better and they are in a better position to enforce these requirements on the suppliers. This concerns such matters as delivery frequency, delivery time, whether or not prices are pre-priced, packaging, and promotional campaigns. In response, the supplier has usually appointed an account manager who shapes the policy with respect to these (major) accounts and coordinates the activities within the supplier's organization for those accounts. Policy making and coordination of implementation is what is usually meant by account management. *See also:* double target group approach.

account manager
The person who is responsible for establishing and implementing the policies for the (major) accounts. The account manager coordinates the policy and implementation in his organization with the product manager, marketing manager, and other account and sales managers.

administered marketing channel system (administered channel)
Distribution channel within which, on the basis of the power of one of the parties, there is an explicitly defined role pattern with regard to the functioning of the different organizations within that channel.

agent (commercial agent)
Independent distributor who, on a contract basis, acts as a mediator for one or more regular connections: he introduces connections to buyers.

Aspinwall classification
The Aspinwall classification is based on the time between purchases, the gross margin, the applications, the consumption time, and the search time. For each of these aspects, some goods are allocated a score. He distinguishes red goods (low scores), orange goods (average scores), and yellow goods (high scores). Depending on the scores, the various categories of goods gradually overlap (continuum). The Aspinwall classification in red, orange and yellow goods, to a certain degree, corresponds with the Copeland classification in convenience, shopping, and speciality goods, respectively. This holds good for their distribution characteristics as well.

assortment
The joint product groups, products, product types, and brands offered by an organization. The assortment can be described on the basis of a number of criteria, namely: the assortment width, depth, length, height, and consistency.

assortment building function (groupage, bulking, joint cargo)
Re-grouping delivered goods for transhipment to the next link in the distribution channel. Usually this takes place in a distribution centre.

assortment consistency
The degree of relationship between the products carried. The criterion for relationship may differ. One criterion, for example, is the relationship in use of the products, purchasing relationship, similarity in production process, and similarity in materials used. The more consistent the assortment, the bigger the probability that the buyer finds what he expects to find.

assortment depth

The average number of products and product types within the product groups of an assortment. The deeper the assortment, the larger the number of product types or brands.

assortment height

The unweighted average price level of the products and brands belonging to the assortment.

assortment length

1 The average stock of the products carried in the assortment.
2 The total number of products the assortment is composed of.

assortment width

The number of different product groups that make up the assortment. The more different product groups, the wider the assortment.

auction

Concrete market where goods (usually) in kind are supplied and traded under the management of an auctioneer. The goods or their samples may be judged by the would-be buyers. At an auction many buyers always face one seller.

availability

Degree to which consumers have to bridge difference in place, time, quality, and quantity in order to acquire specific products. Availability may be quantified with such distribution ratios as the distribution spread and the selection indicator.

average turnover share

The average of the turnover shares of a particular supplier with the different distributors or buyers.

backward integration

Type of integration whereby a distributor acquires the ownership and exploitation from a previous participant (assuming the physical product flow) in the channel.

breaking bulk

Breaking down consignments into lots/sizes requested by buyers.

broker

Middleman in the trade concluding a transaction (entering a deal) in his own name, but by order of a customer, at a reimbursement of his expenses, and a percentage of the turnover. At the same time the broker is in charge of all the additional matters such as transport and insurance. The broker operates as an independent person. There is no fixed relationship between him and the client.

buying share

Share (in money or volume) which the turnover/market of a supplier has in the total purchase of a specific consumer (retailer or industrial consumer).

cabotage

Within the physical distribution: using the capacity of means of transport on their 'way back'. For example: a retail chain delivering products at branches, collecting products 'on the way back' from a supplier.

captive distribution

Distribution situation in which the distributor does act in his own name, but given the existing balance of power within the distribution channel, complies entirely with the producer's wishes as far as policy is concerned. *See also:* channel captain.

cash and carry wholesaler

Type of wholesale whereby the customers have to retrieve the products from the warehouse themselves, have to pay immediately in cash (no credit facilities), and have to transport the products to their own business.

category management
Analysis, planning, implementation and evaluation of marketing activities by an organization with relation to (part) assortments or product groups. It is no longer thought of in terms of individual products/brands, but in terms of complete, consistent and coherent (part) assortments and/or product groups. When category management is used within an industrial column by both manufacturers and retailers, it can lead to closer attuning of (collective) marketing activities.

channel captain
Organization in the distribution channel carrying out activities in order to affect the strategy and activities of the other members of that distribution channel.

channel competition
Competition between participants within the same channel (intra-channel competition) or between different channels (inter-channel competition).

channel conflict (distribution conflict)
Situation within a specific distribution channel whereby the behaviour of one or more distributors conflicts with the interests of other distributors in that channel, or prevents these other distributors from accomplishing their objectives. In this case conflicts between participants within the same channel (intra-channel conflict) and between participants of different channels (inter-channel conflict) are distinguished.

collection trade
Distributor (wholesaler or exporter) buying (usually small) lots from different organizations, and thus building a supply programme which is attractive to pass on to the next link (other organizations, distributors, importers) in the distribution channel.

consignment
System of delivery and payment for products supplied by suppliers to their distributors. When products are supplied on consignment, this means that the distributor does not need to pay for them until he has sold them himself. Products which he has not sold are taken back by the supplier. In North America, book sales only become final two years after the book has been purchased by the store. Within that period returns can, and do, take place.

contractual market channel system
Distribution system in which, on the basis of voluntary co-operation, there is an explicitly defined role pattern with regard to the functioning of the different organizations within that channel. *See also:* vertical marketing system.

contribution margin (coverage contribution)
Selling price of a product less the variable costs. (Profit) mark-up (in money/percentage) which is supposed to cover the constant costs, and the profit (usually per product unit).

conventional marketing channel (classical marketing channel)
At least two subsequent, independent distributors fulfilling one or more marketing functions with regard to the distribution of a specific product.

Copeland classification
Copeland distinguishes different categories of goods on the basis of the necessity or the willingness of the consumers to make larger or smaller purchasing efforts to buy these goods. He distinguishes: convenience goods (products for which consumers are willing to make only little purchasing effort), shopping goods (for which they are prepared to make some purchasing effort, they do some 'shopping'), and speciality goods (consumers put in great purchasing efforts).

copy
Written and visual expression of an advertising message.

copy briefing
Detailed wording of the objectives of a communication or series of communications, with the intention to make copywriters aware of these objectives and to test various copy proposals using these objectives.

copy platform
Main theme of the text in a communication expression.

customer service
The value added to the physical product as a result of service support. Distinguished are pre-transaction, transaction and post-transaction service elements. Prior to the transaction, the service concerns the convenience with which the buyer can make the deal and the terms of delivery. During the transactions, the degree of service is shown by such features as reliability, keeping promises. After the transactions, the service is shown by the way maintenance and failures are dealt with.

dealer
Distributor of more or less durable production and consumer goods in the case of limited distribution (selective or exclusive distribution) by the producer. A distinction can be made between single brand dealers and multi-brand dealers.

dealer development
The producer's policy with regard to promoting the expertise and quality of selected dealers for his products.

dealer support
The producer's sales and marketing management support system for dealers of his products.

differentiation
An organization's moving activities and associated parts of an organization to independently working organizations existing at a higher or lower level of the industry sector.

direct distribution (direct channel)
Distribution type whereby the producer supplies end users directly, without using distributors. In that case both the wholesale and the retail trade are excluded.

direct-product-profitability (DPP)
Direct (gross) profit contribution/profitability per product/product group within retail trade.

direct-product-profitability method (DPP method)
Costing method in retail trade, whereby the corrected gross margin on a product/product group (= gross margin minus obtained discounts) is reduced by the direct distribution costs (direct costs of: transport, distribution centre/warehouse and the shop operation). This consequently leaves a contribution to the still not attributed share of the overhead costs and the company profit.

distribution
Bridging differences in place, time, quantity and quality for a specific product between various market parties. In the distribution process a number of different distribution functions are executed by different distributors. The distribution decisions within marketing especially address the question as to who will fulfil which functions (choice of channel) and how intensively the product has to be distributed (intensity of the distribution), which individual distributors will be selected, together with the way in which distributors are to be dealt with (push or pull strategy, account management). *See also:* customer service.

distribution analysis
Method to gain an insight into the way in which distribution takes place. Matters investigated include which functions are executed by whom and which path the flow of goods takes and also how intensively distribution is effected. The results of the analysis can be shown with the aid of a distribution chart and distribution ratios.

distribution centre (central warehouse)

Warehouse where, in addition to the storage function, also other distribution functions are performed. Usually, here grouping and transhipment takes place as well.

distribution channel

One or more distributors performing the same trade function within the distribution channel. Thus, the joint exporters form one link. This also applies for the joint importers, the joint agents, the joint commission agents, the joint brokers, the joint wholesale companies, and the joint retail businesses, respectively.

distribution channel decision

Decision on the length and composition of the distribution channel. *See also:* direct distribution, indirect distribution.

distribution diagram

Schematic display of the distribution structure in a particular area for a particular product using a flow chart.

distribution functions

In the distribution process the following functions can be distinguished: transport, storage, information supply, promotion, negotiation, ordering, financing, taking risks, payment and transferring ownership. Distribution functions can be performed using indirect distribution or direct distribution.

distribution instrument

Means that can be used to bridge the differences in place, time, quality and quantity of products as part of marketing policy, for various market parties. Within the distribution instruments the following partial instruments can be distinguished: nature, type, and number of distribution channels, nature, type and number of the separate distributors to be employed in each selected channel.

distribution intensity

The degree to which a product is available. Dependent on the efforts a consumer is prepared to make to obtain the article in question, an article should be available conveniently, at short distance, so in many outlets, or it can be distributed with a lower intensity. A producer or supplier can choose between intensive or limited distribution of his product(s). Within limited distribution, a distinction is made between selective and exclusive distribution. A measure of distribution intensity is market coverage.

distribution management

Analysing, planning, implementing, and controlling distribution functions. Major policy issues here are the choice of:
· the distribution channel and its length;
· the required degree of service of the distribution activities;
· the distribution intensity;
· individual distributors;
· how to co-operate with distributors (account management);
· a push/pull or combined strategy;
· the physical distribution method.

distribution mix

The use of stock levels, ordering systems, depots/warehouses, transportation, etc. to secure effective distribution of a company's products.

distribution outlet

Physical location from which goods are distributed. *See also:* distribution centre.

distribution policy

Analysis, planning, execution and evaluation of activities relating to distribution instruments as part of marketing policy.

distribution position
The position realized by a specific producer or buyer in the distribution channels, or by the different distributors with regard to the distribution of product or brand.

distribution strategy
Involves:
- the choice of the number of different channels with which the producer is going to or intends to maintain a relationship, or the choice for a single channel strategy, a dual channel strategy, or a multi channel strategy;
- the choice of the number of levels (distribution channels) in the chosen channel, or the length of the channel;
- the choice of the number of channel participants per level, or the choice for intensive, selective, or exclusive distribution;
- the choice for the service level of the distribution activities;
- the choice of the types of middlemen, or a choice as to what functions are to be executed by what middlemen; this is also to be considered a choice for shop type, shop concept and wholesale type;
- the choice for a specific form of collaboration between channel participants themselves, the organization form of the distribution channel;
- the choice of types and values of discounts granted to distributors;
- the choice for a push or a pull, or a strategy in between these two.

distribution structure
Nature, number, scope, and coverage of the various distributors in a specific sector or area with regard to all products or to a specific product. The structure can be displayed in a distribution diagram.

distributive trade
All distributors in the distribution channel(s) between the producer and the end user.

distributor (channel participant)
Organization filling a trade function in the distribution channel between producer and end user. This may be an exporter, importer, agent, broker, middleman, commission agent, wholesaler, retailer, or comparable organization.

distributors-portfolio-analysis (DPA)
Portfolio analysis whereby the relative position of the different distributors in the respective distribution channels, in particular the turnover share of the producer with these distributors and its developments are taken into account.

double target group approach
A producer's market operating strategy in which not only a distinction is made by different target groups of end users, but in which the distributors (wholesale and/or retail) are considered separate buyer groups having their own specific requirements and demands.

drop shipper
Type of wholesale with a limited function. With retailers, orders are collected which are then passed on to the producers. The producers themselves take care of delivery. So, the drop shipper does not keep any stocks.

dual channel strategy (dual distribution)
Distribution strategy whereby the producer uses two channel types simultaneously for the distribution of his products.

economic order frequency
That frequency of placing orders where the total amount of storage costs and ordering costs are lowest at the demands of reliability of delivery put.

economic order quantity (EOQ)
The number of products ordered each time, whereby the total cost of ordering, and total storage cost are the least at the required/pursued reliability of delivery. *See also:* economic order frequency.

EDI (Electronic Data Interchange)
Electronic exchange of structured and standardized data between the computers of, for example, the supplier, consumers and logistic service providers as a result of concluding and settling sales transactions.

end user
End user or final consumer of a product. Usually this term is used to denote the consumer.

European Article Numbering (EAN)
Standardized article coding (bar code), pursued by the European Article Numbering Association. *See also:* Uniform Product Coding.

exclusive distribution
Form of limited distribution whereby the market coverage is very low. Of the total number of potential outlets, only a limited number is chosen. The producer or supplier puts relatively high quality demands on the outlets chosen. On the other hand, the selected outlets are granted exclusive rights of sale within a specific area. The image and assortment of the outlet play a major role in the choice.

FIFO (first-in-first-out)
Stocking theory whereby the products which were stocked first will be delivered first. The FIFO-system is derived from a stock accounting system whereby the transaction profit is calculated on the basis of the assumption that the products received first are also delivered first.

forward integration
Type of integration whereby a distributor acquires the ownership and exploitation of a subsequent participant (given the physical product flow from producer to final consumer) in the channel.

franchising
A contractual agreement in which one party (the franchisor) sells the right to market goods or services to another party (the franchisee). McDonald's and Kentucky Fried Chicken are examples of successful retail franchising, the fastest growing form of retailing in America and gaining in popularity in the UK. The franchisee is usually given exclusive selling rights in a particular area.

full function or service wholesaler
Wholesale type whereby all distribution functions are executed, such as bridging time, quality, location, quantity differences and offering assortment, but also financing stocks, and taking stock, and sales risks, together with making contacts, effecting payment, and taking care of transportation of the goods.

grading
Trade function, whereby commodity products are divided according to (standard) quality and/or weight classes.

handling costs
Costs relating to the internal transport of products; both the cost of the physical acts and the associated administrative activities are considered to be part of it.

horizontal cartel (horizontal price maintenance)
Mutual agreement, usually with regard to prices, between different channel participants on the same level in a distribution channel.

horizontal marketing system
Distribution channel(s) in which organizations collaborate on the same level. The collaboration can take place on a voluntary basis or can be enforced.

in-store communication
Sales promoting communication for particular products or brands at the point of purchase/in the shop. For example, displays, advertising on shop trolleys, on/near the shelf, on video screens, and so on.

in-store promotions
Sales promoting activities in the form of selling out promotions or consumer promotions for specific products or brands at the point of purchase/shop. For example, special displays/offers, coupons, presents.

incentive
Reward for particular performances by channel participants. Usually this concerns a reward in the form of a present (a bonus, a study tour, a holiday trip).

indirect distribution
Distribution by a producer involving one distributor or intermediate link becoming the owner of the goods before the product reaches the final consumer.

indirect long channel (long channel)
Distribution by a producer involving at least two distributors or intermediate links becoming the owners of the goods before the product reaches the final consumer.

indirect short channel (short channel)
Distribution by a producer involving one distributor or intermediate link becoming the owner of the goods before the product reaches the final consumer. *See also:* indirect distribution.

institutional approach
Stream within the distribution theory whereby in particular the institutes operating within a distribution channel and their right to exist are taken into consideration.

integrated marketing system (integrated channel)
Distribution channel within which, on the basis of ownership relations, there is an explicitly defined role pattern with regard to the functioning of the different organizations within that channel.

integration
Adopting (part of) the tasks of a preceding or following link in the distribution channel by an organization.

intensive distribution (mass distribution)
Distribution strategy whereby the market coverage is very high. Usually, this strategy is used for convenience goods.

inter-channel competition
Competition between two different distribution channels, for example, between the long channel (such as wholesalers, and radio/tv-shops) on the one hand, and a short channel (such as direct from producer to audio/video discount shop) on the other hand.

inter-channel conflict
Channel conflict between participants of different distribution channels. Usually these conflicts are associated with inter-channel competition. *See also:* channel conflict.

intra-channel competition
Competition between participants within a specific distribution channel. For example, competition between radio/TV-shops. Using a system of recommended retail prices and minimum prices, a producer/supplier tries to prevent this type of competition.

intra-channel conflict
Channel conflict between participants in a same channel. This may be a vertical channel conflict, for example, between a retailer, and a producer, or a horizontal channel conflict, for example, between retailers. *See also:* channel conflict.

inventory function
Keeping goods in stock. A function of a distribution centre or warehouse.

inventory system
One of the three sub-systems within physical distribution. The inventory system concerns the size of stocks for each link in the distribution channel. *See also:* warehouse system, transport system.

inventory turnover (sales price)
Inventory turnover (at cost) of the stock at sales value. In formula:

$$\text{inventory turnover} = \frac{\text{purchase or selling value (sales value) of the turnover in a year}}{\text{purchase or selling value of the average stock in that year}}$$

jobber (trader)
Agent keeping products in stock, if necessary. Jobbers tend to be involved to sell parcels of products through distribution channels which are unusual in the branch.

just in time (JIT)
Distribution method aimed at delivering to the suppliers the required products of the required product quality, and in the required quantities, and at the very moment they are required by the buyer. Improvements are continually sought in order to simplify control, shorten throughput times, and reduce or eliminate stocks and thus costs.

LIFO (last-in-first-out)
Stocking theory whereby the products which were stocked last will be delivered first. The LIFO-system is derived from a stock accounting system whereby the transaction profit is calculated on the basis of the assumption that the products received last are delivered first.

limited distribution
Distribution strategy for which a small market coverage has been chosen. This strategy is especially applied to products for which buyers are prepared to make some purchasing effort, and whereby distributors are required to comply with quality demands. Within the limited distribution strategy, selective or exclusive distribution may be chosen.

logistics (business logistics)
All activities within the framework of the physical distribution of goods in the industry sector.

logistics management
Analysing, planning, implementing and controlling the flow of goods from original manufacturer to end user.

mail order company
Distribution channel whereby the buyer is contacted through catalogues and brochures. The buyer can place orders by telephone, in writing, or by computer, and in due course the products will be delivered to the required location (for example, to home). For up to eight days after delivery, the buyer has the right to return the goods if they do not come up to expectations.

mail order sale
Sale through a mail order company, i.e. type of distribution whereby the transactions and the delivery are realized at arm's length, usually telephone or mail. The goods offered are shown and described by means of mailings or a catalogue.

market coverage (sales coverage, distribution degree, distribution intensity, numeric distribution, unweighted distribution, unweighted market coverage)
Ratio indicating the intensity of the distribution of a specific product or brand by a specific producer. The market coverage is the ratio between the number of distributors of the branded article in question, and the number of sellers of the product class. In formula:

$$\text{market coverage} = \frac{\text{number of distributors of the branded article}}{\text{number of distributors of the product class}}$$

See also: intensive distribution.

market reach (effective distribution, weighted distribution, weighted market coverage)
Distribution ratio indicating what the relative position is of the chosen/involved distributors of a particular producer for a specific product or brand, with respect to all existing distributors of the product class. This indicates the share of the chosen distributors in the market. In formula:

$$\text{market reach} = \frac{\text{sales in the product class by the chosen or one's own distributor}}{\text{sales in the product class by all distributors}}$$

The market reach can also be calculated using the distribution ratios, and the following formula: market reach = market coverage × selection indicator.

market share (sales share)
Ratio indicating the market position of a particular producer or supplier in relation to the total market. The market share is defined as the sales (in volume or numbers), or turnover (in money) of a particular company or a particular brand, expressed in a percentage of the total sales or turnover in the market of all suppliers of that product. The market share can also be calculated using the following formula: market share = turnover share × market reach.

materials handling
Activities concerning taking delivery of goods, warehousing goods, storing, and associated removing activities, retrieving goods from stock, preparing goods for dispatch and dispatching goods.

materials management
Analysing, planning, implementing, and evaluating activities which are developed to drive the flow of raw materials, and semi-manufactures as efficiently as possible to and through the production process, and processing the associated flow of data, together with the tasks to bring about the most efficient usage of the means of production possible.

merchandise display
Stand, holder, drum, container or any other promotional tool provided to a retailer to draw attention to a brand at point of sale.

merchandiser
Function identification for a representative carrying out a, mainly, sales supporting task for the retailer, rather than a selling task from the producer. This sales supporting task includes all activities which improve a product's accessibility at the point of sale. *See also:* merchandise display.

merchandising
In distribution policy, all the activities at the point of sale developed by producer or wholesaler to improve the accessibility and availability of the brand.

middleman (intermediate) (intermediary)
Personal organization mediating and providing services in some way or other, in the bringing about of exchange transactions between suppliers and buyers.

missionary salesman
Representative employed by a producer or distributor (exporter, wholesaler) whose major task it is to inform distributors so that more points of sale may be obtained for the brand. *See also:* merchandising.

multi-brand dealer
Dealer who has obtained, usually exclusive, rights of sale from different producers, and for different (competing) brands.

multi-channel distribution (multi-channel strategy)
Distribution type whereby the producer has chosen for the distribution of his product(s) to involve at least two different types of distribution channels.

normal inventory level
The inventory level that should be available, given a demand which is assumed to be known, in order to be able to meet the demand.

order acquisition (order getting)
Getting orders in the building stage of a relationship with a new customer.

order keeping (order supporting)
Maintaining a good relationship with the buyer by developing different activities within the framework of sales support.

order picking
Retrieving from store the products ordered, and preparing deliveries.

order picking method
Guidelines according to which the products ordered are retrieved from the warehouse and are put together to form a dispatch corresponding with the orders.

order processing
The joint administrative and physical tasks performed by an organization to process an order. For example, taking the order by telephone, typing up the order, taking out the order form (in triplicate), checking the delivery note, packing the products, dispatching them, the internal check of the buyer's credit rating, and terms of payment.

order size
The volume and value of products ordered on a single occasion. This quantity can be determined for a particular period, but also for a particular group of buyers.

order taking
Taking down a routine repeat order for an existing customer.

parallel-import
Import of products through an unofficial or illegal importer.

Pareto rule
Rule of thumb assuming that 20% of the products in the assortment will take care of 80 per cent of the turnover. *See also:* ABC method.

performance bonus
Deferred discount, whether or not granted at the end of a specified period, on the basis of the extent to which the distributor in question has performed the distribution functions which belong to his task. Criteria used to assess the value of the bonus include:
· the distributor's attention for the producer's assortment
· the distributor's product knowledge of the producer's product range
· the distributor's willingness to co-operate with the producer.

physical distribution
Movement of finished products from the manufacturer to the user. This concerns such activities as internal and external transport, materials handling, storage and stock policy

with all channel participants. Within physical distribution, three subsystems can be distinguished, namely, the warehouse system, the transport system, and the stock system. *See also:* logistics.

physical distribution management
Analysing, planning, implementing, and controlling decisions with regard to managing the flow of goods between producers and consumers in such a way that the products arrive with the buyers at the right time in the right place and in the right quantities and qualities.

point of purchase (POP)/**point of sale** (POS)
Interchangeable terms denoting the place where the product may be bought.

POP activities
All activities at the point of purchase, i.e. sales promotion in a shop.

POP display
Display at the point of purchase, usually a merchandise display.

prestige good
Product which is kept in the assortment by the distributor, even if it does not contribute to the profit, because it is essential for the image of the organization in question to carry this article in the assortment.

price distribution
Distribution strategy whereby the producer selects only those distributors who are chosen for a low price/low margin retailing strategy.

public warehousing
A forwarder's contracting out of the total physical distribution, and the associated information function to a distribution organization specialized in it.

pull strategy
Combined distribution and communication strategy in which the producer communicates directly with the consumer, and thus builds up a preference for the brand. This stimulates the selective demand for this product by the buyers, so that distributors are forced, as it were, to include the brand in their assortment. Thus, buyers are pulled, as it were, to the channel, and the product or brand is pulled through the channel.

purchase co-operation
Horizontal marketing system whereby, for example, co-operating retailers, by bundling their orders, order direct from the manufacturer thus obtaining more favourable terms and conditions.

purchase organization
Purchase combination with articles of association and corporate personality.

push strategy
Combined distribution and communication strategy whereby the producer influences, in particular, the distributors, and stimulates them, with discounts, and support, to include, and promote the sale of the particular product or brand. The product or brand is pushed, as it were, through the channel to the buyers.

quantity discount
Discount on the basis of order size. More substantial orders receive higher discounts.

rebate system (rebate ladder)
Arithmetical rule to determine the amount of the rebate at the end of a specified period. The rebate ladder indicates what rebate percentage is to be received for what total quantity ordered in a specific period.

reciprocity
Situation in which supplier and buyer buy each other's products.

reliability of delivery
The degree to which a distributor or supplier lives up to the terms of delivery (speed, quantity and quality) agreed on.

retail
Outlet supplying products, usually in small quantities, to final consumers. It is the last link in the distribution channel.

retail audit (distribution research, Nielsen-distribution panel research)
Constant monitoring of a representative group within the retail trade, on the basis of which data on purchase, stock, sales and returns of different products or brands, insight into the size and structure of the market and the distribution structure those products or brands is obtained. This research method has been developed by Nielsen and is also called Nielsen-distribution panel research.

retail marketing
Marketing activities carried out by retail businesses.

route plan
Planned sequence to call on buyers, often on the basis of an optimation programme. In this way it is tried to increase the number of calls per representative per day, or to cover the smallest distance a day to deliver orders subject to the available capacity limitations.

route planning
Method to determine the (optimum) sequence of calls to be made, in order to enable the preparation of a route plan.

safety stock
Extra stock which is needed to absorb any fluctuations in demand. The size of the demand can never be fully predicted, but fluctuates, and because distributors usually want to maintain a particular level of service, this extra stock is necessary. However, only public utility companies need to supply 100 per cent level of service to customers. Others will adopt a 95 per cent service as being the highest commercially attainable.

sales outlet
Last link in the distribution channel created by the retail trade. The sales outlet is usually a retail shop.

sales share
Distribution ratio indicating which average share forms the sales of a brand/product of a particular supplier of the joint turnovers in the product class realized by that supplier's distributors. The sales share is a measure of the power which the supplier has with the distributors. A large sales share indicates much power. In formula:

$$\text{sales share} = \frac{\text{sales of the brand}}{\text{sales product class by chosen or own distributors}}$$

selection indicator (size indicator)
Distribution figure indicating whether the products or brands of a producer are distributed through distributors which are either relatively large, or relatively small in relation to the average size of all distributors of the product class in question. In formula (SI = selection indicator)

$$\text{SI} = \frac{\text{average turnover in the product group of the distributors of the brand}}{\text{average turnover in the product group of all distributors}}$$

The selection indicator can also be calculated using the distribution figures: SI = market reach: distribution range.

selective distribution
Type of limited distribution whereby the market coverage is relatively low. Of the total number of potential points of sale, a limited number is chosen. The producer or supplier

puts certain quality demands to the points of sale chosen. In the choice of the points of sale such considerations as the image, the size, the expertise, the location, and the assortment of the point of sale, play a major role. *See also:* exclusive distribution, intensive distribution.

service distribution
Distribution strategy whereby the producer selects only distributors who have chosen for a service retailing strategy.

service level
Degree of certainty with which it can be guaranteed that specific delivery requirements will be met. *See also:* customer service.

service merchandiser (rack jobber)
Person employed by/by order of a producer or distributors/wholesaler who, in addition to a wholesaler task (supplying products) also carries out retail trade activities. He advises the retail trade in question on the price and composition of the assortment, the shelf presentation, replenishes the stock in the shop, and takes care of the shelf. Service merchandisers are mostly involved when the retail trade is insufficiently specialized in the product group as far as the purchase or physical distribution field is concerned. *See also:* merchandiser.

service merchandising (rack jobbing)
Type of wholesale whereby a service merchandiser carries out his task. *See also:* service merchandiser.

single brand dealer
Dealer who has received exclusive rights of sale from one producer, and exclusively for products/brands of that producer, and also sells the products/brands of that one producer only. For example, a Fiat, Rover, or Peugeot motor-car dealer, a Benetton clothing shop. *See also:* exclusive distribution, multi-brand dealer.

single channel strategy
Strategy whereby the producer uses one channel type only for the distribution of his products.

sorting-out
Regrouping a number of homogeneous components into a large heterogeneous assortment.

speculative trade
Trade activities having as their only or major goal taking advantage of differences in price and price fluctuations for products in time. So, in speculative trade it is not about offering an assortment or bridging differences in place, time, quality or quantity.

storage method
Guidelines by which incoming goods are stored in the warehouse.

trade margin
Difference between purchase price and selling price of distributors.

trade marketing
A producer's marketing activities directed at (potential) distributors (retail trade, wholesale trade) of his products.

trading down (down-trading, downward stretch)
Expanding an assortment with relatively cheap products, so that the entire assortment radiates a lower quality, provided the price structure allows.

trading up (up-trading, upward stretch)
Adding relatively more expensive products to the assortment, so that the entire assortment radiates a higher quality.

transhipment

Physical distribution activities requiring many different forms of transportation, sometimes called intermodal transportation. It involves goods handling from road to rail to sea to air freight and consequent handling and warehousing costs.

transport system

One of three sub-systems within physical distribution. The transport system concerns the decisions with regard to whether or not transport should be contracted out, the choice of the means of transport, the loading of the means of transport, and planning the routes those means of transport have to take. *See also:* warehouse system, inventory system.

turnover bonus (cumulative quantity discount, rebate)

Discount granted later on, based on the turnover realized in a particular period. The bonus increases according to a rebate ladder. The period by which a bonus is calculated varies from, for example, a month (monthly bonus) to a year (annual bonus).

turnover share

Distribution ratio indicating which parts form the sales (in money) of a brand/product of a particular producer with a particular distributor or a particular channel of the total sales (in money) of that distributor or that channel in the product class in question. The turnover share can be considered a producer share in the turnover of his distributor(s). In formula:

$$\text{turnover share} = \frac{\text{turnover of the brand}}{\text{turnover of the product class with the chosen own distributors}}$$

Uniform Product Coding

Universally accepted coding of products (in the foodstuffs sector) complying with the agreements made in the Uniform Product Coding Foundation. *See also:* European Article Numbering.

van seller

Representative/salesperson calling on (usually smaller) distributors, and selling and delivering products straight from his van.

vertical cartel

Mutual agreement, usually with regard to prices, between subsequent links in a distribution channel.

vertical differentiation

Passing on an activity to a following or previous link in the distribution channel as done by a distributor. Usually this results in a longer distribution channel. *See also:* differentiation.

vertical marketing system

Professionally managed and centrally laid out network of organizations which jointly seek to acquire the largest market impact possible for a particular product or assortment. The market impact may be based on voluntary co-operation (contractual systems), on the power of one of the parties in the distribution channel (administered systems), or on the ownership relations in the channel (corporate systems).

vertical price fixing (retail/resale price maintenance)

System of price agreements for products whereby producers can enforce the retailers to charge a consumer price fixed by them (producers).

warehouse

Building in which products are stored. If the storage time of the products is relatively short, and the regrouping, and transfer function are substantial, it is called a distribution centre. *See also:* warehouse system.

warehouse system
One of the three sub-systems of physical distribution. The warehouse system concerns the decisions with regard to the choice of a location for a warehouse or a depot. *See also:* transport system, inventory system.

wholesale marketing
Marketing by a wholesale organization directed at the consumers (other distributors). In wholesale marketing the different marketing mix elements can be identified as the wholesale mix.

wholesale organization
Middleman between producer and retailer. As basic functions for the wholesale organization can be seen collecting and distributing. The distribution process, however, comprises more additions, and therefore more functions than the two functions mentioned above. On the basis of differences in the execution of the functions, the following wholesale types can be distinguished:
· cash and carry wholesale
· drop shipper
· jobber
· broker
· service merchandiser (rack jobber)
· full service wholesale organization
On the basis of the collecting aspect, an American classification has been made:
· general merchandise wholesaler (wide range of products)
· single line wholesaler (narrow assortment)
· speciality wholesaler (specific marketing knowledge) *See also:* collection trade, distributive trade.

wholesaler owned brand
A specific type of a distributor brand owned by a wholesale organization, and which is (almost) exclusively sold within that organization and/or affiliated organizations.

References and further reading

Bunt, J., A.R. Dreesman and C. Goud, *Dynamiek in de distributie*, Kluwer, Deventer, 1989.

Dikken, I. and H.A.M. Liesker, *Detailhandelsmarketing*, Wolters-Noordhoff, Groningen, 1991.

Peelen, E. and A.R. van Goor, *Customerservice als uitgangspunt voor het distributiebeleid*, Stenfert Kroese, Leiden, 1990.

Pelligrini, L. and S.K. Reddy, *Retail and Marketing Channels*, Routledge, New York, 1989.

Roosenbloom, B., *Marketing Channel Systems, a Management View*, The Dryden Press, Chicago, 1986.

Schuurmans, A.J., *Marktgerichte distributie*, Academic Service, Schoonhoven, 1991.

Ster, W. van der and P.J. van Wissen, *Marketing en Detailhandel*, Wolters-Noordhoff, Groningen, 5th edition, 1993.

Stern, L.W. and A.I. El-Ansary, *Marketing Channels*, Prentice-Hall, Englewood Cliffs, New Jersey, 1988.

9 COMMUNICATION POLICY

Concept overview

above the line activities
account
account executive
account planner
accountability
AD-VISOR
adaptation
advertisement response matrix
advertising
advertising agency
advertising agency billing system
advertising budget
advertising campaign
advertising objective
advertising plan
advertorial
advocacy advertisement
affect
AIDA model
art director
artwork
association
atmosphere
average reach
awareness model

below the line activities
billboard
block-reach
body-copy
brand awareness
brand positioning
briefing
broadcast ad
bursting
bus shelter
business magazine

campaign advertisement
campaign communication
campaign evaluation
campaign turnover
capitalized returns
carry-over effect
cash refund campaign
club promotion
co-operative advertising
collaborative advertising
commission system
communication
communication budget
communication capacity
communication instrument
communication mix

communication model
communication objective
communication plan
communication policy
communication process
communication strategy
communication target group
company bulletin/newsletter/magazine
comparative advertising
concept
concept development
concept test
consumer promotion
contact frequency
contact weighting
controlled-circulation magazine
copy test
copywriter
corporate identity
corporate image
cost-plus system
costs per thousand (costs/1000)
coupon
coverage
creative director
cumulative reach
current reach

DAGMAR
day-after recall
decay effect
direct advertising
direct mail
direct response advertising
display
dissonance reduction theory
drip strategy
duplication

effective reach
Elaboration Likelihood Model
exhibition
exposure
external communication
external pacing

FCB matrix (Foote, Cone and Belding matrix)
First Time Read Yesterday method (FRY method)
fixed profit percentage system
fixed-amount system
flexible profit percentage system
free publicity
frequency

full service
fund raising

generic advertising
global advertising
gross rating point
gross reach
guidance

house-to-house leaflet
house-style

identity
image
image building
image tracking
immediate response (to an ad)
impression management
in-store communication
incentive
insert
integrated communication
internal communication
involvement
involvement model

joint promotion
junk mail

laddering
Lavidge–Steiner model
lobby
logo

mass media
means-end-chain
media advertising
media buying agency
media commission
media mix
media plan
media planner
(media) target audience
media type
medium
medium reach
merchandising
minimum effective frequency
misleading advertising
mnemonic devices
multi-media strategy

net reach
noise

office income
opportunity to see (OTS)
outdoor advertising

pack shot
pay-off
perception
personal selling
persuasion model
point of purchase
position (to)
positioning
post-test
pre-test
premium
primary affective reaction (PAR)
print advertisement
product placement
promotion plan
propaganda
proposition
public affairs
public relations

ratings
reach
reach build
recall
recall research
Recency method
recognition
redemption
relationship management
repositioning
retailers' promotion
Rossiter–Percy model

sales force promotion
sales management
sales promotion
sales promotion objective
sales promotion plan
sales response model
sample
scanning and focusing model
script
selective advertising
self-liquidating premium
selling-in activities
selling-out activities
share of voice
source effect
special interest magazine
split-run test
sponsored magazine
sponsored medium
sponsorship
spot
Starch model

story board
sweepstake

tailor-made promotion
teaser
telemarketing
television sponsorship
testimonial advertising
thematic communication
top of the mind awareness
total reach
trade advertising

trade fairs and shows
trade promotion
two-step flow of communication

unique selling proposition (USP)

videotext

wear in
wear out
word of mouth communication

zapping

Concept descriptions

above the line activities
Marketing jargon meaning mass marketing advertising expenditures. *See also:* below the line activities.

account
All activities which the customer contracts out to the advertising agency. The customer is also called the account.

account executive
The person responsible for the coordination of all activities executed for a certain account in an advertising agency. The AE is also responsible for all communication between the account's co-workers and the co-workers of the agency, third parties called in by the agency such as photographers, directors, etc.

account planner
Person in an advertising agency attempting to link the briefing on the one hand, with the work of the creators on the other. Use is made of, amongst others, the knowledge the account planner possesses in areas such as advertisement effects and market research.

accountability
Being able to account for certain (marketing) activities by showing a relation between a certain marketing effort and its effects.

AD-VISOR
Type of post-test research into the effects of advertising. Memory, persuasive effect, clarity and originality of, and involvement in the advertisement are measured.

adaptation
Adapting a foreign advertisement for local use.

advertisement response matrix
Matrix in which advertisement effects are arranged along two dimensions, developed by Franzen and Goessens. The first dimension concerns the term in which the effects occur (immediately, short and long term). The second dimension distinguishes between psychological advertising and brand response, behavioural brand response, and market response (turnover, supplement and so forth).

advertising
Any communication which uses the media, is paid for by some interested party and is intended to inform and persuade.

advertising agency
Specialists in planning and handling advertising and sales promotion on behalf of clients.

advertising agency billing system
With regard to an advertising agency: the basis on which the advertiser has to pay the advertising agency for services rendered for example: 15 per cent fee, cost-plus system, fixed profit percentage system, flexible profit percentage system, and flat rate system.

advertising budget
Part of the marketing communication budget.

advertising campaign
Plan for a series of advertisement and associated expenditures for a specific brand or organization.

advertising objective
Derived from marketing communication objective(s) which may be related to generic demand, brand awareness, brand attitude, and purchase intention.

advertising plan
Derived from the marketing communication plan. Contains an analysis of, amongst others, the buyer and the product, the determination of the advertising target group, advertising objectives, advertising strategy, campaign development, media plan, and advertising budget.

advertorial
Advertisement presented in the style of an editorial text. As a result the distinction between advertisement and editorial contents becomes blurred.

advocacy advertisement
Part of institutional communication. Advertising expression in which an organization defends itself against existing, and especially impending accusations.

affect
Emotional contents of a marketing communication expression.

AIDA model
Classical hierarchic model on the effects of communication in which the customer goes through a number of stages in compulsory order before proceeding to purchasing. These stages are: *a*ttention, *i*nterest, *d*esire, and *a*ction. *See also:* Lavidge–Steiner model, Starch model.

art director
Position in the creative sector of an advertising agency. This creative sector consists of different creative teams of copywriters and designers (art directors). Together they work on the development of advertising concepts. The art director is responsible for the design.

artwork
Actual elaboration of the (outlined) creative concepts into reproduction material: photos, drawings and so forth. The artwork is combined with the rough drawing of the textual part into the final reproduction material to be printed. *See also:* concept development.

association (brand association)
Process whereby someone associates an object or brand with something else.

atmosphere
The influence created by a newspaper or magazine which impacts on advertising messages by them.

average reach
The average number of people who, at one time or another during a broadcast and/or placement are confronted with the communication expression.

awareness model (salience model)
Advertisement operation model based on a strong link between brand awareness and purchasing behaviour. Starting point is that the advertisement is especially aimed at attracting attention, and providing a topic of conversation. This model is particularly useful for describing and explaining the advertising effect of impulse products, new products to be introduced, and products showing little difference from alternatives.

below the line activities
A term used by marketeers to mean sales promotion expenditure.

billboard
Board on which outdoor advertisement posters can be pasted; usually in a place with frequent passers by. *See also:* outdoor advertising.

block-reach
Number of people (usually expressed as a percentage of the total number that could have been reached) who are confronted with a number of collective advertising messages (advertising block) on radio and television.

body-copy
Textual part of an advertisement (this is excluding heading and closing line).

brand awareness
The degree (measured in percentage) to which the target group is able to recognize the brand and/or characteristics of the brand within a product class. With regard to the brand name the following distinctions are made: unawareness, aided awareness or recognition of submitted brand names, unaided awareness, in which the individual reproduces the brand name on his own initiative, and 'top of the mind' awareness, in which a consumer spontaneously names certain brands first.

brand positioning
Positioning of a brand. *See also:* positioning.

briefing
Instructions in which the account informs the advertising agency about the product, market and organization, the target group, advertising objectives, proposition (main sales argument), guidelines for, amongst others, texts, visuals, design, media, budget, and time planning. The briefing is actually a continuous process. Apart from this external briefing there is also an internal briefing, namely between the account/strategy department and the creative department.

broadcast ad
Advertisements on radio and television transmitted during commercial breaks.

bursting
Placement scheme whereby advertisements are broadcasted frequently or placed together within a very short period of time.

bus shelter
Shelter at bus and tram stops with illuminated panels for outdoor advertising. *See also:* outdoor advertising.

business magazine
Magazine aimed at specific professional groups, branches and/or lines of industry.

campaign advertisement
Advertisement supporting sales promotion activities.

campaign communication
Part of the marketing communication mix, especially aimed at directly influencing behaviour. The communication is aimed at increasing the turnover by stimulating purchases. Sales promotion, displays, direct marketing communication, article presentation, packaging and personal sales are considered part of campaign communication. Direct marketing communication and packaging can also be used thematically.

campaign evaluation
Advertising impact research in which the effect of a (running) advertising campaign is determined in terms of awareness, attitude, purchasing intention, etc.

campaign turnover
That part of the annual turnover obtained during campaign period(s).

capitalized returns
With regard to an advertising agency: the number representing the relative size of an advertising agency, which is equal to 100/15 (of the 15 per cent arrangement) × office income. Has lost its meaning as, among other things, the 15 per cent arrangement is applied rarely nowadays. The capitalized turnover is not equal to the invoiced turnover. *See also:* office income.

carry-over effect
The phenomenon of previous advertising having a longer lasting impact than planned, as a result of which the effect of current advertising is more difficult to measure.

cash refund campaign
Type of sales promotion in which the customer will be reimbursed a sum of money after returning one or more product purchase tokens to the supplier.

club promotion
Form of sales promotion and direct marketing communication directed at strengthening the tie with current customers. Membership of the club usually brings along certain benefits which should lead to a stronger relationship. In the case of benefits, think of receiving free magazines, discounts, and information on events. For example: Sugar Puff's Honey monster adventures, and the M&S credit card.

co-operative advertising
Type of collaborative advertising of producer and reseller for the same product. The costs can be shared in different ways.

collaborative advertising
Joint advertising by several enterprises not directly competing with each other (i.e. textiles and washing powders). A distinction is made between horizontal combination advertising in which two or more organizations co-operate on the same level in the industry sector, and vertical combination advertising in which co-operation takes place between organizations on different levels in the industry sector.

commission system
Oldest billing system of advertising agencies. In this system the direct (creative) hours are calculated using prevailing hourly rates, purchase is raised by a mark-up, and the 15 per cent commission received on the media is supposed to cover the indirect (account) hours. *See also:* advertising agency billing system.

communication
Transferring information. A process in which information is exchanged between people, organizations and instruments. During this process a transmitter transfers information (a message) either directly or through a medium, to a receiver. The communication process is completed as soon as the receiver has processed the information in some way or other. In the course of the communication process, 'noise' may occur due to various causes.

communication budget
Amount allowed to be spent on marketing communication within a certain period; specification of the amount can be made on the basis of brands, regions, and media. The most common methods to determine the budget are: the percentage turnover method, anticyclic budgeting (changes in the level of expenditure are inversely proportionally related to changes in the turnover), the balance method, the parity method (spending runs alongside that of competitors), and the task setting method (the amount necessary to realize the communication objective).

communication capacity
Degree to which a medium is suitable for conveying a specific advertising message. The suitability is determined by, amongst others, atmosphere, communicative quality (movement, colour, sound, image) of the medium, confrontation situation (circumstances under which the contact is established) and the bond between the receiver and the medium.

communication instrument
Means which can be applied to convey information between sellers, buyers, and other parties. The following tools can be distinguished: advertising, sales promotions, trade promotions, consumer promotions, sponsoring, direct mail, personal sale, trade fairs, and exhibitions.

communication mix
The corporate communication mix consists of corporate public relations, internal communication and institutional communication, i.e. advertising and sponsorship. The marketing communication mix (at product/brand level) is composed of advertisements, personal sales, promotions, packaging etc. relating to the product or brand.

communication model
Model describing the working of (marketing) communication. Well-known models include: The Lavidge–Steiner model, the AIDA-model, the Starch model, the VOCATIO-formula, the dissonance reduction theory, and the Elaboration Likelihood Model. The first four are called classical hierarchic models, as the customer has to go successively through a number of stages (from awareness to affection, to action) before proceeding to buying. In the last two models this compulsory order is not present.

communication objective
Derived from the marketing objective. Description of the desired communication effects preferably in measurable terms of generic demand, brand awareness, brand attitude, and buying intention.

communication plan
Derived from the marketing plan. This plan deals with communication analysis, communication objectives, communication strategy, communication mix and communication budget.

communication policy
Analysis, planning, implementation, and evaluation of activities regarding communication instruments as part of marketing management.

communication process
Way in which communication is achieved. The communication process goes through a number of elements which can be arranged in a model. These elements are: the transmitter or source, information, encoding (converting information in symbols which fit the field of experience of the receiver), the message (encoded information), the medium (the channel through which the message is transmitted to the receiver), the receiver, decoding (process in which the receiver filters the information intended by the sender from the message), the response (reactions of the receiver after receiving the message), feedback (that part of the response noted by the sender), and noise (unforeseen interferences during the communication process).

communication strategy
Basic choice of how, when, and to whom which message should be conveyed in order to realize communication objectives.

communication target group
Defined group of people or organizations the message is aimed at. The target group may, amongst others, consist of current and prospective buyers, and 'influencers' who induce others to buying.

company bulletin/newsletter/magazine
Medium internal to the organization which is distributed free of charge to employees and those connected with that organization which is meant to inform and involve them in the organization.

comparative advertising
Type of advertisement in which two or more specifically named brands from the same product category are compared explicitly to one another. Is allowed solely when: a comparison is made with 'comparable' products, there is no question of misleading, the comparison is complete and objective, it does not discredit other products, and does not contain competing brand names. An exception can be made on the last point in situations where the message under no circumstance can be understood without mentioning competing brand names.

concept
Creative idea which forms the starting point of an advertising campaign or communication expression. *See also:* concept development.

concept development
Translation of the proposition into a creative idea (concept), consisting of subject matter, style, tone, words, and images. It is the broad determination of the message.

concept test
Research into the communicative effect of a certain concept in the communication target group.

consumer promotion
(Temporary) price/value improvement of the offer to the consumer. Usually aimed at increasing the short-term turnover by stimulating the consumer's purchases. In the last few years, more and more promotional activities have appeared which are not primarily aimed at increasing turnover, but at enhancing the brand image.
These consumer promotions mainly consist of rise in value or of rumour around the brand. *See also:* sales promotion.

contact frequency
The number of times within a certain period of time that the target group is confronted with the medium or the message. *See also:* frequency.

contact weighting
Measurement of the (absolute) contact frequency with regard to qualitative aspects such as wear in and wear out. Wear in causes the effective reach to increase after the message has been observed more frequently (weighting factor rises to 1.0); wear out causes the message to lose its effectiveness by abrasion (weighting factor drops).

controlled-circulation magazine
Magazine which is distributed free among a defined target group.

copy test
Research into the effect of the commercial message in an advertisement. Two forms are distinguished: The pre-test and the post-test. In the pre-test, prior to the start of the campaign, it is investigated whether the campaign appears to perform the communication task adequately. In the post-test, effect measurement takes place during or after the campaign.

copywriter
Position in the creative section of an advertising agency. The creative section consists of different creative teams of copywriters and designers (art directors). Together they work on the development of advertising concepts. The copywriter is responsible for the textual part of advertising.

corporate identity
The image of an organization.

corporate image
The collection of facts and perceptions by which an organization is known, and with which people describe, remember, and discuss this organization.

cost-plus system
The billing is completely tuned to the services rendered. All hours are calculated using the prevailing hourly rate (in which a mark-up, the so-called plus, is calculated), as well as the purchase including a mark-up. *See also:* advertising agency billing system.

costs per thousand (costs/1000)
Media costs per thousand individuals reached (in the communication target group). *See also:* reach.

coupon
Type of sales promotion. When purchasing the named brand, the buyer will receive the discount indicated on the coupon.

coverage
Number of people from the communication target group reached by a certain medium, expressed as a percentage of that target group.

creative director
(Management) position in the creative sector of an advertising agency. The creative director is responsible for the creative management of the advertising agency, and for the output of creative teams, the RTV department, traffic and production.

cumulative reach (cumulated reach)
The number of people (often as a percentage of the total number that could have been reached) who after several appearances or broadcasts have been confronted with the medium at least once. *See also:* reach.

current reach
Number of people who, within the publication interval of a medium, for example, a magazine, are confronted with the medium. Is important for time-based advertising. For example, an advertisement for Mother's Day is not relevant when seen after Mother's Day.

DAGMAR
*D*efining *A*dvertising *G*oals for *M*easuring *A*dvertising *R*esults. Model whereby it is assumed that advertising effects can only be measured if the objectives have been determined in advance. The model suggests that buyers will go successively through a number of fixed stages before proceeding to a purchase. Specific objectives apply to every stage. The stages are unawareness, awareness, understanding, persuasion, and action. *See also:* AIDA model, Starch model, Lavidge–Steiner model.

day-after recall
Research (by telephone) on the day after a broadcast and/or placement into the recollection of that advertisement.

decay effect
The effect of a brand falling into oblivion, if its awareness is not maintained by communication.

direct advertising
Advertising in which the advertisement is the medium at the same time. Opposite of medium advertising. For example: direct mail, direct non-mail, telemarketing, and sponsored magazine.

direct mail
Personalized mail message targeted at individuals sharing similar characteristics.

direct response advertising
Advertising in which the receiver is asked for a written, electronic or telephonic response.

display
Presentation of brands in such a way as to promote sales.

dissonance reduction theory
Non-classical model of the way in which communication works. A theory describing the information seeking and processing behaviour of individuals who have found their beliefs or attitudes to be in conflict with their experiences. For example: shortly after purchasing a product, because of feelings of doubt, the buyer will look for information convincing him or her that the particular buying decision was the right one.

drip strategy
Placement scheme in which the broadcasting or placement of advertising is spread out over a longer period. Often applied to prevent the product from being forgotten.

duplication
The number of people receiving advertising messages from more than one medium. Often expressed in a percentage: the number of people is then divided by the net reach.

effective reach
Reach figures corrected after contact weighting. *See also:* contact weighting.

Elaboration Likelihood Model
Model of Petty and Cacioppo describing the processing of persuasive communication. The degree to which an individual processes persuasive communication depends on the motivation and capability of the individual to process the message. If the message is processed on the grounds of contents and arguments, the central route is followed. The individual is then motivated and capable of processing the message. If the individual's motivation and/or capability are limited, the peripheral route is followed in which the individual mainly relies on the form aspects of the message.

exhibition
Showing products or services during an event specially organized for that purpose.

exposure
The opportunity to observe a communication expression. In English the term Opportunity To See (OTS) can be used for this.

external communication
Communication of the organization with individuals and organizations outside the organization.

external pacing
Circumstance in which the receiver of the medium does not have any influence on the speed and order in which she or he wants to receive the message. For example, via television.

FCB matrix (Foote, Cone and Belding matrix)
Classification of products by areas of interest such as affective versus cognitive values for buying decision, and the involvement of the buyer during the purchase. The position in the matrix affects the way in which the marketing communication is processed, and gives leads for formulating marketing communication strategy.

First Time Read Yesterday method (FRY method)
Type of reach research based on reading habits of yesterday. The average reach within a period of time is the sum of the number of people who, within this particular period, read the magazine, newspaper and so forth 'for the first time yesterday'.

fixed profit percentage system
In respect of billings an agreement is drawn up between the advertising agency and the customer regarding the net profit limit as a percentage of the capitalized turnover. *See also:* advertising agency billing system.

fixed-amount system
Customer and advertising agency agree on a fixed compensation as a fee per period. The media commission is settled on the basis of this amount. *See also:* advertising agency billing system.

flexible profit percentage system
In the scope of billing, an agreement is drawn up between the advertising agency, and the account on the margins of the net profit as a percentage of the capitalized turnover. An account does not need to pay extra afterwards, and neither does he have money

refunded to him when the net profit turns out to be within the margins. The aim of this arrangement is to stimulate the advertising agency to work more efficiently. *See also:* advertising agency billing system.

free publicity
Type of coverage in the media concerning companies, product or brand which is free but not directed. Free publicity is created by the medium (which therefore need not be positive), or can be stimulated by the source, by way of public relations activities, such as transmitting press reports and product information and holding press conferences.

frequency
The number of times the target group receives the message or the medium within a specific period. *See also:* media plan.

full service (advertising agency)
Organization where (integrated) communication advice, concept development, campaign production, media planning, and the purchasing of media can be found for a range of marketing communication instruments such as advertising, sales promotions, public relations, advice, and direct marketing communication. Usually off-shoots of advertising agencies.

fund raising
Activities of an non-profit organization to collect contributions for a previously determined goal.

generic advertising
Advertisement aimed at increasing the demand for the type of product, the primary demand. Often collective advertising. *See also:* selective advertising.

global advertising
Communication by an organization (multinational) for several countries, with more or less identical advertising insertions.

gross rating point
Medium/advertising reach measurement for radio and television. Is the sum of the number of people reached within a certain period for one particular type of medium, measured as a percentage of the full extent of the medium target group.

gross reach
Sum of the reach figures of different media. Double counting can occur as some individuals are confronted with more than one broadcast or publication of a medium, or with several media.

guidance
Assisting behaviour involving the conveying of information, usually with the premeditated objective to influence attitude and behaviour in order to contribute to the realization of certain management objectives.

house-to-house leaflet
A paper distributed free, which in the first place is an advertising medium, and in addition also distributes news on a regional, local or borough level.

house-style
Part of the corporate communication mix. External appearance of the organization that can be derived from, for example, logo, use of colour and typography.

identity
Joint permanent characteristics of a brand or organization, as seen by the participants within the organization. Distinguished are corporate identity and brand identity or personality.

image
Joint subjective images, ideas, feelings and experiences, imagined or not, by a person or group of people with regard to a certain object (product, person or organization).

image building
Adding and/or strengthening subjective images, ideas and feelings of a person or group of people with regard to an object (brand, product or organization) by way of marketing communication.

image tracking
Determining to which campaigns or advertising expressions certain parts of the image are to be attributed.

immediate response (to an ad)
Immediate reaction of an observer to a marketing communication expression. For example: attention or affection.

impression management
Analysis, planning, execution, evaluation, and control of the organization's performance with regard to groups of the public aimed at improving the image. Corporate image and brand image can be distinguished.

in-store communication
Collective name for marketing communication within the shop, both by the retailer and by the producer. Instruments include: article presentation, display, packaging, demonstrations, trolley advertising, and personal sales.

incentive
The prospect of a reward (in the shape of a discount or a gift, a trip or something similar) offered as an extra incentive for the buyer or salesperson. *See also:* sales promotion.

insert
Folder or reply card stapled or folded in a magazine or newspaper.

integrated communication
Integration of all forms of marketing communication by the organization across the media.

internal communication
All communication between individuals and groups of individuals within (the open boundaries) of an organization, usually aimed at promoting education, information, and motivation of personnel.

involvement
The degree to which a (potential) buyer expects that the choice and purchase of a product or brand will have major consequences and risks for him. The involvement is especially influential on the buying efforts which a consumer is willing to make. The involvement of the buyer can be influenced by the type of product, person and situation. *See also:* Rossiter–Percy model.

involvement model
Advertisement effect model whereby it is assumed that the receiver is personally involved with the brand (psychological brand response). Starting point is that the presentation is more important than the content of the message. Suitable for situations in which the expansion of the brand personality is focused on.

joint promotion
Sales promotion activity jointly executed by two or more organizations, and aimed at increasing the impact and/or distribution of costs. The organizations do not necessarily have to produce the same products, nor do they have to come from the same line of business.

junk mail
Type of unaddressed direct advertising distributed to everyone, door to door, with a possibility to respond direct in writing, by telephone or electronically.

laddering
Research technique used to devise significance structures.

Lavidge–Steiner model
Classical hierarchic model of the working of communication in which the customer goes through a number of stages in compulsory order before proceeding to purchase. The stages are: unawareness, awareness, knowledge, liking, preference, conviction and purchase. Before a customer proceeds to purchase, the marketing communication will successively have to change unawareness into awareness, awareness into knowledge, and knowledge into the different degrees of preference (liking, preference, and conviction) for the product. *See also:* AIDA model, Starch model.

lobby
Part of the activities of public relations and public affairs companies, exercising political pressure, often through personal contacts with politicians and other policy makers.

logo
A symbol which identifies the organization and can consist of a combination of certain letters, words, images, colours and illustrations, represented as one entity.

mass media
Non-personal communication, for example, radio, newspapers and magazines, television, cinema, and billboards (outdoor advertising).

means-end-chain
Systematic reflection of the way in which a customer experiences a product. Three to six different levels of meanings are distinguished. These run from product attributes via consequences to instrumental and final values. Consequences reflect the functional and emotional advantages of the product for the individual, the values reflect what people pursue or consider valuable in life. *See also:* laddering.

media advertising
Magazines, newspapers, television, and radio. Opposite of direct advertising.

media buying agency
Agency specialized in buying (on a large scale) media space in order to obtain better conditions for its customers and buyers.

media commission
Discount percentage of 15% on the publishing costs of advertisements, commercials etc. which is received by an advertising agency. This discount is often partly passed on to the advertiser. *See also:* advertising agency billing system.

media mix
Composition of media selected for an advertising campaign.

media plan
Plan in which objectives specify the selection of medium types, and individual media, usage of the media (colour, format, frequency etc.), costs budget, and publishing scheme.

media planner
Person in an advertising agency who decides which media are most suitable to communicate a certain message.

(media) target audience
Group of people the medium is aimed at. *See also:* communication target group.

media type
Visual media (for example, the press, outdoor objects, and direct (non-) mail), auditive media (for example, radio, telephone, and megaphone), and audio-visual media (such as television, video, and cinema) can be distinguished.

medium
Channel through which information is transmitted, for example, radio, TV, press etc.

medium reach
Number of people (often expressed in a percentage of the total number of people that could have been reached) confronted with the medium. To be distinguished from advertisement reach. *See also:* reach.

merchandising
Merchandising refers to efforts to increase sales of goods in retail outlets by the use of point of purchase displays.

minimum effective frequency
Minimum appearance frequency of a marketing communication manifestation, with the aim of changing the buying intention into a definite purchase.

misleading advertising
Advertisements giving incorrect or incomplete information so as to persuade either an individual or organization to purchase.

mnemonic devices
Characteristically distinctive elements in image and/or sound, which are quickly logged in the memory and aid in recall.

multi-media strategy
Simultaneously using different media types when transmitting a message in order to increase the reach, improve the synergy etc. *See also:* media mix.

net reach
Sum of reach figures of different media, corrected for double counts arising from the fact that there are individuals who will receive more than one medium.

noise
Disruption of the communication process. Noise can occur at different stages during the communication process and may cause the message to be disturbed and therefore misunderstood.

office income
Office income of an advertising agency: sum of media commission, the direct (creative) hours charged multiplied by the prevailing hourly rate and the mark-up on the purchase. *See also:* capitalized returns.

opportunity to see (OTS)
In marketing communication: opportunity to observe a communication manifestation. In addition this is also used in relation with products. *See also:* exposure.

outdoor advertising
Form of visual communication for commercial objectives using any object which is permanently outside. Examples: posters on shelters, lamp posts, vehicles, and billboards, as well as visual news, flags, and banners.

pack shot
Picture of a product and/or packaging in an advertisement.

pay-off
Closing line of an advertisement.

perception
Mental activity in which an individual selects, processes and integrates sensory stimuli into an experience or meaningful and coherent picture of a certain object or action. Perception includes the information processing stages of exposure, attention, retention and understanding.

personal selling
One of the marketing communication instruments. The personal contacts, without interference of media, between enterprises and their customers with the conclusion of a (sales) transaction as their final goal.

persuasion model
Advertisement effect model whereby it is assumed that advertisement primarily has a short term behavioural effect, often consisting of (experimental) purchases of non-customers. Secondly, it is assumed that a confirmation of the behaviour of customers is realized. The Persuasion Model, just like DAGMAR, assumes there is a gradual rational influence on the consumer. Suitable for products with a primarily instrumental function with problem solving qualities.

point of purchase
Merchandising display located at point of sale (POS) or point of sale (POS) which is designed to encourage impulse buys of the produce in question.

position (to)
Conscious efforts by an organization to accomplish a particular relative position for the organization, an SBU, a brand or a product in the perception of consumers, in relation to comparable competitors.

positioning
The position of an organization, SBU, brand or product in the perception of consumers, relative to comparable competitors.

post-test
Communication impact research in which the effect or result of a communication expression is measured after the communication campaign has started.

pre-test
Research into advertising impact in which the testing of the message takes place before executing the campaign. Is aimed at the question of how the message will come across, and if any communication barriers exist. *See also:* post-test.

premium
Unsolicited article, handed out or distributed to customers by the organization within the scope of a sales drive. The article does not need to be an example of the products produced or sold by the organization. There are also premiums for which the buyer will have to pay extra, if he wishes to receive these. The price will then fall below the normal selling price. *See also:* sample.

primary affective reaction (PAR)
One of the first stages during processing of marketing communication by receivers, in which communication expressions are judged on a broad and sensory level.

print advertisement
Advertising message in a printed medium, separated from editorial, in which the space is paid for and filled in by the advertiser.

product placement
Exposing a new product to trial in the market place i.e. by placing a new product in a retail outlet.

promotion plan
Derived from the marketing communication plan. Contains analyses, choice of target segment, objectives, strategies, actions, budgets, and time schedule with regard to promotion.

propaganda
Communication aimed at convincing the target group of the correctness of a certain point of view in the area of, for example, culture, politics, upbringing and religion.

proposition
Within communication policy, the description of the (main) advantages, i.e. the use of a product for the (prospective) customer. These may concern both the instrumental and expressive product aspects and the other aspects of product supply.

public affairs
Management function regarding social and political relations of the organization. In fact, part of (company) public relations.

public relations
Maintaining contacts with interest groups aimed at promoting mutual understanding in order to keep up or improve the market position. Distinctions are made between company public relations, and marketing public relations. In the former, the concept holds a central position with regard to the organization as a whole, in the latter it is limited to marketing activities.

ratings (viewing figures)
Number of people who have watched for a certain minimum part of a time unit on which a ratings report can be made. The smallest timed unit for the purposes of television ratings is 10 seconds. It is possible to get ratings from 10 seconds and subsequent 10 second breaks (e.g. 20, 30) up to 2 minutes which is usually the maximum commercial break.

reach
Number of people (usually expressed as a percentage of the total number of people that could have been reached) who are confronted with the medium or advertisement. The reach can be divided into medium reach, which describes the confrontation with the medium, and advertisement reach, which describes the confrontation with the part of the medium in which the advertising message is included. A large number of variations to measure the reach are known. The best-known and most widely spread are: Current reach, block-reach, gross reach, coverage, cumulative reach, net reach, advertising contact, effective reach, total reach and gross rating points (GRPs).

reach build
Pattern according to which the cumulative reach develops in the period after the appearance or transmission of a communication expression(s). Important to choose the right moment to measure the reach.

recall
How much consumers remember about advertisements.

recall research
Research into consumer recollection of an advertisement in both aided and unaided tests.

Recency method (Recent Reading)
Type of reach research in which the pictures of the title page of daily or weekly papers, magazines and so forth are offered to respondents. When the respondent recognizes it, he/she is asked whether it was read during the most recent appearance period; the person will then be included in the average reach.

recognition
Recalling information stored in the memory, for example, as a result of a learning process. One method to search the memory contents for the result of a learning process, is to determine what the individual has remembered (recollection) and what has been forgotten. With this method, the individual is offered a series of names, words and/or symbols, whereby he/she has to indicate which of these names, words or symbols have been recognized.

redemption
Number of coupons (as a percentage of the number of coupons distributed) submitted to the supplier.

relationship management
Analysis, planning, execution, and evaluation of activities aimed at establishing, maintaining and improving durable relations between the organization and the different market parties and interest groups such as suppliers, customers, intermediaries, shareholders and key figures in the social environment.

repositioning
Conscious effort by the supplier of a brand to change the positioning of a brand.

retailers' promotion
Temporary price/performance improvement in the offer (discount, bonus, incentive, joint promotion) to the retailer, the aim being to increase the short-term turnover within, particularly by improving the turnover share, stock position and/or article presentation. *See also:* trade promotion.

Rossiter–Percy model
Buyer behaviour model developed by Rossiter and Percy on the basis of which communication management can be formulated. Products are classified according to decision type (low involvement versus high involvement) and type of motivation (informational or negative versus transformational or positive).

sales force promotion
Sales promotion directed at its own sales personnel. By way of incentives, competitions etc. the enterprise encourages the individual and total sales effort.

sales management (sales force management, sales management)
Management activities aimed at selecting, appointing, training, and motivating personal sales people, determining objectives with regard to the activities of different sales people, coordinating their activities, and evaluating their performances.

sales promotion
A tactic to improve short-term turnover by improving the price/value ratio of a product whether a discount, or a (temporary) increase in value (for example, 10 per cent extra contents, incentives). Examples of sales promotion are: discounts, sample, coupons, premium, self-liquidating premium, competition, refund actions, savings stamps, sweepstake, joint promotion, club promotion, incentives, etc.

sales promotion objective
Derived from communication objectives. Objectives with regard to consumer promotions can be: attracting new customers, keeping present customers, increasing the expenditure per customer, promoting product use, supporting theme advertising and introducing new brands. Usually, the objectives for trade promotions are obtaining support of the trade during consumer promotions, improving shelf positions, increasing or decreasing trade stock, introducing more and new product varieties, and improving trade relations.

sales promotion plan
Derived from the marketing communication plan. It contains an analysis of, amongst others, the product, distribution, and customer, the determination of the promotion target group, promotion objectives, promotion strategy, and its effect (including: which distributor to co-operate with, and how), promotion budget, and evaluation.

sales response model
Model describing the effect advertisements have on the conclusion of purchase transactions (advertisement effect).

sample
Type of sales promotion whereby a product sample is distributed among prospective buyers to introduce them to this product.

scanning and focusing model

Model reflecting the processing of marketing communications by consumers. According to this model, the consumer first goes through a stage in which he or she selects advertisements to take a closer look at or to listen closer to based on relevance and attractiveness. The selected advertising will be looked at in more detail, and analysed further during the focusing stage.

script

Written version of a radio or television commercial.

selective advertising

Advertising aimed at influencing the demand for a certain brand. Opposite of generic advertising.

self-liquidating premium

Type of sales promotion in which the costs of the action are eventually paid for by the customer, because he has to pay compensation for voluntarily receiving a premium.

selling-in activities

Communication activities with the objective of causing the trade to add the products to the assortment, and pay the necessary attention to these products.

selling-out activities

Communication activities aimed at increasing the speed of turnover in the trade.

share of voice

Share (in time) of a certain advertising expression during the full transmission time for advertising expressions during a certain period, and in a certain product class.

source effect

Influence of the presenter of the message on the acceptance of its contents. For example, authorities and intimates as a source in the communication expression can be more reliable than parties involved in the transaction. *See also:* testimonial advertising.

special interest magazine

Paper (magazine) aimed at specific hobbies, activities, spare time activities, areas of interest etc.

split-run test

Test between a pre-test and a post-test. This test is conducted during the campaign. The circulation or transmission is divided into two (or more) parts. A different communication expression is placed in each part. Every communication expression contains a response facility (usually a coupon). On the basis of the response to every communication expression, the difference in effectiveness of these expressions is determined.

sponsored magazine

Magazine (paper) produced by order of a supplying organization in which the choice of target group and editorial contents are subservient to the market objectives of the account involved. For example: Sainsbury's Magazine. *See also:* sponsored medium.

sponsored medium

Medium produced by order of a supplying organization in which the choice of target group and editorial contents are subservient to the realization of the marketing communication objectives of the account involved.

sponsorship

The subsidizing of an event, usually sporting or artistic, by a company for advertising purposes.

spot

Broadcasting time bought by a medium for the transmission of a commercial.

Starch model
Classical hierarchical model on the working of communication in which the customer goes through a number of stages in compulsory order before proceeding to a purchase. The stages are: noticing, observing, believing, remembering, action. Before a buyer will proceed to purchasing, he will first have to see the advertisement, then read or hear it, believe it, and remember it. *See also:* AIDA model, Lavidge–Steiner model.

story board
A series of pictures illustrating the story in a draft commercial.

sweepstake
Competition in which the participants are sent a randomly drawn number free.

tailor-made promotion
Trade promotions specifically targeted at a certain retailer.

teaser
Message which is meant to create curiosity in the receiver. References to the coming message are made. It is assumed that by arousing curiosity, people will listen to, or read the actual message following it with more interest. Sometimes the actual message appears a few days later, sometimes it is printed a few pages further on.

telemarketing
Selling directly into the home using either the telephone or television.

television sponsorship
Financial support for a television programme production in return for mentioning the organization or brand name and/or showing the respective product during the programme. *See also:* sponsorship.

testimonial advertising (celebrity endorsement)
Authorities, celebrities, pseudo-intimates function as a source in the advertising expression. These authorities render positive information about the quality of a product or brand on the basis of expertise or personal experience. This working method stimulates the source effect. As the manufacturer stays in the background during the advertising message, the message makes a more credible impression. *See also:* source effect.

thematic communication
Part of the (marketing) communication mix; includes advertising, marketing public relations and sponsoring. These communication instruments are especially used to positively influence the knowledge and affection of the target group. Using these instruments, long-term effects are aimed at.

top of the mind awareness
Unaided brand awareness: usually relating to the first brands in a product category which can be reproduced without aid.

total reach
The number of people (usually as a percentage of the total number that could have been reached) who will at one time have been confronted with the medium.

trade advertising
Advertising aimed at trade and commerce.

trade fairs and shows
Collective name for temporary, usually periodically organized events, in which exhibitors, for payment, can rent a stand to show their products to interested parties, consumers (public trade fairs) or organizations (professional trade fairs). Sometimes direct sales will take place.

trade promotion
Sales promotion aimed at trade and commerce. *See also:* sales promotion.

two-step flow of communication
Communication model showing that information reaches the target groups through, amongst others, influencers and advisers (opinion leaders), other people or organizations (followers).

unique selling proposition (USP)
The concept, less popular than it used to be, that a product should have some unique feature about it, able to be communicated to consumers through advertising, that would differentiate it from its competitors. A continuous stream of products with unique features important to consumers, however, is in practice hard to produce and USP have given ground to newer ideas of positioning less tied to actual produce features.

videotext
A two-way TV cable system in the US enabling a television viewer to access information from a database in a central computer and to transmit information back. Videotext can therefore be used for survey research, for opinion polling and for ordering from a store or a catalogue displayed on the TV screen. It makes tele-selling possible.

wear in
Phenomenon in which a communication expression only reaches its maximum effect after the communication target group has become accustomed to it (= wear in).

wear out
Wear and tear in an advertising message incurs, causing the effect of it to diminish in the course of time.

word of mouth communication
Verbal communication between (prospective) buyers about a product, brand or organization. It is viewed as being powerful, impartial and objective and commonly regarded as the most effective means of communication.

zapping
Using the remote control of the television to quickly switch from one channel to another as soon as a programme becomes less attractive, for example, during commercials.

References and further reading

Aaker, D.A., R. Batra and J.G. Myers, *Advertising Management*, Prentice-Hall, Englewood Cliffs, New Jersey, 1992.

Floor, J.M.G. and W.F. van Raaij, *Marketing-communicatie Strategie*, Stenfert Kroese, Leiden, 2nd edition, 1992.

Franzen, G., *Mensen, produkten en reclame*, Samsom, Alphen a/d Rijn, 1987.

Hasper, W.J.J., *De persoonlijke verkoop*, Samsom, Alphen a/d Rijn, 1986.

Meiden, A. van der, *Reclame en ethiek: hoe leren we de reclame mores*, Stenfert Kroese, Leiden, 1985.

Petty, R.E. and J.T. Cacioppo, *Communication and Persuasion: Central and Peripheral Routes to Attitude Change*, Springer Verlag, New York, 1986.

Pieters, R.E. and W.F. van Raaij, *Reclamewerking*, Stenfert Kroese, Leiden, 1992.

Riel, C.B.M. van, *Identiteit en Imago*, Academic Service, Schoonhoven, 1992.

Rossiter, J.R. and L. Percy, *Advertising and Promotion Management*, McGraw-Hill, New York, 1987.

Severijnen, O., *Communicatiemiddelen, inventarisatie en begrippenlijst*, Stenfert Kroese, Leiden, 1992.

Soeterboek, L.P.A. and J.W. van der Hoek, *Encyclopedie voor Reclame en Marketing*, Kluwer, Deventer.

10 SALES MANAGEMENT

Concept overview

account
account manager
account objective
account profile
action-oriented selling method
action-reaction method
active selling method by telephone
ADAP-matrix
after sales
alternative question
area division
area sales manager
assessment-centre method

back order
back-door selling
body language
broker
buying function
buying signal
buying stages

call back
call order
canned sales pitch
canvassing
cash discount
category management
checking function of the salesperson
checking questions in the sales talk
CIS
client rating
closing signal
closing technique
coaching
coalition strategy
cold call
commission
complaints handling
contact resistance
cooling off
cost per call
credit limit
credit manager
credit term

differentiated selling method
double call
draft contract

empathy
endless chain method

head representative
hedgehog

high pressure selling
hot prospect

identification technique
incentive

lead
leading question
low pressure selling

missionary selling method

needs-oriented selling method
negotiation process
non-verbal communication

opening question
order approval
order confirmation
order details
order entry
order processing
orders-calls ratio

paraphrasing technique
pedestal question
personal power
personal selling
plateau
position power
problem-solving selling method
process-oriented selling method
prospect
prospect rating

receptive selling
reflecting question
relation building
relation-advice selling method
relationship management
reminder approach
representative
resistance mechanism
resistances
role adaptation
role behaviour
role conflict
roll out strategy
rolling forecast

sales analysis
sales arguments
sales audit
sales budget
sales demonstration
sales dyad

sales engineer
sales external staff
sales forecast
Sales Information System (SIS)
sales internal staff
sales management
sales manager
sales objectives
sales plan
sales quota
sales returns
sales strategy
sales support system
sales tactics
sales talk
sales talk levels
salesperson
sandwich method
SASS (Sales Support System)
SDS (Structured Decision System)

SDSS (Sales Decision Support System)
second sourcing
selling costs
selling methods
selling stages
selling stages method
SMSS (Sales & Marketing Support System)
sourcing
standard sales talk
starting price
style flexing

total sales potential
TPS (Transaction Processing System)
trade discount
trial and error selling method
trial close

willingness to close the deal
win-win strategy

Concept descriptions

account
A buyer who regularly buys the products or services from a supplier (a regular customer).

account manager
A salesperson who will be held responsible for the selling activities towards one or more major customer.

account objective
Objective which a company wishes to achieve within a given period with a particular account, usually in terms of turnover or sale.

account profile
Description of the commercially relevant characteristics of an account. This will include the turnover- and/or outlet category he/she belongs to, the type of goods or the services he/she buys; purchasing procedures, buying decision procedures, personal details of the DMU, payment performance, credit limit and any further particulars.

action-oriented selling method
A selling method aimed at short-term results, in which special activities are carried out to realise an increase in sales. Usually this has to do with promotional activities, but it may also relate to activities outside the normal framework of the organization, such as selling at shows.

action-reaction method (stimulus-response method)
A way of selling based on the concept that the salesperson suspects what stimuli the prospect responds to and how he/she reacts on them. The stimuli may consist of product information, questions, demonstrations, special actions, etc.

active selling method by telephone
A selling method used to sell (smaller) quantities and to maintain relationships, including supplying service and making appointments for calls by representatives. In this case, the initiative is taken by the selling party.

ADAP-matrix
Sales technique to match the arguments of the salesperson as carefully as possible with the needs of the buyer. The letters stand for Attribute of the product, Difference from competitive products, Advantage with regard the alternative and Proof; the test of the argument or the attribute.

after sales
The stage after the sale has been closed. This includes service, follow-up, relationship building, relationship management and leads. The follow-up is supposed to include ancillary parts, extensions, etc. In this context, the term leads refers to obtaining the addresses of other potential users of the product, so to actively exploit the customer's network.

alternative question
An alternative question offers a customer the possibility pick from various answers. The salesperson has set up his question in such a way, that he/she will have a counter-argument ready for any possible answer.

area division
Division of the joint market area in parts, called areas. For each area, a salesperson is appointed who will be responsible for the sale in that area, and for gathering and providing information about the area.

area sales manager
A salesperson on middle management level, who manages a number of salespersons in a limited area.

assessment-centre method
A method used for selection and capability assessment of staff and for management development. This method consists of simulation techniques (including role playing used to be able to assess candidates on their suitability for a specific function).

back order
An order (or part of an order) which cannot yet be delivered, because the product is not in stock.

back-door selling
A way of selling in which the salesperson by-passes the purchasing department and directly contacts the department which is going to use the products.

body language
The phenomenon that people are able, consciously or unconsciously, to communicate by means of (the composure of) their body, or parts of their body (eyes, arms, legs, etc). Understanding body language may help the salesperson interpret non-verbal signals with regard to acceptation, refusal, (lack of) interest of a prospect. *See also:* non-verbal communication.

broker
A person who brings together buyer and seller. This term is regularly used in the selling of real estate and insurances, but also in the selling of raw materials, agricultural produce and food.

buying function
The buying function includes the following tasks:

research:	This may be both market research and technical research, filing of supplier documentation belongs to the research function.
negotiating:	The buying function must see to it that its organization receives the right goods at the right price at the right time and in the right place.
order control and processing:	Orders must be executed as per the contract of sale; the checking of the invoices and the timely payment conclude the purchase.

buying signal
A verbal or non-verbal signal issued by the customer (consciously or unconsciously) to indicate that he/she intends to proceed to the purchase. For the salesperson this is the signal to embark on his/her closing procedure. *See also:* closing signal.

buying stages
Division of the selling process, distinguishing the following stages:

offer stage:	in this stage the prospective buyer is made the offer;
transaction stage:	in this stage the prospect decides to buy the product offered and the transaction takes place;
relationship stage:	the prospect has become a buyer, delivery is effected, received and payment is made and the selling organization is going to develop the relationship.

call back
1 A conversation or appointment following the first visit to a prospect, intended to achieve a final contract of sale.
2 Calling on a customer after the sale has been closed, to find out to what extent the customer is satisfied with the purchase.

call order (blanket order)
An order in which it is agreed that delivery will be effected when the buyer asks (calls) for it.

canned sales pitch (canned presentation)
A sales talk which has been completely learned by heart and is reproduced verbatim for a prospect.

canvassing (house-to-house selling)
Canvassing is a form of non-store trade whereby products are demonstrated and sold at the door. Typical of canvassing is that the buyer is unprepared, that he/she is presented with a unique offer, that he/she cannot compare the limited assortment on hand with any other assortment, and that, usually, the canvasser (salesperson) meets the buyer only once.

cash discount
A price reduction offered if the buyer settles the invoice within a fixed period.

category management
Analysis, planning, implementation and evaluation of marketing activities by an organization with regard to (part) ranges or product groups. In this context, the organization does not think in terms of individual products/brands any more, but in terms of complete, consistent and coherent (part) ranges and/or product groups. If category management is used by both manufacturers and retailer in a sector of industry, this may lead to a better matching of the (joint) marketing activities.

checking function of the salesperson
Checking by the salesperson, after a complaint has been dealt with, to ascertain whether the complaint has indeed been dealt with well.

checking questions in the sales talk
Questions a salesperson should ask during and after rebuttal of the customer's objections. In his/her rebuttal, he/she asks for any objections and at the end he/she asks if there are any objections left.

CIS
Commercial Information System. Integrated system in which all commercial information is stored electronically. Is used instead of a separate Marketing Information System (MIS) and Sales Information System (SIS).

client rating (customer portfoliomix)
Arranging buyers by assessing them by specific criteria, such as turnover/sales share for the company, or payment performance. This division is used to match with the selling activities, and can serve as a basis in the construction of a customer pyramid.

closing signal
A verbal or non-verbal signal the customer (consciously or unconsciously) issues to indicate that he/she has taken a decision.

closing technique
The method of executing the final stage (the closing) of the sales talk.

coaching
Accompanying and encouraging (often 'on the job') salespersons to enable them to perform better.

coalition strategy (coalition technique)
Entering into informal alliances by salespersons with their clients to react against third parties, usually their own organization. This strategy can be used by the salesperson to win the customer's confidence.

cold call (cold canvassing)

Paying an unannounced sales visit intended to land a customer or prospect. The word 'canvassing' means: trying to get a new customer.

commission

A financial reward for salespersons or middlemen, depending on the performance achieved. For example, a percentage of the turnover.

complaints handling

The skill of a salesperson is often to act as a buffer between the customer and his own organization and placate customers.

contact resistance

Objections of customers to appointments for calls. For example, 'I have no time; you're calling too early; you're calling too late'; etc.

cooling off

Period, laid down by law, within which a buyer can revert to a buying decision in house-to-house selling.

cost per call

An index figure used to check efficiency of the salespersons. The index figure is obtained by dividing cost, usually the salaries and travel expenses, by the number of calls made.

credit limit

The highest outstanding balance a client is allowed to have.

credit manager

Somebody whose specific task it is to monitor the payment performance of the debtors. Although payment is an intrinsic part of the sale, the credit manager is usually part of the finance department.

credit term

Part of the contract of sale in which is arranged by what date the good or the service has to be paid for at the latest.

differentiated selling method

Method in which buyers from the separate categories are treated differently. The division of the buyers/prospects takes up a central place. The salespersons are required to be able to assess the potential of buyers and also to be able to report this properly. To be able to use this method it is necessary to keep information systems up to date.

double call

Joint call to one or more customers by a higher member of the sales staff. Objectives may be evaluating the sales, including the building the relation with the buyer or coaching on the job.

draft contract

Agreement in which a number of issues has been broadly arranged, but need to be further elaborated. For example, the prices and the total quantity have been agreed, the exact articles and delivery dates will be agreed on in due course.

empathy

The ability to place oneself in somebody else's situation and feelings.

endless chain method

Method to identify prospects by asking customers and prospects the names and addresses of other prospects and by then repeating this question with each prospect who is called on.

head representative

Used to be someone managing a small team of representatives. Nowadays, this function is represented by the term sales manager. Sometimes also a term to identify a senior-representative, who has no line assistants under him/her, but receives this title as a kind of 'promotion'.

hedgehog

A counter-question to a question indicating a buying signal from the customer. For example:

Prospect: 'Within what term do you think you could deliver?'

Salesperson: 'What quantity are we talking about?'

high pressure selling

The perception of prospects that a salesperson is not able to recognize the needs of a customer, that the salesperson is too assertive in summing up the product advantages, and/or that the salesperson is too aggressive when forcing a buying decision.

hot prospect

A prospective customer who is very likely to place an order shortly.

identification technique

Technique intended to find, in collaboration with the client, an answer to the question what the real need of the customer is.

incentive

Special reward for salesperson (or middleman) when a particular (sales) objective has been reached.

lead

A sales prospect.

leading question

Questions in which the answer is built in. Their goal is to avoid fierce standpoints of the salesperson.

low pressure selling

Change which arose in the second half of the 1940s after the high pressure selling in America. Skills and salesmanship were increased, causing a substantial growth of effectiveness.

missionary selling method

Method which tends to be used if there is not yet a relationship between a selling company and a prospective buyer. This method is aimed at obtaining insight into prospective buyers. It is the salesperson's task to determine which prospective buyers may become interesting relations for his organization.

needs-oriented selling method

Selling method in which the (possible) needs of the prospect take up a central position. These needs are not yet known to the salesperson. In some cases, the needs may be only latently present with the prospect. That is why the salesperson must achieve an understanding of the needs and requirements of the customer first. Is it a latent need, then he/her must make the customer aware of that need. It is not until the needs of the customer are clear, that the salesperson will be able to communicate the advantages of his/her product or service. *See also:* problem-solving selling method, process-oriented selling method, relation-advice selling method.

negotiation process

A process in which two parties attempt to achieve a mutually acceptable solution of a problem in which the two parties are involved. The problem may be inducing a prospect to place a substantial order. The process consists of different stages:

Preparation stage:	at this stage as much information as possible is gathered, the negotiation targets are decided, any priorities established and the minimum objectives to be achieved; finally the strategy is established.
Opening stage:	parties meet constructively and express the desire to come to a solution; the agenda is prepared.
First position choice:	parties explain their visions and indicate their positions.
Stock-taking stage:	At this stage the parties put each other through the mill.
Option stage:	parties think up as many options serving mutual interests.
Option choice stage:	parties determine which options qualify from the joint interests and from that of buyer and seller.
Deadlock stage:	parties do not always reach agreement; at this stage they will usually split up or call in the assistance of others.
Closing stage:	when agreement is indeed reached, the results will be laid down and made as follow-up appointments.
Cast-off stage:	parties celebrate the result reached.

non-verbal communication

All forms of communication with the exclusion of the spoken or written word. *See also:* body language.

opening question

Open question to start a sales talk with or to change the subject.

order approval

Approval of an order by the buying party. The approval will especially relate to the conditions agreed upon with the salesperson.

order confirmation

A message sent to the client, in which it is confirmed that his/her order has been entered into the order processing system is (goods), or that the order has been executed at the time indicated (services).

order details

The details an organization wishes to have at its disposal, before it accepts an order or a delivery. The necessary details may be required by both buying and the selling organization. Usually this is done by both. The salesperson should see to it that all details are known to the organization.

order entry

The process of entering the order into the order processing system of the selling party.

order processing

The joint administrative and physical tasks executed by an organization in the processing of an order. For example, taking orders by telephone, typing up the order, extracting (in triplicate) the order form, checking the packer's number, packing the products, forwarding the goods, checking internally the credit rating and terms of payment of the buyer.

orders-calls ratio

This ratio represents the relationship between the number of orders booked and the number of calls. The result is a measure for a salesperson's efficiency.

paraphrasing technique

A discussion technique in which the salesperson repeats in his/her own words what the customer has said. Usually this is done to determine if the salesperson has clearly understood the customer. The technique can also be used to seduce the customer to making a statement.

pedestal question
Question in which a compliment has been included in the question in such a way, that the answer requires the attention of the customer so that, as a result, he/she will have no opportunity to take the compliment as flattery. For example, 'Do you remember the name of the architect who designed this splendid, yet functional office?'

personal power
The power which somebody possesses by the perceived personal characteristics of this person (reference power) or by having information, on which someone else depends, but to which the other person himself does not have access (information power). *See also:* position power.

personal selling
One of the marketing communication tools. The personal contacts, without intervention of media, between the company and its buyers with as final goal closing a (sales) transaction.

plateau
Stage in the career path in which members sales staff find themselves when their development as professional salespersons has come to a stop.

position power
The power he/she has received on account of his/her position to manage others. This power can be subdivided as follows:
legitimate power: this power is based on a specific function/position in the organization, to which the power is related;
reward power: the authority to be able to reward staff members;
punishment power: the authority to be able to keep something back from or take something away from staff members;
connection power: having a connection with others who have punishment and/or reward power.

problem-solving selling method
Selling method in which it is assumed that, if the supplier is capable of solving the customer's problem, a sales transaction will indeed be closed. This selling strategy is based on the concept that the customer recognizes his/her problem, can define it and will indeed discuss the problem with a possible supplier. Besides the fact that the prospect wants to solve his problem, he/she will have to have a certain amount of trust in the supplier's possibilities to solve his/her problem, or to fill his/her needs. If this is not the case, then the prospect will not be able to discuss his/her problem or need with this supplier. *See also:* needs-oriented selling method, process-oriented selling method, relation-advice selling method.

process-oriented selling method
Selling method in which the exchange process takes up a central position. In this case it is the salesperson's task to control this process and direct it. He/she should then pay special attention to the reactions of the buying party and try to follow the thought process. If salespersons control the course of the different processes, they can anticipate them in their offer. *See also:* needs-oriented selling method, problem-solving selling method, relation-advice selling method.

prospect
Prospective buyer; person or organization with whom there is a mutual communication, but who have not yet decided to purchase.

prospect rating
A division of prospective buyers by an arrangement running from the prospect with the greatest chance to sell to (hot prospect) to the prospect with the smallest chance to sell to.

receptive selling
Way of selling in which the selling party waits for the buyers to come to him/her.

reflecting question
Repetition or exaggerated stance of the customer in question form, asked with some amazement, but without any aggression. An example is:
Prospect: 'I don't want to do business with you, because you never keep your promises.'
Salesperson: 'We never keep our promises?'
Prospect: 'Well, never may be exaggerating things a bit, but when I last . . .'

relation building
Systematically working on entering into relationships with buyers. In general this also includes the maintenance of the relationship, because this becomes stronger in the process of maintaining the relationship.

relation-advice selling method
Selling method on the basis of a very solid knowledge of the needs and work of the buyer. An intensive contact is necessary here. The role of the salesperson is primarily aimed at maintaining contacts. The salesperson thinks along with the company of the buyer. Is it about a highly specialized offer to industrial companies, then they will have to anticipate the needs of the customers of their buyers. This may lead to assisting in the development of new products, techniques and/or fields of application. For these buyers it is often necessary that salespersons have a good technical background to be able to think along and join the conversation on the level of the customer. *See also:* needs-oriented selling method, problem-solving selling method, process-oriented selling method.

relationship management
Managing a customer database in order to secure a long-lasting relationship with the customer.

reminder approach (reinforcement style)
When the customer is already aware of the product advantages (for example, through advertising or promotion) the sales talk should be aimed at evoking the knowledge the customer has about the product.

representative
Salesperson, whose task it is to sell products and close contracts. A representative's tasks include: establishing personal contacts with prospective buyers (pioneering), informing, selling and taking orders, merchandising, selling-out activities, instruction and demonstration and the supplying service.

resistance mechanism
Inclination of some prospective buyers to cut themselves of, in advance, for a salesperson, so as to protect themselves from entering a commitment they may regret afterwards.

resistances
Reaction of the customers on the offer that a salesperson makes. The different reactions can be arranged by:

impossibility:	the customer he/she cannot afford the offer;
indifference:	the customer does not perceive any advantage in the offer;
objection:	the customer has a genuine objection to the offer;
misunderstanding:	the objection the customer has to the offer is due to a misunderstanding;
doubt:	the customer doubts the advantage he/she is offered;
negotiating:	the customer wants to negotiate the offer.

role adaptation
Adaptation by the salesperson in the sales talk to the customer's behaviour by means of interactive techniques in the communication on relationship level. If the salesperson handles it consciously, this will lead to a greater personal effectiveness.

role behaviour

Behaviour that the salesperson shows with regard to the customer. A good salesperson will show the following role behaviour:
- information provider, talker;
- information gatherer, listener;
- enthusiastic, friendly;
- self-confident, positive;
- thinking along.

Less good salespersons will also or in stead of this, show:
- modesty (docility);
- negativity, fear, indecisive attitude;
- dominance, aggression;
- impulsive behaviour, etc.

role conflict

A conflict occurring because, during a (sales) talk with the customer, the salesperson is in different roles which are conflicting. For example, a conflict between the loyalty which the salesperson has with regard to his own organization and his/her loyalty with regard to the customer.

roll out strategy

Strategy which can be used when the market is much bigger than the processing capability of the organization. Then it is obvious to work only part of that market and to try and conquer more of that market step by step. If the proper choice is made in the initial stage, then it will generate sufficient profits to help taking the following step in financial terms.

rolling forecast

A method of predicting in which is looked into the future over a fixed period, for example, three or five years. The details predicted of the first period will be the most accurate, those of the last will be especially helpful to determine the trend. Since the later forecast periods gradually move towards the first period, they will be more accurate for each new forecast.

sales analysis

Periodic analysis/report of the sales results. Here the sales per buyer, results, discounts, attributes costs and the result usually per month (or per period) also accumulated for the current year represented in report form. In addition to the details for each buyer, also the details for each department are set up to the total for the organization.

sales arguments

Reasons and/or proofs the salesperson can bring out to convince the prospect that the offer contains an advantage for him/her.

sales audit

A comprehensive, systematic and preferably independent periodic thorough study and evaluation of the realized sales objectives, the sales policy applied, the selling activities and the sales organization.

sales budget

Financial budget of the sales department. On the one hand this relates to the estimated turnover which has the character of an objective, and on the other hand the estimated costs by cost category (salary cost, travelling expenses and hotel expenses, telephone expense, etc.).

sales demonstration

Showing of a product or the way it works in support of the sale of that product.

sales dyad
Interaction between two persons in a sociologically significant relation. For example, interaction between salesperson and prospect.

sales engineer
Salesperson who sells products for which it is essential to have technical knowledge of the products and their applications. For example, a representative in the market of machinery, raw materials, (usually technical) products and semi-manufactures.

sales external staff
Part of the sales organization set up and maintained to call on (prospective) buyers from that organization in their own location intended to realize and to maintain the sales for that organization.

sales forecast
The sales volume which an organization expects to sell in a particular market, over a particular period.

Sales Information System (SIS)
A collection of internal and external data relevant for sales, usually stored with the aid a computer in such a way that the information is easily accessible again.

sales internal staff
Part of the sales organization effecting routine sales from within the company and supports the external staff.

sales management (salesforce management)
Management activities comprising analysis, planning, elaboration and checking of the activities, mainly aimed at realizing sales objectives of an organization.

sales manager
The person who is in charge of managing part of the sales organization. Usually is in immediate charge of a number of salespersons and he/she reports to a director of sales. He/she is responsible the execution of part of the sales plan and contributes to the creation of the sales plan.

sales objectives
The objectives intended to be achieved with the sales department within the planned period. The major objectives relate to the sale, the turnover and the contribution or profit.

sales plan
Policy document in which the internal and the external environment of the goods or services to be sold are mapped and analysed. Using this analysis the sales possibilities are determined. They form the basis for the sales objectives, the core of which consists of the sales forecast. On the basis of the internal and external analysis and the insight of management strategies are set to achieve the objectives. The strategies are elaborated into sales tactics, of which the targets per salesperson and per period form the core. The plan will indicate the methods and the points for checking and evaluation of the objectives and the way in which they are achieved.

sales quota
Quantitative sales objective, set in absolute values, which has to be accomplished in a particular area by a salesperson, an account manager or by another member of the sales department.

sales returns
Goods returned to the supplier because they have been rejected by the buyer.

sales strategy
The way in which the organization attempts to achieve the sales objectives with intended medium-term and long-term implications, usually longer than one year.

sales support system
The support a company offers its salespersons to achieve the planned sales quotas. This system consists amongst others of prospect lists, sales training and instructions and information on advertising campaigns.

sales tactics
Further elaboration of the sales strategy, in which the approach to achieve the objectives relates to the short term, usually less than one year.

sales talk
A conversation in which the salesperson tries to induce the prospective buyer to buy his/her product. The following three basic types of sales talk are to be distinguished:

standard conversation: a conversation built up along a fixed pattern; it can be used to sell standard products to like-minded buyers who have the same needs.

spontaneous conversation: a type of conversation which particularly depends on the way in which the prospective buyer enters the conversation. The risk of this kind of conversation is the routine story the salesperson tends to make of it and the risk that he/she forgets particular matters such as closing the deal.

phased conversation: the way in which the salesperson structures his/her conversation is emphasized. The sale runs according to a more or less fixed pattern.

sales talk levels
Within the communication process we distinguish three levels on which communication takes place:

Content level: only the content of the message is relevant.

Procedure level: with this the rules of the game applied to the communication are meant.

Commitment level: this is used to indicate the atmosphere in which the communication takes place.

salesperson
Other name for representative. The indication salesperson has received a bad ring to it, due to the high-pressure type of selling in the past. For that reason many fancy names have been thought up such as area manager, sales executive, etc.

sandwich method
Selling method which can be used to 'sandwich' the price between the value of the product and the advantages:
1 the salesperson makes the customer aware of the value of the product, preferably the value which the product has for the customer;
2 then he/she mentions the price;
3 if possible, the price will be related to a unit, so that it can be expressed in a low figure (reduction technique) and attempts will be made to relate this figure to a much higher amount which is connected with the offer. For example, the cost of a desk in relation to the annual salary of the staff member who has to work at it;
4 then the most important advantages of the offer will immediately be repeated.

SASS (Sales Support System)
The support a company offers its salespersons to achieve the planned sales quotas. This system consists amongst others of prospect lists, sales training and instructions and information on advertising campaigns.

SDS (Structured Decision System)
An interactive computer system in which (sales) information is gathered and stored. Subsequently the system can take particular routine decisions in advance without further intervention of third parties.

SDSS (Sales Decision Support System)
An SMSS primary aimed at the sales function. *See also:* SMSS.

second sourcing
An organization's looking for a second supplier or expert. There may be several reasons for this: the wish to be independent of one supplier; they are not satisfied with the present supplier; they want to be able to use new developments; they have to compensate for fluctuations in the demand as a negotiating option with the present supplier.

selling costs
In a limited sense, the costs incurred by the sales department. In a broader sense the internal recovery costs of the other departments are added to it.

selling methods
Systematic approach of the interaction of a prospective buyer with a salesperson, in which the salesperson leads the customer to the decision to buy. Broadly, the following methods are distinguished:
· needs-oriented selling method
· process-oriented selling method
· problem-solving selling method
· relation-advice selling method
· sandwich method
· trial and error selling method
· selling stages method

selling stages (selling cycle)
Subsequent stages in the activities performed by a salesperson to sell his product. The main stages are:

preliminary stage: at this stage the discussion objectives are set and as much information as possible about the buying company and the conversation partner is gathered;

opening stage: this stage is the greeting, introduction stage when efforts are made to create a good atmosphere;

information stage: at this stage mutual information is exchanged, the customer presents his/her needs and the salesperson presents his/her offer;

transformation stage: this stage relates to the translation of the offer into fulfilling the needs and meeting the customer's requirements;

closing stage: this stage is marked by the customer giving buying signals; his/her attitude with regard to the offer has become positive; the salesperson should zero in on this by accompanying the customer to the order;

relation stage: after first actual sale has been closed and the conversation has been ended, building the relationship with the buyer starts.

selling stages method
In this selling method the way in which the salesperson structures his/her conversation is emphasized. This method is partly based on the mental stage selling method. Moreover, the selling method strongly emphasizes the selling activities of the salesperson. The sale runs according to a more or less fixed pattern. *See also:* selling stages.

SMSS (Sales & Marketing Support System)
Interactive computer system which helps marketing and sales decision makers use data and models to solve little structured problems. The major objective of an SMSS is making sales and marketing problems translucent, so that better quality decisions can be taken.

sourcing
The looking for a sales organization offering a particular product by an organization.

standard sales talk
A sales talk made up of fixed parts and should be kept according to that structure.

starting price
The price with which a salesperson starts his/her price negotiations in the sales talk.

style flexing
Communication style/technique in which during a (sales) talk a similar posture or attitude is adopted to that adopted by the conversation partner, intended to tune into or stay at the same wavelength as the other person. This technique can also be used for language, rhythm of speech, rate of speech and breathing.

total sales potential (sales potential)
The maximum sales volume that can be achieved in a particular market, over a particular period. This volume is based on data from sales and/or marketing research.

TPS (Transaction Processing System)
Computer system in which (sales) information is gathered and stored in such a way that this information will be easily accessible again. The function of a TPS is to place at the disposal of those concerned within an organization the same information.

trade discount
Discount granted to the trade as a reward for cost saving, as encouragement to increase turnover or sales either to direct the sales or to influence the way in which functions are carried out and to influence performance (controlling discount).

trial and error selling method
Selling method which can be used when an organization has no understanding of the market and when there is no time and/or means to explore the market through market research or via other ways. The method means that first the market is split up by market segments and by the influence of the companies within them. The organization can then determine who is (likely) to be the leader in a particular group or in a particular area. These companies will be called on first. On the basis of knowledge and experience gained during these calls sales management can decide to go working those companies, or rather stop doing so. In that way the market will be handled at a relatively high rate and the selection will be more and more refined. Essential in such an approach is a good feedback procedure.

trial close
Attempt of a salesperson, on the basis of feedback, to encourage the prospect to close a sale before the end of the presentation.

willingness to close the deal
The inner readiness of a prospect to close the sale.

win-win strategy
Strategy in negotiation situations in which both parties gain advantage. In a sales situation both the buyer and the salesperson are under the impression that they have closed a good deal.

References and further reading

Balsley, R.D. and Birsner, E.P., *Selling Marketing Personified*, The Dryden Press, New York, 1987.

Churchill, G.A., Ford, N.M. and Walker, O.C., *Salesforce Management.* Irwin, Homewood Illinois, 1993.

Dalrymple, D.J. and Cron, W.L., *Sales Management: Concepts and cases*, Wiley, New York, 1995.

Stanton, W.J., Buskirk, R.H. and Spiro, R.L., *Management of a Salesforce*, Irwin, Homewood, Illinois, 1995.

Wage, J.L., *Psychologie en Techniek van het Verkoopgesprek*, Samsom, Alphen a/d Rijn, 1994.

11 BUSINESS-TO-BUSINESS MARKETING

Concept overview

acquisition
actual value
agent
application engineering
approved vendor
array and review strategy
assembly plant
auxiliary materials

backward integration
bartering
buffer stock
bulk goods
bundle
business logistics
business re-engineering
business-to-business marketing
business-to-business services
buygrid matrix
buying situation

CAD/CAM
catalogue
CE marking
certification
CIM
co-design
co-manufacturing
co-operative model
complementary utilization costs
conformity
consultative sales approach
convergent industry
custom-made goods
customer service

Decision Making Unit (DMU)
derivative
derived demand
design specification
direct account
DMU-PSU relations
dual sourcing

EDI (Electronic Data Interchange)
end-use analysis
engineering
escalation contract

fighter model
final product
financial lease
fitness for use
functionality

gatekeeper's role
global sourcing

high-end product
high-tech marketing

industrial buying process
industrial rights
initiator
installed base
interaction process
invited bid

just in time (JIT)

labour intensity
lead time
low-end product

macro segmentation
main supplier
make or buy
manufacturing specification
market pull
Materials Requirements Planning
micro segmentation
mock-up
modified rebuy
modular product design
MRO (Maintenance, Repair, Operating)
multiple sourcing

new buy
new task buy

off-shoot
offer
operational lease
original equipment manufacturer (OEM)
outsourcing

piece-goods
problem solving unit
problem specification
purchasing officer
putting out to tender/tendering

reciprocity
relationship management
reliability engineering
role of the decider
role of the influencer

sales engineer
semi-manufacture
service
short list

single sourcing
specials
spiff
straight rebuy
sub-contracting
supplier research
systems selling

team selling
technology push

tendering
time-to-market
turn-key project

user's role

value analysis
value-added reseller (VAR)
vendor rating

zero defects

Concept descriptions

acquisition
Process of acquiring orders and connections.

actual value
The subjective value which a product has for a customer at a specific moment.

agent (broker)
Intermediary in the trade who on request from a client will conclude a sales transaction (takes on a trade agreement) in return for a fee and a percentage of the turnover. The agent operates independently. There is no fixed relation between him/her and the client.

application engineering
Adapting an existing product design for a specific field of application.

approved vendor
A supplier who is included on a preferred list of suppliers.

array and review strategy
Purchasing strategy whereby both current and any other suppliers are asked to make an offer.

assembly plant
Company whose manufacturing process mainly consists of assembling parts and components bought elsewhere.

auxiliary materials
Materials which are used or applied in a manufacturing process, but which are not included in the product itself. For example, lubricants for machines.

backward integration
An organization's strategy to produce a product (raw material, semi-manufacture, service) within its own organization, rather than obtaining it from a third party. To be accomplished, for example, by taking over a supplier.

bartering
Exchange of goods and/or services for other goods and/or services, so not involving money.

buffer stock
Stock to bridge contingencies.

bulk goods (commodities)
Goods usually supplied in large quantities and which have to meet particular basic specifications.

bundle
Identification for the total performance a supplier provides a buyer with: product plus product transfer.

business logistics
The sequence of materials handling, starting at the purchase and, through the production line and wholesaler, ending on the shelves of the retailer.

business re-engineering
The adaptation of business processes, the starting point of which is that an optimum connection with the desires of the consumers should be created. By structuring the business processes around the consumers, activities which initially would have been distributed by the organization, are now often concentrated in one person or department. In order to realize this, a drastic adaptation of the information structure and flows is also necessary. Business re-engineering is aimed at achieving, amongst other things, larger efficiencies and shorter reaction times.

business-to-business marketing (industrial marketing, organizational buying behaviour)
Marketing activities of one organization aimed at other organizations.

business-to-business services
Provision of services between industrial organizations, such as transportation and distribution.

buygrid matrix
Identifies the most important criteria at each stage within the decision-making process of buyers. On one dimension, the matrix distinguishes between the various buying situations a prospective buyer may find himself in (new task, modified rebuy, and straight rebuy), and the other dimension includes the eight stages in the buying process.

buying situation
Situations of the buying organization which are also decisive for the course of the buying behaviour and buying process. A frequently made classification is the following: new task, modified rebuy, and straight rebuy situations.

CAD/CAM
Computer Aided Design/Computer Aided Manufacturing. Design and manufacturing method whereby the design specification obtained using the computer is automatically converted into a computer driven manufacturing specification.

catalogue
The complete range of products which a supplier is able to offer by mail including prices, terms of delivery and ordering information.

CE marking
The CE brand (Conformité Européenne) is a technical hallmark valid in all EU member states, concerning environmental protection, safety, health and other consumer protection. The gradual technical harmonization within the EU will in future replace and surpass the national hallmarks.

certification
Certification establishes that an organization conforms to a certain threshold standard (for example ISO 9000 standard).

CIM
Computer Integrated Manufacturing. Production method whereby the manufacturing process is linked by computer to major customers who can order direct via the computer.

co-design
A product designed by the supplier and buyer together.

co-manufacturing
Production carried out by supplier and buyer together (or geared to one another).

co-operative model
Working method whereby attempts are made to solve problems through co-operation. *See also:* fighter model.

complementary utilization costs
That part of the total cost made for the purchase and use of a product on top of the purchase price of a product: labour costs, costs of waste/drop out, energy costs, service costs, etc.

conformity
Where the degree of variance between the actual product supplied and the specifications offered is low, there is conformity with specifications.

consultative sales approach
Identifying and solving the buyer's problems with the customer. The underlying goal is to build a lasting relationship resulting in orders.

convergent industry
Collection of companies manufacturing products which, by means of some kind of assembly, are composed of raw materials, and/or semi-manufactures supplied by third parties.

custom-made goods
Situation in which goods, services, and systems are made specifically for one customer.

customer service
The value added to the physical product as a result of distribution activities. The distinction is made between pre-transaction, transaction, and post-transaction service elements. Prior to the transaction, the service relates to the convenience with which the buyer can conclude the order and the terms of delivery. During the transaction, the degree of service is apparent from such things as reliability or meeting appointments. After the transaction, the service is expressed in the way maintenance and repair is dealt with.

Decision Making Unit (DMU, buying centre)
Informal group in an organization engaged in the buying decision with regard to one specific product. In general, the DMU consists of persons from different parts of the organization depending upon the newness of the intended purchase in question and its total value. Within the DMU various roles may be distinguished: the adviser's role, the influencer's role, the initiator's role, the decision maker's role, the gatekeeper's role, the user's role, and the buyer's role.

derivative
Semi-manufacture derived from raw material.

derived demand
Demand for goods and services by organizations arising in consequence out of the demand by final consumers for a specific product. The level of demand for industrial goods, for example, is derived from the demands for products made using the industrial goods in question.

design specification
That part of the product specification in which it is stated what technologies and materials will be used for the manufacture of a product.

direct account
Buyer of a (semi) manufacture with whom business is done without involving middlemen.

DMU-PSU relations
Network of relations between members of the DMU (see Decision Making Unit) on the consumer side and members of the PSU (see problem solving unit) on the sales side.

dual sourcing
Method of working the buying process whereby two suppliers are deliberately maintained, mainly in order not to be dependent on either. *See also:* multiple sourcing.

EDI (Electronic Data Interchange)
Electronic exchange of structured and standardized data between computers of, for example, the supplier, consumers and logistic service providers as a result of concluding and settling sales transactions.

end-use analysis
Analysis of the application possibilities of a specific (semi) manufacture by the needs and requirements of the buyers, and users of finished products in which that (semi) manufacture could be included.

engineering
Process within an organization whereby the buyer's requirements are translated into a technically feasible solution.

escalation contract
Contract in which price rises are allowed to be passed on if the cost price of intermediate products used in production rises.

fighter model
Working method which attempts to solve problems mainly by starting a fight with the business relation. *See also:* co-operative model.

final product
The final product created after a number of tests and iterations. Intended to be used in this form by the final user.

financial lease
A legal agreement for not more than the economic life cycle of an object whereby the legal ownership remains with the money-lender, but in which the borrower is the economic owner. On the balance sheet of the lessee (the user/borrower) the object is capitalized while the debt in question is included as well. *See also:* operational lease.

fitness for use
The degree to which a product matches intended specifications of use.

functionality (ease of use or operation)
Degree to which a product is user friendly.

gatekeeper's role
One of the roles within the DMU. The staff member who has a gatekeeper's role mainly tries to contribute to the buying decision process by controlling the information flow to, from, and within the DMU.

global sourcing
Suppliers from around the world are considered prospective suppliers of goods and services.

high-end product
Product or system which is supposed to meet high demands and demanding specifications.

high-tech marketing
Using advanced technology solutions for customer problems. This has dramatic consequences for the way in which a marketing function has to be structured, and elaborated.

industrial buying process (organizational buying behaviour)
From identifying the buying problem, through to the evaluation of the product delivered. Usually, the process comprises several stages, dependent on the nature of the buying situation. In general, the following stages may be distinguished: decision making with regard to the necessity of the purchase, preparing an inquiry for an offer, selection of the suppliers to be invited, evaluation of the offers submitted, negotiation, choice of the supplier, delivery, and installation, implementation, and evaluation of the product delivered.

industrial rights
Possession of proprietary technology, knowledge, or manufacturing process(es).

initiator
One of the roles within the DMU: the person taking the initiative in the (purchase) decision making process.

installed base
The number of products, usually capital goods, which a supplier has sold in total, and which are still in use.

interaction process
Social process in which it is being recognized that the buyer and supplier do exchange information and need to work together.

invited bid
Method of working in the buying process whereby a number of suppliers are invited to submit competitive bids.

just in time (JIT)
Distribution method aimed at delivering to the suppliers the required products of the required product quality, and in the required quantities, and at the very moment they are required by the buyer. This method is mainly aimed at simplifying control, shortening throughput times, and reducing or eliminating stocks.

labour intensity
Extent to which labour is necessary to perform a specific function or stage within manufacturing process.

lead time
The time period necessary to design, test, produce, and deliver the first of a new product.

low-end product
Product or system which may meet relatively low demands and less demanding specifications. *See also:* high-end products.

macro segmentation
Type of market segmentation in business marketing whereby, as a first step in the segmentation procedure, the total market is broken down into buyer groups with common characteristics such as size, sector, SIC-code, and location. In a next stage, each of the macro segments might be broken down into more sub-segments. *See also:* micro segmentation.

main supplier
Key supplier of components or systems to Original Equipment Manufacturers; often acts as co-producer.

make or buy
Perennial question as to whether the company should carry out activities itself or should contract them out. This problem is often raised in an organization, and at many levels. This may lead to an organization being in competition with its (prospective) suppliers.

manufacturing specification
That part of the product specification describing the techniques and materials which have to be used in production.

market pull
Stimulus for product innovation may come from two sides. In market pull, the innovation is initiated and stimulated from the side of the buyer, unlike technology push, whereby the stimulus primarily comes from technology.

Materials Requirements Planning
Logistics planning system whereby a company plans its production and buying activities based on its (expected) sales.

micro segmentation
Type of market segmentation in business marketing whereby the macro segments are further broken down into sub-segments based on similarities in the buying behaviour of the organizations, the size of the decision making unit, the extent of buying complexity, etc. *See also:* macro segmentation.

mock-up

A representation or a prototype model of a product, building or installation, which is as realistic as possible.

modified rebuy

Situation in which an organization finds itself when it has bought a specific product previously, but wishes to look around for the next order period, or wishes to implement modifications. For example, changed product specifications, different price, or new supplier. In the modified rebuy situation, the complexity of the buying process in general is less than in the situation of new task, and greater than in the situation of straight rebuy. *See also:* new task buy, straight rebuy.

modular product design

Design whereby a product is built up from part systems which are easy to take apart, and replace.

MRO (Maintenance, Repair, Operating)

Products needed for maintenance, repair and sustenance of the production and remaining equipment.

multiple sourcing

A buying policy whereby the purchases are spread across various suppliers to reduce dependence, to spread risk, to facilitate price negotiation etc.

new buy

The first time that a customer buys a product which is new for him or her.

new task buy

Purchasing a specific article or specific service for the very first time. The greater the accompanying (financial) risk, the more complex and more extensive the buying decision process.

off-shoot

Product which arises as a derivative of a particular technological development.

offer

The (written) offer of a supplier to supply specific products or services, stating the prices and other conditions (of sale, and delivery). *See also:* tendering.

operational lease

Lease of a limited duration with a right to extension. The supplier is responsible for maintenance and service.

original equipment manufacturer (OEM)

Manufacturer who produces/assembles goods, in which he will use other suppliers' brand products as components. When marketing his own product, the manufacturer can then use the suppliers' brand as an (additional) selling argument. An example of this is the slogan 'Intel inside' for computers which have Intel chips/processors built in during assembly.

outsourcing

Obtaining components, products, services or systems from specialized suppliers, rather than providing these in-house.

piece-goods

Goods that are produced as single items (or as a few items only).

problem solving unit

Group of specialists in an organization which has been formed in order to sell a product to another organization. The *Problem Solving Unit* (PSU) is the counterpart of the DMU, and may consist of staff members from different levels, and from different disciplines in order to meet the specific needs of that buying organization (or DMU).

problem specification
The problem which is expected to be solved by the product.

purchasing officer
A staff member in industrial companies or other organizations charged with the buying process. Synonymous with such terms as 'buyer' or 'purchasing manager'.

putting out to tender/tendering (tender system competitive bidding)
Frequently used method in business marketing whereby several suppliers can tender to supply a specific product or to execute a particular project. The offer includes the prices and other terms and conditions of the delivery.

reciprocity
Situation in which supplier and buyer buy each other's products.

relationship management
Analysis, planning, execution, and evaluation of activities aimed at establishing, maintaining and improving durable relations between the organization and the different market parties and interest groups such as suppliers, customers, intermediaries, shareholders and key figures in the social environment.

reliability engineering
Approach whereby 100 per cent reliability is pursued, aiming for 'zero defects' as a result.

role of the decider (decision maker's role)
One of the roles within the DMU. The individual who eventually settles what product is to be bought. As the newness of the product and its value increases, then the decision will be taken further up the organization, perhaps by the MD or Board.

role of the influencer (influencer's role)
One of the roles within the DMU. The individual who has an influencer's role tries to contribute towards the buying decision by giving an opinion, for example, on the alternatives for the product to be bought and the supplier to be chosen.

sales engineer
Salesperson selling products whereby technical knowledge of the product and its features is essential.

semi-manufacture
Product which results from processing raw materials and which is meant to be processed further.

service
(In a technical sense) providing services aimed at error-free operation of products, machines and production processes.

short list
Number of prospective suppliers for whom, after a first broad evaluation round, a certain preference exists, and who will be considered for a certain task.

single sourcing
A purchasing policy whereby a particular product is bought from one supplier only. Contrary to multiple sourcing.

specials
Products or services which have been especially developed for one particular buyer.

spiff (bonus)
An incentive given to retail sales personnel by a manufacturer.

straight rebuy
Routinized rebuy of a particular good or a particular service without any modification of the product specifications and conditions of sale. In this buying situation, the buying process is relatively simple. *See also:* modified rebuy, new task buy.

sub-contracting
The acceptance and execution of (shared) activities by a supplier who works for the principal contractor.

supplier research
Research into suitability of (prospective) suppliers and their products. *See also:* vendor rating.

systems selling
Selling a packaged solution to a problem.

team selling
Selling products by a team of people, each a specialist in some aspect of the product.

technology push
The incentive for product innovation may arise from two sides. In technology push, the innovation is initiated and stimulated by technology unlike market pull, where the stimulus arises with the buyer.

tendering
Method whereby companies are invited to submit an offer to supply a specific good or service and indicate their terms and conditions.

time-to-market
The development time needed to bring a new product to market.

turn-key project
A newly constructed production plant commissioned by the supplier where equipment has been provided and staff trained so that effective handover can be achieved by a target date once all contractual obligations have been met.

user's role
One of the roles within the DMU. The staff member who has a user's role mainly tries to contribute to the buying decision process by providing arguments arising from the factual use of the product to be purchased.

value analysis
An approach to cost reduction seeking to standardize and/or simplify components in order to reduce the cost of production.

value-added reseller (VAR)
Retailer purchasing products from a manufacturer and/or supplier and (in the eyes of the consumer) adds to the value by assembly, service, guarantee, installation, adaptation to the desires of the customer, etc. For example, when non-standardized computer packages are adapted to customer specification.

vendor rating
Ranking suppliers by rating them by specific criteria, such as price, quality level, product experience, service dependability, reliability and location.

zero defects
Policy aimed at making entry checks superfluous through error-free delivery to the production line.

References and further reading

Alexander, R.S., J.S. Cross and R.M. Hill, *Industrial Marketing*, Irwin, Homewood, Ill., 1987.

Biemans, W.G., *Industriële Marketing*, Wolters-Noordhoff, Groningen, 1992.

Corey, E.R., *Industrial Marketing, Cases and Concepts*, Prentice-Hall, Englewood Cliffs, New Jersey, 4th edition, 1991.

Hutt, M.D. and T.W. Speh, *Business Marketing Management*, The Dryden Press, Chicago, 4th edition, 1992.

Kympers, L.P.V.M., e.a., *Toegepaste Industriële Marketing*, Kluwer, Deventer, 1992

Ogilvie, R.G., *Industriële Marketing: planning en strategie*, Stenfert Kroese, Leiden, 2nd edition, 1989.

Reeder, R.R., E.G. Brierty and B.H. Reeder, *Industrial Marketing*, Prentice-Hall, Englewood Cliffs, New Jersey, 1991.

Tettero, J.H.J.P., *Commerciële beleidsvorming & industriële markten*, Kluwer, Deventer, 6th edition, 1991.

12 SERVICES MARKETING

Concept overview

access time
additional services
alternative options

Buyer Seller Interaction

capacity utilization
commitment
consumer co-production
consumption system
contact personnel
contracting-out service

efficiency measurement

front office
functional quality

inseparability
intangibility
internal marketing

judgement measurement

knowledge based service

machine-related services
market relationship
marketing instrument

off-peak demand
output measurement

peak-shaving
people based services
perishability
personnel
professional service

recommendation
relationship life cycle

satisfaction
service
service concept
service delivery
service marketing
service offer
service sector
services continuum
SERVQUAL
servuction
substitute option
switching cost
system based services

technical quality
throughput time

waiting time

Concept descriptions

access time

The time which elapses from the moment when a client asks for attention from a service organization, to the moment attention is given, or the first contact takes place.

additional services

Services which are added to the core service and have as a function to increase value to the customer by making the package now offered more attractive. They form a part of the service offer.

alternative options

Degree to which a consumer has the possibility of choosing from alternative suppliers to obtain a service.

Buyer Seller Interaction

Actions of buyer and supplier which impinge upon each other. This interaction is important for service organizations because the buyer and the supplier must jointly contribute in order to produce and consume the service. *See also:* consumer co-production.

capacity utilization

The extent of present capacity utilization. In hotels, capacity utilization is room occupancy, in restaurants, tables and public transport, seats. Stockpiling is impossible for service organizations, capacity utilization is subject to daily changes in demand.

commitment (loyalty)

The extent to which two parties in a relationship pursue continuity of a relationship, irrespective of any changes which may occur in the environment and/or with the other party. Loyalty is dependent on satisfaction and level of switching costs.

consumer co-production

The finished product is produced with a contribution by the buyer (e.g. IKEA furniture).

consumption system

The entire process of service delivery together with the connected goods/services, which determine the experience and appreciation of the service by the consumer. For example: a package holiday contains not only the flight and accommodation, but other elements such as: transport to and from airport, meal facilities, recreation provisions and courier services.

contact personnel

Employees who have regular contacts with the customer, more of whom will be working in the front office.

contracting-out service

A kind of service which the buyer would be able to carry out in-house, for example, cleaning the house or an office but chooses to contract out.

efficiency measurement

Type of quality measurement in the services and the not-for-profit sector, whereby the efficiency of delivery is measured. This concerns reaching the right target groups using the right activities/actions.

front office

That part of the organization in which staff maintain direct contacts with buyers. Service people in the front office have to be skilful with regard to the executive tasks, and should have good communication and commercial skills.

functional quality

The quality of the service delivered to the buyer. In functional quality it is all about 'how' the service is delivered. For example, does the waiter wait on the table with a friendly face or not? *See also:* technical quality.

inseparability
Fact that production and consumption may converge. *See also:* consumer co-production.

intangibility (immaterial)
One of the specific characteristics of services. Services do render a concrete result or effect, but 'the' service has no material appearance. This is a major reason why it is often difficult to envisage what a service really comprises.

internal marketing
Type of marketing whereby the exchange transactions are set within one's own organization, i.e. marketing activities by divisions of an organization aimed at other divisions of the same organization.

judgement measurement
Type of qualitative quality measurement in the services and not-for-profit sector, whereby the judgement of the participants/consumers on the delivered actions/activities is measured. Judgement measurement forms part of satisfaction measurement.

knowledge based service (skill-based service)
A type of service for which the service organization has specific professional knowledge at its disposal, for example, the work of a medical specialist. Usually it is about a combination of knowledge and craft.

machine-related services
Services which, for a major part, are produced by machines, not by people. Think, for example, of cash dispensing machines. *See also:* people based services, system based services.

market relationship
Mutual alliance of services because they are part of a larger consumption system for certain clients. For example, road transport and rail transport sometimes overlap.

marketing instrument
Means used to promote, facilitate and expedite exchange transactions. Generally, in service organizations five Ps are distinguished, namely: product (or service), price, promotion, place, and/or personnel.

off-peak demand
The demand for services outside the peak, or the high season. Many service companies will stimulate off-peak demand, leading to better capacity utilization.

output measurement
Type of quantitative quality measurement in the services and not-for-profit sector, whereby in particular the production is measured in terms of number of activities, number of visitors, and market/turnover.

peak-shaving
Shaving the peak demand by shifting some demand to low-season or 'off-peak hours'. This results in more even utilization.

people based services
Services, which, for a major part, are produced by people, and not by machines, for example, dental care. *See also:* machine-related services, system based services.

perishability
Due to their intangibility, the finished products of service organizations cannot be stored. Think, for example, of a seat on a flight. If there is no demand for this seat on a Saturday, it cannot be kept in store, and be 'sold' on Sunday. *See also:* service marketing.

personnel

Fifth p of the marketing mix of service organizations. Due to the relatively influential and intensive Buyer Seller Interaction, personnel is considered a marketing instrument in services marketing.

professional service

Knowledge based or skill based services provided by highly qualified, professional staff. The services are characterized by many interactions with the buyer, and a high degree of customized work.

recommendation

Situation in which a consumer on the basis of, for example, a purchase experience, gives publicity to his experience, judgement and feeling towards a specific service provider.

relationship life cycle

Pattern according to which a relationship between buyer, and supplier changes under the influence of the Buyer Seller Interaction. Analogous to the product life cycle, Peelen breaks down the life cycle into four stages, namely the introduction, the growth, the maturity, and the decline stage.

satisfaction

One of the variables determining the strength of the relational loyalty. Satisfaction results from the degree to which the relation between a buyer and a supplier meets expectations.

service

Exchange object consisting of activities usually targeted at persons or goods but designed to add value. A service is a specific phenomenon of (part of) a product without tangible qualities. The following types of services are distinguished: contracting out services, facilitating services, knowledge or skill services. *See also:* services continuum.

service concept (basic service)

The translation of the service benefit concept into the basic offer of the service organization. Thus, for a hotel offering accommodation is the basic service, for a forwarding agent it is the transport of persons or goods.

service delivery

Process of subsequent activities carried out to provide the service. During the delivery of the service a distinction is made between the access time, the waiting time, and the throughput time. *See also:* Buyer Seller Interaction.

service marketing (marketing of service organizations)

Marketing activities of organizations whereby the objects to be traded are services. Services are characterized by inseparability (they are produced and consumed at the same time) by intangibility (they cannot be seen, tested, tasted before consumption) by perishability (they cannot be stored for later sale) and by variability (quality varies greatly depending upon the provider).

service offer

A detailed elaboration of the service concept by a more accurate specification of the elements of the service, and its quality and quantity level.

service sector (service industry)

Organizations whose main activity is providing services. For example, forwarding agents, hospitals, restaurants, and banks.

services continuum

Scale emphasizing that the product or supply of organizations hardly ever consists of goods or services only. The position of supply on the scale indicates the percentage of the supply which consists of services versus the goods part.

SERVQUAL

Instrument which measures how the buyer perceives the quality of the service. The perception is measured using five dimensions, namely, the tangible aspects of the service (the physical environment), the reliability (living up to expectations), the willingness to help (meeting buyer requirements quickly), the 'assurance' (knowledge, and politeness of staff, degree to which staff makes a trustworthy and reliable impression), and the empathy (involvement with buyer, individual attention for buyer problems).

servuction

Concept from services marketing introduced by Eiglier and Langeard. The word is franglais, a conjunction of the French 'service', and 'production', and means the production of the service.

substitute option

The possibility a consumer has to choose for another type of service, including not contracting out, or using a product providing for the same need, instead of a certain service.

switching cost

One of the components determining the strength of the relational involvement. The switching costs consist of the thresholds that accompany terminating and starting a relationship. Think of terminating memberships, making a buying effort, and investments already made.

system based services (organization based services)

Services the manufacturing process of which is, for a major part, both dependent on people and machines. Typical of system based services is the complex interface between the front and the back office. *See also:* people based services.

technical quality

The quality of what the buyer receives during the service delivery process. With technical quality it is all about 'what' is delivered, for example, the room in a hotel, or the meal in a restaurant. *See also:* functional quality.

throughput time (response time)

The time elapsing between the moment an order for a service is placed and the time when the service is supplied.

waiting time

The time between a first contact and the moment the service is delivered.

References and further reading

Aa, W. van der and T. Elfring, *Dynamiek in de dienstensector*, Kluwer, Deventer, 1988.

Boomsma, S., *Interne Marketing. Hoe marketing effectief werkt in de eigen organisatie*, Kluwer, Deventer, 1991.

Faes, W. and C.A.H. van Tilborgh, *Marketing van diensten*, Kluwer, Brussel, 1989.

Grönroos, Chr., *Service Management and Marketing*, Lexington Books, 1990.

Heskett, J.L., W.E. Sasser and C.W.L. Hart, *Service breakthroughs. Changing the rules of the game*, The Free Press, New York, 1990.

Heuvel, J., *Dienstenmarketing*, Wolters-Noordhoff, Groningen, 1993.

Kotler, Ph. and P.N. Bloom, *Marketing Professional Services*, Prentice-Hall, Englewood Cliffs, New Jersey, 1984.

Lovelock, C.H., *Managing Services. Marketing, operations and human resources*, Prentice-Hall, Englewood Cliffs, New Jersey, London, 1992.

Lovelock, C.H., *Service Marketing*, Prentice-Hall Int., London, 1991.

Peelen, E., *Relaties tussen consument en aanbieder, dissertatie*, Erasmus Universiteit Rotterdam, 1989.

Tettero, J.H.J.P. and J.H.R.M. Viehoff, *Marketing voor dienstverlenende organisaties, beleid en uitvoering*, Kluwer, Deventer, 1994

Tilborgh, C.A.H. van, *Marketing van diensten*, Kluwer, Deventer, 1992.

Zeithaml, V.A., A. Parasuraman and L.L. Berry, *Delivering Service Quality: balancing customer perceptions and expectations*, The Free Press, London, 1990.

Zemke, R. and D. Schaaf, *The service edge, 101 companies that profit from customer care*, NAL Penguin Inc., New York, 1989.

13 NOT-FOR-PROFIT MARKETING

Concept overview

budget subsidy

collective goods
commercial activity
customer satisfaction management

demand level
demarketing
direct benefit principle
donor
donor target group

effectivity measurement

judgement measurement

lump-sum financing

network
non-monetary price
not-for-profit organizations
not-for-profit sector

operational deficit financing
organization orientation
output measurement

price policy in not-for-profit
  organizations
price signal
privatization
productivity measurement
profit-oriented organization
psychological threshold
public sector

social marketing
societal marketing concept
sponsorship
subsidy

target group
time threshold

Concept descriptions

budget subsidy
On the basis of a submitted plan and a budget a not-for-profit organization may be allocated a budget for a period of three to five years. The organization will have a large degree of freedom in the way the budget is spent.

collective goods
Goods and services that are provided for general as opposed to individual benefit such as police, fire protection and roads.

commercial activity
Term indicating that a certain activity is aimed at profit making. This concept is used within certain not-for-profit organizations to indicate that an activity undertaken by themselves, is also offered by commercial organizations with the aim of generating profit. An example is the emergence of private clinics in health care.

customer satisfaction management
Type of productivity measurement checking whether the consumer is satisfied with the service and the way in which it was delivered.

demand level
Organizations may encounter various demand levels from negative demand, lack of demand, and latent demand to excessive demand and unhealthy demand. For each of these demand levels, the organization does its best to manage that demand. Not-for-profit organizations engage more in such activities than profit-oriented organizations.

demarketing
Specific marketing efforts by suppliers, not-for-profit organizations or government aimed at reducing temporarily or permanently the general demand or the demand from specific consumer groups for a specific product or a specific product type.

direct benefit principle (principle of consumer-paid services)
Principle assuming that a consumer of government services is charged a fee which corresponds to the benefit received.

donor
Person or organization providing funding. The gift or subsidy may be subject to restrictive conditions with regard to its use. Examples are donations and legacies to foundations and organizations and government subsidies.

donor target group
As distinct from regular consumers of the not-for-profit organization (target group) a group of persons or organizations which can be identified as donors for a not-for-profit organization.

effectivity measurement
Measurement indicating to what extent the organization has succeeded in accomplishing its objectives, such as output measurement, result measurement and judgement measurement.

judgement measurement
Type of qualitative quality measurement in the services and not-for-profit sector, whereby in particular the judgement of the participants/consumers on the delivered actions/activities is measured. Judgement measurement forms part of satisfaction measurement.

lump-sum financing (lump-sum subsidy)
Type of funding. On the basis of a submitted plan and a budget (for a period of three to five years) the organization will be allocated a lump-sum subsidy for a period of three to five years. The organization will have a large degree of freedom in the way the budget is spent. Any credit balance may, in principle, be retained, any loss balance must be replenished by the organization itself.

network

Formal or informal complex of relations between various people and/or organizations who have a common characteristic or interest, or work together.

non-monetary price

All sacrifices which (cannot or) are not expressed in money which buyers have to make in order to be able to buy a product. Examples include the distance the consumer has to bridge, the time and effort he has to go to (time threshold), and the fear or uncertainty he has to conquer (psychological threshold). Many not-for-profit organizations charge prices which fall short of cost recovery or do not charge any monetary price at all. The influence of the non-monetary price on the buying decision of a consumer of not-for-organizations is therefore larger than with consumers of products of commercial organizations.

not-for-profit organizations

Organizations not pursuing profit. These organizations do not aim at acquiring profits or a credit balance for the benefit of the suppliers of their capital or other participants in the organization, including members of the board, management, and co-workers. Usually, not-for-profit organizations have been founded to perform specific social functions. They may be private or public organizations.

not-for-profit sector

Not-for-profit organizations are mainly found in the following sectors
  · health care: hospitals, nursing homes, medical day care centres;
  · welfare work, social work: socio-cultural training centres, institutions for community work;
  · arts/culture: theatres, museums, orchestras, theatre, drama and ballet companies;
  · education and research: schools, some educational institutions, universities, research institutes;
  · sports: (amateur) sports clubs, some sports accommodations;
  · recreation: public open space planning, some recreational centres, broadcasting corporations financed from public funds;
  · interest groups; trade unions, employers organizations, trade organizations, consumer organizations, patients organizations, environment and nature conservation organizations, action groups political organizations, professional organizations;
  · charity organizations: organizations to combat diseases, poverty;
  · religious organizations; religious communities, sects.
Some not-for-profit organizations are difficult to classify. Thus, libraries may be classified under the sectors culture, education and research as well as under recreation.

operational deficit financing (exploitation subsidy)

Type of funding activities by a subsidizer. On the basis of a submitted plan and a budget (for a period of three to five years) the organization will be allocated a subsidy for a period of three to five years. The organization will have a large degree of freedom in the way the budget is spent. Any credit balance will be deducted from the next term's subsidy, any loss balance will be replenished by the subsidizer.

organization orientation

The tendency of an organization to force consumers to adapt to the rules which the organization has set to function better internally, but which do not necessarily lead to that customer's needs being satisfied better.

output measurement

Type of quantitative quality measurement in the services and not-for-profit sector, whereby in particular the production is measured in terms of number of activities, number of visitors, and market/turnover.

price policy in not-for-profit organizations

A not-for-profit organization often has fewer starting points for and less freedom in determining the prices of its services than a profit-oriented organization. The nature and the objectives of the organization usually imply that a price is charged to the customers which does not cover the cost, so that an incomplete price signal is issued to the market. Subsidy conditions or government regulations for a specific sector may also strongly restrict freedom. In this case the non-monetary price will play a more substantial role.

price signal

Not-for-profit organizations often fix their (monetary) price at a level below the cost price of the service, or do not charge anything at all. Then, the price does not represent the real scarcity, or in other words the value of the production factors the supplier has sacrificed. This results in the consumer receiving an incomplete price signal with respect to the way in which to spend his money.

privatization

Transferring activities from the public sector (government) to the private sector (whether or not commercial organizations, clubs, foundations). This may coincide with the conversion of collective goods into individualizable goods, for instance transferring police tasks to private security firms. Sometimes these tasks are performed on an not-for-profit basis.

productivity measurement

Form of productivity measurement whereby it is checked to what extent particular concrete objectives of the organization have been accomplished by its activities. In this case the direct effects of the service on the consumer are meant, for example, the fact that a patient has recovered as a result of medical treatment.

profit-oriented organization

Profit seeking organization. One of the major objectives in this organization's policy is realizing profit.

psychological threshold (psychological price)

The perceived barriers, such as fear and uncertainty, the consumer has to conquer before he proceeds to buying the service. The psychological threshold is a form of a non-monetary price.

public sector

The category of service organizations within the national economy without a motive of profit. Since the major part of the not-for-profit organizations are service organizations, these are usually considered to belong to the public sector.

social marketing

The concept that states that any marketing organization must consider not only customers' long-term interests, but society's long-term interests as well. Social responsibility may be exercised by non-commercial and not-for-profit organizations.

societal marketing concept

An American term for social marketing (see above).

sponsorship

The subsidizing of an event, usually sporting or artistic, by a company for advertising purposes.

subsidy

Placing money at the disposal of not-for-profit organizations, in order to maintain or promote facilities which are not or inadequately borne by the market.

target group

The group of persons or organizations which this organization aims its activities at. To be distinguished from donor target group.

time threshold (time price)

The barrier formed by time which the consumer has to sacrifice in order to obtain and consume a specific service. For example, the total time a patient needs to visit an out-patient clinic, including time of treatment and waiting time. The time threshold is a type of non-monetary price.

References and further reading

Block, S.R., *The Discipline of Non-profit Organizations*, Lyceum, Il., New York, 1991.

Hart, H.W.C. van der, *Leveren zonder Prijssignaal*, Nuenen, 2nd edition, 1984.

Heskett, J.L., W.E. Sasser and C.W.L. Hart, *Service Breakthroughs. Changing the rules of the game*, The Free Press, New York, 1990.

Kotler, Ph. and A.R. Andreasen, *Strategic Marketing for Non-profit Organizations*, Prentice-Hall, Englewood Cliffs, New Jersey, 3rd edition, 1991.

Lovelock, C.H., *Managing Services. Marketing, operations and human resources*, Prentice-Hall, Englewood Cliffs, New Jersey, 1992.

Zemke, R. and D. Schaaf, *The Service Edge, 101 Companies that Profit from Customer Care*, NAL Penguin Inc., New York, 1989.

14 RETAIL MARKETING

Concept overview

affiliation system
automatic vending machine sales
auxiliary service

business location/site research
business-to-business marketing

canvassing
catalogue showroom
category killer
category management
chain level
choice assortment
co-operative
community shopping centre
concessionaire
consumers' market
convenience store
core assortment

dealer
dealer display
department store
direct product costs
direct product profit
direct product profitability (DPP)
direct-product-profitability method (DPP
   method)
discounter
distribution structure
distributor
distributor marketing
distributor owned brand
double target group approach
down-grading

external store presentation

facings
family
family grouping
franchising system
fun shopping

house party
hypermarket

impulse goods
in-store communication
in-store promotions
interior display
internal store presentation

local shopping centre
location choice
low-margin retailing strategy

mail order company
mobile shop

multiple shop organization
mystery buyer

national chain
national multiple shop organization
non-store retailing

one-stop shopping
outlet

presentation

regional chain store
regional shopping centre
retail
retail brand policy
retail chain
retail concentration
retail formula strategy
retail life cycle
retail marketing
retail mix
retailer
retailer owned brand
routing

scanner
served area
service retailing strategy
shop in a shop
shop test
shopping centre
sight shelf zone
speciality store
store formula
store image
store layout
store retailing
store type
supermarket
superstore

telemarketing
teleshopping
town shopping centre
trade marketing
turnover/gross profit

up-grading

variety store
voluntary chain

wheel of retailing
wholesale brand
wholesale marketing
wholesale trade
wholesaler marketing
wholesaler owned brand

Concept descriptions

affiliation system
System whereby small retailers buy their products from a multiple shop organization. The multiple shop organization, therefore, performs the wholesale function for these small retailers, for example, Spar and VG.

automatic vending machine sales
Type of non-store trade. Sale through machines. Usually this concerns impulse and emergency goods (cigarettes, snacks, confectionery, condoms, etc.).

auxiliary service
Additional service during the materialization of the core service. For example: in the case of an airline the core service can be formulated as the air transport of goods and people; auxiliary services can then be: care of the tickets, luggage processing, catering, etc.

business location/site research
Research into the various aspects of a business site. Taken into consideration are the size of the served area, the composition of the population in the served area, the expenditure and spending patterns of these (prospective) group of consumers, the competition present or to be expected, accessability by public transport as well as by car (parking space, and so on).

business-to-business marketing
Marketing activities of an organization aimed at other organizations.

canvassing (house-to-house selling)
Canvassing is a form of non-store trade whereby products are demonstrated and sold at the door. Typical of canvassing is that the buyer is unprepared, that he/she is presented with a unique offer, that he/she cannot compare the limited assortment on hand with any other assortment, and that, usually, the canvasser (the salesperson) meets the buyer only once.

catalogue showroom
Shop in which of each product in the assortment, only one item is shown. The shop also has a catalogue featuring the entire assortment. On purchase, the article is delivered straight from the warehouse. The purchase is effected for cash payment. Service is very limited: information is only provided through the catalogue, the articles are not always guaranteed.

category killer
The term given to chains of high volume, low price stores such as K-Mart who are committed to low prices rather than product ranges or lines.

category management
Analysis, planning, implementation and evaluation of marketing activities by an organization with relation to (part) assortments or product groups. It is no longer thought of in terms of individual products/brands, but in terms of complete, consistent and coherent (part) assortments and/or product groups. When category management is used within an industry column by both manufacturers and retailers, it can lead to closer attuning of (collective) marketing activities.

chain level (channel level)
One or more distributors performing the same trade function within the distribution channel. Thus, the joint exporters form one chain. This also holds good for the joint importers, the joint agents, the joint commission agents, the joint brokers, the joint wholesale and the joint retail organizations, respectively.

choice assortment
Part of the store assortment which can be used to add to the core assortment, in view of the store formula of the retailer in question.

co-operative
Horizontal marketing system whereby, for example, co-operating retailers, by bundling their orders, order direct from the manufacturer thus stipulating more favourable terms and conditions. Associated primarily with the Co-operative Movement founded in the UK in 1844.

community shopping centre
Shopping centre serving a community, i.e. approximately 12,000–20,000 inhabitants living at a walking distance of 10 to 15 minutes from the centre.

concessionaire
Independent retailer leasing space in an existing retail shop (usually a department store or a supermarket), and running a speciality shop there, independently and for his own risk.

consumers' market (cash and carry store)
A discounter for consumer goods with a very limited assortment, low prices and little service.

convenience store
Originally, American store type where convenience goods are sold and where customer convenience is taken care of by, particularly, long business hours.

core assortment
That part of the assortment which consists of articles with a relatively high rate of turnover. Usually those products are considered to belong to the core assortment which represent the top 20 per cent of all articles carried, in terms of turnover.

dealer
Distributor of more or less durable production or consumer goods, in the case of a limited distribution (selective or exclusive distribution) by the producer.

dealer display
Display provided by the producer to the retailer or dealer.

department store
Large retail business with a relatively wide and deep assortment, and a shop surface of 10,000 to 20,000 m². Department stores will typically be found in large city centres and in shopping centres in the suburbs. Usually they are self-service shops, but service staff is present. Examples of department stores are: Harrods, Marks & Spencer (M&S), La fayette.

direct product costs
Costs to be allocated directly to an article or article group. A distinction is made between the costs of the distribution centre, the transport costs, and the costs of the shop operation (especially applicable to distribution problems).

direct product profit
Profit resulting from an article or article group. This is the gross margin less the direct product costs.

direct product profitability (DPP)
Direct (gross) profit contribution/profitability per product/product group in the retail trading. *See also:* direct-product-profitability method.

direct-product-profitability method (DPP method)
Costing method in retail trade, whereby the corrected gross margin on a product/product group (= gross margin minus obtained reductions) is reduced by the direct distribution costs (direct costs of: transport, distribution centre/warehouse and the shop operation). This consequently leaves a contribution to the not yet attributed share of the overhead costs and the company profit.

discounter
Department store with a limited, shallow assortment, low prices and very limited service.

distribution structure
Nature, number, size, and spread of the various distributors in a specific area with regard to all products or a specific product.

distributor
Organization performing a trade function in the industry sector, such as an exporter, an importer, an agent, a broker, a commission agent and other middlemen, a wholesale trade, a retail trade.

distributor marketing
Marketing by a distributor directed at consumers. If the distributor is a wholesaler, then it can be called wholesale marketing, if the distributor is a retailer, then it is called retail marketing.

distributor owned brand
Brand for a product or different product groups which is owned by a distributor, and which is (virtually) exclusively sold by that distributor and/or the affiliated organizations. A distinction can be made on the basis of wholesaler brands and retailer brands.

double target group approach
A producer's market operating strategy in which not only a distinction is made by different target groups of end users, but in which the distributors (wholesale and/or retail) are considered separate buyer groups having their own specific requirements and demands.

down-grading (grading down)
Changing a more service retailing oriented strategy into a more low margin retailing oriented strategy.

external store presentation
Part of the 'presentation' retail mix element containing factors outside the shop, such as the shop front and the shop environment. *See also:* retail mix.

facings (shelf facings)
The number of packagings which, being present on the shop shelf, can be seen by the consumer. For the number of facings, only the length and the height in the shelf are decisive, not the depth.

family
In distributor marketing the group of products which are seen by buyers as belonging together. If this is taken into account when the shop and the shelves are laid out, the consumer will be able to find the articles looked for quickly.

family grouping
The formation of (product) families in the layout of the shop and the shelves. *See also:* family.

franchising system (franchising)
Type of collaboration whereby a franchise agreement is concluded between a franchisor, and a franchisee, in which the franchisor grants to the franchisee the right to apply an exclusive exploitation system developed or used by him for a fee, to which application the franchisee binds himself in pursuance of the said agreement. Examples of franchise organizations are: Holiday Inn hotels, McDonalds, The Body Shop and Benetton. The franchise system is a contractual (vertical) marketing system.

fun shopping (recreational shopping)
Situation in which a consumer considers shopping a form of pastime or recreation.

house party
Sales venue in the family circle where an adviser/the host demonstrates and sells articles to guests (usually family, relatives, friends, acquaintances). This is a kind of house-to-house selling.

hypermarket
Retail business with a (very) large shop surface (2000–5000 m^2), usually situated outside large residential areas, with ample parking space. The hypermarket is a combination of a supermarket and a department store. In addition to foodstuffs, the assortment also contains durables and other non-food products.

impulse goods
Goods which, in general, are bought by consumers, on the spur of the moment, and often after having been confronted with them.

in-store communication
Sales promoting communication for particular products or brands at the point of purchase/in the shop. For example, displays, advertising on shop trolleys, on/near the shelf, on video screens, and so on. Not quite appropriately, this is sometimes referred to as in-store marketing or in-store promotion.

in-store promotions
Sales promoting activities in the shape of selling out promotions or consumer promotions for specific products or brands at the point of purchase/shop. For example, special displays/offers, coupons, presents.

interior display
Display used within the shop. This may be both a dealer display and a merchandise display.

internal store presentation
Part of the 'presentation' retail mix element. It includes the atmosphere of the shop, as well as the physical layout of the space.

local shopping centre (shopping strip, strip mall)
Shopping centre in a town having a district serving function. The established shops usually sell products filling the daily buying needs (usually fresh produce). The served area at a walking distance of five minutes averages 3500–5000 people.

location choice (site selection)
Selecting the site for a shop. This is what is meant in the 'site' retail mix element. *See also:* retail mix.

low-margin retailing strategy
Strategy of a retailer whereby he chooses for a wide target group which prefers low prices. In this strategy, the retailer is satisfied with a low margin, carries a wide and shallow assortment, has low buying costs, and employs few and not highly skilled personnel.

mail order company
Distribution by an organization whereby the buyer, through catalogues, brochures, and so on, is informed on the supply of the (trade) organization. The buyer can place orders by telephone, in writing, or by computer, and in due course the products will be delivered. The buyer has a right to return the goods within a specified period of time if they do not come up to his expectations. This is a kind of 'home shopping'.

mobile shop
Type of door-to-door retailing whereby a large van, laid out as a shop, drives up to the consumer's front door, so that they can do their shopping there. The assortment consists mainly of convenience goods, and the shops usually operate on a self-service basis.

multiple shop organization (multiple shop chain)
Large retail organization (on the basis of turnover, number of employees and/or number of locations). For many products in the assortment, multiple shops have integrated the wholesaler function with the retailer function. National chain stores and department stores are considered to be multiple shop organizations. A distinction is made between national multiple shops and regional multiple shops.

mystery buyer
Person (usually employed by a producer, importer, wholesaler or research agency) acting as an ordinary customer of a retail shop, assessing the shelf positions, service, quality and the staff's selling efforts for a specific product or brand in the assortment. *See also:* shop test.

national chain (store)
Retail organization with more than seven branches. *See also:* multiple shop organization.

national multiple shop organization (national chain)
Large retail organization (on the basis of turnover, number of employees and/or number of locations) in a particular country. *See also:* national chain.

non-store retailing
Type of retailing without a fixed location. This includes: market and street trade, mobile shops, door-to-door selling, pedlars or non-store trade for shipping, selling by telephone, mail order businesses and selling through machines.

one-stop shopping
Specific buying behaviour of consumers who prefer to do the major part of their shopping (in particular of convenience and shopping goods) in one location. The retail trade can meet this requirement by settling in shopping centres or shopping malls, establishing larger (self-service) department stores, hypermarkets, or entering into certain kinds of co-operation.

outlet
Place where buyers can buy their products. For end users or final consumers, this tends to be a retail shop.

presentation
Element from the retail marketing mix. *See also:* internal store presentation, external store presentation.

regional chain store
A relatively large retail organization (on the basis of turnover, number of employees and/ or number of locations) in a specific area/region. *See also:* national chain.

regional shopping centre
Shopping centre serving a regional area which is 2.5 times as big as a district shopping centre.

retail
Trade supplying the final consumers (end users) with products. The last link in the distribution channel.

retail brand policy
Retailer brand as a counterpart of the manufacturer brands (A brand, B brand, C brand, generic brand, free brand). Objective of the retail brand policy is to be able to stress ones distinctive features in respect of the competition. Using a retail brand, a distinctive advantage may be created in respect of the competition in the field of price of quality and store loyalty may be built up. Retail brands occur in two forms:
· brand names having the name of the company or a variation of it
· brand names having individual brand names

retail chain (store)
A retail organization with different branches (locations) which are owned by this retail organization. These branches usually show a high degree of assortment similarity, internal and external shop presentation. *See also:* national chain.

retail concentration
Process in retail as a result of which an ever growing part of the retail turnover (in a particular line of business or sector) is realized by an ever decreasing number of retail organizations (in that line of business or sector).

retail formula strategy
Marketing policy of a retail organization with regard to the specific store formula which will be used in the retail location(s).

retail life cycle (life cycle)
Description of the (restricted) life cycle of shop formulas. The retail life cycle consists of four stages: early growth (introduction), rapid development, maturity, and decline. The 'wheel of retailing' concept explains the retail life cycle.

retail marketing
Marketing by retail organizations. In retail marketing, the elements of the marketing mix in question are identified as the retail mix.

retail mix
The six variables which the retailer can manipulate in his marketing policy, namely:

place:	store location aspects including parking space, accessibility, premises, stocking facilities, centre/suburb/shopping centre;
product:	brand policy, assortment policy;
presentation:	external shop presentation (shop front, shop environment), and internal shop presentation (shop atmosphere, physical division of space, shop layout, shelf layout);
staff:	recruitment, selection, training;
price:	pricing of the assortment;
promotion/ communication:	communication, advertising, promotions, campaigns, shop window display, point-of-purchase display, dealer display.

retailer
Owner of and/or manager in a retail business running this business for his own account and risk.

retailer owned brand (own brand, house brand, shop brand)
Distributor brand owned by a retail organization, and which (virtually) exclusively is sold in that organization or the organizations affiliated to it.

routing
The order in which the different products and article groups ('families') are located in the shop and the (often forced) walking route the clients have to take in order to pass through the shop.

scanner
Gadget used at the check-out to read the UPC code. The scanner is not only used to read the price, but usually also to monitor the stock.

served area (served region, served district)
The geographical area in which the inhabitants may be considered the (prospective) customers of a particular shop or shopping centre.

service retailing strategy
Strategy of a retailer whereby a narrow target group is chosen which has a preference for quality and service. In this strategy, the retailer prefers an exclusive and narrow assortment with a higher margin, relatively high purchasing costs, offering service, advice and expertise, and working in an exclusive, luxurious environment.

shop in a shop
Separate selling unit in a larger retail site (department store). Such a separate selling unit is usually a served unit, whereas payment is effected separately. Usually this is performed by a concessionaire e.g. perfume counter.

shop test
Shop research whereby a pseudo-buyer buys an article in the shop to be investigated and, by asking some questions, tests the retailer's or the staff's service. *See also:* mystery buyer.

shopping centre (shopping mall)
Site where a number of different shops are established together. *See also:* community shopping centre, town shopping centre, regional shopping centre, local shopping centre.

sight shelf zone
Part of the shop shelf between 1.20 and 1.60 m, so that the majority of the customers may be faced directly with the products on the shelf, and do not have to go to much trouble to take the product from the shelf.

speciality store
Served store with a deep assortment, extensive service and relatively high prices.

store formula
Total proposition used by the retailer to attract and hold on to a particular group of buyers. The store formula can be identified using three components: the type of assortment (what is sold), the target group (to whom is sold), and the market position (in respect of the competition).

store image
The ideas, feelings and judgements a customer has with regard to a particular store. This is the subjective perception of the store concept.

store layout
The division of the store surface by its different functions. For the store layout, decisions are made with regard to the area of sales space, the area for operational destinations such as warehouse, canteen, office and the so-called service surface (aisles, waiting room, information desk) and the checkout service.

store retailing
Retailing with a fixed place or location, unlike non-store retailing.

store type
Description of a store on the basis of objective criteria relating to the prices of the products in the assortment, the width and depth of the assortment as such, type of service, location of the site and the surface of the shop.

supermarket
Self-service shops primarily in food retailing with a surface of less than 25,000 sq. ft.

superstore
Specialized store based on hypermarket model, located out of town near a major road network and beside other major retailers. Usually more than 25,000 sq. ft of selling space.

telemarketing
Established term wrongly used to identify a type of marketing. It concerns using the telephone merely to support selling and communication activities.

teleshopping
Preparing and executing the purchasing decision at home, such as placing the order, and taking receipt of the order using catalogues, telephone, computer (Internet), videotext, order forms, and other response facilities.

town shopping centre
Usually the historically developed concentration of shops. Often clothing shops, department stores, furniture shops, and hotels and restaurants.

trade marketing
A producer's marketing activities directed at (potential) distributors (retail trade, wholesale trade) of his products.

turnover/gross profit (shelf division product grouping system)
Shelf division system whereby maximization of the gross profit per metre shelf space is pursued. The selection criterion to include products in the assortments is the gross profit of a particular product per shelf space.

up-grading
Changing a low margin retailing oriented strategy into a dedicated service retailing strategy.

variety store
American name for a type of shop where in addition to non-food and convenience articles also a limited food assortment is present, for example, Woolworths.

voluntary chain
Organization of a large number of retailers who, on a voluntary basis, buy centrally from one or more wholesalers, and use one name, presentation, logo, and retailer owned brand in their external presentation. The associated retailers remain independent entrepreneurs. The initiative for a voluntary chain is usually taken by the wholesale trade.

wheel of retailing
Model describing and explaining the succession of the store formulas. In this model an original store formula with minimal added value proceeds to upgrade to a store formula with more added value. After further upgrading all shops become comparable again and space will be created at the bottom end of the market (shop with minimal added value), and the cycle can restart and newcomers can enter the market.

wholesale brand
Distributor brand which is owned by a wholesale organization, and which is (virtually) exclusively sold within that organization and/or the associated organizations.

wholesale marketing
Marketing by a wholesale organization directed at the consumers (other distributors). In wholesale marketing the different marketing mix elements can be identified as the wholesale mix.

wholesale trade
Middleman between producer and retailer with as basic functions collecting and distributing.

wholesaler marketing
A producer's or distributor's marketing activity directed at the (prospective) wholesalers of his products.

wholesaler owned brand
A specific type of a distributor brand owned by a wholesale organization, and which is (almost) exclusively sold within that organization and/or affiliated organizations.

References and further reading

Bunt, J., A.R. Dreesman and C. Goud, *Dynamiek in de distributie*, Kluwer, Deventer, 1989.

Cook, D. and D. Walters, *Retailmarketing, Theory and Practice*, Prentice-Hall, Englewood Cliffs, New Jersey, 1991.

Dikken, I. and H.A.M. Liesker, *Detailhandelsmarketing*, Wolters-Noordhoff, Groningen, 1991.

Pelligrini, L. and S.K. Reddy, *Retail and Marketing Channels*, Routledge, New York, 1989.

Schuurmans, A., *Marktgerichte distributie*, Academic Service, Schoonhoven, 1991.

Ster, W. van der and P.J. van Wissen, *Marketing en Detailhandel*, Wolters-Noordhoff, Groningen, 5th edition, 1993.

15 DIRECT MARKETING

Concept overview

address agency
after sales mailing
auto-dial

block dominance theory
break-even response
brochure
bulk mailing
bundling

catalogue
CD-Rom (Compact Disc Read Only
  Memory)
CDI (Compact Disc Interactive)
central reply card
client pyramid
clustering
cold call
cold prospect
combi mailing
compact mailing
company magazine
compiled list
continuity offer
control address
control pack
conversion ratio
costs per order
costs per response
costs per thousand (CPM)
coupon advertising
credit scoring
cross-selling
crossing
customer loyalty card
customer profile

data file
data file holder
data file manager
data file protection
data file supervisor
database
database marketing
deep selling
direct advertising
direct mail
direct mailing campaign
direct marketing
Direct Marketing Association (DMA)
direct marketing communication
direct non-mail
direct response advertising
direct response commercial
direct response television

direct selling
double duty advertising
drop date
dry test

EDI (Electronic Data Interchange)
electronic mail
endorsed mailing

file enhancement
flyer
follow-up mailing
freepost
frequent customer reward programmes
front-end analysis
fulfilment
fulfilment house
full service direct marketing agency
fund raising

gadget
gain(s) chart
gimmick

head-to-head test
home shopping
hot list
house list
house to house circulation

in-bound telemarketing
in-house magazine
incentive
infomercial
insert
interactive marketing
interactive media
internal data file

junk mail

labelling
lead
lead generation
lead qualification
letter shop
lifetime value
likely addresses
list broker
list compiler
list management
loyalty programme

mail merge
mail order advertising
mail order sale
mail package

mail preparation activities
mailing
mailing list
main mailing
match code
matching
MDS envelope
members store
membership card
membership formula
merge-purge
more step approach
multi-mailing
multi-shot mailing
multi-stage campaign
multimedia

NAR data
negative option
network marketing
new member introduction rewards
non-response
non-response analysis

one-shot mailing
one-stage campaign
order-card
ordering behaviour
orders per thousand (OPM)
out-bound telemarketing
outsert
overkill

partner card
party post
pay per view
personalization
personify
phone monitor
piggy back
point of decision theory
positive option
postage paid
postcode segmentation
prospect

qualified leads

record layout
relationship life cycle
relationship management
relationship marketing
reminder
reply card
reply coupon
reply envelope
reply form

response
response analysis
response carrier
response curve
response device
response filter
response intensifier
response list
response medium
response per thousand (RPM)
retention marketing
return processing
returns
RFM
Robinson list
roll-out

sales resistance theory
selective binding
self-mailer
single variable test mailing
source code
split run
sticker
streamer
streaming test
sweepstake
synchronous insertion
syndication

target group selection in direct marketing
teaser mailing
tele-selling
tele-support
telemarketing
telephone script
teleshopping
teletext
test mailing
testing
touch screen
traffic analysis
TV home shopping
twin spot

unaddressed mailing
underkill

video on demand
videotext
videotext service
voice response system
voice-to-voice communication

wet test
world wide web (www)

yes/no option

Concept descriptions

address agency (list broker)
Organization having at its disposal files with addresses, arranged according to demographic, psychographic and geopraphical variables in order to make them accessible to third parties against payment (usually for single usage).

after sales mailing
Mailing sent to individuals who have concluded a transaction. The aim of the mailing is to create a closer relationship with the customer or increase the satisfaction of the user, to create a positive image, hence indirectly stimulating future sales.

auto-dial
This is a technique used in telemarketing. The computer generates a combination of numbers and has a program which can be used to phone a telephone number at a predetermined time. This is often used in telemarketing programmes. *See also:* voice response system.

block dominance theory (isolation factor theory)
The more dominant the presence of a direct response commercial within a block (because of length, twin spots, and so on), the bigger the response possibility. *See also:* direct response television.

break-even response
Response to be realized to recover the total costs of a campaign.

brochure
Folded printed matter suitable for the communication of more complex product and supply information.

bulk mailing
Final version of the main mailing, usually based on the results of various tests.

bundling
Division of postal parcels into one or more bundles, for example, according to postcode. For a discount, part of the work is taken off the distributor's hands.

catalogue
Classified inventory of all the products which can be supplied by an organization. The summary can also include prices, conditions of delivery, ordering information.

CD-Rom (Compact Disc Read Only Memory)
An optical storage medium in the shape of a compact disc. The storage medium is intended for storing large amounts of computer data in digital form.

CDI (Compact Disc Interactive)
A term referring to both a multimedia standard, a storage medium and a hardware platform. CDI combines compressed sound, (moving) image, text and software on one optical disc. With the use of a CDI player image and sound can be played back synchronously on a television set. Apart from the compression and decompression of moving images, the power of the system lies mainly in the interaction between programme and user.

central reply card
Reply card often to a publisher requesting information on various products and/or advertisers.

client pyramid
Division of the market into a number of (customer) categories according to the length of the relation, the turnover per time unit and the sales per time unit.

clustering
The grouping together of prospects or customers who show a large degree of similarity on one or more relevant variables.

cold call
Approaching cold prospects without prior announcement or appointment.

cold prospect
Addressee about whom no definite information is known as to whether he or she is interested in the offers of the organization. The activities involved in approaching these prospects are called canvassing activities.

combi mailing (card deck, card pack, co-op mailing, mailbag, multibag, multimailing)
Combined mailing in which a supplier offers various products/services, or in which several suppliers make an offer to the addressee.

compact mailing
Combined envelope, folder, sales letter and reply card. To be opened, for example, by way of a perforated seal.

company magazine
Medium of the organization which is sent without request and for free to employees and/ or relations of the organization with the objective to inform them on and involve them in the organization.

compiled list
Address list of people or organizations, compiled from several different sources. The organizations or people all display characteristics which can be identified (for example, home owners), but it is not known whether or not they are interested in a specific offer. Directory not owned by the organization. Usually rented direct from the data file owner in question, or via a listbroker.

continuity offer
An offer during which more than one transaction is concluded over time, for example, a series of books or a (book, CD, etc.) club membership.

control address (hide address)
Addresses to be added to the address directories by the address supplier with the objective of establishing whether the direct marketing organization actually uses the directory in compliance with what was agreed.

control pack
Standard basic mailing included in a test to give a reference point for measuring the influence of test variables.

conversion ratio
The conversion of enquiries into actual orders.

costs per order
The (direct marketing) costs to be allocated to the order divided by the number of orders. This is a good cost measure in cases where the action is mainly aimed at sales. *See also:* costs per response.

costs per response
The (direct marketing) costs incurred divided by the total response, in the shape of both orders and requests for information.

costs per thousand (CPM)
Costs per thousand mail pieces sent. In formula
CPM = (total costs of the mailing/edition of mailing) × 1000

coupon advertising
Advertisement containing a coupon, giving the opportunity to ask for more information or the product itself. People are given the chance to react instantly.

credit scoring
Evaluation whereby, on the basis of internal and external sources, calculations are made beforehand as to whether a prospect or customer is eligible for credit.

cross-selling
Sales of other than the goods already purchased, or services to existing customers.

crossing
Overlap of address directories obtained through merge-purge. *See also:* merge-purge.

customer loyalty card
Card distributed by the supplier meant to achieve customer loyalty, building up a relationship, and recognizing good customers. The card is meant for all 'good' customers only. The card contains at least NAR data. The card can offer the owner benefits such as easy payment (the card then takes the function of a payment card), credit facilities, pre-sale information and discounts. The card offers the supplier such features as direct communication, analysing the type of customer and purchasing patterns.

customer profile
Description of the specific characteristics of the customers. These characteristics are used to define the target group and the method of communication with them.

data file
Collection of data, compiled according to a certain structure and with a common characteristic.

data file holder
The person in control of the (personal) data to be stored in the file.

data file manager
Person appointed by the data file holder to be in the day-to-day charge of the file, i.e. changing and keeping files up to date.

data file protection
Precautions ensuring that unauthorized persons cannot access the file.

data file supervisor
Person appointed by the data file holder who supervises the administration, functioning, protection and proper usage of the registration(s) of persons which the holder controls.

database
Electronic 'card-index box' containing various data. In direct marketing this concerns data such as contact details, customer profile, purchase or order behaviour.

database marketing (direct marketing)
Alternative term for direct marketing, emphasizing that the use of a database is essential.

deep selling (up selling)
Increasing the sales to existing customers, for example, by offering premiums or incentives. The campaign is aimed at a product or service which is already used by these customers. *See also:* cross-selling.

direct advertising
All advertising aimed directly at a target group: addressed and unaddressed letterbox advertisements, commercial messages by telephone, and other interactive media. An example of addressed direct advertising is direct mail, and an example of unaddressed direct advertising is the door-to-door distribution of advertising handbills.

direct mail
A personalized written commercial message. Direct mail contains, for example, an envelope, a letter, information material, and a reply envelope.

direct mailing campaign
Campaign in which the target group is approached by direct mail.

direct marketing
Type of marketing aimed at realizing a specific transaction and/or obtaining and maintaining a durable, structural, direct relationship between supplier and customers. The marketing instruments play their own specific role, of which direct communication and/or direct delivery are the most characteristic.

Direct Marketing Association (DMA)
American professional association for direct marketing.

direct marketing communication
All communication between supplier and customer in the range of building and maintaining a direct relationship between the supplier and customer. Is often aimed at response, but mediums such as newsletters and promotional magazines, can also be regarded as direct marketing communication.

direct non-mail (junk mail)
Completely unfocused direct advertising; unaddressed letterbox advertising distributed with the possibility of responding direct, either in writing, by telephone, or electronically. No knowledge is available as to who receives this communication or replies.

direct response advertising
Advertising in which the receiver is asked to give a direct response either in writing, or by telephone or electronically.

direct response commercial
A commercial containing a directly measurable and behaviour influencing element, in which the viewer is asked to react immediately, often by using a (free) 0800 number. The reaction can concern a request for information or an order. The length of such a commercial can vary strongly. *See also:* infomercial.

direct response television
Indicating the launching of direct response commercials on television.

direct selling
Method for selling and distributing consumer goods and services by means of personal face-to-face sales conversations, usually conducted at the buyer's home and not in the company.

double duty advertising
Advertising with both thematic and active aspects. For example: a television commercial offering a response possibility in the form of a telephone or reply number.

drop date
Date when the mailing is offered to the post office for delivery.

dry test
Conducting a test to determine the response to a direct marketing campaign in which a product is offered which at that moment does not yet exist, and hence cannot yet be delivered.

EDI (Electronic Data Interchange)
Electronic exchange of structured and standardized data between computers of, for example, supplier, customers and logistical services as a consequence of concluding and settling sales transactions.

electronic mail
Communication by computer. The message is sent via a cable or telephone line from one computer to another. This text can then be read direct, or in a different file.

endorsed mailing
Mailing as a consequence of the co-operation between a directory owner and an organization wishing to use the file. The directory owner introduces the other party.

file enhancement
Adding data at record level to a file, as a result of which better selections and/or (profile) analysis are made possible.

flyer
Printed matter circulated freely or enclosed in a mailing package. Particularly cheap but completely unfocused so a low response rate can be anticipated.

follow-up mailing
Mailing in which non-respondents to a previous mailing are urged again to respond.

freepost
System of post-paid postage in which the respondent does not have to pay the postage. Afterwards, the company pays the post office the postage (including a surcharge) for the mail returned through the freepost number. Can be applied both nationally and internationally.

frequent customer reward programmes
Term used for activities aimed at identifying, maintaining, and where possible, increasing the profits generated by the best customers, by means of long term interactive value added relations. The essence is rewarding customers who buy regularly and/or large amounts. *See also:* loyalty programme, relationship marketing, retention marketing.

front-end analysis
Financial analysis aimed at measuring the initial costs of, and the response to, a direct marketing activity; primarily concerns the costs of recruiting new customers, members, etc. It concerns criteria such as costs per thousand, response per thousand, orders per thousand, costs per response and costs per order.

fulfilment
Finalizing the sequence of response and order processing. This sequence starts with activities such as collecting and registering reactions and can finish by mailing the requested information or products.

fulfilment house (agency)
Agency taking care of all activities resulting from the processing of the response to direct marketing activities.

full service direct marketing agency
Agency which develops direct marketing campaigns, advises on the choice of media, renders services with regard to the development and management of the database and mediates in obtaining addresses, sending mailings, out-bound telemarketing and fulfilment.

fund raising
Activities of mainly non-profit organizations to gather donations through actions, collections, direct mail, advertisements and publicity for a preset determined goal. The application of DM techniques for fund raising is considered a unique speciality within direct marketing.

gadget
Small article sent prior to a mailing, to induce interest in the mailing. Can also be sent simultaneously with the mailing. *See also:* gimmick.

gain(s) chart
A table or figure showing the estimated response to a campaign by various parts of the target group. To this end, historical data is used to calculate the chance of response for each address. Subsequently, the addresses are arranged from high to low according to the estimated chance. The addresses are then often categorized according to classes of similar size (of, for example, 10 per cent, indicated in deciles) and the average chance of response per class is calculated. Afterwards, using the break-even analysis, the position of the cut-off point is calculated, i.e. who should and should not be mailed.

gimmick
Small article of little value, enclosed with a mailing, intended to attract attention in the mailing.

head-to-head test
Test in which research is conducted simultaneously into two variables. *See also:* test mailing.

home shopping
Products or services, offered by means of a mailing, the telephone, a catalogue (printed or available via electronic media), or as a result of direct response commercials on radio and television, may be ordered by mail or telephone, fax or computer.

hot list
A list consisting of the best responding individuals.

house list
Personal list containing data of people who have made a purchase from the organization, or have reacted to direct response advertising. The data can concern the response and payment performance, (geographic) demographic and psychographic data. *See also:* internal data file.

house to house circulation (door-to-door circulation)
Type of direct advertising in which unaddressed printed advertising matter is distributed.

in-bound telemarketing
Incoming telephone calls of respondents to a DM organization. *See also:* telemarketing.

in-house magazine
Unsolicited medium of the organization which is sent to that organization's co-workers and their relatives with the objective of informing and involving them in the organization.

incentive
Reward (in the shape of a discount, present, or trip) offered to the customer, distributor or representative as an extra incentive to influence behaviour.

infomercial (program length advertising)
A long (for example, 20 minutes) direct response commercial varying in length from 3 to 30 minutes which often contains a product demonstration (or an extensive explanation of the service offered) and which offers the possibility to respond.

insert (tip-in)
DM advertising sewn in or inserted in a medium with its own reply card or referring to a central reply card; these are, for example, supplements in newspapers and magazines.

interactive marketing
Alternative term for direct marketing, which emphasizes that interaction between supplier and consumer is essential.

interactive media
Media enabling two-way communication between supplier and customer. Examples are: direct mail, telephone and interactive television.

internal data file

Data file containing information on individuals with whom the organization has had contact in the past. These concern both customers of the organization (those who purchased at least one product or made at least one donation in the past), and the people who have requested information on the offers of the organization. The contact data may also have been obtained through coupon advertisements, inserts, by telephone (people requesting information, reactions to commercials offering a response facility). Often, apart from contact data, the internal data file also contains information on purchasing and payment performance. Furthermore, the file can contain data in relation to the response sensitivity of individuals to previous direct marketing activities and resulting (geographic) demographic and psychographic data.

junk mail

Any unsolicited general mailing or circular which is not targeted at any particular group but just the general public. It is unfocused and will irritate many recipients.

labelling

Type of syndication in which the sender sends his or her own paper, with which his or her name is linked.

lead

Person or organization who has shown an interest in an offer by responding with a request for further information. *See also:* lead qualification.

lead generation

Finding leads with the help of, for example, coupon advertisements or (cold) mailings. Before taking further action, lead qualification can take place first.

lead qualification

Determining the degree to which a lead is interested in the offer of the organization. If the reply card or coupon does not already give this information ('short term purchasing plans', 'interested in information only', 'would like representative to call'), qualification can be established, for example, by using the telephone. For the sake of well qualified leads more sales efforts can be made, for example, a visit by a representative or a telephone call.

letter shop (mailing house)

Agency specialized in, amongst other things, addressing and printing mailings, inserting, sorting and bundling, address wrapping, foil wrapping, addressing and prepostal processing of magazines, filling and preparing for despatch cardboard tubes and other, non-mechanically processable mailings.

lifetime value

The net cash value of the profit from a customer. Is important mainly in the decision-making on recruiting and reactivating customers, for example, the determination of the degree to which (new) investments in customers are profitable.

likely addresses

Addresses complying with certain criteria, as a result of which they are more likely to respond to specific campaigns. In the gains chart analysis, for example, these are the addresses above the 'cut off point'.

list broker

Intermediary who, either for his own account or for the account of the directory owner or directory customer, establishes transactions especially in connection with hiring and renting directories and directories with the accompanying address characteristics for one or more directory customers and more than one data file owner.

list compiler

Organization or person engaged in compiling directories with the accompanying address characteristics. *See also:* compiled list.

list management
Organization and management of the list with the objective of executing and evaluating direct marketing activities on the basis of contact details and other relevant data, and learning from these for future activities. The higher the quality of the file, the lower the costs per order will be.

loyalty programme
Interpretation of frequency marketing. *See also:* frequent customer reward programmes.

mail merge
Compilation of an address directory and a text. This will enable people to send personalized letters. *See also:* personalization.

mail order advertising
Direct response advertisements with direct sales being the objective. The coupon functions as an order coupon.

mail order sale
Selling through a mail order company; i.e. a type of distribution in which the transactions and the delivery are effected through the post. The goods offered are displayed and described by way of mailings or catalogues. *See also:* teleshopping.

mail package
Referring to the direct mail package. Collection of all separate mailing components to be enclosed in an envelope. Elements which normally form part of the package are: an envelope, a letter, a leaflet and a response carrier.

mail preparation activities
Actions to be carried out before a mailing can be sent: folding and inserting of the constituent parts of the mailing, sealing of the envelope, sorting and bundling of the mailings according to the postal rules, stamping, delivery at the post office. This can also include addressing.

mailing
Each type of communication sent via the mail, fax or on-line computer connection, whether or not with NAR data. Often used as a synonym for direct mail (in which case, obviously, it will be addressed).

mailing list
List containing NAR data, selected and compiled once only for a campaign, and not to be stored afterwards. An exception to this is the addresses which, on the grounds of reactions received, can be transferred to one's own address directory.

main mailing
Mailing in which the actual sales proposition is defined and distributed to existing and prospective customers.

match code
Code according to which comparisons are made when matching addresses.

matching
Comparing addresses from one or more directories with the aim of establishing the existence, and subsequent removal of duplications.

MDS envelope
Envelope with Modern Printed Matter Sealing, in which printed matter can be sent with a sealed flap. Such an envelope can be opened discreetly from the side, so that the post office, if necessary, can check whether it actually contains printed matter.

members store
Point of sale in which goods are sold exclusively to club members.

membership card

Proof of membership of an organization. Membership of a (commercial) organization can provide certain benefits.

membership formula

(Direct) marketing strategy, based on the principle that a person first has to become a member of the organization before orders can be placed and delivered by this organization.

merge-purge

Compilation of address directories whereby duplications are removed as accurately as possible.

more step approach

Mailing with different stages in which an order is booked in several steps; firstly, for example, an enquiry is made, subsequently a quotation is requested, and finally an order is placed.

multi-mailing (card deck)

Mailing in which one supplier offers several products, or in which several suppliers co-operate.

multi-shot mailing

Mailing action consisting of more than one stage, in which every consecutive stage aims at getting the receiver of the mailing more interested in the mailing and/or inducing him to buy.

multi-stage campaign

A campaign whereby the communication course consists of more than one part, for example, several mailings (preparatory, main mailing, follow-up, after sales, cross sell), a mailing followed by a follow-up by telephone, or an action whereby information can be requested first, but an order is placed only at a later stage (for example, after a follow-up mailing).

multimedia

Integrated interactive use of text, graphic pictures, moving image and sound using a tele-vision, computer, cable and/or combinations of these.

NAR data

Data concerning name, address and residence (including postcode). Address directories and lists contain NAR data only.

negative option

Ordering method in which the customer/member/subscriber who does not undertake any action, automatically receives an article from the supplier (such as the Editor's Choice in Book Club mailings).

network marketing

Type of personal sales, whereby use is made of independent dealers for whom rewards are partly dependent on turnover.

new member introduction rewards

Method of recruiting new customers/members, in which existing customers/members are requested, whether or not for a reward, to introduce new customers/members.

non-response

The number of receivers of a direct marketing communication expression (telephone message, mailing, etc) who have not reacted to the message addressed to them. Mainly expressed as a percentage of the total number of copies.

non-response analysis

Research aimed at determining the profile (characteristics) of the non-respondents, to obtain possible reasons for the lack of response.

one-shot mailing
A mailing which has not been announced but goes out to its target audience once only and is not the subject of any follow-up mailing.

one-stage campaign
A campaign with a single commercial message aimed at response.

order-card
Card used to place an order. The order card is smaller than an order form. The card can be returned either with or without a stamp (using freepost). *See also:* response device.

ordering behaviour
Behaviour pattern of a customer which can be derived from the number of orders of, for example, the type of product, the time of ordering, the size of the order. *See also:* RFM.

orders per thousand (OPM)
The number of orders per thousand mailings sent. In formula
OPM = orders/(edition/1000) for a one-step campaign, and
OPM = [response/(edition/1000) × conversion percentage for a multi-step campaign.

out-bound telemarketing
Outgoing telephone calls in a DM organization. Service and sales conversations aimed at the customers in which the initiative is taken by the supplier. *See also:* in-bound telemarketing.

outsert
Printed information concerning a product, service or idea on the outside of a product, magazine etc. *See also:* insert.

overkill
Addresses which, during a merge-purge operation, are wrongly marked as duplications. *See also:* underkill.

partner card
A reply card affixed between two sections in a magazine, consisting of a left-hand side and a right-hand side. When the supplier needs either of the two halves, a partner will have to be found to use the other half.

party post
Identical postal parcels, offered in large quantities, which are subject to special rates. The minimum number for this is 50 copies (regional mail).

pay per view
A television service via cable television channels, only accessible to members. The subscriber can, by means of sending orders via the cable, decide for him/herself what he/she wants to watch (movies, documentaries, music programmes, and so forth). The subscriber pays for the programme delivered.

personalization
The addition of NAR and other specific data from the data file to the mailing.

personify
Using as much of the known data as possible to produce an offer aimed at the individual.

phone monitor
Interactive information exchange in which the telephone is visually supported by an individualized teletext application.

piggy back
A DM distribution method in which an envelope or a personalized reply card is stuck on the wrapper of a magazine.

point of decision theory
Indicates at which moment during a long infomercial, the offer should be communicated, given the supposition that viewers will often not be captivated for longer than seven to eight minutes.

positive option
Ordering method in which the purchase is based on a definite preference for a certain product. Opposite of negative option.

postage paid
Method of payment for sending postal parcels in which the sender does not affix stamps on the parcels, but pays the postage when the total number of parcels are posted.

postcode segmentation (geodemographic segmentation)
System in which the characteristics of residential areas and the characteristics of the residents (including family composition, wealth) are determined within postcode areas. By linking the postcode of customers with the characteristics recorded in the database, a profile of existing customers can be developed with, for example, family composition, wealth and lifestyle characteristics. In addition, postcode areas, in which the characteristics of the residents resemble those of their own customers, can be selected; these households can then be approached by way of, for example, a mailing with an offer. Postcodes include up to twenty people in a complete postcode.

prospect
Person or organization with whom a two-way communication exists, but with whom a transaction has not yet been concluded. *See also:* lead qualification.

qualified leads
Leads emerging positively from a lead qualification; also referred to as hot prospects.

record layout
The way in which different elements of the NAR and other data are stored in an information carrier, such as a tape for addressing or merge-purge.

relationship life cycle
The course of a relationship between supplier and consumer described according to quantitative criteria. The quantitative and qualitative description of the course of a relationship between a supplier and buyer. The development of this relationship is phased in time.

relationship management
Analysis, planning, execution and evaluation of activities aimed at establishing, maintaining and improving long-term relationships between the organization and the different market parties and interest groups such as suppliers, consumers, intermediaries, shareholders and key figures in the social environment.

relationship marketing
Type of marketing aimed at building, maintaining, and commercializing relationships in such a way that the objectives of both parties are realized. The objective of relationship marketing corresponds with that of direct marketing. In addition, direct marketing also provides the equipment to realize these objectives.

reminder
Mailing or telephone call in which the receiver is reminded of an article or service, or a submitted offer. Is aimed more at an individual situation than at a follow-up mailing. *See also:* follow-up mailing.

reply card
Card which the interested individual can use to respond to a (direct) marketing communication expression received. *See also:* response device.

reply coupon
Part of a direct marketing communication expression which the receiver of the message can fill in and return to the sender. *See also:* response device.

reply envelope
Special envelope enclosed with mailings, which an individual or organization can use for returning a reply card, coupon, order card, etc. *See also:* response device.

reply form
Large reply coupon or reply card. Often a list of questions has to be answered. *See also:* reply coupon, response device.

response
The number of reactions to a DM action, usually expressed as a percentage of, for example, the total number of mailings sent. *See also:* non-response.

response analysis
The analysis of the response to one or more (DM) actions, in order to select the best responding groups from (larger) directories for future mailings, to determine the characteristics of those who reacted, to determine the best time for an action, and to analyse the offer and the execution of a package and so forth, in order to improve the response and financial results with regard to (one or more) future actions.

response carrier
Part of the mail package to be used for response. This could be, for example, an order form, reply coupon, reply card or reply form.

response curve
Figure reflecting the number of reactions received per day. Often has the shape of an S curve.

response device
A method in which a reaction can be given to a direct marketing communication expression. The following ways can be distinguished: written (reply coupon, reply form, reply card, order card, sticker, central reply card, partner card), by telephone (for example, a free number) and electronically (e-mail, Internet or videotext).

response filter
Element in the text of a commercial expression which operates as a negative response signal, i.e. which reduces the chance to respond. *See also:* response intensifier.

response intensifier
Element in the text of a commercial expression which operates as a positive response signal, i.e. which increases the chance to respond. *See also:* response filter.

response list
List containing NAR data of organizations or individuals who have reacted to a DM action of another supplier, thus indicating they have some interest in the offer.

response medium
The object with which the receiver of the message may respond, for example, using a reply card, reply coupon or order form. *See also:* response device.

response per thousand (RPM)
The response per thousand mail pieces sent. In formula
OPM = response/(edition/1000)

retention marketing
Concept used to explain that retaining customers should be essential to any marketing strategy.

return processing

Processing NAR corrections in the directory on the basis of returned mail, or informing the file owner of the number and (incorrect) NAR data of the returned mail with the aim to qualify for a refund of the rent or purchase sum of the NAR data.

returns

Mail returned to the sender.

RFM

Recency, frequency, monetary value scoring model describing the purchase history of customers. Recency is the variable measuring how long ago an individual purchased something from the organization. Frequency indicates how often an individual has made a purchase within a certain length of time. Monetary value reflects the value of the items purchased. The sum of the scores with regard to recency, frequency and monetary value will determine the selection of NAR data for the next DM action.

Robinson list

Internationally used term for an address list of people who wish not to receive mailings.

roll-out

The distribution of the final mailing after initially one or more test mailings have been sent.

sales resistance theory

Viewers are least inclined to react to a direct response commercial when they are watching their favourite programme. It is better to realize reaction behaviour at moments when they are watching television with less motivation.

selective binding

Assembly or binding of different sections of a standardized package at the request of the target group, so that printed matter is created which is more relevant to the interests of the groups addressed.

self-mailer

Mailing consisting of only one part, for example, a postcard, which can immediately be used as a reply card.

single variable test mailing

Mailing in which only one variable is tested. *See also:* test mailing.

source code

Unique code in a file with regard to the origin of an address, i.e. to which campaign in which medium the customer reacted.

split run

Division of the edition of a daily paper or magazine in two or more parts, whereby every part contains a different version of an advertisement. In daily papers the division is often made according to editions; in magazines it is possible to take systematic samples from the subscribers file. Advertisements are evaluated according to the response.

sticker

Reply card stuck onto an advertisement which can easily be removed.

streamer

Short, captivating text on the outside of the envelope.

streaming test

Measuring the effect of consecutive mailings. This can give an indication as to how many consecutive times an address can be approached within a certain period.

sweepstake
Competition in which the participants are sent a randomly drawn number free. Prior to despatch, the winning numbers are determined at random. The winning numbers will only later be published.

synchronous insertion
Inserting several (personalized) items in one single envelope.

syndication
The offering of products by a supplier whereby use is made of the medium and the name of another supplier, and which is aimed at a synergetic effect, consisting of one supplier radiating on the other, or the (unexpected) offer of the goods of one supplier to the customers of the other.

target group selection in direct marketing
The selection of likely addresses from a data file. The collection of likely addresses concerns a group of people or organizations who, given an expected probability of the purchase of a product, will provide an expected turnout greater than the total costs of the direct marketing action.

teaser mailing
Mailing arousing the curiosity of the reader in a certain area without revealing too much. Precedes the main mailing or a message in mass media.

tele-selling
Selling products, services or ideas by telephone.

tele-support
Supporting activities with the help of the telephone, such as making appointments for the representative.

telemarketing
Incorporated term wrongly indicated as a type of marketing. It concerns the systematic use of telephones as a marketing communication instrument. There is mention of incoming telephone calls (in-bound, also referred to as passive telemarketing) as well as outgoing telephone calls (out-bound, also referred to as active telemarketing).

telephone script
A fully copied out text of a (commercial) telephone conversation in which for each answer to be given a specific continuation possibility is included.

teleshopping
Preparation of the buying decision at home, placing the order, and taking receipt of the order at home with the help of catalogues, telephone, videotext, fax, e-mail, web page, order forms and other response devices.

teletext
Electronic medium in which data is transmitted in one direction (contrary to videotext) by the television. Using a remote control, the receiver can select which data are to be displayed on screen.

test mailing
Testing of the characteristics of the offer of the mailing itself, by sending the mailing (different versions of it) to a number of members of the target group. A large number of tests are possible. They will, for example, be in relation to target groups (list test), the product (concept test) or the price (price test).

testing
Research into the effect on the response of the used list, the characteristics of persons or organizations approached, the time of the direct marketing action, the characteristics of

the offer, the direct marketing communication expression, etc. To this end, different direct marketing communication expressions, for example, mailings (different versions of it) are sent to members of the target group(s).

touch screen
Screen acting as a monitor and input medium. By touching the screen with your finger, certain operations can be executed. By touching the screen, a current or infra-red beam is interrupted. This enables the computer to determine the place, after which an instruction can be carried out.

traffic analysis (telephone)
Analysis showing exactly how often, and during which period, people have tried to phone a certain telephone number. Especially relevant when analysing the efficiency of, for example, direct response commercials. Is undertaken by Telecom companies.

TV home shopping
Sales method based on recommending goods or services in a television programme (infomercial) whereby viewers have the possibility to immediately order the goods or services shown by telephone.

twin spot
Two commercials belonging together, whereby one supports the other, often in a long and short variant (for example, 30 and 5 seconds respectively) broadcasted in one advertisement block, separated by one or more other commercials. The second commercial repeats the response method.

unaddressed mailing
Mailing without NAR. *See also:* direct non-mail, house to house circulation.

underkill
Address which, inappropriately, has not been marked during a merge-purge operation as a duplicate. *See also:* overkill.

video on demand
A system whereby information (in the shape of a video which can be played) is delivered on request. Order and delivery can take place either on-line or off-line.

videotext
Collective name for a number of patterns of long-distance interactive communication between human and computer. The connection with the computer can be effected through a PC using modem and software, television and telephone (television videotext), two-way television cable and a specific videotext terminal.

videotext service
Service offered by an organization consisting of information, conversation and/or order facility offered by an organization via videotext.

voice response system
Computer system which, by means of (digitally) recorded human messages or computer simulation, verbally answers questions on a specific topic. Uses keyboards and/or voice-to-voice communication.

voice-to-voice communication
Dialogue in which the spoken word gives instructions to a computer which subsequently replies with a 'human' voice. *See also:* voice response system.

wet test
Testing of a product already developed.

world wide web (www)
Increasingly popular computer modem communication which enables access to different 'home pages' for companies, products and services and enables the customer to have

access to full-colour graphics, text and sound. Orders can be placed and delivery details entered on-line.

yes/no option
Response facility enclosed with a mailing. Even if the receiver of the mailing is not (yet) interested in the offer, he/she can indicate this by crossing the no-option on the reply card or coupon. An example of this is the so called no-envelope.

References and further reading

Curry, J., *Customer Marketing*, De Management Bibliotheek, Amsterdam, 1991.

Dresmé, P.B. and J.A.M. Krützmann, *Het eerste Nederlandse boek over direct respons televisie*, Amsterdam, 1994.

Dorland, A., *Digitaal*, Valkierser Publishing BV, Hilversum, 1993.

Hoekstra, J.C., *Direct Marketing*, Wolters-Noordhoff, Groningen, 1993

Hoge, C.C., *The Electronic Marketing Manual*, McGraw-Hill, Inc., New York, 1993.

IPN, *De DRTV-Encyclopedie*, Amstelveen, 1994.

Kotler, Ph., *Marketing Management, Analysis, Planning, Implementation and Control*, 8th edition, Prentice-Hall, Inc., Englewood Cliffs, N.J., 1994.

Molenaar, C.N.A. e.a., *Handboek Direct Marketing*, Samsom, Alphen a/d Rijn, 1988.

Molenaar, C.N.A., *Interactieve marketing; het einde van de massamarketing*, De Management Bibliotheek, Amsterdam, 1993.

Postma, P., *Het direct marketing boek*, De management bibliotheek, Amsterdam, 1990.

Raaij W.F. van e.a., *De direct mail demonstratiecampagne*, PTT-post, Den Haag, 1988.

Roberts, M.L. and P.D. Berger, *Direct Marketing Management*, Prentice-Hall, Englewood Cliffs, New Jersey, 1989.

Roomer, J. and A. Hessels, *Direct marketing begrippenlijst*, Kluwer Bedrijfswetenschappen, Deventer, 1992.

Roomer, J., *DM-theorie, methoden en technieken van Direct Marketing*, Samsom Bedrijfsinformatie, Alphen aan den Rijn, 1990.

Rosenbloom, B., *Marketing Channels; A Management View*, 4th edition, The Dryden Press. Chicago, 1991.

Stone, B., *Successful Direct Marketing Methods*, 5th edition, NTC Business Books, Lincolnwood, Ill., 1994.

Vögele, S., *Handbook of Direct Mail*, Prentice Hall International (UK) Ltd, Hemel Hempstead, 1992.

16 INTERNATIONAL MARKETING

Concept overview

area management
area-centric approach
ASEAN
ATA carnet.

balance of payments
bartering
Belgio-Luxemburg Economic Union
 (BLEU)
Benelux
BERI index
bill of lading (B/L)
bonded warehouse
buy-back transaction

Caribbean Common Market (Caricom)
Central American Common Market
certificate of origin
Certificate re goods transit
CIF
clearing
commercial agent
commodity agreements
concentrated diversity strategy
concentrated similarity strategy
contract manufacturing
contraction method
counter purchase
countertrade
cultural empathy
cultural reasonableness
culture
currency risk
currency-risk insurance
customs union

diamond model
differentiated export policy
differentiated international marketing
 strategy
direct entry strategy
direct export
direct market approach strategy
documentary collection (D/A, D/P)
documentary credit (L/C)
dumping

Economic and Monetary Union
Economic Union
ECU (European Currency Unit)
EFA (export-financing arrangement)
embargo
entry strategy
ethnocentric approach
Eurobranding
Euroconsumer

Euromarketing
European Coal and Steel Community
 (ECSC)
European Economic Area (EEA)
European Economic Community (EEC)
European Free Trade Association (EFTA)
European Union (EU)
expansive method
expatriates
export
export audit
export cartel
export co-operation
export consortium
export credit insurance
export management
export merchant
export policy
export policy plan
export promotion

filter model
Financing Association for Developing
 Countries
First World
FOB (free on board)
free trade
free trade zone

GATT (General Agreement on Tariffs
 and Trade)
General Preferential System Certificate
 (GPS certificate)
geocentric approach
global localization
global marketing

homeland
host country

import
import agent
import tariff
incidental export
Incoterms
indirect entry strategy
indirect export
indirect market approach strategy
international management
international market segmentation
international market selection strategies
international marketing
international public relations
international trade
international transfer price

joint selling
joint venture

Letter of Credit
licensing

market approach, forms of
matching fund
mercantile house
MITI
mixed credit
mono-marketing
multi-country research
multi-market marketing
multi-marketing
multinational company
multiple diversity strategy
multiple similarity strategy

Newly Industrialized Countries (NIC)
non-tariff barriers

offshore banking
Organization for Economic Co-operation
    and Development (OECD)

parallel-import
piggy back
political risk

political union
polycentric approach
protectionism
proto-international

quotas

Second World
single country research
sogo shosha
standardized export policy
standardized international marketing
    strategy
strategic goods
surveyor

tax holiday
Third World
trading policy
traditional export policy
transit trade

UNCTAD
UNIDO

voluntary export restriction (VER)

World Bank
World Trade Organization (WTO)

Concept descriptions

area management

Analysing, planning, and implementing part of the company's export policy with regard to a specific part of the international market which a manager or team of persons within a company is responsible for.

area-centric approach

Company view whereby it is assumed that countries can be geographically grouped on the basis of cultural relationship and product/market characteristics. Experiences in one country within such a group of countries or area are considered to be transferable to the other countries.

ASEAN

Economic union, founded in 1967, consisting of the countries Indonesia, Malaysia, the Philippines, Singapore, and Thailand. ASEAN is an abbreviation of *A*ssociation of *S*outh *E*ast *A*sian *N*ations.

ATA carnet

A document with which goods can temporarily be imported and exported from/to countries which have joined the 'ATA convention'. This carnet is issued by the Chambers of Commerce of the affiliated countries.

balance of payments

Summary of all the transactions with foreign countries during a specific period generating payments and receipts. The balance of payments consists of five part balances: the balance of trade (export and import of goods); the balance of services (expenditure and receipts with regard to services received or delivered to a country), and the returns on capital or income balance (expenditure and payments on interests, dividends, primary income and income transferences); the capital balance (capital import, capital export, respectively), and the gold and foreign exchange balance (influx of gold and foreign exchange, or drain of gold and foreign exchange). The former three part balances together are called the current account of the balance of payments.

bartering

One form of counter trade whereby goods are exchanged for other goods.

Belgio-Luxemburg Economic Union (BLEU)

Co-operation between Belgium and Luxemburg in the field of economics.

Benelux

Economic union between the countries Belgium, The Netherlands and Luxemburg.

BERI index

Scaling method assessing the risk and the (un)attractiveness of doing business with specific countries. Each country is judged by a number of criteria (fifteen). The total score for a country equals the sum of the country scores multiplied by weighting factors.

bill of lading (B/L)

Shipping document representing title to the goods shipped. The B/L is the only negotiable transport document. Ownership of goods is transferred to the new owner of the Bill of Lading by handing over this document. Usually this is sent separately by courier or registered mail.

bonded warehouse

A separate space with goods which have not yet been cleared by customs and which has, therefore, been closed off by the customs authorities. Goods do not pay duty until they leave the bonded warehouse. Whisky as alllowed to mature for years in a bonded warehouse and pay duty only when it leaves the bonded warehouse.

buy-back transaction (buy-back compensation)
One type of counter trade whereby the supplier of the capital goods is paid in branded goods manufactured by the means of production supplied.

Caribbean Common Market (Caricom)
Economic union, founded in 1973, consisting of the former British colonies in the eastern Caribbean.

Central American Common Market
Partnership, founded in 1960, pursuing the economic integration between the member states, namely Costa Rica, Guatemala, El Salvador, Honduras and Nicaragua.

certificate of origin
An official declaration, required by the importing country, in which it is declared by a authorized/recognized authority in the exporting country that the goods originate in the country in question. In Britain, this declaration is issued by the Chambers of Commerce.

Certificate re goods transit
Official legal proof indicating the origin of goods. This certificate is issued by the customs of the exporting country. It is fiscal proof which is used to obtain part or full exemption of import duty in the country of import.

CIF
*C*ost, *I*nsurance and *F*reight: one of the Incoterms (international common terms devised by the International Chamber of Commerce). Concerns a term of delivery in an international contract of sale to the effect that all costs (including insurance and transport) are for a supplier's account, up to the moment that the goods have been unloaded from a ship/lorry/plane, in a place of delivery agreed upon.

clearing
One type of counter trade whereby two countries agree to buy each other's goods at a fixed rate of conversion of the two domestic currencies for a fixed period.

commercial agent (agent, export agent)
Someone who makes it his business to act as an intermediary in the creation of certain agreements between someone he has a regular relationship with (principal) and third parties, or of concluding such agreements for and on behalf of the principal. The term 'regular relationship' does not imply employment. The principal characteristic of the commercial agent is his independence with regard to his principal. The concept of the commercial agent, for that matter, is defined differently in the laws of various countries.

commodity agreements
Agreements between exporting and importing countries aimed at realizing and maintaining a reasonable stability in the raw materials situation. Commodity agreements have been concluded for tin, wheat, coffee, sugar, cacao, olive oil, and latex. The UNCTAD (UN Committee on Trade and Development) is in charge of these commodity agreements.

concentrated diversity strategy
International market selection strategy whereby the company chooses for a relatively small number of international markets with characteristics which the company considers different.

concentrated similarity strategy
International market selection strategy whereby the company selects a relatively small number of international markets featuring a high degree of mutual uniformity, from the point of view of that company.

contract manufacturing
Kind of indirect entry strategy whereby a producer in a host country manufactures products and/or product components for a producer abroad. Various governments subject entry of their geographical market area to this condition.

contraction method
Market selection method whereby, in principle, a selection of all (approximately 220) countries of the world are used as a starting point. Subsequently, selection finds place by elimination. *See also:* expansive method.

counter purchase (parallel transaction)
One form of counter trade whereby, in principle, only cash payment for goods is used. The supplier, however, undertakes to buy other goods in the buying country representing a specific percentage of the value of the goods supplied perhaps even to the total value.

countertrade
A generic term to describe a phenomenon in international trade whereby the buying party pays with a combination of goods and money. There are different forms: barter, counter-purchase, buyback, compensation and clearing.

cultural empathy
An individual's capacity to identify with and live in a different culture.

cultural reasonableness
The consistence and coherence of thought, feeling and dealing within a specific culture.

culture
Classical definition: complex entity of knowledge, convictions, art, laws, norms and values and other behaviour, skills and customs, which is typical of the members of a particular community. There are three characteristics: culture (1) is acquired and transferred from generation to generation; (2) has a strong mutual coherence between parts of the culture, and (3) is shared by the members of the community in question and is distinct from other communities.

currency risk
Financial risk which an organization may encounter if the foreign currency is weak and inflation is prevalent.

currency-risk insurance
Applicable where the time frame of a credit exceeds two years. Then, the NCM takes out an insurance to cover the currency risks run by the exporter.

customs union
Co-operation in which the participating countries undertake internal free trade and so undertake not to levy import duties but also to operate a common external tariff. An example of this is the Central American Common Market (CACM).

diamond model
A Porter model containing the factors which determine the competitive capacity of nations. Distinguished are: (1) the organization strategy, structure and rivalry (the way in which organizations are set up and managed in a nation, and the mutual competition); (2) the 'demand conditions' (the home market); (3) the 'factor conditions' (a nation's competitive advantage with regard to input factors), and (4) the related and supporting lines of business (their presence and international competitive capacity). Outside of this were the two external factors: government and chance.

differentiated export policy
Policy in which the export activities and the usage and application of marketing instruments within the different export countries vary considerably.

differentiated international marketing strategy
Strategy whereby for each international target group a specific marketing policy is prepared and executed.

direct entry strategy (direct market entry strategy)
Strategy whereby an organization creates a starting position under their own responsibility and with own means in a foreign market. In this entry strategy, there is maximum control of the marketing instruments from headquarters. *See also:* indirect entry strategy.

direct export
The organization takes responsibility for the market in the host country itself, for example, by means of a sales office or plant of their own.

direct market approach strategy
Strategy aimed at expansion by the company itself of the starting position already created in the host country, to a sufficiently large and defendable market position.

documentary collection (D/A, D/P)
One of the Incoterms. Concerns a method of payment included in the trade agreement. The seller obtains the documents, and therefore the title, on payment to the exporter's bank (D/P, *D*ocuments against *P*ayment), or against acceptance of a long-dated bill (D/A, *D*ocuments against *A*cceptance).

documentary credit (L/C)
One of the Incoterms. Concerns an agreement of a bank with the seller to pay the selling price to him on his handing over the documents mentioned in the letter of credit and on his meeting all the other conditions included in the contract, or to accept drafts, or have them accepted, or grant an advance on the full draft amount. Often identified with 'Letter of Credit' (L/C).

dumping
Selling goods in an importing country or host country at prices below the real cost prices in the home market of the exporting company often causing injury to local domestic companies.

Economic and Monetary Union
Co-operation and mutual matching of economic and monetary politics.

Economic Union
Co-operation between countries with regard to the harmonization of economic, monetary, tax and social politics in combination with the creation of supranational institutions. Examples include the Benelux, the EU, ASEAN and Caricom.

ECU (European Currency Unit)
The monetary unit used within the European Union which is linked to the currency (weighted value) of the member states. So far, the ECU has only functioned as a unit of account. In the framework of the European Monetary Union, the ECU is in fact intended to be introduced as an instrument of payment.

EFA (export-financing arrangement)
In an export transaction of any consequence, for example, in the case of capital goods, usually payment is effected in instalments. When determining these part payments, the interest is taken into account. The market interest, however, differs per country. This results in an exporter in a high interest country having a disadvantage as compared with an exporter in a low interest country. In order to avoid undesirable effects, the so-called consensus interest has been introduced. This interest is determined every six months by OESO in combination with the duration of the export credits. If the market interest is higher than the consensus interest, the exporter can ask his bank to reserve 'space' with the Dutch Central Bank under the export financing arrangement. This means that, under a number of conditions, he qualifies for the profitable EFA interest rate.

embargo
Total ban on the import of a particular product from a certain source country. This may be seen as a special kind of contingent regulation, whereby the quota is set at a maximum import of zero units of the product in question.

entry strategy
Strategy aimed at acquiring a starting position in a host country. To be distinguished are the indirect entry strategy and the direct entry strategy.

ethnocentric approach
Company concept in which the home country is considered superior to any host country, and that therefore the strategies so far applied in the home country may be copied direct to these countries. *See also:* geocentric approach.

Eurobranding
Trading products in different markets in Europe under a common brand name.

Euroconsumer
Term used to indicate the possibility that groups of consumers from various European countries are to be considered one group (Euro segment) in that they respond fairly homogeneously to the marketing proposition of a supplier.

Euromarketing
European marketing policy whereby the segmentation, target group determination, and positioning is determined and filled in from a European perspective. *See also:* Euroconsumer.

European Coal and Steel Community (ECSC)
European co-operation in the production of coal and steel as predecessor of the European Community, later the European Union. At the time, the participating countries were: the Benelux, Germany, England and France. *See also:* European Union.

European Economic Area (EEA)
Agreement between the EU member states and the countries of the EFTA, whereby a free movement of people, goods, and services is pursued between the countries involved.

European Economic Community (EEC)
European co-operation (1-1-1958) with regard to economic co-operation, as a predecessor of the European Community, later European Union. At the time, the participating countries were: the Benelux, Germany, Italy and France. *See also:* European Union.

European Free Trade Association (EFTA)
Free trade association in which Finland, Liechtenstein, Austria, Norway, Sweden, Switzerland, and Iceland participate. The EFTA was founded in 1960.

European Union (EU)
Economic union whose fifteen members are Belgium, Luxemburg, Denmark, Finland, Germany, France, Greece, Ireland, Italy, Spain, the Netherlands, Portugal, the United Kingdom, Austria and Sweden. Originally it consisted of six countries who since 1957 had been co-operating in the area of coal and steel production (ECSC) and later in the economic area (EEC). Afterwards it expanded to include Italy and later Denmark and Ireland. Greece, Spain and Portugal joined in the eighties. After the name was changed in 1993 from the European Community (EC) to the European Union (EU), Finland, Austria and Sweden joined as new members.

expansive method
A market selection method whereby the company selects host countries showing a similarity with the home country, or those countries in whose markets the company is already operational. *See also:* contraction method.

expatriates
A company's employees sent out to a host country overseas.

export
All border crossing transactions with regard to goods and services whereby the compensation affects the other country's balance of payments.

export audit
Method a company can use to analyse whether and to what extent it is 'fit' to (start) export(ing). Components of this analysis are: organization, production capacity, financial capacity, and market approach.

export cartel
Co-operation between various organizations aimed at collective arrangements with regard to the export of more or less homogeneous goods with a view to regulating price and controlling supply.

export co-operation
Co-operation between producers remaining economically independent with regard to export activities. Co-operating producers may originate from the same channel of the industry sector (horizontal co-operation), or from different channels (vertical co-operation). *See also:* export promotion.

export consortium
Co-operation in the framework of an indirect entry strategy whereby a loose, informal group of exporting companies will perform one or more marketing and sales functions for companies remaining independent. This is done by founding a central institution, and aimed at realizing reduction of costs and expansion of turnover for all participating companies.

export credit insurance
If an exporter grants credit to a buyer, he may obtain security on the instalments agreed upon by taking out a credit insurance with a designated institution. In the United Kingdom, ECGS (Export Credit Guarantee Scheme) is the appropriate institution.

export management
Management with regard to the delivery of goods and services across the border of the home country.

export merchant
A person who makes it his business to conclude agreements at his own risk in his own name, or firm, and for a certain remuneration or commission by order and for the account of someone else.

export policy
Analysis, planning, execution and evaluation of activities of an organization with regard to exchange transactions between this organization and customers in countries other than in the homeland of this organization.

export policy plan
Collective name for the different kinds of export plans matching the various stages in the internationalizing process.

export promotion
Stimulating foreign trade undertaken by a national government by means of supplying information, trade missions, etc.

filter model
Technique to select a number of prospective host countries on the basis of general and more product/country specific criteria. Subsequently, these deserve specific attention from the company as options within the internationalizing process. The selection is also indicated with priority countries.

Financing Association for Developing Countries
Association aimed at promoting the economic and social progress in the developing countries, by means of such activities as participation in countries and/or acting as an investment partner.

First World
All industrialized countries united in the OECD.

FOB (free on board)
One of the Incoterms. Concerns a term of delivery in an international contract of sale whereby all costs are for the supplier's account up to the moment the goods are loaded on board a ship/lorry/plane in a place agreed upon.

free trade
Trade policy whereby international trade is fully determined by supply and demand.

free trade zone
Group of countries co-operating in the economic field having agreed on an unrestricted exchange of goods between the members states, but who operate their own policy with regard to non-member states. This has resulted in the use of certificates of origin becoming necessary. An example of this is the EFTA.

GATT (General Agreement on Tariffs and Trade)
International agreement in which the politics of free trade is laid down (precursor to the World Trade Organization which supplanted it in 1993). Approximately 100 countries have signed this agreement. Multilateral trade negotiations take place in so-called rounds.

General Preferential System Certificate (GPS certificate)
Official fiscal proof of origin on the basis of which preferential tariffs are granted. Within the GATT conference the industrialized countries granted general preferential tariffs to developing countries. These countries have to submit this General Preferential System Certificate when importing. These certificates are only issued by specially appointed authorities in the developing country in question.

geocentric approach
Business concept in which no country is deemed superior or inferior to other countries in the world. Differences between the countries are respected as such. The attitude of the company may be typified as 'the world is our home market'. *See also:* ethnocentric approach.

global localization (glocalization)
Strategy whereby products are offered globally in a standardized way, if necessary with limited adaptations to the requirements or needs of local consumers.

global marketing
Marketing activities by organizations aimed at target groups scattered over a large number of countries whereby the highest possible uniformity in marketing activities is pursued.

homeland
The country in which the main office of an internationalized company is established.

host country
Each country, apart from the home country of the organization where this organization operates.

import
Importation of goods and services in a host country.

import agent
Commercial agent working in the country of the importing company, and therefore being familiar with the commercial practices, customs and traditions.

import tariff
Tax or duties on the import of a product. This increases the price as a result of which the import is limited. The joint general terms and conditions being part of the international contract of sale. These conditions take care of three aspects, namely, the distribution of costs, the distribution of risk, and the distribution of task. Frequently used Incoterms are CIF and FOB.

incidental export
The incidental and unplanned trade of surplus production to foreign markets.

Incoterms
Collection of general terms and conditions being part of the international contract of sale. These conditions take care of three aspects, namely: division of costs, division of risk and division of task. Frequently used Incoterms are CIF and FOB.

indirect entry strategy (indirect market entry strategy)
Strategy whereby a company leaves the organizing and performance of all activities to obtain a starting position in a host country to local third parties established in that country. As a result, the marketing strategy defined by that company is less controllable than with a direct entry strategy. *See also:* joint venture, piggy back.

indirect export
Kind of exporting whereby the market approach in the host country is performed by organizations not belonging to the company in the host country. Indirect export includes the stage of the indirect entry strategy and that of the indirect market approach strategy.

indirect market approach strategy
Strategy aimed at supporting the involved locally established third party in such a way that the starting position already created in the host country is developed to an adequate size and a defendable market position.

international management
Analysing, planning, implementing and controlling/adjusting border crossing company activities.

international market segmentation
The splitting up of the international market in segments which do not necessarily converge with country borders, but which have common characteristics relevant for the marketing policy. *See also:* Euroconsumer.

international market selection strategies
Strategic starting points in the quest for market opportunities abroad, based on specific skills of the company. Distinguished are the concentrated similarity, the concentrated diversity, the multiple similarity and multiple diversity strategy.

international marketing
Marketing activities (of organizations) aimed at target groups which are present in more markets than only their own national market.

international public relations
Systematic maintenance of international contacts with persons or organizations on whose judgement the international company is largely dependent.

international trade
Border crossing exchange process of goods and services.

international transfer price
Fixing the price of products where it concerns deliveries between at least two plants abroad belonging to the same company.

joint selling (assortment exchange)
Kind of exporting whereby an exporting company uses the local selling channels of a company established in the host country. The latter company uses selling channels at home of the former company in the same way.

joint venture
Specific indirect entry strategy whereby the exporting company enters into a co-operation with a distributor at home or abroad. In addition to share capital, the parties involved often contribute other assets as well, including technical know-how, management, sales machinery, etc. All partners in the joint venture have a say in the policy to be executed.

Letter of Credit
Documentary credit as security to obtain purchase money or contract price. Concerns information from a bank to the selling party that it will be paid a sum of money under specific conditions. On presentation of the required documents, payment will be effected.

licensing
Specific indirect entry strategy whereby a foreign company is granted the right to use industrial propriety rights according to an agreement which defines production limits, geographical sales territories and royalty payments.

market approach, forms of
Organizational international set up of the marketing approach on foreign markets. The accompanying export activities may be split up into direct export and indirect export.

matching fund
If an exporter can show that there is distortion of competition due to interest subsidy of the government in question and also the EFA is inadequate, than he may, under certain conditions, apply to the matching fund of the department of economic affairs.

mercantile house (trade agent)
Organization which approaches for its own account and responsibility particular (export) markets or market segments with products supplied by other (exporting) organizations.

MITI
Japanese Department of Trade and Industry.

mixed credit
Combination of a loan at commercial conditions together with a concessional loan from the budget of Development Co-operation, in one credit offer.

mono-marketing
Standardized international marketing strategy whereby the company will serve those market segments which show a strong similarity with the target groups in the home market.

multi-country research
Type of international market research whereby different countries may be compared by their appeal for a company.

multi-market marketing
Kind of international marketing whereby the activities in a large number of countries, and just as many national marketing plans are integrated and are tuned to each other in the multi-market marketing plan.

multi-marketing
Differentiated international marketing strategy whereby the starting point for the company is that target groups in the various countries differ from the home market and require a separate market approach.

multinational company
Company having subsidiaries in more countries and performing long-term operational activities there.

multiple diversity strategy
International market selection strategy whereby the company chooses for a relatively large number of international markets with greatly diverse characteristics.

multiple similarity strategy
International market selection strategy whereby the company chooses for a relatively small number of international markets with a large degree of similarity in characteristics.

Newly Industrialized Countries (NIC)
Group of developing countries distinguishing themselves by a strong growth of the industrial production on the basis of initially low labour costs. Usually these include Brazil, Korea, Malaysia and Mexico.

non-tariff barriers
Invisible import restrictions encountered upon entry. These include bureaucratic delay techniques and restricting import licences due to necessary inspections relating to safety or health and hygiene standards.

offshore banking
Trading in a different currency by a foreign banking institution from the currency of the country it is located in.

Organization for Economic Co-operation and Development (OECD)
Organization whose members are the governments of the industrialized countries, the so-called first world. The OECD is concerned with economic and social issues of the members. Founded in 1960 by 24 rich, industrialized countries.

parallel-import
(Re)importation of goods by non-official distributors.

piggy back (carrier, rider)
Specific indirect entry strategy whereby an exporting country (rider) uses the distribution channel and any sales organization of another (exporting) company (carrier).

political risk
Risk of a reduction or even complete stagnation of the economic activities in a host country, due to an uncertain political situation or unforeseen political changes. This may jeopardize the export to that country resulting in a fall in the sale and turnover of the companies exporting to that country.

political union
Co-operation pursuing the integration of political decision-making of the member states. Example: the European Political Union (EPU).

polycentric approach
Company view whereby branches of a company in various host countries prepare and perform the local policy to a high degree, because experiences in the home country are not deemed transferrable to the host countries.

protectionism
Trade policy whereby the government, through measures such as excises, levies and non-tariff barriers, protects the home market and industry.

proto-international
Company with the majority of its sale and a substantial part (10 per cent to 15 per cent) of its staff abroad.

quotas
Quantity restriction on the import of a given good (usually textiles or footwear) imposed by the government of the host country.

Second World
The Eastern European countries, formally organized in the COMECON.

single country research
Kind of international research whereby the research method is specifically tuned to the country in question.

sogo shosha
Japanese trading houses. There are nine including Mitsubishi and Mitsui.

standardized export policy
Policy in which the export activities, and the usage and application of marketing instruments within the different export countries do not vary considerably or to only a limited degree.

standardized international marketing strategy
Strategy whereby the same marketing policy is used for each international target group.

strategic goods
Goods normally exported only with Government approval and licensing.

surveyor
Sworn and expert person who may issue a declaration on goods recognized by government authorities.

tax holiday
Phenomenon that the government offers the possibility to a foreign company to be exempt from paying taxes or to pay only little tax on the profit realized in that country during a pre-set (starting) period.

Third World
Developing countries many of which are found in Africa, Latin America and Asia. *See also:* Second World.

trading policy
Measure which the government of a country takes, or may take with the intention to influence in this way the process of international trade, in the framework of its macro economic objectives.

traditional export policy
Export on the basis of a product-oriented approach without any adaptation to the foreign market whereby all marketing decisions are left to the foreign promoter of the company's interest.

transit trade
Trade in goods which are forwarded on to other countries.

UNCTAD
*U*nited *N*ations *C*onference on *T*rade and *D*evelopment, a pressure group of developing countries within the United Nations.

UNIDO
*U*nited *N*ations *I*ndustrial *D*evelopment *O*rganization: (part) organization of the United Nations whose main objective is to expedite the industrial development of developing countries and to promote industrial co-operation between regions and countries.

voluntary export restriction (VER)
Export policy whereby the host government voluntarily imposes its own industry quantitative export restrictions, so as to avoid harsh(er) protective measures from other countries.

World Bank

Organization playing an important role in financing projects in developing countries. Its largest institution is the International Bank for Reconstruction and Development.

World Trade Organization

Organization developed in 1993 out of the General Agreement on Tariffs and Trade (GATT).

References and further reading

Albaum, G. et al., *Marketing and Export Management*, Addison-Wesley, Mass., 1989.

Bakker, B.A., *Export & Marketing: naar een exportbeleid voor Nederlandse ondernemingen*, Samsom, Alphen a/d Rijn, 1980.

Bakker, B.A. and J.F. Lanman Trip, *Handboek Internationalisatie*, Samsom, Alphen a/d Rijn, 1991.

Bradley, F., *International Marketing Strategy*, Prentice-Hall, Englewood Cliffs, New Jersey, 1991.

Dahringer, L. and H. Muelbacher, *International Marketing: a global perspective*, Addison-Wesley, Mass., 1991.

Hoogenraad, P. and H.J. Scholten, *Juridische aspecten van de export*, Wolters-Noordhoff, Groningen, 1993.

Jain, S.C., *International Marketing Management*, Thomson Information/publishing group, Boston, 1990.

Jeannet, J. and H.D. Hennesey, *International Marketing Management*, Houghton Mifflin Cy, Boston, 1988.

Keegan, W.J., *Global Marketing Management*, Prentice-Hall, Englewood Cliffs, New Jersey, 1989.

Kokelenberg, A.R. and J.A. Algera, *Financiële aspecten van de export*, Wolters-Noordhoff, Groningen, 1993.

Kympers, L.P.V.M., A.C.G.M. Bastiaansen, F. Hauwert, K. Hofstra, L.P.O. Kloosterman and G. Rumph, *Exportmanagement: Exporteren/Internationaliseren*, Wolters-Noordhoff/Fenedex, Groningen 1991.

Ohmae, K., *The Borderless World, Power and strategy in the interlinked economy*, Harper Business, New York, 1980.

Paliwoda, S.J., *International Marketing*, Butterworth-Heinemann, Oxford, 1989.

Schmetz, H.L.J.M., *Internationale marketing*, Wolters-Noordhoff, Groningen, 1989.

Toyne, B. and P.G.P. Walters, *Global Marketing Management: a Strategic Perspective*, Allyn & Bacon, Boston, 1989.

17 FINANCIAL ASPECTS

Concept overview

accounting principles
added value
asset structure
assets

balance sheet
benefits
bond
book value
break-even point
budget

capital budgeting
capital compensation costs
cash flow
cash management
cash value
change in accounting principles
change-over costs
compound/cumulative interest
consolidated balance sheet
consolidated profit and loss account/
   results
consolidation
contribution margin
convertible bond
cost price of the turnover
cost-effectiveness, value of capitalized
   value
credit insurance
current ratio
current value

debt servicing capacity
debtor management
debtors
default risk
deferred loan
depreciation
depreciation, methods of
direct costing
dividend
dividend policy

economic stock
expenditure/expenses

factoring
financial lease
financial leverage
fiscal result
fixed assets
fixed costs
fixed financial assets
fixed liabilities
floating assets

floating liabilities
free reserves
future value

goodwill
gross margin
guarantee capital

historic cost

income
incremental cash flow
index number
intangible fixed assets
interest coverage ratio (ICR)
internal financing
internal rate of return (IRR)
intrinsic value
issue

lease
leverage factor
leveraged buy-out
liquidation value
liquidity
loan capital
long-term loan capital

management buy-out
market value
marketing budget
matching principle

negative goodwill
net cash value (NCV)
net equity
net returns
net turnover
non-cash item

off-balance sheet financing
operational lease
opportunity costs

participation
pay back period
price/profit relationship
productivity indicators
profit
profit share
profitability on total capital
provisions

quick ratio

replacement value costs
reserve
return value
returns

sale and lease-back
sensitivity analysis
share
share capital
share premium reserve
short-term loan capital
solvency
state of origin and spending
stock management
supplies

tax allowances
terms of payment
turnover
turnover rate of capital

value of money over time
variable costs

working capital
working capital management

Concept descriptions

accounting principles (valuation principles)
The method according to which the assets and liabilities which by nature are not expressed in nominal money, are converted into a value. The best known principles are: historic cost, replacement value, return value, actual value, profitability value, and liquidation value. Typical of the valuation or accounting principles is that they explicitly pay attention to the issue of how much (net) equity must be maintained before there is a surplus (profit). According to historic cost, profit is the surplus on top of the original nominal capital in money. According to replacement costs, actual cost and profitability value there is no profit until the substance (the assets) of the organization are retained or enlarged. The return and liquidation value do not start from the going-concern idea. The profit is determined by the amount which is obtained from selling the assets. The profitability valuation principle differs from the other principles in that it is directed at calculating the future profits (ex ante) instead of the profits of the past (ex post).

added value
In economics: all the returns obtained by a company less the costs which have to be paid to other organizations; by definition this equals the sum of the incomes earned by means of that company (staff incomes, money lenders, government and returns retained in the company).

asset structure
The mix of the different net equity and loan capital components in financing. For example, the composition of the shares issued, the relative proportion of short-term capital, long-term capital, and net equity.

assets
All the property of a company included in the balance sheet. Broken down into fixed assets and liquid assets.

balance sheet
A statement indicating the size and composition of the total assets owned at a specific time. The balance sheets provides a survey of the company's property, its debts and its net assets at a specific moment. The balance sheet is basically the following accounting equation: assets = liabilities + equity.

benefits
In everyday usage synonymous for the difference between turnover and cost.

bond
Participation in the (long-term) loan capital of a company whereby the borrowing company provides particular collateral. Redemption is effected according to a preset programme. *See also:* convertible bond.

book value
A technical term, not a valuation standard, used to specify the balance sheet value of a (durable) asset. The book value equals the balance sheet value of the asset, which is the difference between the purchase price and the cumulative depreciation.

break-even point
The point (in a graph) at which there is neither a profit nor a loss. In this point the size of the production and/or the turnover of such that the total cost is exactly equal to the total return at a specific price.

budget (financial budget)
Financial plan in which the expenses and receivables over a specific period are determined. An approved budget also serves as an authorization for expenditures within the framework and the limits of the content of the budget.

capital budgeting
Periodically evaluating and selecting future investments.

capital compensation costs
Weighted average percentage compensation which an organization has to pay by period (for each capital) to providers of loan capital and net equity. The capital compensation costs may also be seen as opportunity costs; in that case, the factor equals the returns missed, expressed in a percentage of the investment amount, by not investing in another project.

cash flow
Earnings less expenditure over a specific period. The size of the cash flow may be derived from, amongst others, the statement of source and application of funds. Using the balance sheet, the cash flow may also be calculated as the sum of profit (after taxes) and depreciations. This operating cash flow may either be decreased or increased by the balance of the desinvestitures and investments, the mutations in the loan capital and the working capital.

cash management
Financial analysis, planning and management of money streams whereby a trade-off is made between the profits and losses of liquidity, the efficiency of the collection of debts, and the payment of debts is optimized and whereby the relationships with banks play a major role.

cash value
The present value of a future money stream, discounted at an appropriate capital cost factor.

change in accounting principles
Principles to determine the profit should remain unchanged from one period to another, so that a comparison between periods is possible.

change-over costs
Costs (also in time and management attention) which have to be met in order to change a production line over to another variety.

compound/cumulative interest
Interest which is earned on both the original principal amount and the interest itself which is earned with the original principle amount in previous periods. The interest earned in a period will become part of the principal amount in the following period.

consolidated balance sheet
Merged balance sheets of the company and its subsidiaries (more than 20 per cent participation). In this case the share capital and the reserves of the companies in which is participated, are eliminated. Also eliminated are the items participation with the holding company and the mutual receivables and debts. *See also:* consolidation.

consolidated profit and loss account/results
Merged profit and loss account of the organization and its subsidiaries (more than 20 per cent participation). In this case intergroup transactions are eliminated so that the turnover in respect of third parties is accounted for as turnover. In particular as a result of this purge, the consolidated profit is lower than the sum of the separate profits of all group companies. *See also:* consolidation.

consolidation
Merging the balance sheet and the profit and loss account of an organization and its subsidiary companies in such a way that a picture of the group as a whole is created. When the merged balance sheet and profit and loss account is prepared, mutual deliveries, receivables and debts are eliminated.

contribution margin
Selling price of a product less the variable costs. (Profit) mark-up (in money/percentage) which is supposed to absorb the fixed costs and the profit (usually per product unit).

convertible bond
Bond which, at the request of the lender, and within a specified period, may be converted into shares at a specific rate of exchange.

cost price of the turnover
The manufacturing or purchasing costs of the products sold or to be sold. This amount may relate to one product unit or to the total number of products sold in a period.

cost-effectiveness, value of capitalized value
Valuation principle whereby the value of assets is equalled to the cash value of the future cash flows to be generated with the assets. The profitability value can be calculated using the formula below:

$$PV = \frac{W_1}{1 + i} + \frac{W_2}{(1 + i)^2} + \frac{W_3}{(1 + i)^3} + \ldots \frac{W_n}{(1 + i)^n}$$

$W_{1,2,..}$ = profit (after tax) of year 1, 2,..
n = number of years in which a profit is expected
i = interest rate to be used. (*See also:* opportunity costs).
PV = profitability value

credit insurance
Insurance covering losses on debtors. It is usual to take out an insurance covering foreign debtors in particular, but also domestic debtors are more and more insured against.

current ratio
Ratio providing an indication on a company's capacity to meet its short-term obligations (term < one year).

The current ratio can be calculated in this way:

$$\text{current ratio} = \frac{\text{current assets}}{\text{current liabilities}}$$

current value
Principle of valuation in which the value of an asset is based on the amount that has to be paid now in the market in order to buy an identical asset.

debt servicing capacity
The capacity to meet the obligation of paying interest and redeeming the principal amount in respect of the loan capital.

debtor management
Financial analysis planning and management of customer receivables. The two main issues in this field are how to determine the conditions of sale and the terms of payment, and how to determine which debtors will be allowed credit facilities.

debtors
A company's customer receivables.

default risk
The probability that interest or principal amount cannot or only partly be paid on the due date.

deferred loan
Loan capital the supplier of which, in case of the company's bankruptcy, is not paid until other debts have been settled and any financial means remain.

depreciation
Fall in value of a durable means of production as a result of use and/or the elapse of time.

depreciation, methods of
Way in which the difference between the purchase price and the residual value is spread over the useful life. Three groups of methods include: linear depreciation (a fixed percentage of the purchase price), degressive depreciation (the amount of the depreciation falls each year) and the progressive depreciation (the amount of the depreciation rises each year).

direct costing (partial cost system)
Cost system whereby only the variable costs are differentiated by cost unit (for example, a product). The fixed costs are not allocated to separate cost units, but are debited to the profit and loss account.

dividend
Payment by the company to its shareholders/owners either in cash or in shares. Dividend is that part of the net profit which is paid to shareholders/owners as an award for their participation in the company.

dividend policy
Line of conduct expressing which part of the realized profit is to be placed at the disposal of the shareholders as dividend.

economic stock (inventory)
The stock running a price risk, at a particular moment. It equals the technical stock of goods plus the goods ordered but not yet received goods less the decrease of stock due to delivery of goods following contracts of sale already concluded.

expenditure/expenses (cash-out-flow, out-of-pocket expenses)
Spending of financial means.

factoring
Type of financing for companies whereby the factoring company does not only take over the management, the administration and the collection of the debtor portfolio, but also the entire risk of payment.

financial lease
A non-terminable contract for no longer than the useful life of an object whereby the legal ownership remains with the money lender, although the borrower is the economic owner. On the balance sheet of the lessee (the user/borrower) the object is carried as an asset while the debt in question is entered at the same time. *See also:* operational lease.

financial leverage (gearing)
Using loan capital in order to increase the expected return on the net equity.

fiscal result
Profit calculated in accordance with the valuation principles of the tax authorities.

fixed assets
Property of an organization with the useful life of more than one year. Fixed assets tend to be broken down into tangible fixed assets, intangible fixed assets and financial fixed assets. *See also*: intangible fixed assets.

fixed costs
Costs which in their entirety are fixed for a specific period. They are independent of the number of goods or services produced during that period.

fixed financial assets
Shares in connected companies, connected company receivables, participations, third-party receivables, long-term investments, other receivables, and shares in the company bought by that company itself (in as far as these may be capitalized).

fixed liabilities
Net equity, provisions and debts with a term of more than one year.

floating assets
Property which is present as money or of which it may be expected that it is capable of being converted into money within a year (such as stocks and debtors). *See also:* fixed assets.

floating liabilities
Debts which have to be paid within one year (short term loan capital). *See also:* fixed liabilities.

free reserves
Reserves which do not belong to the legal or statuary reserves and from which no payments can be effected to shareholders.

future value
The value of a present sum of money at a moment in the future by investing it over the intermediate time span. To be calculated by increasing the present amount by the compound interest.

goodwill
That part of the purchase price of a company which exceeds the intrinsic value of that company.

gross margin
Difference between the retail price and the variable costs (in the retail trade usually the purchase price) of a product or product group. The gross margin can be expressed in an absolute money sum or a percentage of the retail price. *See also:* contribution margin.

guarantee capital
Apart from the net equity, this includes subordinated loans as well. The guarantee capital includes other liability items which need not be paid (redeemed) in case of an organization's failure, like, for example, the amount on the equalization account investment premium and the tax allowances provision. From the viewpoint of the provider of loan capital, a relevant measure for the solvency equals the guarantee capital/total asset.

historic cost
Valuation principle whereby the value of an asset is based on the price at which the asset was bought.

income (cash-in-flow)
Receipt of cash.

incremental cash flow
Difference between cash flows of an organization with and without an additional project or an additional investment.

index number (ratio)
Number (usually a ratio) characterizing a specific aspect of an organization. Best known are the ratios for profitability, solvency, and liquidity.

intangible fixed assets
Intangible property with a useful life of more than one year. Includes: costs of research and development, goodwill, patents, licences, copyrights, brands, trade marks, concessions, permits, preparation and start-up costs.

interest coverage ratio (ICR)
Profit before interest and tax, divided by interest costs. Is used to judge how much a company can deteriorate before interest payments are jeopardized.

internal financing
Financing emanating from retained profits and depreciations. This concerns the internally generated cash flow.

internal rate of return (IRR)
Return factor whereby the cash value of an investment equals zero. The height of the IRR indicates the appeal of an investment.

intrinsic value
The difference between assets and liabilities.

issue
A company's issuing new shares or bonds.

lease
Contractual agreement to use a specific object. Occurs as financial lease and operational lease.

leverage factor
The degree to which the expected profitability on the net equity is increased as a result of loan capital financing. To be calculated as: profitability net equity: profitability loan capital.

leveraged buy-out
Take-over of an organization often by its personnel or its management, using loan capital.

liquidation value
Principle of valuation. Value of an asset or assets in direct sale as a result of the company being closed down.

liquidity
The degree to which an organization is able to meet its payment obligations in the short term. To manage the working capital, a liquidity budget of incoming and outgoing money streams is essential. Nevertheless some understanding of the course of liquidity may be obtained on the basis of the balance sheet using a (combination of) current ratio asset tests, working capital, inventory days, average term of credit allowed and average term of credit received.

loan capital
The capacity to borrow money from third parties on a temporary basis at a pre-agreed compensation and conditions.

long-term loan capital
Debts with a term of at least one year. This may also include provisions.

management buy-out
Take-over of an organization by its management. *See also:* leveraged buy-out.

market value
The stock exchange value of a listed company is the product of the number of issued shares times the price on the stock exchange.

marketing budget
Budget with regard to marketing activities of an organization.

matching principle
Principle to the effect that the costs of a transaction are allocated to a period in which also the returns are accounted for.

negative goodwill
Created when the purchase amount of a company if lower than the value of the assets less the loan capital.

net cash value (NCV)
The balance of the present and future incoming and outgoing money stream to be generated by means of investment and discounted at the prevailing capital costs factor.

net equity

A company's total property less the claims on this property by third parties (not being shareholders) or: the total volume of assets less the loan capital. *See also:* intrinsic value.

net returns (operating results, result on sales)

Profit from ordinary operations. The profit from operations may be calculated before or after deduction of the balance of financial benefits and expenses.

net turnover

The return on the basis of delivery of goods and services (excluding VAT) less discounts, and so on.

non-cash item

Cost item which is deducted from a return, but which does not result in a cash mutation. Examples: depreciations, additions to the tax allowances provision, revaluations led through the profit and loss account.

off-balance sheet financing

Financing which cannot be found under the debts (loan capital) in the balance sheet (operational lease, sale and lease back constructions, etc.).

operational lease

Lease contract of a limited duration, with a right to extension. The supplier is responsible for maintenance and service.

opportunity costs

The profit which is lost or the loss which is suffered because the financial means have not been used in a different way.

participation

The long-term and direct or indirect retaining or shares of certificate of shares in a company for one's own account (at least 20 per cent of the issued capital) for the company's own operational activities. When a company owns more than 20 per cent of the other company's capital, there is a legal suspicion of participation. However, this suspicion is refutable if it can be shown that the criteria of capital provision, permanence and service for the company's own activities are met.

pay back period

Period in which the cost of a particular investment (for example, the expenses for the development and introduction of a new product) is recovered by an organization.

price/profit relationship

Ratio used by investors to evaluate shares. An investor with a less optimistic expectation for the future who has made allowance for this in the share price, will consider the share relatively expensive, so unattractive and the other way around. The price/profit relationship is to be calculated as:

$$\text{price/profit relationship} = \frac{\text{price on the stock exchange}}{\text{profit per share}}$$

productivity indicators

Indicators enabling the efficiency of a particular organization's activities to be measured. For each organization it must be determined which indicators make sense. Here are a few random examples: percentage of non-productive hours, capacity usage percentages of machines, waste and drop-out percentages, maintenance percentage per machine, return on material, number of offers accepted, number of calls/orders per representative, turnover/profit per m^2, per staff member and so on, and so forth.

profit

Increase of the net equity as a result of operational activities. In accounting terms the profit can be calculated from the profit and loss account, as the balance of turnover and the costs over a particular period from the balance. From the balance sheet, the profit can be determined on the basis of the increase in the size of the net equity within a particular period, corrected for other funds raised or paid back. From a business administrative point of view there are various valuation principles which can be used to calculate the profit.

profit share (bonus)

Part of the profit which is paid to a company's staff.

profitability on total capital

Ratio used to determine what profit rate is realized on the total capital. The profitability on total capital can be calculated as follows:

$$PTC = \frac{\text{profit before interest and tax}}{\text{total capital}} \times 100$$

provisions

A cost equalization account set up for obligations or losses the size of which and the moment at which they will occur is not sure, but whose absolute height may be reasonably estimated. Frequently occurring forms: guarantee provisions, provisions for bad debts, pensions, tax allowances, insurance own risk and reorganizations.

quick ratio (acid test ratio)

Ratio as a standard for liquidity. The quick ratio equals the difference between current assets and stocks divided by the current liabilities. Traditionally the minimum value for this ratio is considered to be the number 1. *See also:* current ratio.

replacement value costs

Valuation principle whereby the value of an asset is based on the price which, at this moment, has to be paid to replace the asset with an identical item (corrected for depreciations).

reserve

Net equity which is present on top of the amount of the paid off capital and results from, amongst others, premium, re-valuation and retained profit.

return value

Valuation principle whereby the value of an asset is based on the price it fetches when it is sold. *See also:* liquidation value.

returns

The entire income allocated to a particular period.

sale and lease-back

An organization sells a specific asset which it owns to a lease company, which subsequently leases it back to the organization, either as a financial, or as an operational lease. Usually restricted to property or real estate.

sensitivity analysis (feasibility analysis)

Analysis of the effect on the cash flows of an investment, if changes should occur in critical items such as sales and costs.

share

Participation in a company's net equity.

share capital

Capital permanently placed at the disposal of a company by shareholders in the form of ordinary shares, priority shares, preference shares and cumulative preference shares. This makes the shareholder owner of the company's net assets. In the case of ordinary shares the dividend depends on the results and the dividend policy.

share premium reserve

Reserve created because shares are issued above par or bought below par. If the shares issued are bought at a price which is above par the share premium reserve must be written off for the difference between the two prices times the number of shares bought. If the difference is larger than the premium, the profit will have to be debited for the remaining amount (share premium reserve discount amount).

short-term loan capital

Debts with a term of not more than one year.

solvency

Indicates the degree to which the assets are financed with net equity or with loan capital. The best known and most commonly used ratio is:

$$\text{solvency} = \frac{\text{net equity}}{\text{total capital}} \times 100\%$$

Nowadays, a ratio of net equity/total capital of 30 per cent is considered reasonable; for capital intensive and cyclically sensitive companies this should be substantially higher and for trading companies it may be lower. An indication whether or not a company is financed with too much loan capital, also displays the interest coverage ratio (ICR). *See also:* guarantee capital.

state of origin and spending (statement of source and application of funds, funds flow statement)

Overview of the investments in a period and of the way these are financed. Starting point of the cash flow, which amount, together with the increase of the net equity other than retaining of profit and with long-term loans can be used to invest in fixed assets and extension of working capital.

stock management

Optimizing the level of stock, given, amongst others the costs of purchasing and production and variable series sizes, the opportunity costs of the working capital used to maintain the stocks and the costs of not being able to sell in the case of inadequate supplies.

supplies

A floating asset consisting of raw materials and/or work on hand and/or finished product.

tax allowances (tax allowances provision)

The fiscal claim which weighs upon the valuation of the assets. This is subject to settlement with the tax authorities at some time. Prior to this settlement a tax allowances provision may be created. It is an improper provision because the height of the amount can be calculated exactly according to the prevailing tax laws and regulations.

terms of payment

Specification of the terms within which and the way in which the net amount of a debt has to be settled. The time allowed to a buyer before payment is due; it is part of the total offer of the company (such as price, quality, time of delivery, etc.). Essential part of debtor management.

turnover

The income from sales transactions allocated to a particular period.

turnover rate of capital

Ratio indicating the relationship between the turnover and the total capital in a particular period.

value of money over time (discounted value)

The time value of money expresses the opportunity costs of missing out on the return of a riskless investment.

variable costs
Costs which vary directly with the size of the operational activities and show a tendency of becoming zero when there is no activity.

working capital
Measure for liquidity. The working capital equals the floating asset less the floating liability.

working capital management
Financial analysis, planning and management of floating assets and floating liabilities. Components include credit management, debtor management, stock management and cash management. Resources include: the statement of origin and expenses, ratios such as the quick ratio and debtor turnover rate.

References and further reading

Boer, P. de, M.P. Brouwers and W. Koetzier, *Basisboek Bedrijfseconomie*, Wolters-Noordhoff, Groningen, 3rd edition, 1992.

Bulte, J., J. Dijksma and R. van der Wal, *Management Accounting*, Wolters-Noordhoff, Groningen, 1993.

Dijksma, J., *Jaarverslagen lezen*, Wolters-Noordhoff, Groningen, 1993.

Duffhues, P.J.W., *Ondernemingsfinanciering en vermogensmarkten*, 1 and 2, Wolters-Noordhoff, Groningen, 1991.

Halem, C. van and A. van der Pol, *Kosten en kosten*, Wolters-Noordhoff, Groningen, 1993.

Schlosser, M., *Corporate Finance, a model building approach*, Prentice-Hall, Englewood Cliffs, New Jersey, 1989.

Slot, R., *Elementaire Bedrijfseconomie*, Stenfert Kroese, Leiden, 11th edition, 1991.

Tijhaar, W.A. and P.A.M. Bertens, *Bedrijfseconomie in bedrijf*, 1 and 2, Wolters-Noordhoff, Groningen, 2nd edition, 1991.

Vecht, J.M., F. van der Wal and R. Slot, *Zicht op cijfers: inleiding tot de analyse van jaarrekeningen*, Stenfert Kroese, Leiden, 11th edition, 1992.

18 ORGANIZATIONAL ASPECTS

Concept overview

account director
account executive
account manager
agent
area manager
art director

bottom-up planning
brand manager
bureaucracy

centralization
commission agent
concessionary store
contingency planning
controlling management
copywriter
corporate communication
corporate identity
corporate image
critical mass

database manager
decentralization
delegating responsibility
directing decisions
directing management
division structure
dual planning

field service manager
flat organization
formal organization
franchisee
franchisor

incentive
inertia
informal organization
inside service staff
intrapreneurship

joint venture

line organization structure
line staff-organization structure
logistics manager

management by exception (MBE)
management by objectives (MBO)

marketing audit
marketing controller
marketing director
marketing management
marketing manager
marketing services
marketing services manager
matrix-organization structure
media planner

national account manager

organization
organizational chart
organizational culture
outside service staff

platform
product group manager
product management
product manager
public relations manager

quality action teams

regional account manager
reseller
route planner
route seller

sales engineer
sales manager
sales representative
salesforce
service merchandiser
span of control
span width
strategic business unit (SBU)
strategic planner
synergy

theory X
theory Y
top-down planning
Total Quality Management
traffic manager

venture team

zero defects

Concept descriptions

account director
Senior executive responsible for account managers and account executives. Leads, and is generally responsible for, (the relationship with) a group of major customers.

account executive
The person responsible for the coordination of all activities on behalf of a certain account in an advertising agency. The account executive is also responsible for all communication between the account's co-workers and the co-workers of the agency, third parties called in by the agency such as photographers, directors, etc.

account manager
The person in an organization who is responsible for the analysis, planning, implementation, monitoring and evaluation of the relationship with one or more major accounts. Is found as a function within an advertising agency; in that case the account manager is in charge of a number of account executives. Is also found as a function with a manufacturer. In that case the account manager is responsible for the policy for the (major) accounts (for example, retail chains).

agent
Middleman operating independently who executes an intermediary role for one or more regular connections on a contract basis.

area manager
Staff member within a geographically structured marketing or sales organization who is responsible for the marketing activities in a particular area. An area may be a border-crossing region, a country or a part of a country.

art director
Position in the creative sector of an advertising agency. This creative sector consists of different creative teams of copywriters and designers (art directors). Together they work on the development of advertising concepts. The art director is responsible for the design.

bottom-up planning
Type of planning whereby objectives and tasks are defined at lower hierarchic levels which are then submitted to a higher hierarchic level for comment, adaptation and approval. The higher level assesses the submitted plans on the basis of the objectives and task set by that level itself. This is an ongoing process which does not stop until top management approves the joint submitted plans. *See also:* top-down planning.

brand manager
Marketing manager responsible for the analysis, planning, implementation, checking, and evaluation of the marketing activities of a specific brand.

bureaucracy
Type of organization characterized by a strong hierarchic structure, a multitude of regulations and rules and a high degree of specialization. There is a strong culture of checking and monitoring with an aversion to change and uncertainty.

centralization
The situation in an organization whereby relatively little decisive power has been delegated, i.e.: whereby any authority has been concentrated in one or only a few persons. Centralization may also be regarded as a process in which the situation described above with regard to bureaucracy is pursued.

commission agent (broker)
A person who makes it his business to conclude agreements at his own risk in his own name, or firm, and for a certain remuneration or commission by order and for the account of someone else.

concessionary store
Independent retailer leasing space in an existing retail shop (usually a department store or a supermarket) and running a speciality shop there, independently and for his own risk.

contingency planning
Method of planning in which management predefines what actions have to be taken in the case of anticipated abnormal, incidental events, such as price wars, a strike or a calamity, so that quick action can be taken if such an event takes place.

controlling management
The part of management responsible for monitoring and evaluating plans and their execution. In practice, this is usually higher management, sometimes this task has been delegated to staff departments. *See also:* directing management.

copywriter
Position in the creative sector of an advertising agency. The creative sector consists of different creative teams of copywriters and designers (art directors). Together they work on the development of advertising concepts. The copywriter is responsible for text.

corporate communication
Management instrument used for attuning as effectively and efficiently as possible all consciously operated forms of internal and external communication.

corporate identity
Symbolic manifestations that create the image of an organization to the market.

corporate image
The collection of characteristics under which an organization is known, and by which people describe, remember, and discuss this organization.

critical mass
Minimum size of an organization in order to be able to operate effectively, timely and profitably.

database manager
Official responsible for the design, management and application of a database to support, amongst others, marketing activities.

decentralization
The situation in an organization whereby relatively much decisive authority has been delegated, i.e.: whereby responsibilities have been divided between a large number of people. Decentralization may also be regarded as a process in which the situation described above is pursued.

delegating responsibility (empowerment)
Transference of tasks and their accompanying authorities and responsibilities by a higher level to a lower level in the organization. The higher level is no longer responsible for the execution of the task, but assumes responsibility for testing and verifying it. The higher level, however, will continue bearing the final responsibility for the result.

directing decisions
Decisions with a once-only and executive character. Directing decisions are made under the regime of constituent decisions which are concerned with creating policy frameworks and strategies.

directing management
The part of management which is responsible for making directing decisions, i.e. executing the policy. It belongs to the task of directing management to implement the policy defined by constituent management. *See also:* controlling management.

division structure
Organization structure found in very large companies which proceed to bundling into divisions strategic business units with a mutual relationship (market, technology, or activity). The bundling is intended to increase the concern's decisiveness.

dual planning
Type of strategic planning in which short-term and long-term plans are developed and executed analogously. A dual plan consists of specific action plans aimed at using short-term (up to three years), and strategic initiatives aimed at the longer term (three years and above), which will create new opportunities as a result of organizational changes, strategy development and the development of competencies.

field service manager
Official leading the department of field services. This department supports marketing and/or sales, in the area of pre sales and/or post sales service to customers. For example, auditing, training, installation, documentation, maintenance, etc.

flat organization
Organization with the minimum number of hierarchic levels which on a medium length term are necessary, given the skills at executive levels and the management capacity at higher levels.

formal organization
The relations and communications (including tasks and responsibilities) within an organization which have been formally defined. Expressions of the formal organization include the formal organization structure and the formal style of management. *See also:* informal organization.

franchisee
Organization exploiting a specific (shop) formula and paying compensation to the franchisor.

franchisor
Organization granting to a franchisee the right to exploit a specific (shop) formula for a certain compensation.

incentive
Reward (in the form of a good or a service) for a particular performance to encourage sales staff, middlemen, customers, and others. The reward and the accompanying acknowledgement are designed to further stimulate certain behaviour.

inertia
Type of psychological slowness causing organizations to abandon strategic choices from the past with only great difficulty, and under pressure of changes in the environment.

informal organization
The relations and communications (including tasks and responsibilities) in an organization which have not formally been defined. The informal organization exists beside the formal organization and may
1 be oriented at the corporate objective (for example, informal brain storming groups)
2 be neutral (for example, coffee conversations) and
3 be opposed to the corporate objectives (for example, an unorganized strike).

inside service staff
Part of the sales organization supporting the representatives, consisting of a separate department or of one or more persons within a company. The inside service does have contacts with external groups (of buyers), but does not necessarily have to leave the company for its work. For example, the inside sales service maintaining contacts with clients by letter or by telephone.

intrapreneurship

Flexible type of organizing whereby managers are encouraged to take initiatives with regard to new ideas. The 'champion of an idea' (intrapreneur) will be allowed scope to elaborate the idea and will be rewarded for taking risks.

joint venture

A type of co-operation between two or more independent companies with regard to a particular activity. Within the framework of the defined objectives, an organization may initiate a particular activity, but it may lack know-how, capital or other facilities. It may approach another organization in order to set up a joint venture which is intended for a special project only and for a fixed term.

line organization structure

A hierarchically structured organizational system with clear authoritative relationships at each hierarchic level. Each member of the organization has a direct line to a higher level where he/she is held accountable; he/she is in charge of one or more subordinates at the same time. A line organization is characterized by a one-person management: each member of the organization has only one superior.

line staff-organization structure

An organizational system whereby specialists (groups) have been added in support to line executives. In a line organization, a staff member may not have sufficient capacity in the shape of knowledge, experience or skills to perform his function adequately or to manage his department properly. In that case, one or more advisers may be appointed in support of the line executive. The group has an advisory/supportive function and has no authority to issue orders or give instructions.

logistics manager

Official leading the analysis, planning, implementation and maintenance of the flow of goods, both within, from, and to the organization.

management by exception (MBE)

MBE is an integrated type of management, based on the following principles:

a The policy makers allow freedom of action to the policy executors, albeit within clearly limited lines of policy.

b Decisions which will exceed the limits of authority require further authorization of other, perhaps higher, levels.

Management by exception puts high demands on policy definition and transference: it should be clear where the division lies between the 'normal' and the 'exceptional'.

management by objectives (MBO)

MBO is an integrated type of management, based on two principles:

a The better people know what goal is to be accomplished, the more they will want to identify themselves with that goal and the bigger the chance that the goal will indeed be reached.

b The better progress can be measured, the sooner any adjustments can be made, so that the goal will still be reached.

Applying MBO means that policy makers and policy executors jointly and in consultation define goals and determine the ensuing responsibilities. The policy maker's responsibility will be directed at providing means. The executors' responsibilities will be aimed at the results to be reached as far as the execution is concerned. The result accomplished jointly will periodically be tested against the goals set.

marketing audit

An extensive, systematic, preferably independent and periodic thorough investigation and evaluation of the marketing function and marketing activities of an organization (part).

marketing controller
Staff member within the financial discipline responsible for the monitoring and evaluation of the marketing expenses and activities. He/she prepares financial analyses of marketing plans and evaluates marketing activities. He/she is also the influencer in contract negotiations with marketing suppliers (advertising, media, merchandising).

marketing director
Staff member managing the marketing and sales function within an organization. Responsible for the coordination between marketing and sales plans. In hierarchy placed above the marketing manager and sales manager and below the general manager.

marketing management (commercial policy-making, marketing policy)
Analysis, planning, execution and evaluation of the marketing activities of an organization. Marketing management may be of a strategic or operational nature.

marketing manager
Marketing person responsible for the analysis, execution and evaluation of an organization's marketing activities.

marketing services
Supporting department(s) or activity(ies) within the market department in, amongst others, areas such as planning, administration and customer service. The marketing services are in particular internally orientated and are especially offered internally.

marketing services manager
Staff member who is in charge of the marketing services function which supports marketing activities. The marketing services are mainly internally oriented (for example, promotions or market research).

matrix-organization structure
Type of organization whereby the staff members are classified in (temporary) work groups, on the basis of projects. This type of organization tends to occur in companies which undertake different activities on a project basis. Since these projects will not often be identical, attempts will be made to allocate people and means by project who will be able successfully to complete the project. How the project group is assessed depends on the degree of knowledge, skill and expertise needed to find a solution. The advantage of the matrix-organization structure is the optimum possibilities to allocate the available capacity. On the other hand, the matrix-organization structure often requires much consultation and time from management and that the organization's personnel must be able to co-operate flexibly as far as knowledge and skills are concerned.

media planner
Staff member within an organization responsible for the selection and application of various communication media.

national account manager
Account manager responsible for the analysis, planning, implementation, checking and evaluation of the relationship with a large group of clients having a central purchasing function. His/her task is to maintain systematically good contacts with a wide variety of connections on different levels and with different disciplines within the buying organizations.

organization (business economy)
All the people, means and activities aimed at achieving certain objectives. Thus an organization distinguishes itself from private persons. For example, manufacturers, retailers and institutions.

organizational chart
A diagram showing the way in which the formal organization is structured.

organizational culture
In general, culture refers to acquired values, standards, symbols and behaviour. In the case of organizational culture it is all about the culture within an organization which is expressed in relationships, communication, styles of management, etc.

outside service staff
Department or persons within the sales organization which maintains contacts with external (buyer) groups. Unlike the inside service staff, the outside service staff's tasks include visiting external groups.

platform
Organized occasion for policy makers (within or outside a company or group of work associations) to exchange information and ideas on an informal basis.

product group manager
Marketing manager responsible for the analysis, planning, implementation, checking and evaluation of the marketing activities of a collection of related products. The relationship between the products may be in the field of filling needs, use, raw materials and/or manufacturing process. It is his/her task to allocate the budgets within the product group, to guard the strategy and the positioning and mediate in conflicts between product or brand managers. In hierarchy placed above the product or brand managers and below the marketing manager.

product management
Type of organization whereby marketing management follows the P-organization structure, i.e. whereby the activities are coordinated around one or more products. *See also:* strategic business unit.

product manager
Marketing official responsible for the analysis, planning, implementation, checking and evaluation of the marketing activities concerning a specific product (including product varieties offered). In the hierarchy this official is positioned below the product group manager and the marketing manager.

public relations manager
Staff member whose task it is to maintain contacts with interest groups in order to promote mutual understanding and to maintain or improve the organization's operation.

quality action teams
Teams which have to put forward proposals for improvement of quality in clearly defined areas.

regional account manager
Account manager responsible for the analysis, planning, implementation, checking and evaluation of the relationship with a group of buyers operating regionally and having a centralized purchasing function.

reseller
Person or company whose function it is to further distribute and/or sell a product. Examples include agents, wholesalers and retailers.

route planner
Staff member making route plannings aimed at optimizing the number of sales or service calls per day and/or minimizing the cost of transport, travel and travel time within (any) promised time of delivery or response. Route planning can be found with, for example, physical distribution, technical service and representatives.

route seller (sales representative, sales agent)
Representative delivering the products sold direct from his/her car (lorry). Also, he/she is partly responsible for the physical distribution of the products sold by him/her.

sales engineer
Salesperson selling products whereby technical knowledge of the product and features is essential. For example, a representative on the machines, raw materials (usually technical) finished articles, and semi-manufactures market.

sales manager
A staff member who is responsible for the analysis, planning, implementation, checking and evaluation of the sales activities. Within a company he/her is in charge of a group of salespersons, is usually part of the marketing team and in hierarchy is placed below the sales director. In particular, the duties include recruitment, selection, training, motivation, rewards, routing and dividing into areas.

sales representative
Salesperson whose task it is to sell products and to conclude contracts. A representative's tasks include: making personal contacts with new prospectives (pioneering), providing information, selling and booking orders, merchandising, selling out activities, instruction, demonstrating and providing service. *See also:* account manager.

salesforce
Persons within the sales organization who have contacts with external groups (buyers).

service merchandiser (rack jobber)
Person employed by/by order of a producer or distributors/wholesaler who, in addition to a wholesaler task (supplying products) also carries out retail trade activities. He/she advises the retail trade in question on the price and composition of the assortment, the shelf presentation, replenishes the stock in the shop, and takes care of the shelf. Service merchandisers are mostly involved when the retail trade is insufficiently specialized in the product group as far as the purchase or physical distribution field is concerned.

span of control
The number of subordinate staff which a leader can directly and efficiently manage. *See also:* span width.

span width
The number of subordinate staff a manager manages directly.

strategic business unit (SBU)
Unit within the organization which functions more or less as an independent (sub)-organization. In general an SBU will have an objective of its own, have its own groups of buyers and competitors and have its own independent management.

strategic planner
Personnel official whose task it is to support the concern management during the strategic concern planning process. In centrally managed organizations the strategic planner in particular has an intrinsic strategic task (preparing strategic decisions). In decentralized management organizations the strategic planner often has a processing and stimulating roll.

synergy
Phenomenon that different activities together are more effective and/or efficient than the sum of the separate activities

theory X
Style of management described by McGregor whereby the style of management is determined by the assumptions it has with regard to the workers' attitude and behaviour. In theory X these assumptions are: most workers hate work and changes; they have to be encouraged, rewarded and monitored; they need direct management and avoid responsibility. *See also:* theory Y.

theory Y
Style of management described by McGregor whereby the style of management is determined by the assumptions it has with regard to the workers' attitude and behaviour. In theory Y these assumptions are: most workers do not hate working; they are capable of coping with responsibilities and of developing, but they need management's encouragement. They have social needs and need respect and self-development. *See also:* theory X.

top-down planning
Type of planning whereby a higher hierarchical level defines plans and objectives which have to be carried out at a lower level. In defining objectives and tasks, higher management uses, amongst other things, information provided by lower levels. *See also:* bottom-up planning.

Total Quality Management (Integral quality care)
Analysis, planning, execution and evaluation of activities within the entire organization (in all units and at all levels) aimed at achieving agreed standards of quality and continuously improving the quality. Often demands adaptation of attitude and behaviour of employees.

traffic manager
Staff member responsible for coordinating and the progress of the activities to be carried out in an advertising agency.

venture team
Type of project organization whereby, usually for the development of a new product, a (multi-disciplinary) group of people is formed. They are (partly or completely) exempt from their normal tasks. The venture team has a certain independence within its own budget and the time frame agreed upon.

zero defects
Working method aimed at making entry checks superfluous through reliable, error-free delivery.

References and further reading

Bonoma, T.V., *The Marketing Edge: making strategies work*, The Free Press, New York, 1985.

Boomsma, S., *Interne Marketing. Hoe marketing effectief werkt in de eigen organisatie*, Kluwer, Deventer, 1991.

Chandler, A.D., *Strategy and Structure*, MIT Press, Cambridge, 1962.

Hasper, W.J.J., *Marketing en organisatie-ontwikkeling*, Samsom Bedrijfsinformatie, Alphen a/d Rijn, 1987.

Heijnsdijk, J., *Vitale organisaties*, Wolters-Noordhoff, Groningen, 2nd edition, 1990.

McDonald, M., *Marketing Plans*, Butterworth-Heinemann, Oxford, 1986.

Mintzberg, H., *The Structuring of Organisations*, Prentice-Hall Int., London, 1990.

Piercy, N., *Marketing Organization: an analysis of information processing, power and politics*, George Allen & Unwin, London, 1985.

Schieman, C.J., J.H. Huijgen and F.J. Gosselink, *Beheersing van Bedrijfsprocessen*, Stenfert Kroese, Leiden, 5th edition, 1989.

Verdoorn, P.J., *Het commercieel beleid bij verkoop en inkoop*, Stenfert Kroese, Leiden, 2nd edition, 1971.

19 LEGAL ASPECTS

Concept overview

advertising
advertising ban
advertising rules
agency agreement
arbitration

brand
brand regulation

canvassing
cartel
cartel policy (European)
CE marking
codes for market research
commission agent
comparative advertising
competition proviso
copyright

dealer contract

European law

factoring
fiduciary property
franchising

general terms and conditions
guarantor position of suppliers

hidden defects
hire purchase

ideal advertising
industrial design protection
industrial property
industrial property law

joint venture

leasing
licence
Luxemburg Court of Justice

misleading advertising

patent
Patent and Designs Act
price control decrees
product liability
public relations

self-regulation
syndicate

Treaty of Rome

Concept descriptions

advertising
Any public recommendation to promote the selling of goods and services or the propagation of ideas.

advertising ban
Usually voluntary ban on advertising specific products and to certain groups of people within society, despite the freedom to trade such products.

advertising rules
Rules for the protection of health with regard to attractive expressions on behalf of alcoholic drinks, tobacco products and sweets.

agency agreement
Agreement whereby one party, the principal, appoints another person, the agent, and the latter binds himself for a specified or unspecified period and in return for payment, to act for him as an intermediary when establishing contracts, and from time to time conclude such contracts in the name of and for the account of the principal without being subordinated to him.

arbitration
A way of settling disputes by arbitrators instead of by regular judges. Arbitration is frequently used in (trade) agreements and will be agreed upon in advance. It may concern the quality of the product supplied as well as legal disputes.

brand regulation (merchandise marks law)
The joint regulations pertaining to the legal protection of marks to distinguish products.

brand (trademark)
Names, drawings, prints, stamps, figures, letters, shapes of products or packagings, and all other signs serving to distinguish the products (goods and/or services) of an organization. To protect it, the brand can be registered with an (inter)national trademark agency.

canvassing (house-to-house selling)
Canvassing is a form of non-store trade whereby products are demonstrated and sold at the door. Typical of canvassing is that the buyer is unprepared, that he/she is presented with a unique offer, that he/she cannot compare the limited assortment on hand with any other assortment or evaluate the company, and that, usually, the canvasser (the salesperson) meets the buyer only once.

cartel
An illicit agreement between organizations which usually produce similar goods and/or services, making arrangements in order to reinforce their joint position. As a rule cartels include:
· condition cartel: arranging conditions of payment and delivery
· quota cartel: arranging manufactured quantities;
· area cartel: arranging the division of outlets;
· price cartel: agreeing on minimum prices;
· calculation cartel: where a specific calculation scheme is operated by the partners.

cartel policy (European)
Legislation laid down in the EU treaty to promote free competition and to ban any restriction of free competition, for example, through binding price, production or sales agreements. This outlaws cartels within the European Union.

CE marking
The CE brand (Conformité Européenne) is a technical hallmark valid in all EU member states, concerning environmental protection, safety, health and other consumer protection. The gradual technical harmonization within the EU will in future replace the national hallmarks.

codes for market research
Codes of conduct observed by members of the Market Research Society.

commission agent (broker)
A person who makes it his business to conclude agreements at his own risk in his own name, or firm, and for a certain remuneration or commission by order and for the account of someone else.

comparative advertising
Type of advertisement in which two or more specifically named brands from the same product category are compared directly with one another. Is allowed solely when: a comparison is made with 'comparable' products, there is no question of misleading, the comparison is complete and objective, it does not discredit other products, and does not contain competing brand names. An exception can be made on the last point in situations where the message under no circumstance can be understood without mentioning competing brand names.

competition proviso
Contractual provision between employer and employee making arrangements with regard to the employee not being allowed to do any competing work during or on termination of the employment contract. Such a provision may also be included in other than employment contracts.

copyright
Legal right possessed by a maker of a published work in the field of literature, science, visual arts or music. The right protects the published work and not the concept forming the basis of the work. The right may be assigned by deed; the usufruct of the right may be assigned as well.

dealer contract
Agreement giving one party the right (whether exclusive or not) to sell the products of the other party.

European law
Laws and regulations applying within the European Union, either directly applicable through treaties or through rules, or indirectly applicable through directives (from Brussels) by way of national legislation in the European country in question.

factoring
Means of financing for companies whereby the factor does not only take over the management, the administration and the collection of debts, but also the entire financial risk.

fiduciary property
Silent (propertyless) security right to, for example, personal property, whereby the owner has the actual disposal of the goods, but has encumbered these with a security right on behalf of, for example, a bank. In the present Civil Code this does not entitle transference.

franchising
Licensing of a proprietary business system.

general terms and conditions
General conditions are written bindings which are expected to be a standard part of the agreements concluded by the author, and which have to be explicitly referred to.

guarantor position of suppliers (guarantee from suppliers)
Promise given by a supplier in writing that the article sold or the service supplied meets certain requirements during a certain period under certain conditions.

hidden defects
A hidden defect can be said to exist when purchasing goods if the object sold does not meet what the customer could, within reasonable limits, have expected from the goods.

hire purchase
Type of purchase whereby payment of the good takes place in two or more instalments and ownership of the good is not transferred until the last instalment has been paid.

ideal advertising (non-commercial advertising, charity advertising)
Advertising for ideal, non-commercial purposes.

industrial design protection
Rules and regulations for the protection of copyright for original industrial designs or creative (artistic) expressions.

industrial property
Not a legal term, but a reference to the ownership of technology, knowledge or manufacturing process(es) whether protected by patents or not.

industrial property law
This includes various international bilateral and multilateral agreements and conventions.

joint venture
Form of legal co-operation between organizations where these organizations separate part of their company assets are then joined into a new organization developing an activity or a market for joint account and risk.

leasing
Renting out of durables whereby the maintenance costs are borne by the lessor. Two type of leasing are distinguished:
   · Operational leasing, whereby, in principle, the lessor remains the permanent owner and the lease contract will apply for only a part of the expected economic life of the good.
   · Finance leasing, whereby, in principle, the lessor is the temporary owner and the ownership of the good is assigned to the lessee in due course.

licence
Formal permission from a patent holder given to others (licensees) to use a patent protected knowhow or property completely or in part. In practice, also used for the right to use someone else's copyrighted property.

Luxemburg Court of Justice
European legal body charged with explaining and applying European treaties. Supranational for the European Union.

misleading advertising
Advertisements giving incorrect or incomplete information, persuading someone or an organization to purchase on incorrect grounds, illegal activities.

patent
Subjective industrial ownership right granted on request by the Patent Board or the European Patent Bureau (EPB) to someone having invented a new product or working method. The patent grants to the patentee exclusive exploitation rights during a specific period. *See also:* Patent and Designs Act.

Patent and Designs Act
Act regulating patent law; the exclusive right granted to a patentee who, as title holder to a new product, a new working method, an improvement of the same, has been registered in the Patents Register. *See also:* patent.

price control decrees
Government regulations in the field of prices for specific products and services, in specific industries or sectors.

product liability
The liability of companies with regard to consumers for the products (goods) put on the market by them. Starting point is the liability of the producer for defects in his product, unless he/she can prove that he/she is not liable. Liability for services, which complements product liability, is being prepared.

public relations
Maintaining contacts with interest groups aimed at promoting mutual understanding in order to keep up or improve the market position. In a legal sense to be distinguished from advertising, as explained by self-regulation and legislation.

self-regulation
Regulations not issued directly by the government, applicable to a specific line of business, created within that line of business, or with the aid of organizations outside that business and/or in collaboration with the government.

syndicate
Agreement between companies determining the size of the individual demand/supply/production and profit for the associated companies, and the distribution of the profit by a common agency afterwards is usually determined by a central sales office.

Treaty of Rome
Officially: European Treaty for the Protection of Human Rights. European treaty in which such things as freedom of speech (and advertising) are laid down, compliance of which is checked by the European Court for Human Rights in Strasbourg.

References and further reading

Brack, A., *Consument, recht en koopkracht: juridische en sociaal-economische verkenningen*, Kluwer, Deventer, 1981.

Hoogenraad, P. and H.J. Scholten, *Juridische aspecten van de export*, Wolters-Noordhoff, Groningen, 1993.

Kneppers-Heynert, E.M., in: Leeflang, P.S.H. and P.A. Beukenkamp, *Probleemgebied Marketing: een management benadering*, Stenfert Kroese, Leiden/Antwerpen, 1987.

Ribbink, G.J., *Reclamenormen en Wettelijke Bepalingen*, Stichting Reclame Marketing.

Index

Break-even point, 324
Break-even point (critical point), 168
Break-even ratio, 168
Break-even response, 288
Break-even sales (critical sales), 168
Break-even turnover (critical turnover), 168
Breaking bulk, 193
Briefing, 215
Broadcast ad, 215
Brochure, 288
Broker, 193, 235
Budget (financial budget), 324
Budget research, 82
Budget subsidy, 269
Buffer stock, 250
Build strategy, 122
Bulk goods (commodities), 250
Bulk mailing, 288
Bundle, 250
Bundling, 288
Bureaucracy, 337
Bursting, 215
Bus shelter, 215
Business buyer (industrial/organizational buyer), 40
Business definition, 122
Business location/site research, 275
Business logistics, 250
Business magazine, 215
Business marketing (business-to-business marketing, industrial marketing, organization marketing, organizational buying behaviour), 3
Business process re-engineering, 122
Business re-engineering, 250
Business unit strategy, 123
Business-to-business marketing, 275
Business-to-business marketing (industrial marketing, organizational buying behaviour), 251
Business-to-business services, 251
Buy-back transaction (buy-back compensation), 309
Buyer, 14, 40
Buyer behaviour, 40
Buyer Seller Interaction, 261
Buyer's credit, 40
Buyers' market, 14
Buygrid matrix, 251
Buying behaviour model, 40
Buying function, 235
Buying motive, 40
Buying power, 40
Buying process, 40
Buying role, 40
Buying share, 193
Buying signal, 235
Buying situation, 251
Buying stages, 235
By-product, 147
Bypass attack strategy, 123

Cabotage, 193
CAD/CAM, 251
Cagi (computer assisted graphical interviewing), 82
Call back, 235
Call order (blanket order), 236
Campaign advertisement, 215
Campaign communication, 215
Campaign evaluation, 215
Campaign turnover, 215
Cancellation rate, 40
Canned sales pitch (canned presentation), 236

Cannibalization, 147
Canonical correlation coefficient, 82
Canvassing (house-to-house selling), 236, 275, 347
Capability, 123
Capacity (normal utilization of), 168
Capacity utilization, 261
Capi (computer assisted personal interviewing), 82
Capital budgeting, 325
Capital compensation costs, 325
Capitalized returns, 215
Captive distribution, 193
Captive market (proprietary market), 14
Caribbean Common Market (Caricom), 309
Carry-over effect, 216
Cartel, 14, 347
Cartel policy (European), 347
Cash and carry wholesaler, 193
Cash cow, 123
Cash discount, 168, 236
Cash flow, 325
Cash management, 325
Cash refund campaign, 216
Cash value, 325
Catalogue, 251, 288
Catalogue price (list price), 168
Catalogue showroom, 275
Categorical system, 82
Categorization, 40
Category killer, 275
Category management, 194, 236, 275
Cati, 82
Causal chronological model, 82
Causal connection, 82
Causal research (testing research), 83
CD-Rom (Compact Disc Read Only Memory), 288
CDI (Compact Disc Interactive), 288
CE marking, 147, 251, 347
Census, 83
Central American Common Market, 309
Central cues, 40
Central reply card, 288
Central route (central path), 40
Central tendency criterion (centre measure, location criterion), 83
Central values, 41
Central-limit theorem, 83
Centralization, 337
Certificate of origin, 309
Certificate re goods transit, 309
Certification, 147, 251
Chain level (channel level), 275
Chamber of Commerce and Industry, 14
Change in accounting principles, 325
Change-over costs, 325
Channel captain, 194
Channel competition, 194
Channel conflict (distribution conflict), 194
Characteristics approach, 41
Checking function of the salesperson, 236
Checking questions in the sales talk, 236
Chi-square test, 83
Choice assortment, 275
Choice criteria (purchasing criteria), 41
Choice set, 41
CIF, 309
CIM, 251
Circular reactions, 168
CIS, 236
Class, 83

Integration strategy, 128
Intensive distribution (mass distribution), 199
Intentional learning, 54
Inter-channel competition, 199
Inter-channel conflict, 199
Interaction (process), 19
Interaction process, 54, 254
Interactive marketing, 293
Interactive media, 293
Interest, 54
Interest coverage ratio (ICR), 328
Interface, 19
Interference, 55
Interference theory, 55
Interior display, 278
Internal communication, 222
Internal cost efficiency, 174
Internal data, 93
Internal data file, 294
Internal environment, 5, 19
Internal financing, 328
Internal marketing, 5, 262
Internal rate of return (IRR), 329
Internal search, 55
Internal source, 93
Internal store presentation, 278
Internal transfer prices, 174
International management, 315
International market research, 94
International market segmentation, 315
International market selection strategies, 315
International marketing, 5, 315
International public relations, 315
International trade, 315
International transfer price, 315
Interval level (interval scale), 94
Interview, 94
Interviewer bias, 94
Intra-channel competition, 199
Intra-channel conflict, 200
Intrapolation, 94
Intrapreneurship, 340
Intrinsic cues, 55
Intrinsic product attributes, 153
Intrinsic value, 329
Introduction stage, 153
Introductory price, 174
Inventory effect, 174
Inventory function, 200
Inventory system, 200
Inventory turnover (sales price), 200
Investment strategy, 128
Invited bid, 254
Involvement, 55, 222
Involvement model, 222
ISO, 153
ISO 9000 certificate, 153
ISO 9000 standard, 153
Issue, 329

Job classification, 94
Jobber (trader), 200
Joint prices (price bundling), 174
Joint promotion, 222
Joint selling (assortment exchange), 316
Joint venture, 19, 128, 316, 340, 349
Judgement measurement, 262, 269
Junk mail, 222, 294
Just in time (JIT), 200, 254

Key success factor (critical success factor), 128
Knowledge, 55
Knowledge based service (skill-based service), 262
Knowledge function of attitude, 55
Kolmogorov–Smirnov test, 94
Kruskal–Wallis test, 94

Label, 153
Labelling, 55, 294
Laboratory experiment, 95
Labour intensity, 254
Laddering, 223
Laddering (analysis of the structure of meaning), 55
Laggards, 55, 153
Late majority, 55, 153
Latent demand, 19, 56
Lavidge–Steiner model, 223
Law of closeness, 56
Law of equality, 56
Law of mutual destiny (Law of common destiny), 56
Law of nearness (Law of proximity), 56
Lead, 238, 294
Lead generation, 294
Lead qualification, 294
Lead time, 254
Lead users, 56
Leader (customer draw, bait, traffic builder), 174
Leader (traffic builder), 153
Leading question, 238
Learning, 56
Learning advantages (experience advantages), 174
Learning curve, 128
Learning curve (experience curve), 174
Learning organization, 128
Lease, 329
Leasing, 349
Left skewed (negative skewed), 95
Letter of Credit, 316
Letter shop (mailing house), 294
Leverage factor, 329
Leveraged buy-out, 329
Lexicographic decision rule, 56
Licence, 153, 349
Licensing, 316
Life cycle, 153
Life-style segmentation, 128
Lifestyle, 56
Lifetime value, 294
LIFO (last-in-first-out), 200
Light users, 56
Likely addresses, 294
Likert scale, 95
Likert scale item, 95
Limited distribution, 200
Limited problem-solving purchasing behaviour (limited problem solving), 56
Line filling, 154
Line organization structure, 340
Line staff-organization structure, 340
Line stretching (product extension strategy), 154
Liquidation value, 329
Liquidity, 329
Lisrel, 95
List broker, 294
List compiler, 294
List management, 295
Loan capital, 329
Lobby, 20, 223
Local shopping centre (shopping strip, strip mall), 278

Mass media, 223
Massification theory, 57
Match code, 295
Matching, 97, 295
Matching fund, 316
Matching principle, 329
Materials handling, 201
Materials management, 201
Materials Requirements Planning, 254
Matrix-organization structure, 341
Maturity stage (stabilization stage, saturation stage), 154
Maximum capacity utilization, 175
MDS envelope, 295
Me-too pricing, 175
Me-too product, 57, 154
Mean (arithmetic mean), 97
Mean absolute deviation, 97
Means-end-chain, 223
Measurement level, 97
Measures of variability, 97
Media advertising, 223
Media buying agency, 223
Media commission, 223
Media consumption, 57
Media mix, 223
Media plan, 223
Media planner, 223, 341
(Media) target audience, 223
Media type, 223
Median, 97
Median test, 97
Medium, 224
Medium reach, 224
Medium users, 57
Members store, 295
Membership card, 296
Membership formula, 296
Memory, 57
Mercantile house (trade agent), 316
Merchandise display, 201
Merchandiser, 201
Merchandising, 201, 224
Merge-purge, 296
Merger, 131
Metric measurement level, 97
Micro segmentation, 131, 254
Micro-environmental matters (factors) (internal environmental factors), 21
Middleman (intermediary), 21
Middleman (intermediate) (intermediary), 201
Minimum effective frequency, 224
Minimum price, 176
Misleading advertising, 224, 349
Mission, 131
Missionary salesman, 202
Missionary selling method, 238
MITI, 316
Mixed credit, 316
Mnemonic devices, 224
Mobile defence strategy, 131
Mobile shop, 278
Mobility barrier, 131
Mock-up, 255
Modal class, 97
Mode, 98
Modelling (vicarious learning), 57
Models of consumer behaviour, 58
Modified rebuy, 255
Modular product design, 255

Monadic product test, 154
Monadic research, 98
Mono-marketing, 316
Monadic approach, 58
Monomorphic social influence, 58
Monopolistic competition, 176
Monopolistic competition (heterogeneous polypoly), 21
Monopoly, 21, 176
Monopsony, 21
More step approach, 296
Motivation, 58
Motivation Research, 58
Motivation type, 58
Moving average, 98
MRO (Maintenance, Repair, Operating), 255
Multi-attribute attitude models, 58
Multi-brand dealer, 202
Multi-channel distribution (multi-channel strategy), 202
Multi-client research (syndicated research), 98
Multi-country research, 316
Multi-dimensional product space, 154
Multi-dimensional scaling, 98
Multi-mailing (card deck), 296
Multi-market marketing, 316
Multi-marketing, 316
Multi-media strategy, 224
Multi-shot mailing, 296
Multi-stage campaign, 296
Multi-stage interaction, 58
Multimedia, 296
Multinational company, 316
Multiple correlation coefficient, 98
Multiple determination coefficient, 98
Multiple diversity strategy, 317
Multiple shop organization (multiple shop chain), 279
Multiple similarity strategy, 317
Multiple sourcing, 255
Multiple-item scale, 98
Multivariate analysis of variance, 98
Mystery buyer, 279

N, 98
NAR data, 296
Nash equilibrium, 131
National account manager, 341
National chain (store), 279
National multiple shop organization (national chain), 279
Natural Grouping, 98
Need, 58
Need, 7
Need competition, 21
Need for cognition, 58
Need, recognition of, 58
Need-driven consumers, 58
Needs-oriented selling method, 238
Negative confirmation, 59
Negative goodwill, 329
Negative option, 296
Negotiation process, 239
Net cash value (NCV), 329
Net equity, 330
Net profit, 176
Net profit margin, 176
Net reach, 224
Net returns (operating results, result on sales), 330
Net turnover, 330